WESTERN EUROPE'S

BEST-LOVED

DRIVING

TOURS

Simon & Schuster Macmillan

The following authors contributed to this book:
Austria – Adi Kraus;
Britain and Ireland – Roy Woodcock, John McIlwain, Susan Poole,
Lynn Gallagher, David Williams;
Germany – Adi Kraus;
Italy – Paul Duncan;
Scandinavia – Kim Naylor;
Spain – Mona King;
Switzerland – David Allsop.

Edited, designed and produced by AA Publishing.

Published by AA Publishing

Published in the United States by Macmillan Travel
A Simon & Schuster Macmillan Company
1633 Broadway, New York, NY 10019

Macmillan is a registered trademark of Macmillan, Inc

ISBN 0-02861567-0

Cataloging-in-Publication Data is available from the Library of
Congress.

Color separation: Daylight Colour Art, Singapore

Printed and bound by G. Canale. & C. s.p.a., Torino, Italy

Opposite: *pleasant streetside façade*

CONTENTS

Left: *detail on Florence's Duomo*

ABOUT THIS BOOK

This book is a compilation of 44 driving tours through some of Western Europe's most fascinating countryside.

It is divided into 8 major sections – Austria, Britain and Ireland, France, Germany, Italy, Scandinavia, Spain and Switzerland. Within each section the tours start in the major towns and cities considered to be the best centres for exploration. At the beginning of each section you will find a brief description of each of the tours, plus essential information for visitors.

Each tour has details of the most interesting places to visit en route, some of which may be open only in summer. Panels catering for special interests follow some of the main entries – for those whose interest is in history, wildlife or walking, and those who have children. There are also panels which highlight scenic stretches of road and which give details of special events, crafts and customs.

The simple route directions are accompanied by an easy-to-use map at the beginning of each tour, along with a chart showing how far it is from one town to the next. This can help you to decide where to take a break and stop overnight, for example. (All distances quoted are approximate.)

Before setting off it is advisable to check with the information centre listed at the start of most of the tours for recommendations on where to break your journey and for additional information on what to see and do, and when best to visit.

Throughout this book the following country distinguishing symbols are used on the maps:

COUNTRY DISTINGUISHING SYMBOLS

A	Austria		I	Italy
AL	Albania		IRL	Ireland
AND	Andorra		L	Luxembourg
B	Belgium		LT	Lithuania
BG	Bulgaria		LV	Latvia
BIH	Bosnia & Hercegovina		M	Malta
CH	Switzerland		MK	Macedonia
CZ	Czech Republic		N	Norway
D	Germany		NL	Netherlands
DK	Denmark		P	Portugal
E	Spain		PL	Poland
EST	Estonia		RUS	Russian Federation
F	France		S	Sweden
FL	Liechtenstein		SK	Slovakia
FIN	Finland		SU	Belorussia
GB	Great Britain		TR	Turkey
GR	Greece		UA	Ukraine
H	Hungary		YU	Yugoslavia
HR	Croatia			

on the road

AUSTRIA

Austria is rich in culture and scenery – from Vienna, city of Strauss and Mozart, to the Vienna Woods and the Blue Danube, and to the snow-capped mountains and pretty villages beyond.

Tour 1

High mountains form the central part of the Tirol, often extending above the snow and ice barrier. The foothills are covered with meadows and pastures which provide a livelihood for the inhabitants – tourism also contributes to the economy. On a wider scale, large hydroelectric schemes not only supply the energy for local needs, but a substantial amount is also exported to the power-hungry industrial areas of Western Europe.

The south of the high central mountain range is influenced by the warm and mild air from the Mediterranean. Vines could not survive the harsh winters of North Tirol, but they grow quite readily on the slopes in the South Tirol, which, as well as being one of the most picturesque regions, also has a thriving fruit-growing industry.

When travelling from

Page 7: top – Johann Strauss in Vienna's Stadtpark; bottom – the Grossglockner Hochalpenstrasse

North to South Tirol remember that the currency in Südtirol is the Italian lire and passports are necessary.

From the capital of Tirol, a small undulating side road runs through villages, the main traffic at a distance further down the valley. After deviating into some lesser-known valleys the main Brennerpass is reached. Südtirol starts immediately after the pass.

The capital of the region, Bozen (Bolzano in Italian) has acquired a strong Italian presence due to Italian immigration after Südtirol was annexed in 1919. The Dolomites now come into view and the drive continues through what is one of the most scenic routes in Europe. Many passes have to be negotiated until the return route enters East Tirol and a tunnel linking up with the province of Salzburg. After a stop at the famous waterfalls, a pass leads back into Tirol and the Ziller valley, at the end of which a left turn leads back to Innsbruck.

Tour 2

The southern part of the Austrian Alps, with an abundance of warm lakes encircled by forests and meadows, is explored in this region. Life is more leisurely than in the north and one of the highest mountain passes crosses the area. Gorges, spas and dramatic-looking limestone ranges are intermingled with green pastures and forests, providing the northern boundaries of the region.

This tour starts from southern Carinthia and leads right up on one of Austria's famous mountain roads. The delightful village of Heiligenblut is a stopping place before the real ascent begins. The well-constructed road should not present any problems, apart from heavy traffic when you branch off to one of the popular view points. The descent into the province of Salzburg leads to the traditional spa of Badgastein. The absence of a road south over the mountains is solved by loading cars on shuttle trains through a tunnel.

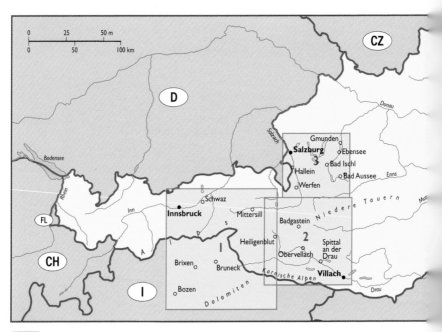

The Pallas Athene Fountain, in front of Vienna's Parlament

our 3

he town of Salzburg has also iven its name to the rovince, which only became art of Austria in 1816. Before en it was under the strong independent rule of its archbishops. Salzburg is a ewel amongst European owns and attracts so many isitors from all over the

world. The yearly festival is a major cultural event and the standard of the performances complements the superb setting and atmosphere of the town.

The region east of Salzburg had grown into a well-known tourist area long before the arrival of the motor car and was favoured by the Emperor Franz Josef himself. The lakes of the Salzkammergut acquired fame as stage settings for operettas and musicals. The opportunities offered for leisure and tranquillity there have a proven track record and with the cultural centre of Salzburg so near, are hard to beat.

This tour starts with visits to a salt mine, rock and ice caves, then some of the country's most romantic lakes, the Gosau and Hallstätter See. Salt is still on the agenda in the area of the 'Ausseer Land', Bad Aussee and Alt Aussee. Turning north the town of Bad Ischl, with its former imperial association, is passed and the route leads past the Traunsee and Attersee to the traditional Salzkammergut resorts of St

Wolfgang. St Gilgen, Mondsee and Fuschl, which still retain their delightful old-world charm, before returning to Salzburg.

Tour 4

The province of Lower Austria covers the area around Vienna and the influence of the former imperial capital is felt everywhere. The final ranges of the Eastern Alps lie across the province of Lower Austria and two of its peaks, the Rax and Schneeberg, are by tradition popular excursion centres for the Viennese. Two pipelines draw water from several springs in the mountains right to the capital's doorstep. Leaving Vienna in a southerly direction reveals the close association of the former ruling Habsburg family; in the church at the abbey of Heiligenkreuz, and the tragic story of Mayerling, where the crown prince decided to end his unhappy life together with his mistress. The foothills of the Eastern Alps near Vienna are covered with vineyards and this glorious setting has no doubt inspired many unforgettable melodies by Beethoven and Schubert.

A tranquil Alpine village with its magnificent mountain backdrop, typical of Upper Austria

10, A-1010 Wien. Tel: (01) 533 3691.
Ireland: Landstrasser Hauptstrasse 2, Hilton Centre, A-1030 Wien. Tel: (01) 7154246.
UK: Jauresgasse 3, A-1030 Wien. Tel: (01) 713 1575–79. Consular section: Tel: (01) 714 6117.
USA: Boltzmanngasse 16, A-1091 Wien. Tel: (01) 31339.

EMERGENCY TELE-PHONE NUMBERS
Fire 122
Police 133
Ambulance 144
Car breakdown 120/123

ENTRY REGULATIONS
EU nationals need a valid passport or identity card. Nationals of Switzerland, Norway, Australia, Canada, the US and New Zealand need only a valid passport.

For stays of over three months, special regulations apply to all visitors, check with appropriate embassies or consulates.

HEALTH MATTERS
Vaccinations are only necessary if arriving from an infected area. In the case of emergencies or sudden illness citizens from other EU countries are entitled to the same benefits as nationals of the country visited. Visitors from the UK should obtain form E111 from a post office before departure. Additional insurance is strongly recommended for all visitors.

MOTORING
Accidents
As a general rule you are required to call the police when individuals have been injured or considerable damage has been

AUSTRIAN TELEPHONE NUMBERS
At present, when dialling Vienna from abroad use the prefix 01. When dialling Vienna in Austria the code is 0222. All Vienna numbers are changing to 7 digits (some still have only 6).

BANKS
Banks are open Monday to Friday 8am–12.30pm; 1.30–3.30pm Monday to Wednesday and Friday; Thursday 8am–12.30pm, 1.30–5pm.

COUNTRY DISTIN-GUISHING SIGNS
On the maps, the following international distinguishing signs indicate countries around Austria:

CH	= Switzerland
CZ	= Czech Republic
D	= Germany
H	= Hungary
I	= Italy
SK	= Slovakia
SLO	= Slovenia

CREDIT CARDS
Major credit cards are accepted in banks, good hotels, shops, restaurants and many petrol stations, and in cash dispensers only when displaying a relevant card sign.

CURRENCY
There are 100 Groschen in 1 Schilling. Coins are in 2, 5, 10 and 50 Groschen, and 1, 5, 10 and 20 Schillings. Notes are in 20, 50, 100, 500, 1,000 and 5,000 Schillings.

CUSTOMS REGULATIONS
Visitors from EU countries are governed by EU regulations and can bring in items for their personal use without paying duty. Limits apply to goods obtained at duty-free shops. Visitors resident outside Europe are entitled to higher allowances and amounts should be verified at the time of purchase.

ELECTRICITY
220 volts, 50 cycles AC, on a continental two-pin plug. UK, Australian and New Zealand appliances need an adaptor; US appliances need an adaptor and a transformer if not fitted for dual voltage.

EMBASSIES AND CONSULATES
Australia: Mattiellistrasse 2–4, A-1040 Wien. Tel: (01) 512 85800, outside office hours 512 73710.
Canada: Dr Karl Lueger Ring

caused. Failure to give aid to anyone injured will render you liable to a fine.

Documents
You must have a valid driving licence, passport, third-party insurance and vehicle registration document. A green insurance card is strongly recommended.

From 1 January 1997 a vignette has to be obtained at the point of entry to pay motorway tax. Visitors staying up to two months can obtain a motorway vignette including tolls for mountain passes and tunnels. Small tolls are often levied for the upkeep of local mountain roads.

Car hire
Car hire is available at most airports, railway stations and in larger towns. Drivers must be over 21 and have driven for at least a year.

Breakdowns
If your car breaks down, try to move it to the side of the road so it does not obstruct traffic flow. A warning triangle is obligatory and hazard lights, if fitted, must be used.

The motoring club ÖAMTC (Österreichischer Automobil-, Motorrad- und Touring Club – Schubertring 1–3, A-1010 Vienna (tel: 0222 711 99–1231), operates a 24-hour breakdown service. Call 120 for Pannenhilfe (breakdown service).

On motorways a patrol can be summoned from an emergency telephone. A small arrow on marker posts on the verges indicates the direction of the nearest one. When calling, ask for Pannenhilfe.

Driving conditions
Drive on the right, pass on the left. There are on-the-spot fines for speeding and other offences.

Many mountain roads require payment of tolls (*Maut*), and some are closed in winter or barred for cars with trailers. Refer to the maps.

Speed limits
Motorways 130kph (81mph); outside built-up areas 100kph (62mph); built-up areas 50kph (31mph).

Traffic regulations are strictly enforced, particularly in relation to speeding and the use of alcohol.

Route directions
Throughout the book the following abbreviations are used for Austrian roads:
A – Autobahnen (motorways)
SS – Schnellstrassen
Bundesstrassen are indicated by their number only.
Landstrassen are not numbered on the maps.

POST OFFICES
Post offices are open Monday to Friday 8am–noon and 2–6pm. On Saturday many open from 8am to 10am. In larger towns main post offices open 24 hours a day, also Sundays and holidays. Letter boxes are bright yellow.

PUBLIC HOLIDAYS
1 January – New Year's Day
6 January – Epiphany
Easter Monday
1 May – Labour Day
Ascension Day
Whit Monday
Corpus Christi
15 August – Assumption Day
26 October – National Holiday
1 November – All Saints' Day
8 December – Immaculate Conception
25 December – Christmas Day
26 December – St Stephen's Day

TELEPHONES
There are separate phone booths for coins and phone cards. Cards can be obtained from post offices and tobacco kiosks (*Tabak-Trafik*). International codes are: Australia 0061, Canada and USA 001, UK 0044, Ireland 00353. Cheap rates apply from 6pm–8am (from 6pm Friday through to 8am on Monday, and public holidays). Calls from hotels are expensive.

TIME
Austria is one hour ahead of Greenwich Mean Time (GMT) in winter, two hours in summer.

TOURIST OFFICES
Australia: 1st Floor, 36 Carrington Street, Sydney, NSW 2000. Tel: (02) 299 3621.
UK: 30 St George Street, London W1R 0AL. Tel: (0171) 629 0461.
US: PO Box 491938, Los Angeles, California 90049. Tel: (310) 477 3332; PO Box 1142, New York, NY 10108–1142. Tel: (212) 944 6880.
For enquiries in Vienna tel: (01) 587 2000.

USEFUL WORDS
The following is a list of useful words and phrases.
English German
yes ja
no nein
please bitte
good morning/day guten Morgen/Tag
goodbye Auf Wiedersehen
excuse me entschuldigen Sie bitte
how are you? wie geht es Ihnen?
very well, thanks; and you? danke, gut; und Ihnen?
do you speak English? sprechen Sie Englisch?
I don't understand Ich verstehe nicht
today heute
yesterday gestern
where is…? wo ist…?
open offen
closed geschlossen
good gut
bad schlecht
big gross
small klein
expensive teuer
cheap billig
how much does it cost? wieviel kostet es?
Monday, Tuesday, Wednesday, Thursday, Friday, Saturday, Sunday Montag, Dienstag, Mittwoch, Donnerstag, Freitag, Samstag, Sonntag
1 to 10 eins, zwei, drei, vier, fünf, sechs, sieben, acht, neun, zehn.

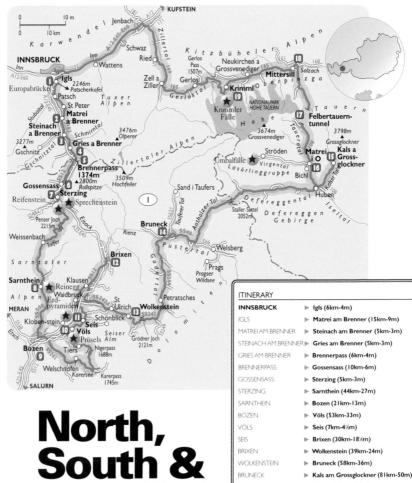

North, South & East Tirol

6/7 DAYS • 576KM • 356½ MILES

Enclosed by the Alps, Innsbruck is one of the most important junctions in Austria, and has been the capital of Tirol since 1363. The Herzog Friedrichstrasse leads through the centre of town, whose focal point is the famous Goldenes Dachl (golden roof), and well-kept, colourful houses line the arcaded main streets.

i *Fremdenverkehrsverband Innsbruck-Igls, Burggraben 3*

SPECIAL TO...

The Goldenes Dachl (golden roof) in Innsbruck, with its balcony below, is one of the main attractions. The roof contains 1,657 gilded copper tiles and was commissioned by Emperor Maximilian I so that he could watch the goings on down below. Things have not changed much over the centuries, only now the people are looking up at the roof instead of the Emperor looking down.

FOR HISTORY BUFFS

On Bergisel, south of Innsbruck, stands a monument to Andreas Hofer, looking down from the scene of the battles he fought so successfully for his country in 1809 against a vastly superior enemy. A pleasant park has been laid around the statue and near by stands the Bergiselschanze, built for the Olympic ski jump in 1964.

FOR CHILDREN

When visiting Innsbruck take the children to the Alpenzoo, on the northern slopes of town. Here you can see animals from all parts of the Alps in a well-arranged natural setting.

▶ *Leave Innsbruck and head south under the motorway to Igls.*

❶ Igls, Tirol
Igls lies only 6km (4 miles) from Innsbruck on an elevated plateau and is probably best known for its winter sports facilities. Its altitude (900m/2,950 feet above sea level) affords visitors an invigorating climate

and welcome retreat from busy Innsbruck, where it can sometimes get very hot in summer.

i *Fremdenverkehrsverband*

RECOMMENDED WALK

From Igls a pleasant walk leads to the next village of Patsch. On the way stop at the Grünwalderhof for a truly stunning view towards the Stubaital (Stubai valley) and the Brenner route. On the right stands the Serles Mountain, called the Altar of Tirol because of its position and shape.

▶ *From Igls continue on a small, narrow road via Patsch, St Peter and Pfons to Matrei.*

❷ Matrei am Brenner, Tirol
Matrei played a part in Celtic and Roman history, when crossing the Alps at the Brennerpass was considered to be the safest and most reliable way. The Romans called it *Matreium* and today it looks like a small medieval village, enhanced by the beautifully painted house façades. A 1916 fire and air bombardments in 1945 caused severe damage, but most of it has been restored. Look out for the partially rebuilt 13th-century castle and the 14th-century parish church.

i *Fremdenverkehrsverband, Reuterplatz 3*

SPECIAL TO...

The Europabrücke (Europa Bridge) near Schönberg is not only a superb technical achievement but also an attraction for visitors. Best seen from the old Brenner road below, it stands 190m (623 feet) above the valley and is counted among the most daring projects of this century.

▶ *From Matrei continue south to Steinach.*

❸ Steinach am Brenner, Tirol
Steinach's interesting parish church is dedicated to St Erasmus. The sumptuously decorated high altar is considered to be among the finest baroque-style choir sections in Tirol. The altar paintings are the work of Martin Knoller, an artist from Steinach.

Turning west under the 700m (2,300-foot) long bridge into the Gschnitz valley and the Gschnitz itself, a pleasant walk then leads via Obertal to the Lapenis Alm, an alpine pasture and starting point for many hikes. Another path leads from Gschnitz uphill to the church of St Magdalena, from where there are fine views over the valley.

i *Fremdenverkehrsverband*

▶ *From Steinach continue south via Stafflach to Gries.*

❹ Gries am Brenner, Tirol
En route to Gries a stop at the small village of Stafflach is recommended as it provides access to two tranquil valleys – the 11km (6½-mile) long Schmirntal and the 8km (5-mile) long Valsertal, which ends in a nature reserve.

Gries is the last stop before the Brennerpass and a starting point for a 7km (4-mile) drive into the Obernbergtal and to the Obernberg village. A half-hour walk leads to the picturesque Obernberger See.

i *Fremdenverkehrsverband*

▶ *Continue to the Brennerpass.*

❺ Brennerpass
Since 1919 the Brennerpass has formed the border between Austria and Italy, when part of Tirol, called Südtirol, had to be ceded to Italy. By AD200 the Romans had laid a narrow path over this important Alpine crossing. Remnants of the old

Roman road can still be seen at the small Brennersee (lake) near by. Nowadays the Brenner crossing carries a large volume of traffic, mainly between Germany and Italy, which unfortunately pollutes the Tirolean countryside.

▶ *From Brenner continue south on the SS12 to Gossensass.*

6 Gossensass, Südtirol
A stop at Gossensass rewards the visitor with a first glimpse of Südtirol. The medieval burghers' houses in the centre are a reminder of the wealth

7 Sterzing, Südtirol
One of Sterzing's attractions are the colourful houses in the Neustadt, the main road in the centre of town. These buildings date back to the periods of late Gothic and Renaissance style in the Middle Ages. Many are adorned with decorative oriels. Look out for the Deutsch-ordenskommende, a 15th- to 16th-century building erected for the Deutscher Orden, a brotherhood founded in 1198 by Christian knights and priests to look after the sick. It is now a museum.

Two impressive castles are in

▶ *Continue south on the SS508 via the Penser Joch to Sarnthein.*

8 Sarnthein, Südtirol
The village of Sarnthein lies tucked away from the main traffic routes. On a gentle slope stands 13th-century Schloss Reinegg, now one of the best preserved in South Tirol. The churches in Sarnthein and the nearby hamlets of Nordheim, Astfeld and Gentersberg were all built in the 12th to 14th centuries in Romanesque style, but Gothic features such as arcades were added later.

Matrei, set in the Tauern Valley, with easy access to alpine beauty spots

created by the local mining industry. A chairlift from Gossensass takes visitors up to the Hühnerspielalm and a section near the top of the Rollspitze, 2,800m (9,186 feet) above sea level, which can be reached from the top in a half-hour walk.

[i] *Kurverwaltung*

▶ *Continue on the SS12 for 5km (3 miles) to Sterzing (Vipiteno).*

the vicinity. Burg Sprechenstein lies 1.8km (1 mile) north in a picturesque setting on a slope. Beautiful frescos decorate the castle's chapel, which contains a winged altar in late Gothic style. Burg Reifenstein stands on a rock 2km (1 mile) south of Sterzing. Still standing from the 12th century are the keep and the living quarters. The Deutsche Ritterorden (Order of the German Knights) erected additional buildings in front of the main castle in the 16th century.

[i] *Verkehrsamt, Stadtplatz*

[i] *Verkehrsverein*

▶ *Drive south on the SS508 for 19km (11 miles) to Bozen.*

9 Bozen, Südtirol
Bozen (Bolzano in Italian) was for centuries an important trading centre. Wealthy merchants here employed Italian artists from Venice and Florence, and together with talented local craftsmen Bozen became a showpiece and meeting place for northern and southern cultures. Even in prehistoric times a settlement stood here and in 15BC the Romans

erected a military post called *Pons Drusi* on this site.

The centre of Bozen is very similar to other Tirolean towns like Meran and Innsbruck, its pavements sheltered by arcades. South of the Waltherplatz (the main town square) stands the parish church on the site of an early Christian church, already in existence in the 5th century. The tower is 62m (203 feet) high; also notable is the 1729 high altar in marble. The old town of Bozen stretches out to the north of the Waltherplatz and is mainly a pedestrian precinct; the market plays an important role in the life of the local population and sells local produce.

For curiosity's sake you should also see the other side of Bozen, the Italian part called Neu Bozen. You enter it turning west across the Talfer river. Mazzini Square contains a fascist victory monument which has withstood several attempts to blow it up. Crossing back over the river you can stroll along the Wassermauer Promenade in a northerly direction to Schloss Maretsch. This is a lovely 13th-century castle, enlarged 300 years later and now a favoured venue for meetings and conferences.

Before leaving Bozen a trip further south should not be missed. Salurn (Salorna) is the last village of the German-speaking South Tirol. Gravestones here indicate it was a settlement during Roman times and the Salurner Klause, a narrow part of the Etsch valley, only 2km (1 mile) wide, represents a natural border. Steep mountains protect the valley, but throughout history this has been the scene of frequent skirmishes.

The parish church of St Andreas in Salurn was first documented in 1215 and its free-standing tower can be seen from far away. A visit to the ruins of Burg Hadersburg is also recommended. The return journey from Salurn to Bozen provides a real treat, a drive

through the vineyards on the Südtiroler Weinstrasse. If you ask for red wine anywhere you will be offered Kalterersee, a light and fruity wine from this region.

[i] *Städtisches Verkehrsamt und Kurverwaltung, Waltherplatz 28*

BACK TO NATURE

East of Bozen a side road leads up to the Rittenplateau and the village of Klobenstein. From here, near the hamlet of Mittelberg, you can see a marvel of nature, the Erdpyramiden. These pyramids, reminiscent of stalagmites in caves, are up to 30m (100 feet) high and their formation is due to erosion of the soil after the Ice Age.

FOR CHILDREN

From Bozen take the cablecar to Oberbozen. From here a rack railway runs through the meadows of the Rittenplateau to Klobenstein, a journey of 12km (7 miles). The railway used to run from the centre of Bozen, but the cablecar and the new road provide faster connections. The whole family will be enchanted by the beautiful countryside and magnificent views from up here, right to the Dolomites.

▶ *From Bozen take the Grosse Dolomitenstrasse (SS241) via Welschnofen and the Karersee to Hotel Latemar, then a sharp left turn towards the Nigerpass, just before the Karer Pass descends via Tiers. Take a right fork soon after Tiers, then turn north to Völs.*

🔟 Völs, Südtirol
At the beginning of the ascent to the Seiser Alm, a well-known pasture, lies the village of Völs, with its late Gothic parish church, and Romanesque St

Peter am Bichl, higher up the village. Some houses dating back to the 15th and 16th centuries are decorated with frescos or ornate portals. Nearby Schloss Prösels, 2km (1½ miles) south, shows interesting features from the 15th century: towers, portals, ramparts and medieval fortifications.

[i] *Verkehrsverein Völs am Schlern*

▶ *From Völs continue north, then the road turns east to Seis.*

🔟🔟 Seis, Südtirol
Seis is the central point from which to explore the Seiser Alm, an alpine pasture with large green meadows surrounded by mountains. The popularity of the area threatens its natural beauty and plans are in hand to make it car-free, with public transport providing the necessary communications. A road east leads 9km (5½ miles) to Schönblick, from where the road is barred to private cars. From Schönblick several chair-lifts transport visitors to enjoy the beauty of this alpine paradise.

[i] *Verkehrsamt Seis*

▶ *Continue north for 3km (2 miles) to Kastelruth, take the first turning west, then north for 8km (5 miles) to Waidbruck, and on the SS12 north to Brixen.*

🔟🔟 Brixen, Südtirol
Brixen is the oldest town in Tirol. Founded in AD901 it soon gained importance and became a bishopric. The inhabitants, however, have not enjoyed their status happily over the centuries: the plague arrived in 1348 and 1636, and in 1444 a fire claimed most of the buildings. At the end of the 18th century Brixen had to endure the occupation of 12,000 French troops. When they were driven out, the Bavarians arrived for eight years, until 1814 when Brixen was reunited with Austria. Later in 1919, after

World War I, South Tirol was ceded to Italy and the Italian occupation continues today.

The cathedral represents one of the most important church buildings in Tirol and its bishops rule over a wide area of the Catholic hierarchy in Tirol. It is well worth a visit – the cloister is particularly outstanding, and there are superb frescos. Located southwest of the cathedral is the former castle of the prince-bishops, which occupies the site of an earlier fortress from 1200. Now called the Hofburg, it was started in 1595 in Renaissance style, and completed only in 1710.

ⓘ *Kurverwaltung, Bahnhofstrasse 9*

Intricately decorated buildings give Matrei a distinctly Austrian air

▶ *From Brixen take the SS12 south towards Klausen, cross the river and take the SS242d to St Ulrich and Wolkenstein.*

⑬ Wolkenstein, Südtirol
The village of Wolkenstein is the last in the Grödner valley, before the Grödner Joch takes you into the next valley, the Gadertal. The ruin of Burg Wolkenstein is a reminder of the former aristrocratic rulers of the area. Their best-known son was the poet Oswald von Wolkenstein, who lived from about 1377 to 1445. The churchyard of Brixen's cathedral contains a plaque carved in stone, dedicated to the poet.

ⓘ *Verkehrsamt Wolkenstein in Gröden*

▶ *Take the SS242 east from Wolkenstein, then turn left on to the SS243, through the Grödner Joch and north on the SS244 down to the Gadertal to Bruneck.*

⑭ Bruneck, Südtirol
One of the most famous medieval painters and woodcarvers, Michael Pacher, was born in Bruneck. His reputation took him far afield from this alpine region and it is considered a great honour to exhibit one of his many masterpieces in churches or museums. Bruneck's delightful centre around the Stadtgasse is now a pedestrian zone.

Directly above the town stands Schloss Bruneck, built between 1251 and 1336. The strong outer walls remain – the inside is interesting too. A regional museum in the suburb of Dietenheim was erected in the grounds of a former large farm, which was called Mair am Hof, and portrays the life and work of the farmers in the valleys of South Tirol.

From Bruneck, try an excursion 14km (8½ miles) north through the Tauferer Tal to Sand in Taufers and its castle. The fortified castle (Burg) was constructed in the 13th century and stands on a commanding hill above the village. Two drawbridges have to be crossed to enter the castle courtyard, which is flanked by the keep and another wide tower, containing the living quarters.

BACK TO NATURE

Before turning left into the Antholz valley after leaving Bruneck, continue on the SS49 further east to Welsberg, then take a right fork which leads, via Prags, to the Pragser Wildsee. This spot is a photographer's dream, with a lake varying in colour from dark green to blue at one end and a steep rock fall at the other forming the backdrop.

The inner courtyard features a small smithy and the chapel is decorated with frescos from the workshop of Michael Pacher.

i *Verkehrsamt, Bruneck*

▶ *From Bruneck take the* **SS49** *east and branch off after 10km (6 miles) north via Niederrasen into the Antholzer Tal (Antholz valley), over the Staller Sattel back into Austria and continue on the* **L25** *through the Defereggental (Defereggen valley) to Huben. Then across the Iseltal on the* **L26** *into the Kalser Tal (Kalser valley) and Kals.*

15 **Kals am Grossglockner,** Osttirol

Kals is a good starting point for many mountain hikes in the area and several huts provide the necessary stopping points. The Grossglockner, at 3,797m (12,461 feet), is the highest mountain in Austria and, weather permitting, can be clearly seen from Kals. For a really magnificent panorama there is a chairlift called Bergbahn Glocknerblick leading up to 2,000m (6,562 feet). From there a world of 30 alpine peaks unfolds.

i *Fremdenverkehrsverband, Kals*

▶ *From Kals return to Huben on the* **L26,** *then turn sharp north on the* **108** *to Matrei.*

16 **Matrei,** Osttirol

Matrei lies well positioned in a wider section of the Tauerntal (Tauern valley), already settled in prehistoric times. Matrei's landmark, Schloss Weissenstein, former outpost of the bishops of Salzburg, stands on a steep rock. It was built in the 13th century, but rebuilt in the 19th. A chairlift provides a pleasant ride up the mountain and from the top easy walks can be taken to enjoy the magnificent alpine panorama.

At Bichl, just outside Matrei, old Roman gravestones are exhibited, dating from 200BC. A trip to the end of the Virgental

A striking view of Austria's highest peak, the Grossglockner

leads to the Umbalfälle (Umball waterfalls), which can be seen from a specially arranged path to get the best views.

i *Fremdenverkehrsverband, Rauterplatz 3*

▶ *From Matrei turn north towards the Felbertauerntunnel on the* **168**.

17 **Felbertauerntunnel,** Osttirol/Salzburg

It was only in 1967 that a road connection was established here through a tunnel, 5km (3 miles) long. From old pictures it can be seen that this crossing over the Alps was used much earlier, when loads were packed on horses and driven in convoys over the narrow trails. These convoys, called *Samerzug,* are still organised from Mittersill to let the tradition live on.

▶ *From Felbertauerntunnel continue north to Mittersill.*

18 Mittersill, Salzburg

Mittersill has become a busy junction where traffic meets from north and south, east and west, but is also a focal point for the National Park region of Hohe Tauern, where measures are taken to protect the environment. Mittersill has a very interesting local museum, the Heimatmuseum, housed in the Felberturm, a square-shaped tower where farmers once came to pay their rents. The ground floor displays agricultural tools and the upper floors exhibit a well-presented collection of alpine minerals and crystals. One of the emeralds found in the Rauris valley in the Hohe Tauern range is set in the British crown, part of the Crown Jewels in the Tower of London.

The castle, on the slopes overlooking the Pinzgau valley, was burnt down during the peasant revolt in 1525 and then rebuilt. It is now a privately owned hotel.

i   Fremdenverkehrsverband, Marktplatz 4

RECOMMENDED WALKS

Between Mittersill and Krimml lies Neukirchen am Grossvenediger. From here a cableway leads up to about 2,000m (6,562 feet) and an area for easy walks and impressive views south to the glaciers of the Hohe Tauern range. Up here is also a favourite take-off point for parasailers.

▶ *From Mittersill continue west on the 165 to Krimml.*

---

19 Krimml, Salzburg

Krimml is well known for its mighty waterfalls, claimed to be the largest in Europe. The water crashes down with tremendous force in three steps over a total distance of 380m (1,250 feet). Photographers should note that the best time for taking pictures is from 10am to 1pm from the upper fall – as the falls are flanked by steep

---

mountains they are in shade for most of the time.

i   Verkehrsverein Krimml, Salzburg

▶ *From Krimml continue on the 165 over the Gerlos Pass to Zell am Ziller, turn right on the 169 to Jenbach, then take the A12 west to Innsbruck.*

SCENIC ROUTES

Soon after leaving Sterzing the route up to the Penser Joch (pass) becomes very enjoyable and leads through some delightful countryside. Try to stop at the top of the pass for the view.

Leaving Bozen the Grosse Dolomitenstrasse leads through some incredibly beautiful countryside, which continues along the Rosengarten range to Tiers.

The thunderous Krimml waterfalls

Over the Alps
to Famous Spas

The old centre of Villach, on the right bank of the Drau river, has a wealth of interesting old buildings. The Hauptplatz (main square) is surrounded by burghers' houses, the most famous being No 18, where physician and scientist Theophrastus Bombastus von Hohenheim (Paracelsus) spent his youth (see page 23); and the parish church of St Jakob, also on the main square, has a 95m (312-foot) Romanesque tower.

4 DAYS • 320KM • 198 MILES

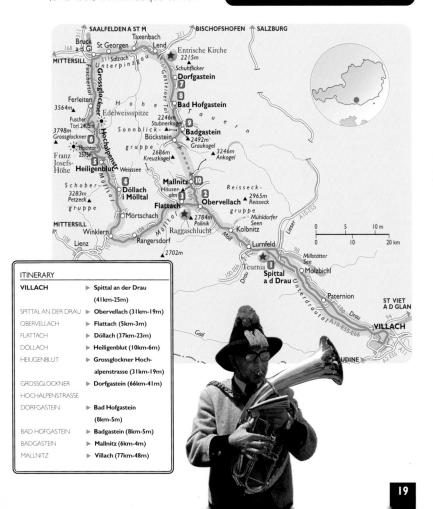

i Fremdenverkehrsamt der Stadt
Villach, Europaplatz 2

FOR CHILDREN

Draupromenade 12 in the
centre of Villach is the location
for the Villacher Fahrzeug
Museum (automobile museum)
which will be of interest to
children and adults alike. The
museum pays homage to the
post-World War II vehicles of
the '50s, when owning a car
was only a dream to many.
The exhibition covers cars,
scooters, motorbikes and
mopeds and is open daily.

▶ From Villach take the 100 to
Spittal an der Drau.

❶ Spittal an der Drau,
Kärnten

The town of Spittal is often
referred to as Spittal am
Millstätter See, due to its proximity to the lake. It lies at the
confluence of the Lieser and
Drau rivers and its name comes
from *Spittel*, an old German
word meaning hospital. In 1191,
a small church and hospital for
pilgrims stood here. Previously
a market place, the town only
received its charter in 1930.
One building outshines the rest,
the Renaissance Schloss Porcia.
It is also called the Schloss
Salamanca after the Spanish
Count Salamanca, who, as chancellor to Archduke Ferdinand of
Austria, had the palace built
between 1533 and 1597. It is
one of the few Austrian buildings in true Renaissance style,
and it incorporates some exquisite Italian designs. The focal
point is the courtyard with
three-storeyed arcades built on
a square base. The upper floors
house the local Bezirksheimat-
museum (District Museum)
which gives information on the
different ruling houses of the
area and local folklore. A miniature castle in the park exhibits a
collection of minerals and a
mining museum.
    The remnants of a Celtic

settlement, called *Teurnia*
(which under the Romans
became *Tiburnia*) can be seen at
St Peter in Holz, about 5km (3
miles) northwest of Spittal. The
scattered remains lie between
the main road and the confluence of the Fischerbach into
the Drau river. The Teurnia
Museum and an open-air exhibition provide additional insight
into the early cultures and civili-
sations of the region.

i Fremdenverkehrsamt,
Burgplatz 1 (Schloss Porcia)

RECOMMENDED
WALKS

Between Spittal and
Obervellach a stop is
suggested at Kolbnitz in the
Mölltal. The Reisseck mountain
railway takes visitors up to the
Reisseck Lake Plateau in 45
minutes. The large and small
Mühldorfer Seen are both
natural alpine lakes and are
now being used as reservoirs.
Well-marked trails lead visitors
through the area for enjoyable
walks and hikes. The
powerhouse at Kolbnitz can be
visited and will be of special
interest to the technically
minded.

▶ From Spittal continue northwest on the 100 to the junction at Lurnfeld and take
the 106 northwest to
Obervellach.

❷ Obervellach, Kärnten
Obervellach became known in
the 16th century for its gold and
copper mining industries. It was
during this time, when the town
flourished, that the local parish
church of St Martin was built
and attracted the famous Dutch
painter Jan van Scorel in 1520, a
pupil of Albrecht Dürer.
Although one of his early works,
the altar triptych in the northern
chapel is judged to be a masterpiece of the Renaissance
period.

i Fremdenverkehrsamt

▶ Continue on the 106 west
to Flattach.

❸ Flattach, Kärnten
Flattach is the starting point for
two popular excursions. To the
south lies the entrance to the
Raggaschlucht (gorge), to which
a visit is highly recommended.
The walk extends over 800m
(2,625 feet) and climbs 200m
(650 feet), but there are very
secured walkways laid out along the
rocks and over bridges, which
make this an enjoyable and
fascinating exercise. The gorge
is open every day between May
and October.
    The trip north leads by road
through the Fragantbachtal to
the Weissseehaus. A cableway
then takes you to the
Wurtenkees glacier. The views
from up here are very rewarding
and extend as far as the highest
peaks of the Eastern Alps.

i Gemeindeamt

▶ From Flattach continue on the
106 to Winklern and then
north on the 107 to Döllach.

❹ Döllach im Mölltal,
Kärnten

Up in the valley of the Möll
river lies Döllach, the main
centre of the newly created
community resort of
Grosskirchheim, which takes in
a number of small villages in
the vicinity.
    The Schloss was built in the
15th century and once housed
the administration of the gold
and silver mining in the area. Its
imposing buildings are interconnected by walls and now
incorporate an interesting
museum, which explains the
development of gold mining in
the Hohe Tauern mountains –
already practised in Roman
times. A collection of minerals,
old furniture, tools, arms and
artefacts from Upper Carinthia
supplement the exhibition.

i Verkehrsamt

▶ From Döllach continue on the
107 north to Heiligenblut.

altar comes from the workshop of the famous Michael Pacher, the man responsible for many of the masterpieces in Alpine churches. The relic is kept in the Sakramenthäuschen, a shrine in the choir section. You should not miss the crypt. Steps lead down to a hall which is impressive in its noble simplicity and style. The church is surrounded by a beautiful churchyard and graves with wrought-iron crosses above them.

> [i] Verkehrsamt

SPECIAL TO...

The tourist office in Heiligenblut hires out equipment for those interested in gold washing in the surrounding streams. The former mines were used until the 15th century when they iced up, but the rocks in the riverbeds still contain particles of gold. You won't get rich, but it is an entertaining pastime, and who knows, someone may be lucky and bring home some grains of the precious metal.

RECOMMENDED WALKS

From Heiligenblut start northwest of the village via Winkl to the romantic Gössnitzal and the 100m (327-foot) waterfall.

> ▶ From Heiligenblut continue on the **107** north to the Hochtor and Fuscher Törl.

Heiligenblut's elegant parish church rises above the resting place of St Briccius, a distinctive landmark among alpine scenery

---

SCENIC ROUTES

The really attractive part of the Grossglockner Hochalpenstrasse (High Alpine Road) begins after leaving Döllach. Meadows and trees gradually give way to alpine pastures and are followed by a region of rocks and ice. The panoramic views from the Edelweissspitze are claimed to include 37 alpine peaks in excess of an altitude of 3,000m (9,843 feet).

5 Heiligenblut, Kärnten
Heiligenblut is perhaps one of the most photographed places in Austria because of its position, its attractive church and superb background. The name means Holy Blood and legend recalls the story of St Briccius, who wanted to take a sample of the blood of Jesus from Constantinople (now Istanbul) back to Denmark. He was killed by an avalanche, but later found and buried. A chapel was erected above his grave and the precious relic was later stored in the parish church of Heiligenblut. The church was erected by the miners' guild with the help of local farmers between 1483 and 1491 in true Gothic style. The wood-carved

6 Grossglockner Hochalpenstrasse, Kärnten/Salzburg
Soon after leaving Heiligenblut the real ascent starts and as the maximum gradient is only 1 in 8 this should not cause any problems, especially as the road is superbly engineered. Problems which could arise are caused by the road's popularity in the

21

Sightseers enjoy magnificent views from the Grossglockner road

summer months, when parking areas near the viewpoints can be full and it is advisable to walk for the last stretch. After 8km (5 miles) the road to the Franz-Josefs Höhe branches off to the left. A hotel stands here and you are overwhelmed by one of the most majestic views in the Eastern Alps from a height of 2,362m (7,086 feet). The Grossglockner, Austria's highest mountain, stands right in front of you and a lift from the car park leads down to the glacier. It is a 9km (6-mile) journey back to the turn-off point and then another 7km (4 miles) of zigzags and bends up to the highest point, the Hochtor, at 2,575m (8,420 feet), which is also the border between the provinces of Carinthia and Salzburg.

From the Hochtor, the road leads down to the Fuscher Törl and a side road from there continues up to the Edelweiss-spitze. This is also a superb viewpoint which should not be missed. From then on it is downhill all the way!

i   *Franz-Josefs Höhe*

▶ *Drive from the Edelweiss-spitze down to Fuscher Törl, turn right and continue on the 107 to Bruck an der Glocknerstrasse. Take a right turn and continue on the 311 to Lend and turn right for the 167 to Dorfgastein.*

FOR HISTORY BUFFS

East of the village of Bruck, after the descent on the Grossglockner Hochalpenstrasse, lies St Georgen. In 1732 a linden tree was planted here to commemorate the expulsion of the Protestants. The tree is still standing and is now a natural monument. Also interesting is the parish church, a neo-Gothic building. It contains a picture of Maria auf dem Eis (Our Lady of the Ice) of around 1500.

---

7 Dorfgastein, Salzburg
When entering the Gastein Tal (Gastein valley) a surprise awaits the visitor. Near the ruin of Klammstein is the entrance to a cave, called the Entrische Kirche (literally translated as the 'frightening church'). It is a large cave, divided into many subterranean halls. An upper floor, recently discovered, is a great attraction. The cave can be visited from June to September.

A short drive leads to the resort of Dorfgastein, a small restful village surrounded by meadows and pastures. A chair-lift leads up to the 1,500m (4,920-foot) Brandlalm.

i   *Verkehrsamt*

▶ *From Dorfgastein continue on the 167 to Bad Hofgastein.*

8 Bad Hofgastein, Salzburg
This spa resort gets its warm water from a nearby spring. The water is known for its healing properties for rheumatic disorders. One of the main attrac-

tions is the swimming pool in the Kurzentrum, where the water temperature in the three separate indoor pools is 32°C and swimmers can reach the outdoor pool without leaving the water. If you find this too warm, the sport swimming pool is kept at 24°C. No spa is complete without a Kurpark, where you can stroll, and the park in Bad Hofgastein is laid out with alpine flora, affording views of the glaciers of the Hohe Tauern mountain range.

The parish church of Our Lady was first built in 894 and was reconstructed several times during the 15th and 16th centuries. It also benefited from donations and gifts during the period 1400 to 1560, when gold

A tranquil village scene in the quiet resort of Dorfgastein, set among alpine meadows

mining created many benefactors of great wealth. The church is now one of the finest Gothic-style buildings in the province of Salzburg. The high altar inside is enriched with a statue of the Madonna sitting on a throne. The Weitmoserschlösschen, southwest of the town, stands in a commanding posi-

tion on a hill, representing a Gewerkensitz (guildhall), and also the residence of mine owners from the boom years during the 16th century, in typical Salzburg style.

ⓘ *Kurverwaltung*

▶ *Continue for 8km (5 miles) on the 167 south to Badgastein.*

9 **Badgastein,** Salzburg
The waterfall of the Gasteiner Ache, the river which gushes through the town, is Badgastein's landmark. If you are stopping overnight it is suggested you stay a certain distance from the falls as the noise of the thundering waters is loud. As in many other spas, the Romans were the first to discover the healing qualities of the thermal springs. The first person, however, to analyse the benefits of the springs, was the physician and researcher Theophrastus Bombastus von Hohenheim. All kinds of cures are available under doctors' orders, especially for sufferers from asthma, rheumatism and circulatory problems. The Felsenbad Gastein offers similar facilities to the one at Bad Hofgastein.

For golfers a nine-hole golf course is available from May to October. As Badgastein is also a winter sports resort a number of lifts are available to take you up to higher altitudes. The Stubnerkogel cableway from the station leads up 2,246m (7,369 feet); the Graukogel chairlift from the Hotel

Schillerhof goes up to 1,985m (6,512 feet); while from the Bellevuehotel, another chairlift provides an easy connection to the Almbar, with an open-air pool. Needless to say, good Austrian catering can be found at all three destinations.

A short way south of Badgastein, near Böckstein, an old gold and silver mine is being used for hot-air treatments. The therapeutic mine shaft has temperatures between 37 and 42°C and humidity of between 80 to 97 per cent. Entry to the Heilstollen (treatment shaft) is strictly supervised and a prior visit to a physician is obligatory.

ⓘ *Kurverwaltung*

▶ *Drive 4km south to Böckstein. Cars are put on shuttle trains and taken through the tunnel to Mallnitz.*

10 **Mallnitz,** Kärnten
It takes about 10 minutes from Böckstein to Mallnitz by train. Mallnitz is a resort just south of the high Alpine peaks of the Hohe Tauern range and a good centre for walking tours and mountain hikes. The town is 1,200m (3,937 feet) above sea level and the mountain air is crisp and clean.

The Ankogel cableway, about 4km (2 miles) north of Mallnitz takes visitors up to 2,722m (8,930 feet) and apart from the breathtaking views over the snow-covered mountains the terrain offers gentle walks and hikes. You can take the double chairlift to the 1,900m (6,234-foot) Häusleralm which starts only 1km (½ mile) south of Mallnitz. Very pleasant walks can be enjoyed from the top terminus on the surrounding plateau.

ⓘ *Fremdenverkehrsverband*

▶ *From Mallnitz take the 105 south to Obervellach, then the 106 southeast to Lurnfeld. Take the 100 east to Lendorf and then join the A10 southeast to Villach.*

Salzburg & the
Salzkammergut

Salzburg's long history has seen occupation by the Illyrians, the Celts and the Romans. But its greatest period began in the 17th century, when architects von Erlach and von Hildebrandt gave the city its baroque beauty. This is also a city of music, whose annual festival is famous worldwide.

6 DAYS • 386KM • 240½ MILES

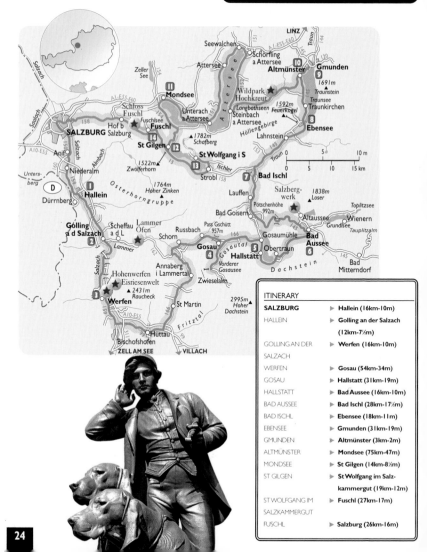

ITINERARY

SALZBURG	▶ Hallein (16km-10m)
HALLEIN	▶ **Golling an der Salzach** (12km-7½m)
GOLLING AN DER SALZACH	▶ **Werfen** (16km-10m)
WERFEN	▶ Gosau (54km-34m)
GOSAU	▶ Hallstatt (31km-19m)
HALLSTATT	▶ **Bad Aussee** (16km-10m)
BAD AUSSEE	▶ Bad Ischl (28km-17½m)
BAD ISCHL	▶ Ebensee (18km-11m)
EBENSEE	▶ Gmunden (31km-19m)
GMUNDEN	▶ Altmünster (3km-2m)
ALTMÜNSTER	▶ Mondsee (75km-47m)
MONDSEE	▶ St Gilgen (14km-8½m)
ST GILGEN	▶ **St Wolfgang im Salz-kammergut** (19km-12m)
ST WOLFGANG IM SALZKAMMERGUT	▶ Fuschl (27km-17m)
FUSCHL	▶ Salzburg (26km-16m)

A general view of Hallstatt, the beautiful waterside village

i Stadtverkehrsbüro, Auerspergstrasse 7

▶ *From Salzburg take the 150 then the 159 south to Hallein.*

❶ Hallein, Salzburg
Hallein is very much connected with the mining and processing of salt. The village of Dürrnberg became part of Hallein in 1938, and it is a spa for cures which depend on saline waters. Its main attraction, however, is the salt mine, which can be visited from May to September. The tour through the mine is extensive and well organised. One shaft even crosses a subterranean border with Bavaria. Overalls and miner's caps are provided and enjoyable slides and rides through chutes are great fun for everybody.

Opposite the parish church on the Gruberplatz stands the house of the organ player Franz Gruber (1787–1863), the composer of *Silent Night (Stille Nacht)* who died in 1863. In the Keltenmuseum (Celtic Museum) you can see local finds and the original score of the famous Christmas carol.

i Fremdenverkehrsverband, Unterer Markt 1

▶ *From Hallein continue south on the 159 to Golling.*

❷ Golling an der Salzach, Salzburg
In the castle look out for the prehistoric cave drawings on show. The village is a good centre for short trips into the outgoing area. The Golling waterfall lies 3km (2 miles) west

and can be reached by pleasant footpaths. The water there cascades down from a height of 76m (249 feet) and this spectacle with its surroundings has inspired many a painter seeking a romantic scene.

Eastwards, a short drive leads to Scheffen, which has a remarkably large church for a small village. Gothic-style ornaments on the door fittings and paintings of horses on the windows refer to the former function of this church as a centre for pilgrimages on horseback, presumably for blessings. Driving further along the valley you reach the Lammer Klause. A secured footpath, chiselled into the rocks, leads through the Lammer Öfen, a narrow gorge of the Lammer stream. The rocks on either side are fascinating, the result of water erosion over thousands of years.

⌑ *Fremdenverkehrsamt*

▶ *From Golling continue south on the **159** to Werfen.*

⓵ **Werfen,** Salzburg

The old market town of Werfen is now a favourite spot for visitors to one of nature's wonders, the Eisriesenwelt (giant ice cave). It claims to be the largest in the world, 42km (26 miles) long. The various monuments in ice are created by a natural airflow. In summer the warm air from outside enters the caves and melts the ice. In winter the molten ice freezes again and both phenomena interact and create spectacular formations, which depend on the direction of the wind. All are given names and are enhanced by clever illuminations. To reach the entrance, take the road north to the Fallstein car park. From here it is a 10-minute walk to the Rasthaus (rest house) and then four minutes by cableway to the Dr F Oedi Haus, the starting point for guided tours through the cave.

Also recommended is a visit to the fortress Hohenwerfen, which was erected in 1077 and

A well-loved prospect: the Vorderer Gosausee, against the backdrop of the Dachstein peak

extended by Archbishop Konrad in 1122. After the peasants' revolt between 1525 and 1526, further defensive measures were taken but the fortress acquired its present-day appearance in 1563 under Archbishop Lang. Emperor Franz I renovated the complex in 1824, as he wanted to retain this 'picturesque remnant of old times'. In 1931 a fire devastated the fortress, but it was restored yet again. The focal points inside are the *palas* (the living quarters) and the bell tower with its 1563 Renaissance bell.

⌑ *Fremdenverkehrsverband, Hauptstrasse*

▶ *From Werfen continue south on the **159** towards Bischofshofen, take a left turn for the **99** east to Niedernfritz, turn left for the **166** and continue to Gosau.*

⓸ **Gosau,** Oberösterreich

After the steep descent from Pass Gschütt, a right turning in Gosau leads to the Vorderer Gosausee, an alpine lake set 937m (3,074 feet) above sea level, which is surrounded by sheer rocks and offers a most stunning view towards the Gosau glacier and the Dachstein mountain beyond. This particular view is very well known in Austria and has been chosen as a motif for many landscape painters in search of a romantic setting.

A cableway from the western shore of the lake is available up to the 1,587m (5,207-foot) Zwieselalm. From here a far-reaching panorama stretches out before you, suggesting many other delightful places to explore.

⌑ *Fremdenverkehrsverband, Gosau*

▶ *Continue on the **166** east to Gosaumühle and south to Hallstatt.*

8 Hallstatt, Oberösterreich

The village of Hallstatt is a rewarding subject for any photographer – especially those prepared to take a boat out on to the lake to get a good shot. The village lies perched between the lake and the foothills of a mountain and its reflection on the surface of the lake provides an unforgettable image. Hallstatt's history goes back to 900BC. Many graves have been found since excavations started in the 19th century. For safety, the people of the early Iron Age lived in wooden houses on stilts on the shores of the lake. Salt mining became a lucrative business here early in village history. A five-minute trip by funicular takes you up to the entrance of the salt mine, which is open to the public from May to October. The visit starts with a slide down to the salt works and finishes with a circular walk round the illuminated salt lake. The museum at Marktplatz is also open from May to October, giving information on prehistoric times and the old methods of salt mining. Also on show are finds from the graveyards of the

Salzberg (Salt Mountain). A regular motorboat service connects with other villages on the lake.

i *Fremdenverkehrsverband, Seestrasse 56*

▶ *Continue south to Obertraun and northeast to Bad Aussee.*

9 Bad Aussee, Steiermark

Bad Aussee owed its growth in the Middle Ages to its large deposits of salt. The Kammerhof on the Oberer Marktplatz houses the museum which exhibits local artefacts and costumes, but also has a special section dealing with cave exploration and salt mining. In the 19th century Bad Aussee's salt water was first used for medical cures. Now it is also a popular tourist resort.

Nearby Altaussee had the first salt works before they were transferred to Bad Aussee by Duke Albrecht in 1290. The old salt mine (*Salzbergwerk*) lies northwest of Alt Aussee and can be visited daily. The guided tours last about an hour and a half. During World War II

the mine was used to store precious works of art.

The Salzkammergut Panoramastrasse (Panorama Road) leads from north of the town to Augstsee (10km/6 miles), an ideal spot for hikers who can climb up to the top of the Loser mountain in about an hour. Superb views from here make it worth the effort. Another lake in the area is the Grundlsee, which is by the village of the same name. You can follow the road to the other end of the lake and further on to the Toplitzsee. Rumour has it that treasures were sunk here before the end of the last war, but so far nothing of value has been recovered.

A detour is suggested from Grundlsee south to the 145 and east to Bad Mitterndorf. From here a narrow road leads up to the Tauplitzalm, a large plateau with many small lakes. Return to Bad Aussee on the 145.

i *Kurverwaltung*

Bad Aussee, once full of visitors seeking salt-water cures, now a favourite centre for tourists

St Wolfgang im Salzkammergut, a traditional village on the lake shore

▶ From Bad Aussee take the 145 northwest to Bad Ischl.

7 Bad Ischl, Oberösterreich
Bad Ischl is a well known spa, the discovery of Emperor Franz Josef I. It was his favourite spot and summer residence, and he had his own villa built here. The Kaiservilla is open to visitors and shows the Emperor's fondness for a simple and disciplined lifestyle. The composer of the operetta *The Merry Widow*, Franz Lehár, also had a house here, now the Franz Lehár Museum.

Bad Ischl flourished in the 19th and beginning of the 20th century, when the European aristrocracy was at its most glittering. There is also another salt mine on view from mid-May to the end of September.

☐ Kurdirektion, Bahnhofstrasse 6

▶ From Bad Ischl continue on the 145 northeast to Ebensee.

8 Ebensee, Oberösterreich
Ebensee lies on the southern end of the Traunsee and is bordered on its west side by the formidable Höllengebirge mountain range. A cableway

leads from Ebensee up to the Feuerkogel peak, 1,594m (5,223 feet) above sea level, which offers fine views of the area. A rewarding side trip leads 8km (5 miles) west of Ebensee to the Langbathseen (lakes), which lie in a designated nature park to preserve their remote and unspoilt environment.

☐ Gemeindeamt

▶ From Ebensee continue north on the 145 to Gmunden.

9 Gmunden, Oberösterreich
Gmunden lies at the top end of the Traunsee and is an old established holiday resort. A bridge over the Traun river connects the two parts of Gmunden and this is also the town centre. Its attractive lakeside position lured many visitors in bygone times and, as a result, a number of castles were built here for the wealthy. In the part of Gmunden called Traundorf stands Schloss Cumberland, which was built between 1882 and 1886 by the last King of Hanover. The most notable castle is Schloss Orth, erected in

the 17th century on an artificial island and connected to the mainland by a 130m (426-foot) wooden bridge. Gmunden's ceramics are well-known in Austria and the Rathaus (town hall) has a unique carillon using ceramic bells.

☐ Kurverwaltung, Am Graben

▶ Drive southwest to Altmünster.

10 Altmünster,
Oberösterreich
Altmünster was founded by the Romans and later became a market town. The name of the town, the 'old minster', refers to an early Benedictine monastery which only had a short lifespan. In the chapel of the parish church of St Benedict is a notable epitaph engraved in red marble, which refers to Count Herbersdorf, who was governor of the area and hated for his cruelty in putting down the peasants' uprising in 1526. A peasant later took revenge and killed him. An old Roman gravestone has been taken into the church to avoid further erosion by the weather.

☐ Verkehrsamt

FOR CHILDREN

The route from Altmünster to the Attersee Lake takes you past the Wildpark Hochkreut, a game park on an elevated meadow. It warrants a stop to see the enclosures with ibex, moufflon and bison which are kept there in relative freedom. Petting animals like ponies and goats will delight the children. Open from the beginning of April until the snows fall.

▶ *Take the L544 southwest to Steinbach am Attersee, turn right on the 152 to Schörfling and continue on the other side of the Attersee on the 151 to Unterach am Attersee and northwest to Mondsee.*

⓫ Mondsee, Oberösterreich
Mondsee is now a thriving holiday resort. It was already a settlement in 3000BC, when people lived in dwellings on stilts by the lakeshore. The finds established the name 'Mondsee Culture' which was given to similar settlements on other lakes in the Eastern Alps. After the Romans left, a Benedictine abbey was founded in AD748 by the Bavarian Duke Odilo II. The former abbey church of St Michael has five baroque-style altars by Meinrad Guggenbichler, one of which is called the Corpus Christi altar and depicts appealing statues of children carrying grapes. Incidentally, this church featured in the film *The Sound of Music*. Three museums can also be visited in Mondsee: the local Heimatmuseum with works by Guggenbichler; and the Austrian Pfahlbaumuseum, which shows stilt dwellings and brings to life the Mondsee Culture period are both located in

The town hall in St Gilgen, birthplace of Mozart's mother

the former abbey; the third museum is called the Mondseer Rauchhaus, an open-air museum which displays one of the oldest farmhouses of the area, fully furnished in the rural style of the time.

ℹ️ *Fremdenverkehrsverband, Dr Franz Müller Strasse 3*

▶ *From Mondsee take the 154 southeast on the west side of the lake to St Gilgen.*

⓬ St Gilgen, Salzburg
A plaque on the magistrates' court in St Gilgen commemorates the birthplace of Mozart's mother, Anna Maria Pertl, who was born here in 1720. Later, Mozart's sister, Nannerl (Marianne), lived here from 1784 to 1801. The Mozartbrunnen (fountain) in front of the town hall is a further reminder of the famous family and has become St Gilgen's landmark. This well-established lakeside resort offers many leisure and sports facilities and hikers can take a 10-minute ride by cableway up the

Zwölferhorn mountain to wander around the top and make the most of the breath-taking view over seven lakes and the glaciers of the Dachstein to the south.

ℹ️ *Verkehrsverein, Mozartplatz 1*

▶ *From St Gilgen take the 158 southeast to Strobl and from there take a left turn to St Wolfgang.*

⓭ St Wolfgang im Salzkammergut, Oberösterreich
As St Wolfgang gets very congested in the summer, it may be advisable – as well as pleasant – to leave the car in St Gilgen and complete your journey by lake steamer. St Wolfgang is perhaps the most famous village in the Salzkammergut area. Music lovers will recognise the setting of The White Horse Inn, the Weisses Rössl, which stands right on the lake. Inside, this old inn is full of tradition and sitting on the lakeside terrace enjoying a meal or a drink is one of the great pleasures of the visit. The parish

Pacher's altar, St Wolfgang church

church can be seen from many points around the lake and the interior contains a splendid work of art in the altar by Michael Pacher. The wood-carved altar was commissioned in 1471 and it took the artist 10 years to complete the work; it then had to be transported over the Brennerpass from Pacher's home in Bruneck, Tirol. This was quite a feat when you consider the height of the altar (12m/39 feet) and the transport facilities of the time. The Pacher Altar is in Gothic style, elaborately worked and painted. The wings are closed during the week, but opened on Sundays, when it is revealed in all its glory. It is worth studying the intricate carving and getting to understand the details, so

perfectly arranged and finely executed on this quite unique masterpiece.

[i] *Kurdirektion*

RECOMMENDED WALKS

From St Wolfgang a cogwheel railway takes visitors up to the top of the Schafberg, north of town. Pleasant walks through alpine meadows are available and panoramic views cover all three lakes in the vicinity, the Wolfgangsee, Mondsee and Attersee. Keen hikers can also climb up from St Wolfgang in about four hours; others have the option of just walking down instead or taking the train back.

▶ Turn back to St Gilgen and continue on the 158 north-west to Fuschl.

14 Fuschl, Salzburg

The village of Fuschl is surrounded by forests and mountains and a comparatively small lake, which makes the area more intimate. On a peninsula above the dark waters of the lake stands Schloss Fuschl, built in the 15th century as a hunting lodge for the Archbishops of Salzburg. Its exclusive position makes it a favourite spot for visitors and it now functions as a luxury hotel. Visitors can sit on the terrace overlooking the lake and surrounding mountains enjoying the view and the delightful atmosphere. In the castle grounds are a hunting and pipe museum and a game park.

[i] *Gemeindeamt*

FOR CHILDREN

From Fuschl you can take the children to the summer tobogganing run, which lies 3km (2 miles) south.

▶ From Fuschl take the 158 west to Salzburg.

SCENIC ROUTES

The route along the Traunsee from Ebensee to Gmunden is very attractive – look out for the imposing Traunstein mountain, dominant on the other side of the lake.
Drive south from Schörfling along the west side of the Attersee to Unterach. The road often leads right along the shoreline of the lake and the scenery gets more and more dramatic the further you go. At Unterach the mountains of the Höllengebirge stand right on the opposite side of the lake and present a stunning picture.

The Southern
Vienna Woods

Few visitors will fail to be stirred by the sight of the magnificent 12th-century Cistercian abbey of Heiligenkreuz; most will be deeply moved by the tragic events at Mayerling, while the spa towns of Bad Vöslau and Baden offer an intriguing glimpse of a past age of glory and elegance.

3 DAYS • 382KM • 236½ MILES

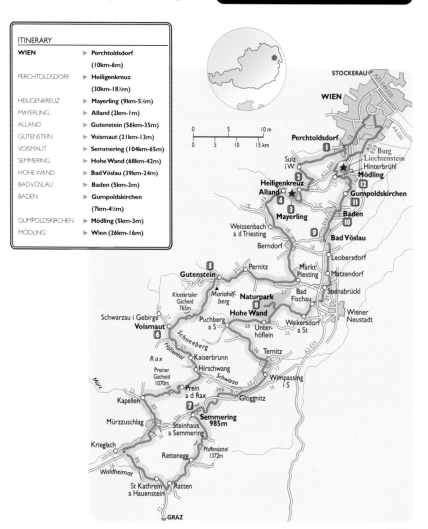

Leafy glade in the Wienerwald

4 Alland, Niederösterreich
Alland lies only 2km (1 mile) from Mayerling. It is known for its long cave with stalagmites and stalactites and is a good stopping place. The cave is open from Easter to autumn.

▶ *Drive on the 11 southwest, then southeast to Weissenbach an der Triesting, continue on the 18 to Berndorf and south to Markt Piesting. Take a right turn and continue on the 21 west to Pernitz and Gutenstein.*

5 Gutenstein,
Niederösterreich
The castle is now a ruin, but there are fascinating views down to the gorges. The Waldbauernmuseum (Museum of Hill Farmers) gives an insight into local lives. From Gutenstein, a winding road leads 3km (2 miles) up to the Mariahilferberg (mountain), which is 708m (2,323 feet) high. On the peak stands a baroque pilgrim church with excellent views.

▶ *From Gutenstein drive 3km (2 miles) west on the 21 and turn left and continue on the LH134 to Voismaut.*

6 Voismaut,
Niederösterreich
The Falkenstein nature park is only a short distance north from Voismaut, at Schwarzau im Gebirge. Here you can get close to nature and enjoy picnics.

⒤ *Schwarzau Naturpark*

FOR CHILDREN

Just before reaching Hirschwang in the Höllental is the terminus of the Raxbahn, one of the oldest cableways in Austria. It leads up to the high plateau of the Rax mountain. An Alpenlehrpfad (alpine lecture trail) is marked.

▶ *From the centre of Vienna drive to the ring road, the Gürtel. Take the 12 to Liesing and turn right via Rodaun to Perchtoldsdorf.*

1 Perchtoldsdorf,
Niederösterreich
On the market square stands the imposing medieval keep and the parish church of St Augustin. The keep houses a museum of local history.

⒤ *Fremdenverkehrsamt*

▶ *Drive west on the LH127 to Sulz im Wienerwald and continue southeast to Sittendorf. Take a right fork due south to the 11 and turn right to Heiligenkreuz.*

2 Heiligenkreuz,
Niederösterreich
The Cistercian abbey of Heiligenkreuz was founded in 1135 and is one of the oldest of this order in Austria. Its name derives from a relic of the True Cross, presented to the monks by Duke Leopold V on his return from the Third Crusade.

The interior of the Stiftskirche shows interesting contrasts in style, the dark Romanesque nave and heavy pillars against the bright Gothic choir section. Both Franz Schubert and Anton Bruckner played the organ here.

⒤ *Fremdenverkehrsamt*

▶ *Take the LH130 south to Sattelbach and turn sharp right on the 210 northwest to Mayerling.*

3 Mayerling,
Niederösterreich
The tragic story of Mayerling unfolded in a lonely hunting lodge on 29 January 1899. The Crown Prince of Austria, only son of Emperor Franz Josef, first shot his mistress Baroness Maria Vetsera, who was only 17 years old, then killed himself. The Emperor then gave orders for the lodge to be converted into a Carmelite convent.

⒤ *Kloster*

▶ *From Mayerling continue on the 210 northwest to Alland.*

Take the **27** south to Hirschwang and the first turning right to the **LH135** southwest via Prein an der Rax to Kapellen. Turn sharp left on the **23** southeast to Mürzzuschlag. Take the **S6** southwest to Krieglach and turn left on the **72** southeast to St Kathrein am Hauenstein, then take the first turning left on the **L117** via Ratten, Rettenegg and the Pfaffensattel to Steinhaus am Semmering and turn right on the **306** to Semmering.

🛐 Semmering,
Niederösterreich

The Semmering Pass forms the border between the provinces of Styria and Lower Austria. Once a fashionable resort for the elegant Viennese, visitors tend to come now out of nostalgia for the good old days. Plenty of modern facilities aid your enjoyment of restful days in good mountain air.

i *Kurverwaltung*

Drive via Maria Schütz to Schottwien and Gloggnitz. Take the **17** to Wimpassing and turn left via Ternitz on the **26** to Puchberg am Schneeberg. Continue on the **26** east to Unterhöflein, turn left to Maisersdorf and left up the mountain road to the Hohe Wand.

FOR HISTORY BUFFS

On the top of the Semmering Pass is a memorial to Emperor Karl VI, the builder of the road over the pass. Another monument commemorates the first flight over the pass in 1912 by Eduard Nittner. In 1848 Carl Ritter von Ghega built the first mountain railway in Europe to cross the pass which runs through 17 tunnels and over several viaducts.

🛐 Hohe Wand,
Niederösterreich

The nature park of the Hohe Wand plateau lies on top of a limestone mountain range, which can be reached by driving over a mountain road. The area is a favourite spot for rock climbers.

i *Grünbach am Schneeberg, Gemeindeamt*

BACK TO NATURE

The nature park of the Hohe Wand covers the whole area of this elevated plateau. The forests of beech, fir and oak are home to deer, mountain goats and marmots, capercaillie and grouse.

From Maisersdorf drive east to Weikersdorf am Steinfelde, turn left and continue on the **LH137** to Bad Fischau. Take the **21** north past Steinabrückl, then turn north via Matzendorf to Bad Vöslau.

🛐 Bad Vöslau,
Niederösterreich

As the name implies, Bad Vöslau is a spa which is fed by a thermal spring producing water at a constant temperature of 24°C. Its heyday was in the 19th century, but visitors are still welcome.

i *Kurdirektion*

Take the **212** north to Baden.

🛐 Baden, Niederösterreich

The thermal springs of Baden bei Wien were known to the Romans. About 4½ million litres of hot water with a high sulphur content are produced daily by 15 springs. The temperature in the large outdoor pools is about 33°C, but it takes some time to get used to the smell of sulphur. At Rathausgasse 10 stands a memorial to the composer Ludwig van Beethoven, who spent the summers of 1821 and

Baden, Austria's principal spa town

1823 here and composed most of his *9th Symphony* in this house. Baden was a popular summer residence for Austrian emperors. The Helenental valley to the west is a favourite spot for romantic walks.

ℹ️ *Kurdirektion*

▶ *From Baden take the LH151 north to Gumpoldskirchen.*

🔟 Gumpoldskirchen,
Niederösterreich

Gumpoldskirchen lies in the foothills of the Anninger mountain. Its sheltered position is favourable for growing vines. It is best visited in the daytime as it gets very crowded in the summer evenings.

ℹ️ *Gemeindeamt*

▶ *Continue north to Mödling.*

🔢 Mödling,
Niederösterreich

Mödling became famous in the 19th century when artists discoverd the beauty of the surrounding area. Composers Beethoven and Schubert, among others, stayed here during the summer months. You can hardly miss the aqueduct, which carried fresh mountain water across the valley of the Mödling river to Vienna. The Freskohaus in Rathausgasse 6 has sgraffito ornaments on its façade. The charnel house in the Kirchenplatz is a 12th-century Romanesque building with an impressive portal.

Perhaps the oldest house in Mödling is the Herzoghof, Herzogstrasse 4. It was the residence of the Duke of Troppau, who was also the town priest.

Three kilometres (2 miles) north of Mödling stands Burg Liechtenstein. The Hinterbrühl area west of Mödling offers a trip on the largest subterranean lake in Europe, by electric motorboat. The cave was discovered by accident in 1912 and guided tours take place all year round. They also include a visit to a shaft which was artificially dried out and where the Germans produced the first jet fighter at the end of World War II.

ℹ️ *Fremdenverkehrsamt*

▶ *Drive west to Hinterbrühl and join the A21 at Giesshübl. Continue northeast to the junction with the A2 and drive north to Vienna.*

Johann Strauss was one of Vienna's most famous sons

JOHAN
STRAV
1825–18
VND DESSEN (
ADE
1856–1

on the road

BRITAIN &

IRELAND

Steeped in history, each country presents a distinct landscape to the world: England's rolling green hills and country villages, Wales's valleys and castles, Scotland's mountains and lakes, Ireland's cliffs and glens.

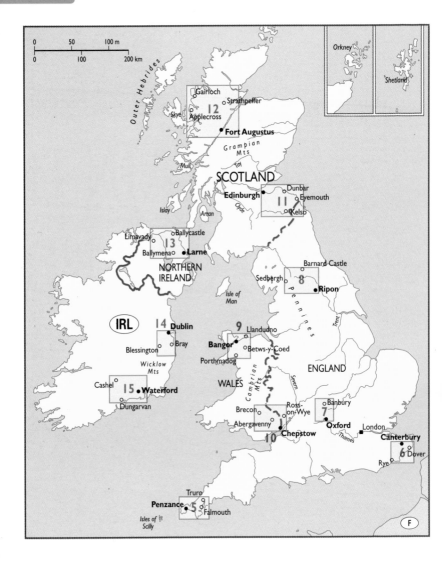

Tour 5

A sequence of cliffs and beaches forms the coastline of Cornwall, with precipitous granite cliffs near Land's End. Copper and tin were important minerals in the region, from Roman times until earlier this century and the history of mining can be traced in the

museums to be found in the area.

Penzance, the most westerly major town of England, enjoys a mild climate which enables palm trees to grow along the coastline. It was immortalised by Gilbert and Sullivan in *The Pirates of Penzance*.

Tour 6

Architectural styles are especially distinctive in Kent, where tile-hung houses can be

seen in many villages, as well as thatched houses and oast-houses. The scenery varies from gentle undulating landscapes and flat marshes to the steep cliffs of Dover and Folkestone, near to which is the terminal of the Channel Tunnel.

Canterbury cathedral dominates the landscape for miles around, but there is much more in this ancient city, often thought of as the birthplace of English Christianity. A walk

Page 35: top – brooding and evocative, Stonehenge remains a mystery; bottom – England's green and pleasant land

around the streets is a walk through history, and a visit to the Canterbury Heritage Exhibition is a good way to start a tour.

Tour 7

In central England the Cotswolds are characterised by the golden, mellow stone of the walls and houses in the area, giving a gentle beauty to farmlands, villages and towns.

Oxford is a captivating place. Its ancient university buildings in their mellow stone have a tranquil dignity, despite being within walking distance of the busy shopping centre. Magdalene, built in the 15th century, is a particularly beautiful college. The 17th-century Ashmolean is Britain's oldest museum and the Bodleian Library, begun in 1598, contains over 5 million books. There are countless other excellent collections and museums and a walk through the streets or along the Cherwell or Thames will convey the city's unique charm.

Tour 8

The North of England is noted for its old industrial towns. Surrounding them, however, is some magnificent countryside including the Pennines, with moorlands, mines and quarries.

Ripon is a busy little town, dominated by its cathedral, one of the oldest in England. An ancient Saxon crypt, thought to date from AD672, lies beneath the cathedral, and inside the fine features include a 16th-century Gothic nave. Another ancient building is the Wakeman's House, built in the 14th century for the man who would 'set the watch' by blowing a horn at 9pm every evening – a practice which continues today.

Tour 9

Wales is a country of great beauty. It is also a country of railways and castles. There are a few main-line railways along the north and south coasts and a scenic cross-country route to Aberystwyth, but there are several small, privately or voluntarily operated lines, such as at Ffestiniog and Llanberis.

The ancient town of Bangor, surrounded by water and high mountains in an area of great natural beauty, is a long-established religious centre: the present cathedral was built on the site of a monastery founded in AD525. The northern college of the University of Wales is based here, on a high ridge overlooking the city. Bangor sits on the Menai Strait, and you can see the island of Anglesey from its restored pier.

Tour 10

South Wales features green valleys, medieval castles and fortresses, a legacy of the country's long struggles against English rule.

Chepstow is a border town which has grown up at a crossing point of the River Wye and is now located conveniently close to the M4. There was an Iron Age as well as a Roman settlement near here, but the town was really created by the Normans. They began to build the castle in 1067, and it still dominates the town from its site over the River Wye. The museum opposite the castle describes the history of the town throughout the ages.

Tour 11

Southern Scotland is dominated by the great mass of the Southern Uplands. Castles and fortified houses serve as reminders of the centuries of border warfare that have shaped the history of the area. The eastern side, with its rugged coastline, beaches and fishing villages is quite spectacular, though in the north of the region the coastal scenery becomes gentler, giving way to fine beaches and grassy links that are ideal for golf.

Tour 12

The sheer splendour of the Western Highlands and Islands, with its grand mountains, heather-clad hillsides and indented coastline, complete with excellent beaches, make this classic touring country.

This tour is the Highlands at its best. Inland, the Great Glen lies in a wide gash in the fabric of the land and this cross-country route has been followed over the millennia by settlers, hunters, missionaries, soldiers – and even sailors!

Tour 13

Ulster is an attractive province of mountains, loughs, coast and countryside, with tranquil villages and friendly people, renowned for their warm welcome. The Antrim Coast road, which clings to the shore, begins a drive of stunning variety, and the Giant's Causeway is an essential destination for every traveller to this part of Ireland.

Tour 14

The lushness of Leinster and variety of its landscapes of lakes, bogs and mountains, are a delight to the visitor. Along the coast are curving bays and sandy beaches, as well as nature reserves.

This route winds its way into the mountains, and visits Glendalough, one of Ireland's most captivating combinations of history and landscape. A highlight of the tour is the profusion of glorious gardens, justifying the claim that this area is 'the garden of Ireland'.

Tour 15

In the province of Munster are soaring cliffs, tiny coves and long stretches of sandy beach; mountains awash with brilliant rhododendrons and the delicate hues of heather, slashed by deep gaps and scenic passes. The lofty Rock of Cashel is a reminder of the days of Celtic kings of Munster and the coming of Christianity.

BANKS

Banks are generally open 9am–4pm weekdays, though times vary from bank to bank; some are open on Saturday mornings until noon.

In Scotland, times vary – some banks have different opening times and some close for lunch.

In the Republic, banks open 10am–12.30pm and 1.30–3pm (9.30am–3.30pm in Northern Ireland) weekdays only. Most banks in Dublin and Belfast stay open until 4pm, and 5pm on Thursdays.

CREDIT CARDS

All major credit cards are widely accepted throughout Britain. In the Republic they may not be accepted by some restaurants and smaller independent retailers and fuel stations. In Northern Ireland, cards other than the Eurocard type are of limited use outside the main towns.

CURRENCY

The unit of currency is the pound (£), divided into 100 pence. Coins are in denominations of 1, 2, 5, 10, 20 and 50 pence and one pound (£1); notes are in denominations of £5, 10, 20 and 50.

In the Republic the monetary unit is the punt (IR£).

CUSTOMS REGULA-TIONS

See **Austria** (page 10).

ELECTRICITY

The standard electricity supply is 240 volts, 50 cycles AC (220 volts, 50 cycles in the Republic of Ireland). Plugs are three-pin. Shavers operate on 240 or 110 volts.

Visitors from Europe, Australia and New Zealand will need an adaptor and US visitors will need an adaptor and transformer if appliances are not fitted for dual voltage.

EMERGENCY TELE-PHONE NUMBERS

Police, fire and ambulance tel: 999.

ENTRY REGULATIONS

Passports are required by all visitors except citizens of EU countries, but they must be able to prove their identity and nationality. Visas are not required for entry into Britain by American citizens, nationals of the British Commonwealth and most European countries.

If you are a British citizen born in the UK no passport is needed to enter Ireland.

HEALTH MATTERS

See **Austria** (page 10).

MOTORING
Documents

You must have a valid driver's licence or an International Driving Permit. Non-EU nationals must have Green Card insurance. If you intend to cross the border between Northern Ireland and the Republic, check that your insurance covers you for both.

Route directions

Throughout this section the following abbreviations are used for roads:
A – main roads
B – local roads
M – motorways
R – regional roads
unclassified roads – minor roads (unnumbered)
Republic of Ireland only:
N – national primary/secondary roads
T – trunk roads *
L – link roads *
* these are gradually being phased out

Breakdowns

Visitors who bring their own cars and are members of a recognised automobile club may benefit from the services provided free of charge by the AA (tel: 0800 887766 for emergency breakdown free-call).

Accidents

In the event of an accident, the vehicle should be moved off the road wherever possible. If fitted with hazard warning lights, they should be used. If available, a red triangle should be placed on the road at least 165 feet (50m) before the obstruction and on the same side of the road.

In the Republic of Ireland, you must stop immediately and exchange particulars with the other party. If this is not possible you must report the accident to a member of the Garda Siochana or at the nearest Garda station.

Speed limits

In built-up areas 30mph (48kph). Outside built-up areas 70mph (112kph) on motorways and dual carriageways; other roads 60mph (96kph).

In the Republic the limits are 30mph (48kph) in built-up areas and 60mph (96kph) elsewhere unless otherwise indicated.

Driving conditions

Driving is on the left. Seat belts are compulsory for drivers and front seat passengers. Passengers travelling in the rear of the vehicle must wear a seat belt if fitted.

Tolls are levied on certain bridges and tunnels.

Car hire

Drivers must hold a valid national licence (with an English translation) or an International Driving Permit.

The minimum age for hiring a car ranges from 18 to 25, depending on the model of car. With some companies, there is a maximum age limit of 70 years.

You may be able to arrange to pick up your car in one town and return it in another.

POST OFFICES

In Britain post offices open 9am–5.30pm or 6pm Monday

Fireworks over Edinburgh

to Friday; 9am–12.30pm Saturdays.

In the Republic: 9am–5.30pm Monday to Friday; 9am–1pm Saturdays; sub-post offices close at 1pm one day a week. Post boxes are green. Republic of Ireland stamps must be used.

In Northern Ireland: 9am–5.30pm Monday to Friday; 9am–12.30pm Saturdays. Post boxes are red and British stamps must be used.

PUBLIC HOLIDAYS

Unless otherwise stated holidays are general throughout Britain and Ireland
(NI) Northern Ireland
(R) Republic
(S) Scotland
1 January – New Year's Day
2 January – (S only)
17 March – St Patrick's Day (NI, R only)
Good Friday
Easter Monday (not S)
1st Monday in May – May Day
Last Monday in May – Spring Bank Holiday (not R)
1st Monday in June – June Holiday (R only)
12 July – Orangemen's

Day (NI only)
1st Monday in August – Bank Holiday (R, S only)
Last Monday in August – August Bank Holiday (not S, R)
Last Monday in October – October Holiday (R only)
25 December – Christmas Day
26 December – Boxing Day

TELEPHONES
Useful numbers:
Operator – 100
Directory Enquiries – 192
International Directory Enquiries – 153
International Operator – 155

To make an international call, from the UK or Ireland, dial 00 (the international code), then the country code, followed by the area code and the local number.

Country codes are: Australia 61; Canada 1; New Zealand 64; Republic of Ireland 353; UK and Northern Ireland 44; US 1. For calls to European countries, omit the first zero.

Phonecards, obtainable from newsagents, can be used in public phone booths to make domestic and international calls.

TIME
The official time is Greenwich Mean Time (GMT).

British Summer Time (BST) begins in late March when the clocks are put forward an hour. In late October, the clocks go back an hour to GMT. The official date is announced in the daily newspapers and is always at 2am on a Sunday.

TOURIST OFFICES
England: English Tourist Board, Blacks Road, Hammersmith, London W6 9EL (tel: 0181 846 9000).
Northern Ireland: NITB, 11 Berkeley Street, London W1X 6BU (tel: 0171 355 5040).
Republic of Ireland: Bord Failte, Baggot Street Bridge, Dublin 2 (tel: 1–602 4000).
Scotland: Scottish Tourist Board, 23 Ravelston Terrace, Edinburgh EH4 3EU (tel: 0131 332 2433).
Wales: Wales Tourist Board, Brunel House, 2 Fitzalan Road, Cardiff CF2 1UY (tel: 01222 499909).

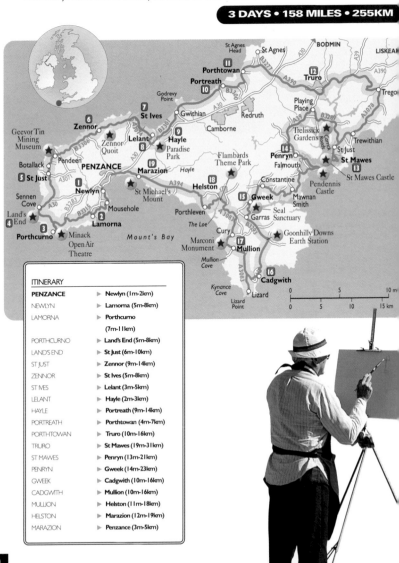

Bays, Cliffs
& Granite

Small bays, sandy beaches and steep rugged cliffs alternate around the Cornish coast on this tour, which then heads inland across undulating countryside, dotted with relics of the mining industry. Granite is everywhere, in the walls and in the villages.

3 DAYS • 158 MILES • 255KM

ITINERARY

i   *Station Road, Penzance*

SPECIAL TO...

A 20-minute helicopter flight from Penzance takes you to St Mary's, the largest of the Isles of Scilly. There is now a summer service to Tresco, the second largest island. Tresco has several miles of deserted golden beaches, but no roads and cars.

▶ *From Penzance, drive south along the coast for a mile (1.6km) to Newlyn, and a little further to Mousehole.*

❶ Newlyn, Cornwall
Really a suburb of Penzance, this is a lively and colourful fishing port, once famous for its artist colony. The Passmore Orion Picture Gallery shows some of their work. Further along the coast is Mousehole. Pronounced 'mowzel', this delightful old fishing village consists of a semi-circle of colour-washed and granite houses round its harbour. Some of the roofs are specially weighted down to combat strong sea winds. Dolly Pentreath, supposedly the last person to speak Cornish as her native language, died here in 1777.

▶ *Continue on unclassified road for 5 miles (8km) to Lamorna.*

❷ Lamorna, Cornwall
Lamorna is a holiday centre. The tempting golden sand of its spectacular cove is surrounded by steep blocks of granite cliffs and rocky outcrops.

▶ *Join the B3315, then at Trethewey turn left on to an unclassified road to Porthcurno.*

❸ Porthcurno, Cornwall
Porthcurno's beach of almost-white sand is overlooked by a remarkable theatre in the cliffs. The Minack is Britain's equivalent to an ancient Greek theatre, set 200 feet (60m) above the waves. It was created by Miss

Rowena Cade, who cut it out of the cliffs in 1931. The theatre has a 16-week season, and can seat 750 on its granite terraces.

▶ *Return to the B3315 and continue for another 4 miles (6km), then join the A30 to Land's End.*

❹ Land's End, Cornwall
England's most westerly point, Land's End is 873 miles (1,405km) from John O'Groats, Scotland's most northerly town. On a fine day the Isles of Scilly, 28 miles (45km) away, can be seen, along with Wolf Rock Lighthouse and the Longships Lighthouse, only a mile and a half (2km) offshore. Land's End is the setting for wild coastal walks and amazing rock formations. Further along is the small village of Sennen, the battle-

The end of England – the haunting majesty of Land's End

ground of the last Cornish fight against invading Danes. Sennen Cove has a good sandy beach and excellent bathing.

▶ *Continue with the A30, then left on to the B3306 for 5 miles (8km) to St Just.*

FOR CHILDREN

The legendary Last Labyrinth at Land's End is a major attraction using electronic equipment and including a life-size galleon with scrambling nets and cabins. You can also watch the glass-blower or wood-carver at work, and there is a fascinating collection of shells.

St Ives' golden beaches attract many holidaymakers in summer

copper trade, but now it is a small industrial town with a good sandy beach, though there are still a few boats to be seen in the harbour. Paradise Park, just off the road before entering Hayle, is a conservation theme park with otters and endangered species of birds. There is also a first-class falconry display.

▶ The **B3301** runs along the coast to Portreath.

RECOMMENDED WALKS

From the B3301 it is possible to walk to Godrevy Point and Navax Point on a circular walk of 3 miles (5km).

5 St Just, Cornwall
This enchanting village and its neighbourhood are rich in antiquities. St Just is noted for the contents of its large medieval church: a stone of the 5th or 6th century inscribed with XP, the first two letters of the Greek word for Christ, and the shaft of a 9th-century Hiberno-Saxon cross. Abandoned and ruined mines litter the countryside north of the town.

At Botallack, along the B3306, is a deep mine which extended out beneath the sea, and at the Geevor Tin Mining Museum at Pendeen, a little further on, you can take an underground tour of this working mine.

▶ Keep going along the **B3306** to Zennor.

6 Zennor, Cornwall
Zennor, named after St Senara, is a grey stone village huddled round its restored 12th-century church in a wild, bleak landscape. The Wayside Museum, the oldest private museum in Cornwall, recaptures the flavour of this area from 3000BC onwards, with displays on archaeology, tin mining and many other aspects of Cornish life. The writers D H Lawrence and Virginia Woolf both lived here in the 1920s. Zennor Quoit, to the southeast, is a chambered tomb from about 2000BC.

▶ A further 5 miles (8km) along the **B3306** is St Ives.

7 St Ives, Cornwall
St Ives was a prosperous pilchard port in the 19th century, but now is more noted for tourism, with its two fine sandy beaches and many excellent museums and galleries. The town has managed to preserve its old-world charm: quaint houses and narrow streets cluster round the 15th-century church. Be sure to visit the Barbara Hepworth Museum and Sculpture Garden, and the Model Railway Museum.

ℹ The Guildhall, Street-an-Pol

▶ Take the main **A3074** for 3 miles (5km) to Lelant.

8 Lelant, Cornwall
Lelant has a fine Norman and Perpendicular style church with a 17th-century sundial, but is now noted for Merlin's Magic Land, which claims to provide a 'Funtastic' day out for the whole family, with bumper boats, motor bikes and many other attractions.

▶ Follow the **A3074**, then the **B3301** to Hayle.

9 Hayle, Cornwall
During the 18th century Hayle developed as a port for the

10 Portreath, Cornwall
Portreath's tiny harbour cottages cluster around the port and the 18th-century pier, at the foot of windswept cliffs. It is a marvellous place to go walking along the coast path and there are spectacular views from Reskajeage Downs, above.

▶ Turn inland along the **B3300**, then left on unclassified roads for Porthtowan.

11 Porthtowan, Cornwall
Porthtowan is a pleasant little place with a sandy beach and magnificent cliffs to north and south. If you have time, walk up on to the cliffs for fantastic views inland and over the Atlantic.

▶ Follow unclassified roads, then the **B3277** and **A390** to Truro.

12 Truro, Cornwall
Truro is a fascinating town with a mixture of old and new buildings. Lemon Street has many fine Georgian structures, and Walsingham Place is a beautiful early 19th-century crescent off Victoria Place. The whole town is dominated by the cathedral, which has three spires and was

built on the site of the 16th-century church of St Mary. The County Museum in Silver Street is considered to be the finest in Cornwall and now there is also a fine new art gallery.

i *Municipal Buildings, Boscawen Street*

▶ *Follow the **A39** eastwards, then turn right along the **A3078** for St Mawes.*

⒔ St Mawes, Cornwall
Smart shops and houses and many narrow old streets make this an interesting place to wander round. You should try to visit St Mawes Castle, built by Henry VIII in the 1540s to guard the mouth of the Fal estuary. The views across Carrick Roads, a stretch of sea, to Falmouth are particularly impressive.

Trelissick Gardens, north of St Mawes, boasts a fine collection of exotic plants from all over the world.

▶ *Turn north on the **A3078** then the **B3289**, using King Harry ferry, which closes before dusk, then join the **A39** to Penryn.*

⒕ Penryn, Cornwall
Almost everything in Penryn is built of granite – granite buildings, a granite port and granite blocks lying around everywhere waiting to be shipped out. The narrow streets of this old town stretch up the sides of the valley in an untidy but appealing way.

Further on is Falmouth, on one of the finest natural habours in the world. There are beaches to the south of the town, and on the northern side of the peninsula are the docks and 18th- and 19th-century buildings. Pendennis Castle was built at the same time as its twin, St Mawes Castle, to guard the harbour entrance.

i *28 Killigrew Street, Falmouth*

▶ *Leave Falmouth on unclassified roads passing through Mawnan Smith, Porth Navas, Constantine and Brill to Gweek.*

⒖ Gweek, Cornwall
This lovely little stone village with two stone bridges across the channels of the Helford River is now better known as a seal sanctuary. Along the picturesque and tranquil banks of the Helford, sick and wounded seals and birds are treated. There are displays which show the work of the centre, and a safari bus will take you round the park to see the convalescent pool and nursery and exercise areas.

▶ *Travel to Garras on unclassified roads. Then take the **B3293** and unclassified roads across Goonhilly Downs, south to Cadgwith and on to Lizard Point on an unclassified road and the **A3083**.*

⒗ Cadgwith, Cornwall
Attractive thatched cottages clustered round the small beach and harbour create a beautiful setting for local fishermen and tourists. Sandy caves alternate with rugged cliffs along this stretch of coast, but the most dramatic feature is the noisy water of the Devil's Frying Pan, created when a vast sea cave collapsed.

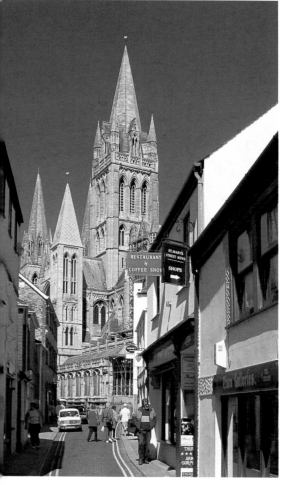

Truro's cathedral was built on the site of a 16th-century church

Cadgwith, a busy fishing harbour
Right: Dover Castle and Pharos

Further on, Lizard Point is the southernmost point in England with dramatic 180-foot (55m) cliffs and a lighthouse, open to the public.

▶ *Head north from Lizard Point for 4 miles (6km) along the A3083, then the B3296 to Mullion.*

RECOMMENDED WALKS

Among the most dramatic walks is the path from Cadgwith towards Landewednack. On the west coast of the Lizard, the coast near Kynance Cove can look most romantic and appealing.

17 Mullion, Cornwall
The village of Mullion boasts a fine 14th- and 15th-century church, whose carved oak bench-ends are worth inspect-ing. The church tower is partially built of the local multi-coloured serpentine. Nearby Mullion Cove is surrounded by steep cave-pocked cliffs and has splendid views.

▶ *Drive on unclassified roads via Poldhu and Cury to the A3083 and on to Helston.*

18 Helston, Cornwall
Radio buffs should visit Poldhu Point before entering Helston, to see the Marconi Monument, which commemorates the first transatlantic transmitting station. The ancient Furry Dance takes place in Helston on 8 May, when there is dancing in the streets all day. In the past this town was a port, before the Loe Bar, a 600-foot (183m) ridge of shingle, blocked it off from the sea. Behind Loe Bar is The Loe, a pretty lake, into which, according to legend, Sir Bedivere threw King Arthur's sword Excalibur.
Nearby Flambards Theme Park provides entertainment for the whole family, open in the evenings in July and August. It features a Victorian village, a simulation of the World War II blitz and many other themes.

▶ *Take the B3304 through Porthleven, then along the A394 to Marazion. Take an unclassified road before the bypass into the village.*

19 Marazion, Cornwall
This ancient port is famous for St Michael's Mount, the granite island located offshore, but is a remarkable place in its own right. Cornwall's oldest char-tered town, it has the safest beach in Cornwall and some of the best wind-surfing in Europe. Henry III granted the town a charter in 1257 and for hundreds of years tin and copper ores were exported from here. The small town still attracts visitors, in spite of the bypass, which has reduced the amount of through-traffic.

▶ *Return to Penzance via an unclassified road to the A394.*

FOR HISTORY BUFFS

St Michael's Mount is accessible by foot at low tide, and you should make time to get across to see the castle and priory, both founded by Edward the Confessor in the 11th century. This was the legendary home of the giant Cormoran, who was slain by Jack the Giant Killer.

BACK TO NATURE

The birdwatching hotspot of Marazion Marsh lies close to the sea just behind the coast road at Marazion. Autumns in previous years have produced regular sightings of aquatic warblers and spotted crakes, as well as occasional records of transatlantic vagrants such as white-rumped sandpipers and lesser yellowlegs.

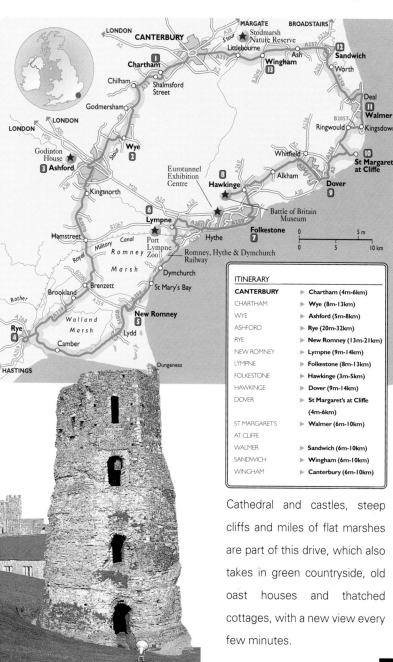

From
Cathedral to Cliffs

2/3 DAYS • 107 MILES • 172KM

Cathedral and castles, steep cliffs and miles of flat marshes are part of this drive, which also takes in green countryside, old oast houses and thatched cottages, with a new view every few minutes.

<i> 34 St Margaret's Street, Canterbury

BACK TO NATURE

Stodmarsh National Nature Reserve lies a few miles to the east of Canterbury. Vast reedbeds and areas of open water attract huge numbers of wildfowl. Reed warblers, Cetti's warblers and bearded tits can be found in the winter, sometimes in the company of short-eared owls.

▶ *Take the* **A28** *to Chartham.*

❶ Chartham, Kent

The valley of the Great Stour, with gravel pits and small lakes, is noted for fishing and bird life, and Chartham is a well-known angling centre. St Mary's Church dates from the 13th century and has one of the oldest sets of bells in the country. Chartham Hatch Craft Centre is just down the road, set in delightful countryside.

Further along is Chilham, where the village square is set at the gateway to Chilham Castle, built for Henry II in 1174. The castle is not open to the public, but you can visit the gardens. There are usually medieval jousting tournaments on Sundays and Bank Holidays. The church has a stone and flint tower, and the largely unspoilt houses around the square are of Tudor and Jacobean style.

▶ *From Chilham return to the* **A28**, *travel south for 2 miles (3km) then turn off on to unclassified roads to Wye.*

❷ Wye, Kent

This village, in its rural setting, is the location of the famous Agriculture School of London University, housed in a college first set up in the mid-15th century by John Kempe, a native of the town, who became Archbishop of Canterbury. The town also has a racecourse, a Georgian mill house and 18th-century Olantigh Hall.

Picturesque timbered Chilham, one of Kent's show places

▶ *Return to the* **A28** *for 5 miles (8km) to Ashford.*

❸ Ashford, Kent

This old market centre for Romney Marsh and the Weald of Kent is now a thriving shopping and touring centre. Medieval, Tudor and Georgian houses still survive and the 14th- and 15th-century parish church retains much of its old character.

Godington House, northwest of town, was built in the 17th century. The rooms are full of Chippendale and Sheraton furniture, and there is fine topiary work in the garden.

<i> 18 The Churchyard

▶ *Follow the* **A2070**, *then the* **A259** *across Romney Marsh for 20 miles (32km) to Rye.*

❹ Rye, East Sussex

Rye is one of the Cinque Ports, a group of maritime towns which were originally responsible for providing ships and men to guard against invasion. At one time Rye was almost encircled by the sea, but the harbour silted up in the 16th century and the water receded. In the winter, when mists roll in across the countryside, Romney Marsh can be sinister and mysterious – a fitting background to tales of the infamous parson and smuggler, Dr Syn.

i *The Heritage Centre, Strand Quay*

▶ *Head back on the **A259** to East Guldeford, then take an unclassified road through Camber to Lydd to join the **B2075** to New Romney.*

5 **New Romney,** Kent
Another ancient Cinque Port, now inland from the sea, New Romney was destroyed in 1287 by a violent storm which changed the course of the River Rother. The Romney, Hythe and Dymchurch narrow gauge railway opened in 1927, with locomotives and carriages which are one-third full size. Toys and models can be seen at New Romney station.

Getting up steam on the Romney, Hythe and Dymchurch Railway

i *Light Railway Car Park, 2 Littlestone Road*

▶ *Take the **A259** again, then unclassified roads for 9 miles (14km) to Lympne, then via the **B2067** to the **A261** which leads eastwards to Hythe.*

6 **Lympne,** Kent
The 11th-century castle at Lympne (pronounced *Lim*) stands on top of a cliff which was once a coastline. Views from here extend across the Channel to the French coast on a clear day. From the castle, the remains of a Roman fort can be seen.

Just outside town is Port Lympne Zoo Park, set in 300 acres (121 hectares) of gardens surrounding a mansion. East of

Lympne is Hythe, another Cinque Port which is now a popular seaside resort and the terminus for the Romney, Hythe and Dymchurch Railway. The town has several historic buildings and summer boating along the old Royal Military Canal.

i *Prospect Road Car Park, Hythe*

▶ *Follow the **A259** from Hythe to Folkestone.*

7 **Folkestone,** Kent
The harbour of this resort handles cross-Channel ferries, and still has a fishing fleet and a fish market. A Museum and Art Gallery in Grace Hill has displays on the town's maritime history, and the Eurotunnel Exhibition Centre explains, with the use of videos, models and displays, this huge project which has been talked about for 200 years. Spade House was the former home of the author H G Wells. The Leas, a wide grassy promenade along the cliff top, has fine views and provides an excellent walk through wooded slopes down to the beach.

i *Harbour Street*

▶ *Head inland along the **A260** as far as Hawkinge.*

8 **Hawkinge,** Kent
Set in the heart of the Downland west of Hawkinge is the Kent Battle of Britain Museum, which conjures up visions of World War II. It houses the largest collection of fragments of British and German aircraft involved in the fighting.

▶ Take unclassified roads eastwards from Hawkinge, eventually running south on to the **A256** for Dover.

⑨ Dover, Kent

Dover, famous for its White Cliffs, was the chief Cinque Port. It was known to the Romans as *Dubris*, and the Painted House, discovered in 1970, dates from about AD200. Among the paintings are several references to the theme of Bacchus, the god of wine. More recent is the Old Town Gaol, which has been restored to show the dismal conditions of Victorian prison life. On Snargate Street you can see the Grand Shaft, a 140-foot (43m) staircase cut into the white cliffs,

built in Napoleonic times as a short cut to the town for troops stationed on the Western Heights. The views across to France can be best seen from Dover Castle, which overlooks the town. The Pharos, a Roman lighthouse, stands within its walls near the fine Saxon Church of St Mary de Castro.

ⓘ Townwall Street

▶ Take the **A258**, then an unclassified road to St Margaret's at Cliffe.

⑩ St Margaret's at Cliffe, Kent

The flint-faced church in the upper part of this village is typical of chalkland buildings.

St Margaret's Bay is a popular start for cross-Channel swimmers

Massive chalk cliffs dominate the scene, and sheltered beneath them is the Pines Garden, created in the 1970s with trees, shrubs, a lake and waterfall, and a statue of Sir Winston Churchill.

Three miles (5km) further is Ringwould, which has another fine church, with an attractive 17th-century tower. Bronze Age barrows can be seen at nearby Free Down, and at Kingsdown there is a lot of flint, both on the buildings and on the shore.

▶ Rejoin the **A258**, then take the **B2057** from Ringwould to Walmer.

Sandwich is one of the oldest
Cinque ports

⓫ **Walmer,** Kent

Henry VIII built the castle here,
along with over 20 other forts to
defend the coast of southeast
England. This fine coastal
fortress, shaped like a Tudor
rose, has been transformed into
an elegant stately home with
beautiful gardens, and is the official residence of the Lord
Warden of the Cinque Ports.
Lord Wellington was Warden
from 1829 to 1852, and his
famous boots are on display.

Further on, Deal Castle, also
built by Henry VIII, is in the
shape of a six-petalled flower,
and tells the full story of the
Tudor castles in the exhibition
room. The Timeball Tower,
which used to give time signals
to shipping is a unique four-
storey museum of time and
maritime communication on the
sea front. The museum in St
George's Street has a collection
of old photographs, model sailing ships and maps.

i *Town Hall, High Street, Deal*
▶ *Take the A258 to Sandwich.*

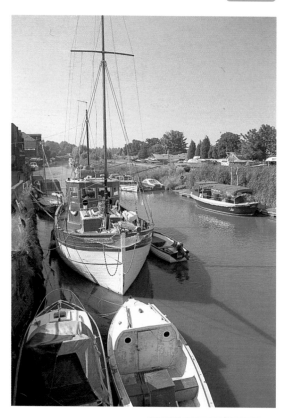

⓬ **Sandwich,** Kent

The oldest of the medieval
Cinque Ports, Sandwich is separated from the sea by 2 miles
(3km) of sand dunes. Its white
windmill dates from about 1760,
and now houses a folk museum
with domestic and farming
exhibits. Sandwich Golf Course,
between the town and Sandwich
Bay, is a world-class championship course.

i *St Peter's Church, Market Street*

▶ *Follow the A257 for 6 miles
(10km) to Wingham.*

⓭ **Wingham,** Kent

This picturesque village
contains a magnificent church
with a green spire, caused by
oxidisation. The Bird Park has
cockatoos, macaws, owls and
waterfowl, all with plenty of
flying space, as well as rare farm
animals and pets. Valuable
research work takes place here
to help endangered species, and
to overcome man's destruction
of natural habitats. A little
further out of town is the village
of Littlebourne. Fruit and hops
are grown around here, and
there is an ancient thatched barn
near the flint-faced church.

▶ *Continue along the A257 for
the return to Canterbury (6
miles/10km).*

Cotswold
Wool & Stone

This is mainly a circuit of Cotswold countryside – a landscape of stone walls surrounding fertile fields and distinctive village architecture. The villages contain many fine churches, but the best known structure is the cross in the centre of Banbury. The family homes of two great men can be seen; one Englishman in Blenheim and one American in Sulgrave.

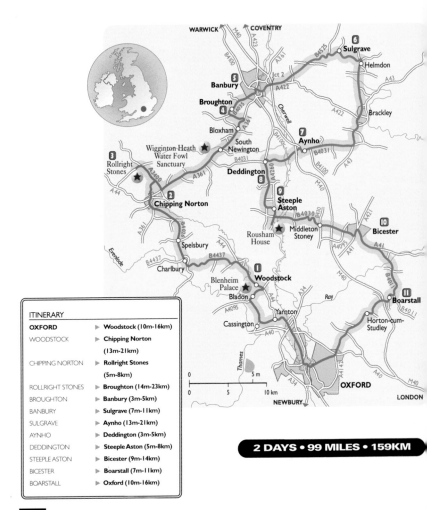

2 DAYS • 99 MILES • 159KM

Bliss Tweed Mill, now flats, near the old wool town of Chipping Norton

[i] St Aldates, Oxford

▶ Leave Oxford on the **A44** and turn left along an unclassified road towards Cassington. Turn right to Bladon on the **A4095** then left on the **A44** to Woodstock.

❶ Woodstock, Oxfordshire

You can stop off in Bladon, to visit the churchyard where Sir Winston Churchill and his wife and parents are buried, before continuing along the road to Blenheim, where he was born. Blenheim Palace was given to the Marlborough family by Queen Anne as a reward for a major victory by the 1st Duke of Marlborough over the French at Blenheim in 1704. Just outside the park is the old town of Woodstock, with its mellow stone buildings. Kings of England used to come here for the excellent hunting in the Forest of Wychwood, but modern visitors have gentler interests. A quiet hour can be spent in the Oxfordshire County Museum, in the town centre, where the history of the people and the changing landscape is conveyed in exhibitions which range from the Stone Age to the present time.

BACK TO NATURE

The grounds of Blenheim Palace, at Woodstock, were landscaped by Capability Brown and comprise rolling, formal parkland and an attractive lake. This harbours breeding dragonflies and is home to Canada geese, mute swans, great crested grebes and kingfishers. In the winter months, look for roaming flocks of siskins, redpolls and long tailed tits in the birch trees.

---

[i] Hensington Road

▶ From Woodstock take the **A44** turning left on to the **B4437** to Charlbury and then the **B4026** to Chipping Norton.

❷ Chipping Norton, Oxfordshire

Gateway to the Cotswolds and historic market town, this was the market for the sheep farmers of the area, and the wide main street is a relic of those days (the name 'chipping' means market). There are many fine old stone buildings, including the church, market hall, pubs and big houses, but it is the fine wool church which dominates the town, one of over 40 in the Cotswolds. Paid for by the proceeds from sheep farming, it is mainly 14th- and 15th-century, but much of its stonework has been restored. Another of the town's landmarks is the chimney of Bliss Tweed Mill which is an important reminder of local history.

[i] 5 Middle Row

▶ Take the **B4026**, then go north along the **A3400** for just over a mile (1.6km) and turn left along an unclassified road signed Little Rollright.

❸ Rollright Stones, Oxfordshire

This Bronze Age circle, which dates from earlier than 1000BC, was nearly as important as Stonehenge in the Neolithic period. Nicknamed the 'King's Men', it measures a full 100 feet (30m) across. Over the road is the King Stone, a monolith, and near by, just along the road, is the group of stones called the Whispering Knights, at the site of a prehistoric burial chamber. The surrounding countryside is

Broughton Castle is a fine example of a gracious Elizabethan Manor

patterned with stone walls of weathered limestone.

▶ *Return to the **A3400** and turn south before branching left on to the **A361**, then turn left in Bloxham along unclassified roads to Broughton.*

FOR CHILDREN

Just before reaching Bloxham, on the road from Rollright to Broughton, you will pass the Wigginton Heath Water Fowl Sanctuary. Conservation is the main aim, with flowers, goats, sheep, lambs and other animals, as well as a bewildering assortment of birds. Various ducks, geese, black swans, owls, doves and peacocks can all be seen at very close quarters. There is also a nature trail and an adventure playground.

4 Broughton, Oxfordshire
Broughton Castle is a fortified manor rather than a castle, turned into an Elizabethan house of style by the Fiennes family in about 1600. Surrounded by a great moat lake, it is set in gorgeous parkland, and has a stone church near by. The present owners, Lord and Lady Saye and Sele, are descendants of the family that has lived here for centuries. Celia Fiennes, the 17th-century traveller and diarist, was a member of this family. William de Wykeham, founder of Winchester School and New College, Oxford, acquired the manor and converted the manor house into a castle. The medieval Great Hall is the most impressive room, and suits of armour from the Civil War are on show.

▶ *Drive 3 miles (5km) east along the **B4035** to Banbury.*

5 Banbury, Oxfordshire
Banbury is a town of charm and character, with its interesting buildings and narrow medieval streets. Famous for the nursery rhyme 'Ride a cock horse to Banbury Cross', the town is also known for its spice cakes, which have been made here since the 16th century. The unusual church with its round tower replaced an older one demolished in the 18th century. There is still a weekly street market, which has been held regularly for over 800 years, and there used to be a livestock market, too, but nowadays the animals are taken to a permanent site on the edge of town, Europe's largest cattle market.

i *Banbury Museum, 8 Horsefair*

FOR HISTORY BUFFS

Banbury's wool industry was helped by the opening of the Oxford Canal in 1790, connecting Banbury with the Midland coalfields and markets in London. The narrow boats on the canals used to be pulled by horses which walked along the towpath, and a family would live permanently on the boat.

RECOMMENDED WALKS

Along the Oxford Canal, near Banbury, is the delightful 9-mile (14km) Banbury circuit, which takes in the villages of Wroxton with its duckpond, Horley, Hornton, Alkerton, an old Saxon village with ironstone houses, Shennington and Balscott.

▶ Take the unclassified road through Helmdon, heading south to Brackley to join the **A43, then shortly** right on to the **B4031** to Aynho.

7 Aynho, Northamptonshire
This limestone village contains apricot trees from which, legend has it, fruit was paid as a toll to the Cartwrights, Lords of the Manor. They lived in the mansion in Aynhoe Park, and there are several memorials to them, including a Victorian marble cross in the church.

▶ From Aynho go west along the **B4031** to Deddington.

8 Deddington, Oxfordshire
Dominating this village, which is built out of the honey-coloured local stone, is the church, with each of its eight pinnacles topped with gilded vanes. Adjacent Castle House was formerly the rectory, and parts of the building date from the 14th century. The area has many links with the days of the Civil War, and Charles I is believed to have slept at the 16th-century Castle Farm near by.

▶ Drive southwards for 5 miles (8km) along the **A4260** and then left on to an unclassified road to Steeple Aston.

9 Steeple Aston,
Oxfordshire
Steeple Aston was winner of the Oxfordshire Best Kept Village Award in 1981 and 1983, and is still an eye-catching village. The village inn, Hopcroft's Holt, had associations with Claude Duval, a French highwayman who worked in these parts. Just beyond Steeple Aston is the Jacobean mansion of Rousham House, built by Sir Robert Dormer in 1635 and still owned by the same family. William Kent improved the house in the 18th century by adding the wings and stable block. In the magnificent garden, the complete Kent layout has survived. There is a fine herd of rare Long Horn cattle in the

park, and you should be sure not to miss the walled garden.

▶ Another unclassified road leads south on to the **B4030** in turn leading to the **A4095** for the 9 miles (14km) to Bicester.

10 Bicester, Oxfordshire
Little can be seen of the Roman town at Alchester, to the south of Bicester, but excavations show that people lived here from about the middle of the 1st century AD until the late Roman period. Bicester itself is a market town with many old streets. Its church contains elements of a 13th-century building, and there was once a 12th-century priory near by.

▶ Take the **A41** following the line of an old Roman road and then the **B4011** towards Thame before turning sharp right to Boarstall.

11 Boarstall, Buckinghamshire
This tiny hamlet is the location of Boarstall Tower, an amazing stone gatehouse which was originally part of a massive fortified house. It dates from the 14th century and is now looked after by the National Trust, who also own Boarstall Duck Decoy. This 18th-century decoy is in 13 acres (5 hectares) of natural old woodland. Attractions include a small exhibition hall, nature trail and bird hide.

▶ Take unclassified roads via Horton-cum-Studley along the edge of Otmoor for the return to Oxford.

SPECIAL TO...

Banbury's cross, in Horsefair, was built in 1859 to commemorate the marriage of Victoria, Princess Royal, and the Crown Prince of Prussia. Its design is based on the Eleanor Crosses, built in the 13th century to mark the resting stages of Queen Eleanor's funeral cortège en route to London for burial.

▶ Head eastwards along the **A422**, turning left after 2 miles (3km) on to the **B4525** to Sulgrave.

6 Sulgrave,
Northamptonshire
The old manor in this attractive stone village was the home of ancestors of George Washington from 1539 to 1659, having been bought by Lawrence Washington, wool merchant and twice Mayor of Northampton. Not to be missed is the family coat of arms with its stars and stripes carved above the entrance porch, and the most treasured possession inside is an original oil painting of George Washington.

SCENIC ROUTES

The A44 from Woodstock to Chipping Norton gives excellent views across rolling countryside. Bloxham and the village of South Newington show Cotswold settlements at their best, especially in the summer, and the skyline of Oxford, with its impressive array of dreaming spires, is unique.

Across the
Backbone of England

The green valleys and wild, often wind-swept moors of Yorkshire provide a rich variety of scenery, with ever-changing views. Curiously weathered rocks add an eerie atmosphere to the landscape of hills and vales, and castles and monastic ruins recall the prosperity of the Middle Ages on this tour.

2 DAYS • 153 MILES • 246KM

ITINERARY	
RIPON	▶ **Masham** (10m-16km)
MASHAM	▶ **Middleham** (8m-13km)
MIDDLEHAM	▶ **Leyburn** (2m-3km)
LEYBURN	▶ **Richmond** (11m-18km)
RICHMOND	▶ **Barnard Castle**
	(14m-23km)
BARNARD CASTLE	▶ **Brough** (17m-27km)
BROUGH	▶ **Sedbergh** (19m-31km)
SEDBERGH	▶ **Hawes** (15m-24km)
HAWES	▶ **Bainbridge** (4m-6km)
BAINBRIDGE	▶ **Buckden** (17m-27km)
BUCKDEN	▶ **Grassington** (11m-18km)
GRASSINGTON	▶ **Pateley Bridge**
	(11m-18km)
PATELEY BRIDGE	▶ **Fountains Abbey**
	(10m-16km)
FOUNTAINS ABBEY	▶ **Ripon** (4m-6km)

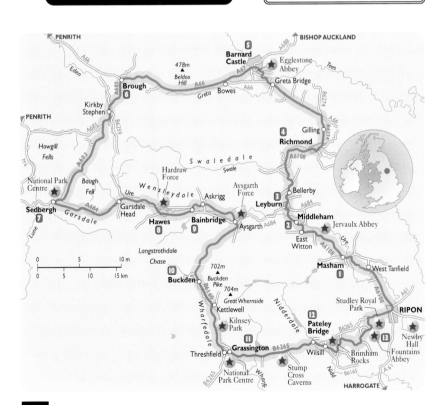

⚐ *Minster Road, Ripon*

▷ *Take the A6108 to Masham.*

❶ **Masham,** North Yorkshire
Masham's importance as a market town is illustrated by the huge market square, dominated by its Market Cross, which survives even though the market no longer takes place. Masham is full of interesting features: a four-arched bridge over the Ure dates from 1754, and St Mary's Church is older, its 15th-century spire standing on top of a Norman tower. The town is the home of Theakston's brewery, famous for its 'Old Peculier' ale.

Five miles (8km) from town is Jervaulx Abbey, in an attractive riverside setting. This Cistercian abbey was founded in 1156 and later destroyed in the 15th century, though enough of it remains to show how impressive it once was.

▷ *Follow the A6108 for 8 miles (13km) to Middleham.*

❷ **Middleham,** North Yorkshire
Grandiose building traditions of the past can be seen in the ruins of 12th-century Middleham Castle, a former seat of the Neville family, where some of the walls are 12 feet (3.5m) thick. This was the childhood home of Richard III and its massive keep is one of the largest ever built. The view from the top is magnificent, looking out across Wensleydale over wild but beautiful moorlands. Now an important horse breeding and training centre, Middleham is a good base for exploring Wensleydale.

▷ *Continue north to Leyburn.*

❸ **Leyburn,** North Yorkshire
Leyburn has developed into a major trading centre for the area. Its appearance is that of a prosperous late Georgian market town, and even though most shop fronts have become largely modern, some 18th-century houses survive, notably around Grove Square; the Bolton Arms and Leyburn Hall are probably the best examples. This is another good Wensleydale centre, and there are fine views from The Shawl, a 2-mile (3km) limestone scar not far from the town centre.

⚐ *Thornborough Hall*

▷ *Keep on the A6108 to Richmond.*

❹ **Richmond,** North Yorkshire
There is much to see in this capital and gateway to Swaledale, thought to be the finest of all Yorkshire Dales. From every angle Richmond Castle dominates the town. This fine Norman fortress, built on to solid rock, was started in 1071 overlooking the Swale, Britain's fastest river, but was never finished. The large, cobbled market place is surrounded by such architectural gems as the Georgian Theatre Royal, built in 1788, which was restored and reopened in 1962. You can see the home of the original 'sweet lass of Richmond Hill', of whom the famous song was written in 1785, and the award-winning Green Howards Museum covers the history of the regiment, including a unique collection dating from 1688 of war relics, weapons, medals and uniforms. Other interesting sights include Greyfriars Tower, the one surviving feature of an old abbey, and the Holy Trinity Church.

⚐ *Friary Gardens, Victoria Road*

▷ *Take the B6274 to the junction with the A66 and continue to Greta Bridge. After crossing the River Greta turn right on to unclassified roads to Barnard Castle.*

❺ **Barnard Castle,** Durham
Medieval Barnard Castle, after which the town is named is now

Middleham's impressive castle ruins

Bainbridge was the centre of the once-great Forest of Wensleydale

a ruin, but in its great days it stood guard over a crossing point of the River Tees. The town boasts one of the finest museums in Britain, Bowes Museum, in a splendid French château-style mansion which was built in 1869 by John Bowes, son of the Earl of Strathmore. It contains an outstanding collection of paintings, porcelain, silver, furniture and ceramics.

A few miles south, off the B6277, are the ruins of Egglestone Abbey, in a delightful setting on the bank of the Tees, and southwest, along the A67, is the village of Bowes, where the local boarding schools gave author Charles Dickens the idea for Dotheboys Hall in his novel *Nicholas Nickleby*. William

Shaw, the unfortunate model for sadistic schoolmaster Wackford Squeers, is buried in the churchyard. The Church of St Giles contains a Roman dedication stone, one of many relics of the Roman invasion in the area. Bowes Castle, like the church, used Roman stone for its building.

ⓘ *43 Galgate*

▶ *Take the **A67** to Bowes and follow the **A66** west along the line of an old Roman route to Brough.*

❻ Brough, Cumbria
Standing on the site of Roman *Verterae*, Brough Castle, now in ruins, was built by William II and later restored by Lady Anne Clifford in the 17th century. This old settlement was a coach-

ing town in the 19th century and used to hold an annual horse fair, now at Appleby. This area has many miles of good walking.

▶ *Take the **A685** to Kirkby Stephen, then the **A683** to Sedbergh.*

❼ Sedbergh, Cumbria
Sedbergh is an old weaving town, and the Weavers' Yard still exists behind the King's Arms. The town is now more important as a tourist centre, and the rich natural history and beautiful scenery of the area have given rise to the creation of a National Park Centre. The Public School has gained a national reputation for its academic standards sporting traditions. The A684 east takes you through Garsdale, whose only community is a line of houses called The Street.

narrow valley, once the venue for brass band competitions.

ℹ️ *National Park Centre, Station Yard*

▶ *Take the **A684** for a further 4 miles (6km) to Bainbridge.*

9 **Bainbridge,** North Yorkshire

This little Dales village, with its lovely stone buildings set round the green, was the former centre of the once great Forest of Wensleydale. Low Mill, on the east side of the green, has been restored and is occasionally open to the public. Brough Hill, a natural grassy hillock to the east is the setting for a Roman fort, and gives fine views of Wensleydale and the village.

A little further along is Askrigg, another charming village, built of local stone and set among hills, valleys and waterfalls. Most of the buildings are 18th- and 19th-century, built as a result of increasing prosperity in the clock-making, lead-mining and textile industries. Waterfalls are numerous, but especially dramatic is Aysgarth Force.

▶ *From Bainbridge cross the River Ure and turn right, continuing on unclassified roads, then at Aysgarth take the **B6160** to Buckden.*

10 **Buckden,** North Yorkshire

Buckden, in Wharfedale, is a very popular holiday and walking area. Kettlewell, further down the valley, was formerly part of the estate of the Percy family, ancestors of the Dukes of Northumberland.

This stretch of road passes the imposing limestone outcrop of Kilnsey Crag, one of Yorkshire's most distinctive landmarks, alongside the all-weather attraction of Kilnsey Park, which has been established as a Visitor Centre.

▶ *Follow the **B6160** south and turn left at Threshfield on to the **B6265** into Grassington.*

ℹ️ *72 Main Street*

▶ *Continue east along the **A684** to Hawes.*

8 **Hawes,** North Yorkshire

Hawes is a centre for sheep-marketing and a focal point of Upper Wensleydale life. Just off the main street are quaint alley-ways and old cottages which have not changed much for 200 years. The National Parks Information Centre is located near the Upper Dales Folk Museum, which is housed in an engine shed of the old railway. Hardraw Force, the highest waterfall in England, is also considered to be the most spectacular, and is accessible only by foot through the grounds of the Green Dragon Inn. The water drops 90 feet (27m) over the limestone Hardraw Scar, into a

11 **Grassington,** North Yorkshire

This is Wharfedale's principal village and another National Park Centre, for the North York Moors. Its small passageways, cobbled market place, medieval bridge and interesting old build-ings all add to the appeal. There are Bronze and Iron Age settle-ments at Lea Green, north of the village, and further east, along the B6265, are the underground caverns of Stump Cross. The main cave has been developed into an impressive floodlit show cave, with wonderful stalagmite and stalactite formations.

ℹ️ *Grassington National Park Centre, Hebden Road*

▶ *Continue along the **B6265** to Pateley Bridge.*

12 **Pateley Bridge,** North Yorkshire

This pleasant town has been the focus of everyday life in Nidderdale since ancient times. The picturesque ruins of Old St Mary's Church stand above the village on the hillside, and the Nidderdale Museum has fasci-nating exhibits including the Victorian Room and a replica cobbler's shop. A mile (1.6km) from town is Foster Beck Hemp Mill, now a restaurant, which features a huge 17th-century water wheel, the second largest in the country.

Above and inset: Fountains Abbey, perhaps England's finest abbey

East of town, along the B6165 (turn off at Wilsill) and unclassified roads are Brimham Rocks. These curious rock formations have been sculpted out of the millstone grit by wind and rain over thousands of years, and there are wide views from the surrounding moorlands.

i *14 High Street*

▶ *Leave by the B6265 turning right after 1 mile (1.6km) on to the B6165. At Wilsill turn left and follow unclassified roads past Brimham Rocks to Fountains Abbey.*

13 Fountains Abbey, North Yorkshire
Founded by Cistercian monks in 1132, Fountains is the largest and perhaps the finest abbey in England. Particularly notable are the tower, nave and lay brothers'

quarters. It was acquired by William Aislabie in 1768 and became the focal point of his magnificent landscaped gardens at nearby Studley Royal Park, which contains typical ornaments of the period, such as a lake, a temple and statues. The park's original house burned down in 1945, but there are still estate cottages, huddled round a 19th-century church designed by William Burges. Deer and other livestock can be seen grazing in the park.

▶ *Return to the B6265 for the journey back to Ripon.*

RECOMMENDED WALKS

The various National Park Centres provide a programme of guided walks at Bank Holidays and during July and August. These start at 2pm and usually last 2½ to 3 hours. Local people with a special interest in some aspect of the Dales act as guides. Information about these walks is given in *The Visitor*, a free publication.

BACK TO NATURE

In the gritstone area of the Yorkshire Dales, above Nidderdale and Swaledale, purple heathers dominate the scene, but in the limestone country round Wharfedale you will find more variety, with the tiny coloured flowers which thrive in the calcite-rich soils. Plants such as yellow pimpernel, giant bell-flower, lily of the valley and ramson grow well in the light shade cast by ash, which grows on the limestone scars, while the unmown roadside verges and hay meadows are favoured by knapweed, sneezewort, early purple orchids and cowslips.

Quarries, Castles & Railways

From Bangor make a brief visit to the island of Anglesey before heading down the coast to Caernarfon and then inland to Snowdonia. The hills are scarred with quarries in places, but still create an overpoweringly beautiful backdrop.

2 DAYS • 113 MILES • 180KM

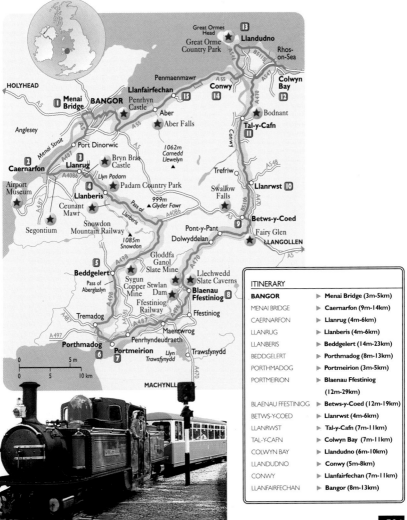

ITINERARY		
BANGOR	▶	**Menai Bridge (3m-5km)**
MENAI BRIDGE	▶	**Caernarfon (9m-14km)**
CAERNARFON	▶	**Llanrug (4m-6km)**
LLANRUG	▶	**Llanberis (4m-6km)**
LLANBERIS	▶	**Beddgelert (14m-23km)**
BEDDGELERT	▶	**Porthmadog (8m-13km)**
PORTHMADOG	▶	**Portmeirion (3m-5km)**
PORTMEIRION	▶	**Blaenau Ffestiniog**
		(12m-29km)
BLAENAU FFESTINIOG	▶	**Betws-y-Coed (12m-19km)**
BETWS-Y-COED	▶	**Llanrwst (4m-6km)**
LLANRWST	▶	**Tal-y-Cafn (7m-11km)**
TAL-Y-CAFN	▶	**Colwyn Bay (7m-11km)**
COLWYN BAY	▶	**Llandudno (6m-10km)**
LLANDUDNO	▶	**Conwy (5m-8km)**
CONWY	▶	**Llanfairfechan (7m-11km)**
LLANFAIRFECHAN	▶	**Bangor (8m-13km)**

[i] *Theatr Qwynedd, Bangor*

▶ *Drive along the A5122 for 3 miles (5km) to Menai Bridge.*

❶ Menai Bridge, Gwynedd

Menai Bridge takes its name from the suspension bridge built by Telford between 1819 and 1826 high above the Menai Strait. Nowadays, traffic on the busy A5 uses Stephenson's Britannia Bridge, whose original tubular structure was rebuilt after a fire in 1970, with a road deck above the railway.

From a lay-by on the A545 beyond Menai Bridge, there are superb views of both bridges, with the mountains of Snowdonia beyond. In Menai Bridge itself is the Tegfryn Art Gallery, which features the work of contemporary Welsh artists.

▶ *Follow the A4080 to the A5, recross the Menai Strait on the Britannia Bridge, then on to the A487 to Caernarfon.*

❷ Caernarfon, Gwynedd

The airport south of Caenarfon is a great all-weather attraction. It used to be an RAF camp during World War II, and is now a hands-on museum, where you

Thomas Telford's graceful suspension bridge over the Menai Strait

can climb into exhibits, touch the controls and use a flight simulator. You can also have a flight over Caernarfon Castle or round Snowdon. In 1969, Prince Charles was invested in the castle, following a tradition set by Edward I, whose first-born son was presented to the people as the Prince of Wales. Inside the castle you can see the investiture robes, and an explanation of the history of the castle and surrounding area, as well as the Museum of the Royal Welch Fusiliers.

Just outside the town, at Segontium, are the remains of a fine Roman fort which served as an important outpost of the Empire for three centuries.

[i] *Oriel Pendeitsh*

▶ *Take the A4086 eastwards and turn on to an unclassified road to Llanrug.*

❸ Llanrug, Gwynedd

The lived-in castle at Bryn Bras, to the south of Llanrug, has spacious lawns, tranquil woodland walks and excellent mountain views. This neo-Norman building on the fringe of Snowdonia was built in the 1830s on the site of an earlier castle, and the majestic gardens are worth visiting in their own right.

▶ *Return to and continue along the A4086 to Llanberis.*

❹ Llanberis, Gwynedd

At Llanberis you can take a 40-minute trip in a narrow-gauge train along the shores of Llyn Padarn, in the Padarn Country Park. The famed modern pump storage hydro scheme is close by at Dinorwic. Dolbadarn Castle is in the town, and less than a mile (1.6km) from the High Street is Ceunant Mawr, one of the most impressive waterfalls in Wales. The most popular footpath up Snowdon starts here, as does the Snowdon Mountain Railway, the only public rack-and-pinion railway, which climbs 3,000 feet (915m) to the summit in less than 5 miles (8km). Each train can take a maximum of 59 passengers and will normally not run with fewer than 25. Services depend on demand and weather conditions, which can be very harsh at the top of Snowdon, even when Llanberis is pleasant and sunny. The views can be superb.

[i] *Amgueddfa'r Gogledd Museum of the North*

▶ *Leave on the A4086, then turn right on to the A498 for 14 miles (23km) to Beddgelert.*

From Llanberis, walk around
the eastern end of Llyn Padarn
at the foot of the Dinorwic
quarries and then along the
northern side of the lake. Visit
the Slate Museum and pass
through the woods and via the
tramway bridge, before going
round the western end of the
lake and back into Llanberis.

5 Beddgelert, Gwynedd
The grave of Gelert is one of the
saddest memorials you are likely
to see. According to legend,
which may actually be a 19th-
century invention, Gelert was a
faithful wolfhound killed by
Prince Llywelyn, who thought it
had killed his son, when in fact
the dog had saved him from a
wolf. Just outside this small town
is the award-winning Sygun
Copper mine, where you can
explore the tunnels of a 19th-
century mine which was once
one of the world's major copper
producers. A guided tour will
take you past veins of ore
containing gold, silver and other
metals. From Beddgelert the
drive takes you through the
picturesque Pass of Aberglaslyn.

[i] *Llewelyn Cottage*

▶ *Follow the A498 southwards
to Porthmadog.*

6 Porthmadog, Gwynedd
Porthmadog was the creation of
William Alexander Madocks,
who hoped to benefit from the
tourist traffic to Ireland; in fact,
the town made its money from
slate. The Ffestiniog Railway,
which runs through magnificent
scenery to Blaenau Ffestiniog,
once carried the slate here to be
shipped abroad, and is now a
major tourist attraction. It uses
horseshoe bends and a complete
spiral at one point to gain height.
Porthmadog also has the little
Welsh Highland Railway, and a
Motor Museum next to the
Porthmadog Pottery.

[i] *High Street*

▶ *Drive along the A487 before
turning right on to an unclassified road to Portmeirion.*

7 Portmeirion, Gwynedd
This Italianate garden village,
surrounded by woods and
beaches, was created by the
Welsh architect Sir Clough
Williams-Ellis. Portmeirion was
used as the setting for the 1960s
cult television series *The
Prisoner,* and now produces a
distinctive range of colourful
pottery.

Italian-style Portmeirion

▶ *Return to and take the A487
eastwards, turning left on to
the A496 at Maentwrog.
Shortly turn right on to the
B4391 which joins the A470
at Ffestiniog. Turn left on to the
A470 and continue to
Blaenau Ffestiniog.*

8 Blaenau Ffestiniog,
Gwynedd
Blaenau Ffestiniog depended
for its livelihood on the slate
quarries, until demand for slate
fell away. Now visitors can get
first-hand experience of the slate
miners' working conditions at
the Llechwedd Slate Caverns,
where the Deep Mine tour will
take you down on Britain's
steepest passenger incline. Just
above the town is the world's
largest slate mine at Gloddfa
Ganol, where you can walk into
the mine and see craftsmen at
work. A modern industry is
established at Tanygrisiau,
where hydro electricity is
produced in a pumped storage

Set on a rock above the town, Conwy Castle is an imposing sight

bridge was designed by Inigo Jones in 1636, and the Gwydir Chapel contains the coffin of Llywelyn, Prince of Wales. Take a tour around the Trefriw Wells Roman Spa, where the water has been used as an aid to healthy living since Roman times, and is said to ease rheumatism and nervous tension. At the Trefriw Woollen Mills, you can see bedspreads and tweeds being manufactured, using electricity generated from the River Crafnant.

> **FOR HISTORY BUFFS**
>
> Trefriw has been known for its spa water since the 1st century, when Roman soldiers tunnelled into the Allt Coch mountains to reach the source. The water is rich in chalybeate, an iron solution; at the Victorian Pump House you can enjoy a sample of the water, which is said to help eliminate fatigue, nervous tension, stress, lumbago and anaemia.

▶ *Continue along the A470 to Tal-y-Cafn.*

11 Tal-y-Cafn, Gwynedd
The 80-acre (32-hectare) garden at Bodnant is claimed to be one of the finest gardens in the world. Now owned by the National Trust, it is located in the beautiful Conwy Valley, with views out to the Snowdon mountains. Throughout the year visitors can find much of interest, with native and exotic trees and flowers, and there is a nursery where plants are propagated.

▶ *Keep going along the A470 and then the A547 to Colwyn Bay.*

12 Colwyn Bay, Clwyd
Colwyn Bay is a lively seaside town, which grew in the late 19th century as a result of the arrival of the railway, the pier, promenade and many hotels and shops date from this period. The town is famous for its parks and gardens. The

scheme. Drive up the mountain road to the Stwlan Dam for the remarkable view along the Vale of Ffestiniog. The Ffestiniog Railway runs through 13½ (22km) scenic miles to Porthmadog, and the more energetic can visit the Rhiwgoch dry ski slope at Trawsfynydd Holiday Village.

ⓘ *High Street*

▶ *Continue along the A470 to Betws-y-Coed.*

9 Betws-y-Coed, Gwynedd
Betws-y-Coed is a popular inland resort set among forested land and magnificent mountains. The River Conwy is met by three tributaries here, and there are numerous bridges, waterfalls, and river pools with walks and

play areas for children. Upstream are the Swallow Falls, one of the most famous of all tourist attractions in North Wales, and downstream is Fairy Glen, a much photographed and painted beauty spot. Back in the centre of the small town, there are many interesting shops and a craft centre. The 14th-century Church of St Mary has a Norman font and an effigy of the great-nephew of Llywelyn the Great. There is also a Motor Museum here.

ⓘ *Royal Oak Stables*

▶ *Leave Betws-y-Coed on the A5, shortly turning right on to the B5106 and follow it north for 4 miles (6km) to Llanrwst.*

10 Llanrwst, Gwynedd
This historic market town is set in a delightful landscape of hills, forests, rivers and lakes. The

The impressive Aber Falls

Welsh Mountain Zoo has chimpanzees, free-flying eagles, a sealion display and jungle adventure land. Other wild animals, though less lively, can be seen in the Dinosaur World in Eirias Park, which contains the largest collection of model dinosaurs in the British Isles.

ℹ️ *Station Road*

▶ *Follow the **B5115** coast road for 6 miles (10km) to Llandudno.*

13 Llandudno, Gwynedd
St Tudno gave his name to the town in the 5th century, and a church still stands on the site of his cell. The town is the largest holiday resort in Wales, with two excellent sandy beaches situated between the headlands of Great and Little Orme. The Great Orme Country Park can be reached on the Great Orme Tramway, which has been taking passengers up to the top of the 679-foot (207m) summit since 1902. The energetic can enjoy the artificial ski slope and the 2,300-foot (700m) toboggan run, and there are fun rides for the children. Llandudno retains some of its Victorian elegance while catering for modern visitors. Lewis Carroll was a visitor and Alice Liddell for whom he wrote *Alice in Wonderland*, stayed here. A White Rabbit statue recalls Carroll's connections with the town, and there is an Alice exhibition in The Rabbit Hole, on Trinity Square.

ℹ️ *Chapel Street*

▶ *Drive south along the **A546** for 5 miles (8km) to Conwy.*

14 Conwy, Gwynedd
Conwy's castle dominates the town, and inside it is a model of the castle and town as they were in the 14th century. This ancient city still has its complete medieval walls, and you can take a pleasant stroll along the ramparts. There are three remarkable bridges crossing the river, including the Conwy Suspension Bridge, designed and built by Thomas Telford in 1826 and renovated in 1990. The smallest house in Britain, a mere 6 feet (2m) wide and 10 feet (3m) high, stands on the quay. There is a Butterfly House in Bodlodeb Park, where exotic varieties fly freely around in a natural environment.

ℹ️ *Conwy Castle Visitor Centre*

▶ *Head west along the **A55** to Penmaenmawr and further along to Llanfairfechan.*

15 Llanfairfechan, Gwynedd
Penmaenmawr has one of the finest beaches in North Wales, stretching between two granite headlands, and this is a fun holiday centre for the children. Further along, at Llanfairfechan, there is a sandy beach and beautiful inland scenery. There are excellent walks near by, notably up to the Aber Falls, 3 miles (5km) west of the town. The village of Aber was once the location of the palace of the Welsh king, Llywelyn the Great.

▶ *Keep on along the **A55** before turning right on to the **A5122** passing Penrhyn Castle on the return to Bangor.*

BACK TO NATURE

The shores of the Menai Strait harbour a rich variety of marine creatures, best looked for at low tide among the seaweeds. This abundance of life supports thousands of birds; waders such as redshanks, dunlins and curlews can be seen feeding alongside gulls and wigeon, and you can scan the open water for divers, grebes and cormorants.

SPECIAL TO...

Contained in the 840 square miles (2,175sq km) of the Snowdonia National Park are mountain peaks over 3,000 feet (915m) high, as well as miles of coastline and sandy beaches, and old mines and quarries, museums, castles and railways add further interest to this remarkable area.

2/3 DAYS • 172 MILES • 277KM

Castles on the
Welsh Marches

This route passes through the Wye and Usk Valleys. The castles built along the Welsh borders are testaments to a turbulent age, when this was an area of constant fighting between the Normans and the Welsh.

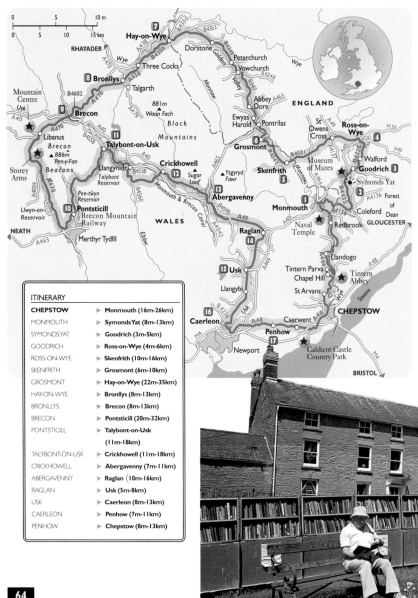

The River Wye, from Symonds Yat
Left: Hay Cinema bookshop

i │ *The Castle Car Park, Chepstow*

▶ *Drive north for 16 miles (26km) on the A466 to Monmouth.*

◻ Monmouth, Gwent
Monmouth was an old Roman settlement, but its main growth came after 1066, and in 1673 the 1st Duke of Beaufort built Great Castle House on the site of the old Norman castle. Near Agincourt Square, dominated by the 18th-century Shire Hall, is a statue of C S Rolls, of Rolls Royce fame, whose family lived near here. East of town is Kymin Hill, where the Naval Temple commemorates British admirals. The walk up to it from town follows the line of Offa's Dyke Long Distance Footpath.

i │ *Shire Hall*

FOR HISTORY BUFFS

Tintern Abbey, just off the road to Monmouth in the Wye Valley, was a Cistercian foundation in 1131 which survived until the Dissolution of the Monasteries under Henry VIII. The abbey church has survived almost intact, and the ruins of many monastic buildings can still be seen.

▶ *Take the A4136, then turn left on to the B4228 just past Staunton. Bear left on to the B4332 after a further ½ mile (1km) to Symonds Yat.*

❷ Symonds Yat, Hereford and Worcester
The scenery of the Wye Valley is among the finest in Britain and Symonds Yat is a particularly impressive beauty spot, above the deep gorge. The river flows for 4 miles (6km) in a large meander before returning to within 400 yards (365m) of the same point. An AA viewpoint on the summit at 473 feet (144m) affords magnificent views.

▶ *Continue north via an unclassified road, turning right on to the B4227 to Goodrich.*

❸ Goodrich, Hereford and Worcester
Imposing Goodrich Castle is a red sandstone ruin which

FOR CHILDREN

As you enter the Jubilee Maze at the Museum of Mazes in Symonds Yat, you will be met by a maze man, wearing Victorian boating costume. There are 12 routes to the centre, where the Temple of Diana awaits you. Evening illuminations create a labyrinth of eerie shadows. The museum tells the history of mazes, and of magic spells and witchcraft.

Cromwell lost to the Royalists during the Civil War, but then battered with a mortar which fired 200lb (90kg) shots. This dramatically situated castle had a moat which was excavated from solid rock, and you can still look down the 168-foot (51km) well in the courtyard.

▶ *Cross the River Wye and take the* ***B4228*** *to Ross-on-Wye.*

4 **Ross-on-Wye,** Hereford and Worcester
The splendid 208-foot (63m) spire of St Mary's Church rises high above the roofs of this attractive town. Interesting old streets spread out from the market place, with its 17th-century red sandstone Market Hall. Notable features include several ancient alms houses and 16th-century Wilton Bridge.

ⓘ *20 Broad Street*

▶ *Leave on the* ***A49***, *then the* ***B4521*** *Abergavenny road to Skenfrith.*

5 **Skenfrith,** Gwent
Skenfrith Castle was built as one of a group of three castles, along with Grosmont and White, to guard the Marches against Welsh

uprisings. Its remains include a central keep enclosed by a four-sided curtain wall and a moat. A small stone village clusters round the castle, with a quaint little 13th-century church and a mill with a working water wheel.

▶ *Continue along the* ***B4521***, *then turn north on to the* ***B4347*** *to Grosmont.*

6 **Grosmont,** Gwent
Set on a hillside by the River Monnow, Grosmont is the site of another Norman fortress, taken and re-taken several times during the Welsh uprisings of the 13th to 15th centuries. The castle ruins can be reached by footpath from the town. Grosmont's 13th-century parish church is noted for its huge but crude effigy of an armoured knight. At Abbey Dore, further along the road, the abbey remains include a vast, atmospheric church, tucked away in the Golden Valley.

▶ *Follow the* ***B4347***, *then the* ***B4348*** *through the Golden Valley and on to Hay-on-Wye.*

7 **Hay-on-Wye,** Powys
Hay stands high above the southern bank of the River Wye.

Hay Castle was built by the Marcher Lord William de Braose

Folk hero Owain Glyndŵr destroyed its castle during the 15th century, but the keep, parts of the walls and a gateway remain. The town's cinema has become the biggest second-hand book shop in the world; in fact the whole town seems to be taken up with second-hand books.

ⓘ *The Car Park*

▶ *Head southwest for 8 miles (13km) along the* ***B4350*** *and* ***A438*** *to Bronllys.*

8 **Bronllys,** Powys
From Bronllys there are clear views of the Brecon Beacons ahead and the Black Mountains, which dominate the scenery to the left. The 12th-century church, now rebuilt, has a very odd detached tower, and a stone-built Malt House is still in excellent condition and contains its original equipment. Bronllys Castle is half a mile (1km) along the A479.

▶ *From Bronllys take the* ***A438***, *the* ***A470*** *and the* ***B4602*** *to Brecon.*

9 Brecon, Powys

Brecon is a pure delight, encircled by hills at the meeting point of the Rivers Usk and Honddu. The cathedral, originally the church of a Benedictine priory, dates mainly from the 13th and 14th centuries, and Brecon Castle is now in the grounds of the Castle Hotel. The County Hall houses the Brecknock Museum, with its wealth of local history, and the South Wales Borderers Army Museum has relics ranging from the Zulu War in 1879 to World War II and later. East of town is the terminus of the Monmouth and Brecon Canal, and to the south is the Brecon Beacons National Park. The Mountain Centre, off the A470, west of the little village of Libanus, is an ideal starting point for exploring the Park.

ℹ️ *Cattle Market Car Park; The Mountain Centre, Libanus*

SPECIAL TO...

Brecon's Brecknock Museum has a superb display of Welsh lovespoons, traditional gifts of betrothal which were carved out of single pieces of wood. From the 17th to the 19th centuries the lovespoon developed into complex and intricate works of art, with keys, bells and other motifs worked into the design.

▶ *Continue southwards along the A470 then take unclassified roads northwards to Pontsticill.*

RECOMMENDED WALKS

A good starting point for walking on the Brecon Beacons is at Storey Arms on the A470, which is at 1,425 feet (427m) above sea-level and gives the shortest route to Pen y Fan, the highest point in the Beacons. Be sure to take an OS map, food supplies and weatherproof clothes, even in fine weather.

---

10 Pontsticill, Mid Glamorgan

Walking and boating are major attractions in this area; or you could have a journey on the steam train of the Brecon Mountain Railway, which runs for 4 miles (6km) down the valley, through splendid scenery.

▶ *Take unclassified roads through hills and forests to Talybont-on-Usk.*

11 Talybont-on-Usk, Powys

This delightful little village is now a tourist centre, especially for walkers and outdoor activities; there is an Outdoor Pursuits Centre in the old railway station. The 18th-century Monmouth and Brecon Canal, which passes through the village, was built to carry coal and iron ore. It eventually closed in 1962, but was reopened by volunteers in 1970 for use by pleasure craft.

▶ *Follow the B4558 to Llangynidr, then the B4560 and an unclassified road to Crickhowell.*

12 Crickhowell, Powys

The name of this little market town is derived from the Iron Age fort Crug Hywel (Howell's Cairn). The town grew up around Alisby's Castle, which was captured and destroyed in 1403 by Owain Glyndŵr, and is now a picturesque ruin. The River Usk is crossed by an old bridge, dating from the 17th century, which appears to have 13 arches on one side but only 12 on the other – the result of 19th-century alterations.

▶ *Take the A40 for 7 miles (11km) to Abergavenny.*

13 Abergavenny, Gwent

At the edge of the Brecon Beacons National Park Abergavenny, the 'Gateway to the Vale of Usk', is overlooked by the Sugar Loaf mountain, 1,955 feet (596m) high, and Ysgyryd (Skirrid) Fawr, 1,595 feet (486m). Its ruined castle was founded in 1090. Impressive buildings in the town include

Working a lock on the Brecon and Monmouth Canal

the stone tythe barn, and the red sandstone Lloyds Bank. St Mary's Church is built on the site of a former Benedictine priory.

ℹ️ *Swan Meadow, Cross Street*

▶ *Continue along the A40 to Raglan.*

14 Raglan, Gwent

One of Britain's finest ruins is 15th-century Raglan Castle which was actually built as a fortified manor. The keep is outside the main castle and Parliamentary troops overcame the Royalists here during the Civil War, by approaching from the opposite side. The castle houses an exhibition on the history of Raglan.

▶ *Follow an unclassified road south to Usk.*

15 Usk, Gwent

Usk is a small market town on the site of an ancient Roman settlement, *Burrium*. Visit the church to see the remarkable restored Tudor rood screen; and, at the other end of the town, the

Raglan Castle was the last to fall to Cromwell in the Civil War

Gwent Rural Life Museum, in an old stone malt barn, which is crammed with exhibits about life in the area. Usk Castle is privately owned but you can visit the ruins of the Priory next to the church.

▶ *Cross the river and continue along unclassified roads for 8 miles (13km) to Caerleon.*

16 Caerleon, Gwent
One of the four permanent Roman legions in Britain was based here, and parts of the Roman city of *Isca* are displayed in an excellent new exhibition room. The major find has been the amphitheatre outside the city walls. This oval earth mound seated 5,000 people, and is the only fully excavated amphitheatre in Britain. The Legionary Museum has more information and relics from the barracks.

▶ *Take the* **B4236***, then an unclassified road to join the* **A48** *for Penhow.*

17 Penhow, Gwent
The oldest inhabited castle in Wales is Penhow Castle, which is perched on a hillside above the main road. Now privately owned, it is open to the public and is an excellent example of the smaller type of fortified manor house.

Three miles (5km) further is Caerwent, on the site of *Venta Silurium*, the only walled Roman civilian town in Wales. Remnants of the wall and mosaic pavements can still be seen. Caldicot Castle Country Park, 2 miles (3km) away, surrounds the 12th-century castle.

▶ *Continue straight along the* **A48** *to Chepstow.*

BACK TO NATURE

The Forest of Dean is an excellent area for the birdwatcher. Woodpeckers, tits and nuthatches can be see, and pied flycatchers are often spotted at the RSPB's Nagshead reserve, where nest boxes encourage the species.

The Border
Country

Few cities can match Edinburgh's city centre: Princes Street and its gardens; Edinburgh Castle; the Royal Mile, with its medieval 'lands', or blocks of flats; the Palace of Holyroodhouse, and the elegant Georgian architecture of New Town. By far the best view of all the city's treasures is from Arthur's Seat, a volcanic hill 823 feet (251m) above sea level.

2 DAYS • 148 MILES • 239KM

☐ *3 Princes Street, Edinburgh*

the old village of Dirleton, claimed by some to be the most beautiful village in Scotland, is dominated by the grand Dirleton Castle which dates back to the 13th century. Perched on top of a rocky platform, it has massive towers and was defended by a moat at least 50 feet (15m) wide.

▶ *Continue on the A198 for 5 miles (8km) to North Berwick.*

❷ North Berwick, Lothian

This seaside golf resort is dominated by the nearby 613-foot (187m) peak of North Berwick Law, which offers splendid views over the town itself and the coast beyond.

The town's main antiquity is the ruin of the old church of St Andrews, where in 1591 the story goes that a gathering of witches and wizards was addressed by the Devil, who appeared in the form of a black

▶ *Continue on the A198 and turn left at a signposted minor road to Tantallon Castle, 3 miles (5km).*

❸ Tantallon Castle, Lothian

The castle stands in a spectacular clifftop position, with three sides protected by the sea and the fourth by thick walls. Two great sieges took place here: the first ended by negotiation (the attackers had run out of gunpowder!) and in the second, General Monk attacked it for 12 days in 1651, damaging the towers. This is the best place on the mainland to view the Bass Rock. The island has huge numbers of gannets breeding there and the colony is so important that the birds' scientific name *Sula bassana* comes from the island.

▶ *Return to the A198 and continue southwards. Turn right at the B1407 to enter Preston.*

▶ *Leave by the A1 and turn left at the A198 to reach Gullane.*

❶ Gullane, Lothian

Gullane is renowned as a golfing centre, with a number of courses including a championship course at nearby Muirfield. There is a Heritage of Golf Museum by the links.
Further east, the centre of

goat. This sinister group apparently sought the death of James VI and a number of the 'plotters' were subsequently brought to trial and burned at the stake. The Devil (who may have been the heavily disguised Earl of Bothwell) escaped a similar fate.

☐ *Quality Street*

The sea provides a formidable defence for Tantallon Castle

❹ Preston, Lothian

On the outskirts of the village stands the charming 18th-century water-driven Preston Mill. Originally a meal mill, the unusual design of its kiln has similarities with an English oast house. The buildings are

Preston Mill, built in the 18th
century and powered by water

constructed of orange sandstone
rubble and roofed with traditional east coast pantiles. A
short walk leads to the
Phantassie Doocot, a dovecot
which once housed some 500
pigeons.

▶ *Leave by the B1047 and turn
left on to the B1377. Turn left
at the A1, then left at the
A1087 to Dunbar.*

5 Dunbar, Lothian
This popular seaside resort is
now a rather peaceful place, a
far cry from the turbulent times
when its castle was of some
importance. The castle was
eventually sacked by Cromwell
in 1650 and its walls torn down,
the stones being used to
improve the harbour. The
remains sit quite forlornly by
the harbour entrance. The
attractive harbour is home to a
busy fishing fleet and there is
a nearby lifeboat museum.
Conservationist John Muir was
born in Dunbar in the mid-19th
century.

[i] *143 High Street*

▶ *Continue on the A1087 and
turn left at the A1 to
Cockburnspath.*

6 Cockburnspath, Borders
The position of this village so
close to the border has meant a
turbulent and rather troubled
history. This was an important
stopping place for horse-drawn
coaches (a mode of travel which
peaked in the 19th century) and
the layout of the village and its
marketplace owes much to this
time. The parish church is
worth a look; it has a fine tower
in the middle of the west gable
and an unusual sundial on the
southwest corner.

The mercat cross is the
finishing point of the Southern
Upland Way, the long distance
footpath that starts at
Portpatrick, over on the west
coast. By following the Way

from its terminus, the path
leads to a group of houses at
Cove, below which is the
picturesque Cove Harbour. The
harbour is reached by going
through a tunnel cut into the
cliff; this was made in the 18th
century and was connected to
cellars probably used for curing
and barrelling fish, and possibly
by smugglers.

▶ *Continue on the A1 and
turn left at the A1107. At
Coldingham, turn left at the
B6438 and follow this to
St Abbs.*

7 St Abbs, Borders
This little fishing village is now
a resort, often busy with divers
who explore the local bays.
Nearby Coldingham has an
ancient priory. Founded in 1098
by King Edgar, the 13th-
century priory church was built
on a site that had a religious
house way back in the 7th
century. Life could hardly have
been peaceful for those that
stayed here during the frequent

outbreaks of hostilities, as the
monks were subject to the
English king and the priors to
the Scots king!

**RECOMMENDED
WALKS**

St Abbs Head offers a pleasant
and interesting walk. Other
good walks can be found in the
John Muir Country Park (west
of Dunbar) and at Barns Ness
(on the coast, southeast
of Dunbar).

BACK TO NATURE

The cliffs at St Abbs Head are
home to countless kittiwakes,
guillemots, razorbills and other
seabirds. A marked path starts
from just before St Abbs village
and leads past the bird cliffs,
allowing a very good view of
the colonies – but stick to
the path!

▶ Return along the **B6438** to Coldingham and turn left at the **A1107**. Turn left at the **B6355** to enter Eyemouth.

8 **Eyemouth,** Borders

This busy fishing port has regular fish markets which are worth visiting. This is home to a large fleet and the local people have been connected with fishing for a very long time. The town's saddest day came on 14 October 1881 when a sudden gale blew up and 129 local fishermen were drowned, some of them in full sight of anxious families watching from the shore. The local museum tells the story of the tragedy.

ℹ️ Auld Kirk

▶ Return along the **B6355**, then follow the **A6105** to Duns.

9 **Duns,** Borders

This long-established village, with its well-built stone houses, makes a useful stopping point for touring this part of the Borders. This was the home town of the world motor-racing champion Jim Clark, who died in a race in Germany in 1968; a small museum in the village has mementoes of his tragically short but fascinating life. Near Duns is the mansion Manderston, which has attractive formal gardens and a marble dairy.

> ### FOR CHILDREN
>
> Crumstane Farm, near Duns, has many animals to interest children, from goats and geese to Clydesdale horses.

> ### RECOMMENDED WALKS
>
> Inland, a road can be followed from Duns to the settlement of Longformacus and then up to the Watch Water Reservoir. From there, the route of the Southern Upland Way can be followed to the two massive Twinlaw Cairns. The view is impressive, and the island of Lindisfarne can be seen from the top.

▶ Leave on the **A6112** for 12 miles (19km) to reach Coldstream.

Preparing the lifeboat, an essential emergency service for the busy fishing fleet of Eyemouth

10 **Coldstream,** Borders

Coldstream stands on the banks of the River Tweed, which at this point marks the border with England. This border was adopted in 1018. The river is crossed by a magnificent seven-arch bridge and on the Scottish side a toll house was the east coast equivalent of Gretna Green, a place where marriages could take place with the minimum of delay. Like so many other little towns in the Borders, Coldstream has a wealth of well-built houses, especially along its main street. The Market Square is a little off this street and in it can be found the Coldstream Museum, which tells the story of the town and the Coldstream Guards.

Outside Coldstream stands the Hirsel Homestead Museum comprising a museum, craft centre and walks in the estate.

ℹ️ High Street

▶ Leave by the **A697** and turn left at the **A698** to reach Kelso.

11 Kelso, Borders

Kelso has one of the most attractive town centres in the Borders, with a huge open square that has often been likened to that of a French town. The town stands at the confluence of the rivers Teviot and Tweed and from the fine bridge which crosses the Tweed there is a good view of Floors Castle, home of the Duke of Roxburghe, a huge mansion built by William Adam between

The remains of Kelso Abbey

1721 and 1725. Kelso Abbey was once the Borders' greatest abbey but only the west end of its stands today. It was founded here in 1128 but its position on the 'invasion route' meant that it suffered frequent attacks.

> ℹ *Town House*

> ▶ *Leave by the A6089. Turn left at the A697 and right at the A68. Follow this to Lauder.*

12 Lauder, Borders

This attractive town has a wide main street in the middle of which stands the Tolbooth. This was originally built in 1318 and the ground floor was used as a gaol up to 1840. Lauder's parish church is an interesting structure in the form of a Greek cross with an octagonal steeple and four arms; it is dated 1673.

Impressive Thirlestane Castle stands close to the town.

This dates from the end of the 16th century but there have been many alterations since then. The castle houses the fine Border Country Life Exhibitions.

The village of Earlston lies only a few miles south of Lauder. This was Ercildoune in medieval days and the home of Thomas the Rhymer who lived during the 13th century. His ability to see into the future was reckoned to be a gift from the Queen of the Fairies with whom it was believed he stayed for a number of years.

> ▶ *Continue on the A68 to Pathhead, then turn left at the B6367 to Crichton Castle.*

13 Crichton Castle, Lothian

Crichton was at one time the home of the Earl of Bothwell, the ill-fated third husband of Mary, Queen of Scots. The

ruins of this substantial structure stand on the edge of Middleton Moor and above the Tyne Water. It dates from the 14th century and one curiosity is a Renaissance-influenced wall erected in the late 16th century. This is an arcade of seven bays topped by diamond-patterned stonework, almost unique in the country. Crichton's church is a fine building, restored in 1896.

> ▶ *Return along the B6367 to Pathhead. Turn left and follow the A68 to Edinburgh.*

The Western
Highlands

The fort at Fort Augustus, built by General Wade in 1730, was named after William Augustus, Duke of Cumberland, who brutally suppressed the Highlanders after the battle of Culloden in 1746. In 1867 it became a Benedictine school; today it is a heritage centre, and Fort Augustus is a popular base for cruisers on the Caledonian Canal.

3 DAYS • 301 MILES • 484KM

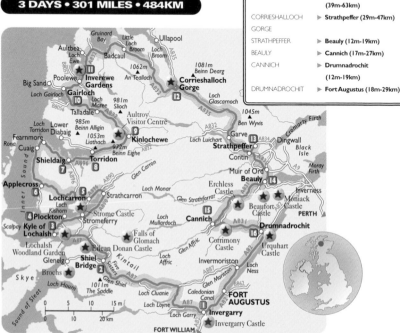

Lochcarron, a tiny hamlet strung along the sea loch's shore

i   *Car Park*

▶ *Head southwards on the* **A82** *for 7 miles (11km) to Invergarry.*

0 Invergarry, Highland
This sleepy-looking village was the home of an important clan, the MacDonnells of Glengarry. To the south lie the ruins of Invergarry Castle; three castles have stood here, the last one having been burnt in 1746 by Cumberland because Charles Edward Stuart stayed here before and after the battle of Culloden. Just to the north of Invergarry stands the roadside Well of Seven Heads, a gruesome reminder of the slaying of seven MacDonnell brothers who had murdered their dead brother's two sons. The story is told on a monument in Gaelic, English, Latin and French.

▶ *Leave by the* **A87** *(to Kyle of Lochalsh) and follow this for 36 miles (58km) to Shiel Bridge.*

2 Shiel Bridge, Highland
The imposing entry to Shiel Bridge is by the magnificent Glen Shiel, on whose north side is the group of mountains known as the Five Sisters of Kintail. The mountains are seen to great advantage at Mam Ratagan, just a little to the west of Invershiel on the Glenelg road. Like many communities in this region, Shiel Bridge is a collection of houses at an important junction, in this case at the head of Loch Duich. Along the northern shore of the loch stands Eilean Donan Castle, whose foundations date back to 1220. Shelled by a British frigate in 1719 during an abortive Jacobite rising, it lay in ruins until rebuilding started in 1912. It is now one of the Highlands' most popular castles and is said to be the most photographed castle in Scotland.

There is an unmanned NTS centre at Strath Croe, to the northeast of Shiel Bridge, with useful wildlife displays explaining the natural history of this wild and beautiful area. A very rough cross-country path from Strath Croe leads to the Falls of Glomach where the water of the Allt a' Ghlomaich tumbles 750 feet (230m).

i   *Shiel Bridge; NTS, Strath Croe*

FOR HISTORY BUFFS

To the west of Shiel Bridge lies the little village of Glenelg. The steep and winding road to it (not for caravans!) has long been of strategic importance, hence the 18th-century military road and the (now ruined) Bernera Barracks at Glenelg. This route was used by Samuel Johnson and James Boswell in 1773 and their steps are followed by many summer visitors heading towards the Kyle Rhea ferry to Skye. South of the village stand two brochs, Dun Telve and Dun Trodden. When built as defensive structures about 2,000 years ago, they were over 40 feet (13m) high and had stairs and galleries built into their circular walls. These are two of the best preserved brochs in the country.

▶ *Continue on the **A87** for 15 miles (24km) to Kyle of Lochalsh.*

3 Kyle of Lochalsh,
Highland

This bustling industrial village is usually thronged in summer as it is the terminus of the railway line from Inverness. The new (and very controversial) bridge that replaced the Skye ferries is reached by the A87. The western part of this peninsula lies within the NTS's Balmacara estate, and one mile (1.5km) after passing the little village of Reraig, the NTS's Lochalsh Woodland Garden is on the left. This boasts a fine collection of mature trees, especially Scots pines, and is developing more exotic species of plants such as bamboo trees.

i   *Car Park, Kyle of Lochalsh*

▶ *Leave by the unclassified road that leads northwards to Plockton.*

4 Plockton, Highland

With palm trees growing by the shore of Loch Carron, Plockton exudes the kind of peace and quiet that has attracted generations of painters; indeed, many would regard it as one of the northwest coast's loveliest villages. The sheltered position

also provides a much-needed haven for yachts sailing along the west coast.

▶ *Return along the approach road to Plockton and turn left to head eastwards towards Stromeferry, following the shore of Loch Carron. Turn left when the **A890** is met. Follow to just beyond Strathcarron railway station then turn left on to the **A896** to Lochcarron.*

5 Lochcarron, Highland

Lochcarron is essentially a long string of houses (and a few hotels) along the shore of the sea loch. To its south is Strome Castle, once a stronghold of the

Above: Kyle of Lochalsh and the controversial bridge to Skye
Left: Plockton, a favourite with lovers of temperate climates

MacDonnells of Glengarry, but destroyed by the MacKenzies in 1602. It commands a fine view of Skye. Just west of the village is Loch Kishorn, a deep and sheltered loch where enormous North Sea oil rigs were once built.

i   *Main Street*

▶ *Continue on the **A896** but turn left at the head of Loch Kishorn to Applecross. This road is definitely not for caravans, but the **A896** from Loch Kishorn to Shieldaig and the minor road from Shieldaig to Applecross are suitable.*

6 Applecross, Highland

Applecross was one of the country's most isolated communities until the coastal road from Shieldaig was built in the 1970s. The traditional route, over the 2,053-foot (626m) pass of Bealach na Ba (Pass of the Cattle), one of the highest roads in Britain, was a formidable obstacle to many vehicles and it is often closed by snow in winter. The zig-zag route slowly winds up to a wonderful wide view towards Kintail.

An Irish monk, Maelrubha, landed at Applecross in the AD670s and founded a monastery which was later destroyed by Vikings. The local church has an ancient cross slab 9 feet (3m) high, with a Celtic cross inscribed. This and others inside the church may date back to Maelrubha's time. An old chapel stands in the graveyard and two rounded stones in front of it mark the traditional resting place of Maelrubha.

▶ Head north on the unclassified road out of Applecross to Shieldaig. Turn left at the **A896**, then bear left to enter Shieldaig.

7 Shieldaig, Highland
This charming village consists of a row of whitewashed houses standing along the loch's shore. Once famous for its herring fishing (its name is Norse for 'herring bay'), it now relies more on tourism to maintain its livelihood. Opposite the harbour lies the small wooded Shieldaig Island. From around Shieldaig, there are wonderful views of some of the Highlands' best scenery. The mountains from Loch Kishorn northwards to Loch Maree are composed of red Torridonian sandstone, some 750 million years old. However, around Shieldaig (and just to the north of it) the rocks are a highly altered variety called gneiss which has been eroded to provide a low, smooth, knobbly platform above which the Torridon mountains soar.

▶ Continue on the **A896** for 8 miles (13km) to Torridon.

8 Torridon, Highland
The houses huddled together in the village are dwarfed by the mass of 3,456-foot (1,054m) Liathach, a mountain to be attempted only by experienced walkers, as its ridge is very narrow and exposed. Composed of Torridonian sandstone, its name, which means The Grey One, is derived from four of its seven tops, that are composed

of the white rock quartzite. An NTS countryside centre is situated just by the main road and this has displays and audiovisual presentations on the local geology and wildlife. Near by, there is a small Deer Museum; deer may be seen near here or even wandering around the village.

ℹ️ *NTS Centre*

The peaceful waters of upper Loch Torridon, ringed by the rugged Highland mountains

SCENIC ROUTES

As a detour, the narrow and twisty road from Torridon to Lower Diabaig is highly recommended as there are splendid views of Loch Torridon. In addition, the small picturesque lochside settlements of Inveralligin and Lower Diabaig are worth seeing.

BACK TO NATURE

About 10,000 years ago when the Ice Age ended, great tracts of land were gradually taken over by the Caledonian Forest. This was the home of bears, wolves and lynxes and the plant life was dominated by the magnificent Scots pine. Man swept out the wild beasts and he also nearly destroyed the Scots pine by felling it for charcoal burning and fuel and by land clearance for agriculture. This tour visits a number of places, notably Torridon, Loch Maree and Glen Affric, where these noble trees are being naturally regenerated.

▶ *Follow the **A896** for 11 miles (18km) to Kinlochewe.*

9 Kinlochewe, Highland

This village stands at the head of Loch Maree, which was once called Loch Ewe, hence the name. To its west lies the Beinn Eighe National Nature Reserve and the reserve's Aultroy Visitor Centre is just along the A832 from the village. Further on is an interesting nature trail which climbs to a fine view over the loch towards Slioch, the 3,217-foot (980m) high mountain that dominates the surrounding district. Loch Maree is one of the country's finest lochs and is steeped in history. The tiny Isle Maree was once a sacred place of the Druids, who are said to have introduced oak trees, one of their religious symbols. In the 7th century, St Maelrubha came and set up his cell here and, for similar reasons, planted holly trees. In later centuries, paganism was practised here and rites involving the sacrifice of a bull occurred on the island as late as the 17th century. The Loch Maree Hotel has a large boulder outside it on which is a Gaelic inscription celebrating a visit by Queen Victoria; a translation is above the hotel's entrance.

▶ *Leave Kinlochewe on the A832 for 20 miles (32km) to Gairloch.*

10 Gairloch, Highland

This widely scattered crofting and fishing community is the district's main centre and it has developed into a popular place for holidays as it combines fine scenery with long stretches of sandy beaches. Fishing is important here and the harbour is well worth visiting when the boats come in. The fishing industry, crofting and other aspects of local life form important displays at the local Gairloch Heritage Museum which was developed from a farmstead with a cobbled courtyard.

[i] *Auchtercairn*

FOR CHILDREN

Gairloch has some of the best beaches in the western Highlands. As well as the beach at the village, there are good ones relatively near by, at Big Sand (to the west) and Red Point (further away to the southwest). For wet-weather activity, there is a swimming pool at Poolewe. The Gairloch Centre has facilities for sports as diverse as climbing, archery, badminton and short tennis. These are some of the few indoor activities for children in the region, something that may have to be considered if the weather is bad.

▶ *Continue on the **A832** to Inverewe Gardens, just beyond the village of Poolewe.*

11 Inverewe Gardens, Highland

In 1862 Osgood MacKenzie started a long labour of love when he began transforming an area of barren ground here into one of Britain's most remarkable gardens. Conifers were planted to form shelter belts, wet land was drained, soil was carried in on men's backs and in 60 years, the local people had created a garden that gives great pleasure to over 100,000 visitors each year. Inverewe lies at the same latitude as Siberia, but here, bathed by the warm Gulf Stream, it boasts palms, magnolias, hydrangeas, rhododendrons and many other plants.

On a summer's day Loch Ewe is a peaceful place, a far cry from the days of World War II when it was a convoy station for ships bound for Russia or Iceland. Aultbea (a little further along the road) was the depot's HQ and remains of gun emplacements have been kept as reminders of the district's role in those dangerous days. Look out for information boards near Aultbea's pier.

[i] *NTS Centre*

▶ *Continue on the **A832** to the **A835**. Turn left and continue for less than a mile (1.5km).*

12 Corrieshalloch Gorge, Highland

Much of the Highland landscape was sculpted by the movement of ice during the last Ice Age. Often the ice smoothed the land, but at Corrieshalloch Gorge its meltwater flowing down the River Broom gouged out this spectacular rugged gorge about one mile (1.5km) long. A narrow bridge crosses the chasm with the water plunging over the Falls of Measach some 150 feet (45m) below – this is not the place for vertigo sufferers! The bridge was built by Sir John Fowler, joint designer of the Forth Rail Bridge, but this is hardly on the same scale and there is a limit to the number of people permitted on the bridge at one time!

The busy fishing port of Ullapool lies further down Loch Broom. This bustling little village was founded in 1788 by the British Fisheries Society to take advantage of the huge shoals of herring found in the nearby seas. It is an important ferry terminal for Stornoway; cruises to the Summer Isles are also available from the harbour.

▶ *Head southeast on the **A835** towards Inverness. Turn left at Contin on to the **A834** to Strathpeffer.*

13 Strathpeffer, Highland

Strathpeffer prospered as a spa in the 19th century after springs (four sulphur and one chalybeate) were developed. The Victorian hotels and large villas date from the spa's heyday and today the hotels still do a brisk trade, catering mainly for bus tours. The spa water can be sampled in a small building by the Square but beware – its taste is even more pungent that its smell! Local handicrafts can be bought at the small shops now occupying the old railway station buildings.

At the northern end of the village is the Eagle Stone, a Pictish stone also said to celebrate a victory of the Munros over the MacDonalds. To the east, the prominent hill of Knockfarrel affords fine views over the district.

☐*i*☐ *The Square*

▶ *Return along the **A834** to the **A835** and turn left. Turn right at the **A832** and at Muir of Ord take the **A862** southwards to Beauly.*

14 Beauly, Highland
Mary, Queen of Scots is supposed to have come here in 1564 and taken a liking to the place; tradition has it she described it as a '*beau lieu*' (beautiful place), hence its name. However, it is more likely Beauly derives from the name given to the 13th-century priory around which the town was built. Beauly Priory was founded in 1230 and the

Once a stretch of arid ground, Inverewe Gardens now boast glorious floral displays every year

present ruins date from the 13th to the 16th centuries. In 1572 Lord Ruthven obtained royal permission to strip the lead off the roof and by 1633 the building was in a ruinous condition. The town's 'modern' planned layout (built around 1840) features a wide market square and a grid street pattern. There are a number of castles to be found in the surrounding district. To the southeast is Moniack Castle, which makes wine from local produce; to the south is Beaufort Castle, built about 1880 in Scots baronial style; and near the road to Cannich stands Erchless Castle, a fine building that was described at the end of the 19th century as 'modernised, yet still a stately old pile'.

▶ *Leave on the **A862** (to Inverness) and turn right at the **A831** and continue to Cannich.*

15 Cannich, Highland
Cannich stands at the head of Strathglass, a glen not normally on tourist routes. The lower part of the glen has an impres-

sive narrow gorge (at An Druim) and there are a number of hydroelectric power stations here.

To the west of Cannich lie some very beautiful glens – Glen Affric, Glen Cannich and Glen Strathfarrar. These can give good walks as the scenery can be spectacularly wild in places: Scots pines are being regenerated and there are chances of seeing red deer.

Corrimony Cairn is found just off the Cannich to Drumnadrochit road. This is about 4,000 years old and has a central grave chamber which can be reached by crawling through the passageway. Standing stones ring the cairn and the large capstone lying on top of it has small circular indentations called 'cup marks' on it. Further along this narrow road, the standing stone known as Mony's Stone can be found, as well as the walled rectangular graveyard of Clach Churadain (St Curadan's Cemetery).

▶ *Continue on the **A831** for 12 miles (19km) to Drumnadrochit.*

century. Its commanding position in the Great Glen gave it immense military importance and part of it was blown up in the late 17th century to prevent it falling into the hands of Jacobites. Further south of the castle, the road passes a cairn erected to John Cobb who died on the loch in 1952 while attempting to set a new world speed record; he achieved the remarkable speed of 206mph (331kph) before the accident.

The village of Foyers can be seen on the opposite shore of the loch. In 1896, Britain's first major commercial hydroelectric power station was built here to provide energy for an aluminium works. These buildings can still be seen though the factory has long since closed. Today, a large pump-storage scheme produces electricity using the power of the water of Loch Mhor, which is on the moorland above the village.

▶ *Head south on the **A82** and return to Fort Augustus.*

16 Drumnadrochit,
Highland

The district round the village attracts huge numbers of visitors, all here hoping to see Nessie, the Loch Ness monster. The loch is only 2 miles (3km) wide at this point but about 750 feet (230m) deep and many 'sightings' have been reported here. In the AD600s, St Adamnan told how Columba drove back a monster when it was about to attack a swimmer. Since then, there have been many reported appearances and frequent scientific expeditions have attempted to find her, but there is still no definite proof

Urquhart Castle, a strategic fort overlooking Loch Ness

that a monster exists; however, even sceptical visitors should keep a loaded camera handy! Loch Ness Centre in Drumnadrochit has exhibits of almost everything connected with Nessie – from explanations of the loch's natural history and equipment used in expeditions to photographs of the beast herself.

Just outside the village stands Urquhart Castle. The site may have been fortified in the Dark Ages but the present structure dates back to the 13th

The Causeway
Coast

Larne is a busy port at the head of Larne Lough, the terminus for the shortest sea-crossing between Northern Ireland and mainland Britain, and the starting point of the Antrim Coast Road. Before the road was blasted in the 1830s, Glens folk looked to Scotland rather than the rest of Ulster, and the Scottish influence remains, especially in the lilting accent. **2/3 DAYS • 163 MILES • 263KM**

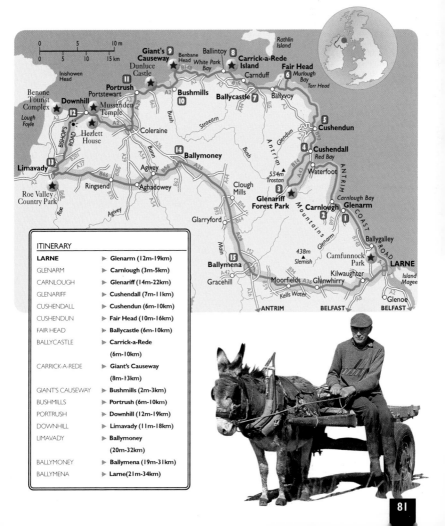

ITINERARY

i *At the harbour; Narrow Gauge Road*

▶ *Take the A2 coastal road north for 12 miles (19km) to Glenarm.*

❶ Glenarm, Co Antrim
The Antrim Coast Road is so attractive that it is difficult to resist its magnetic lure, but leave it for a moment to sample the charm of Glenarm, a village that clings to the glen rather than to the coast. The neo-Tudor Glenarm Castle is the seat of the Earls of Antrim; its barbican and battlemented, buttressed walls of 1825 rise above the river just as it nears

walk up an Antrim glen. This one is narrow, leafy and dense with pathways and waterfalls.

▶ *Take the A2 to Carnlough.*

❷ Carnlough, Co Antrim
Carnlough, at the foot of Glencoy, the least dramatic of the glens, has a good safe beach. A railway used to carry lime from the kilns above the village to the harbour, over the bridge that spans the coast road. The bridge, the clock tower and the former town hall are made from great chunks of limestone. Frances Anne Vane Tempest Stewart, Countess of Antrim and Marchioness of

❸ Glenariff, Co Antrim
The road obligingly provides a perfect route along this magnificent glen. The bay at its foot is 1 mile (1.5km) long and the chiselled sides draw in the fertile valley symmetrically to the head of the glen. There, the Forest Park allows easy exploration of the deep, wooded gorge with its impressive cascades, 'Ess-na-crub' (Fall of the Hoof), 'Ess-na-laragh' (Fall of the Mare) and Tears of the Mountain.

Waterfoot, the little village at the foot of the glen, hosts The Glens of Antrim Feis (festival, pronounced 'fesh') in July, a major traditional arts event.

One of the lovely Antrim Coast Road views, at Glenarm

the sea. The village has twisting streets (Thackeray enjoyed their names), pavements patterned in limestone and basalt, a market house with an Italianate campanile and good, modest Georgian houses and shops.

The forest, through the gateway at the top of the village, gives the first opportunity to

Londonderry, was responsible for many major works, including Garron Tower, built in 1848, once a family home, now a boarding school. She is remembered in the Londonderry Arms hotel, built in 1854.

▶ *Take the A2, following signposts for Cushendall for 9 miles (14km) to Waterfoot. Turn left on to the A43 for 5 miles (8km) to Glenariff Forest Park.*

Between Red Bay and the pier are three caves. Nanny's Cave was inhabited by Ann Murray until her death, aged 100, in 1847. She supported herself by knitting garments and by the sale of *poteen* (an illicit distillation, pronounced 'potcheen'), or 'the natural' as she called it.

▶ *Turn right to follow the B14 for 7 miles (11km) to Cushendall.*

4 Cushendall, Co Antrim
'The Capital of the Glens', Cushendall sits on a pleasant, sandy bay below Glenaan, Glenballyemon and Glencorp and in the curve of the River Dall. The rugged peak of Lurigethan broods over the village, while the softer Tieveragh Hill is supposed to be the capital of the fairies. Cushendall owes much to an East Indian nabob, Francis Turnley, who built the Curfew Tower in the centre as a 'place for the confinement of idlers and rioters'.

In a tranquil valley by the sea just north of the village is the 13th-century church of Layde. MacDonnells of Antrim are buried here, as are Englishmen stationed in these lonely posts as coastguards, and one memorial stone mourns an emigré killed in the American Civil War in 1865 when he was only 18.

▶ Follow the **B92** for 6 miles (10km) to Cushendun.

5 Cushendun, Co Antrim
The very decided character of Cushendun is a surprise. This is a black-and-white village, with an orderly square and terraces of houses that were designed to look Cornish. Lord Cushendun married a Cornish wife, Maud, and commissioned the distinguished architect Clough Williams-Ellis to create a streetscape with style.

A little salmon fishery stands at the mouth of the River Dun, the 'dark brown water'. To the south is Cave House, locked in cliffs and approachable only through a long, natural cave. Castle Carra is to the north, where the clan quarrel between the O'Neills and the MacDonnells caused the killing of the great Shane O'Neill at a banquet in 1567.

▶ At the north end of the village turn on to the road signposted 'scenic route' for Ballycastle by Torr Head. After 9 miles (14km) turn right to Murlough Bay.

6 Fair Head and Murlough Bay, Co Antrim
Paths from the cluster of houses known as Coolanlough cross the barren headland broken by three dark lakes – Lough Doo, Lough Fadden and Lough na Cranagh, which has a *crannóg* or lake dwelling. Fair Head itself is exposed and barren, a place inhabited by wild goats and choughs (red-legged crows). The careful walker can descend the cliff using the Grey Man's Path, which follows a dramatic plunging fissure.

By contrast, Murlough Bay is green and fertile, generous in contours and abundantly wooded. Tradition has it that the Children of Lír were transformed into swans to spend 300 years here. At the top of the road is a monument to the Republican leader Sir Roger Casement, and a row of lime kilns, which would have burned the stone for use in fertiliser, whitewash or mortar.

▶ After 1 mile (2km) turn right for Ballycastle, then right again on to the **A2** to Ballycastle.

7 Ballycastle, Co Antrim
Ballycastle is in two parts – the winding main street which carries you up to the heart of the town, the Diamond, under the backcloth of the beehive-shaped Knocklayd, and Ballycastle by the sea, with its fine beach and lawn tennis courts.

At the foot of the Margy River is Bonamargy Friary, founded by the Franciscans as late as 1500. Sorley Boy MacDonald is buried here. Elizabeth I found that he eluded all her attempts at capture, but in 1575, when he had sent his children to Rathlin for safety, he had to stand on the mainland helpless while they were murdered by Captain John Norris.

At the harbour is a memorial to Marconi, who carried out the first practical test on radio signals between Ballycastle and

Rathlin Island in 1898. You can travel by boat to Rathlin and savour the life of the 30 or so families who live and farm here. The island is a mecca for divers and birdwatchers. Robert the Bruce hid in a cave on Rathlin after his defeat in 1306. Watching a spider repeatedly trying to climb a thread to the roof, he was encouraged to 'try, and try again'. He returned to Scotland to fight on, and was successful at the Battle of Bannockburn.

ℹ Sheskburn House, Mary Street

▶ From the shore follow the **B15** coastal route west to Ballintoy, then turn right, following the sign to Carrick-a-Rede and Larry Bane.

8 Carrick-a-Rede, Co Antrim

A swinging rope bridge spans the deep chasm between the mainland and the rocky island of Carrick-a-Rede, and if you have a very strong heart and a good head, you can cross it. The bridge is put up each year by salmon fishermen, who use Carrick-a-Rede, 'the Rock in the Road', as a good place to net the fish in their path to the Bush and Bann rivers. The rope bridge is approached from Larry Bane, a limestone head which had once been quarried. Some of the quarry workings remain, and the quarry access to the magnificent seascape provides some guaranteed birdwatching. It is possible to sit in your car and get a clear view of kitti-wakes, cormorants, guillemots,

fulmars and razorbills, though you might have to use binoculars if you want to catch sight of the puffins on Sheep Island further out to sea.

Just to the west is Ballintoy, a very pretty little limestone harbour, at the foot of a corkscrew road. A little further west is the breathtaking sandy sweep of White Park Bay. The beach is accessible only by foot, but it is worth every step. Among the few houses that fringe the west end of the beach, tucked into the cliff, is Ireland's smallest church, dedicated to St Gobhan, patron saint of builders.

▶ Take the **B15**, which changes to the **A2**, to Portrush, then take the **B146** for the Giant's Causeway, 8 miles (13km).

9 Giant's Causeway, Co Antrim

Sixty million years ago, or thereabouts, intensely hot volcanic lava erupted through narrow vents and, in cooling rapidly over the white chalk, formed into about 37,000 extraordinary geometric columns and shapes – mostly hexagonal, but also with four, five, seven or eight sides. That is one story. The other is that the giant, Finn MacCool, fashioned it so that he could cross dry-shod from Ireland to Scotland. Generations of fanciful guides have embroidered stories and created names for the remarkable shapes and places to be found – the Giant's Organ, the Giant's Harp, the Wishing Chair, and Lord Antrim's Parlour. The Visitor Centre tells the full story of the geology, the myths and legends, the folklore and traditions.

One story absolutely based on fact is that the *Girona*, a fleeing Spanish Armada galleon, was wrecked in a storm on the night of 26 October 1588. A diving team retrieved a treasure hoard from the wreck in 1967, now on display in the Ulster Museum in Belfast. The wreck still lies under looming cliffs in

Giant's Causeway, a volcanically created landscape which has attracted its fair share of myths

RECOMMENDED
WALKS

There can be few more spectacular walks than the 10-mile (16km) coastal path between the Giant's Causeway and White Park Bay. Magnificent amphitheatres of rocky cliffs, dramatic clefted inlets, basalt sea stacks, an abundance of wild flowers and the company of seabirds add to the pleasure of this walk. A guide will help identify the evocative names for each bay and the historic features, including the remains of tiny Dunseverick Castle.

Port na Spaniagh, one of a magnificent march of bays and headlands on the Causeway. A bus service operates from the Visitor Centre down the steep road to the Grand Causeway, where most columns reach into the sea towards Scotland.

ⓘ *Visitor Centre*

▶ *Take the **A2** to Bushmills.*

🔟 **Bushmills,** Co Antrim
This neat village is the home of the world's oldest legal distillery, which was granted its licence in 1608. The water from St Columb's rill, or stream, is said to give the whiskey its special quality, and visitors can discover something of its flavour on tours of the distillery.

The River Bush is rich in trout and salmon, and its fast-flowing waters not only supported the mills that gave the town its name, but generated electricity for the world's first hydroelectric tramway, which carried passengers to the Giant's Causeway between 1893 and 1949.

▶ *Follow the **A2** west to Portrush.*

⓫ **Portrush,** Co Antrim
Portrush is a typical seaside resort, which flourished with the rise of the railways. It has three good bays, with broad stretches of sand, ranges of dunes, rock pools, white cliffs and a busy harbour.

East of Portrush is a championship golf course, and beyond is Dunluce, one of the most romantic of castles, where a sprawling ruin clings perilously to the clifftop, presenting a wonderfully dramatic profile. The castle was a MacDonnell stronghold until half the

Roll out the barrels: serried ranks of whiskey barrels at Bushmills, the oldest legal distillery in the world

kitchen tumbled into the sea on a stormy night in 1639.

ⓘ *Town Hall*

▶ *Take the **A29** for Coleraine, then follow the **A2** for Castlerock, then on to Downhill, a distance of 12 miles (19km).*

⓬ **Downhill,** Co Londonderry
The feast of magnificent coastal scenery is given a different face at Downhill. Here Frederick Hervey, who was Earl of Bristol and Bishop of Derry, decided to adorn nature with man's art, by

creating a landscape with eye-catching buildings, artificial ponds and cascades, in keeping with the taste of the time. He was a great 18th-century eccentric, collector and traveller, who gave his name to the Bristol hotels throughout Europe. Although nature has won back much of the Earl Bishop's ambitious scheme, the spirit of the place is strongly felt, and Mussenden Temple, a perfect classical rotunda, sits on a wonderful headland.

Near by is 20th-century man's idea of seaside recreation,

at Benone Tourist Complex, beside one of the cleanest beaches in Europe, backed by a duneland park.

📋 *Benone Tourist Complex*

▶ *From the **A2** turn left on Bishop's Road for Gortmore, then after 8 miles (13km) turn right on to the **B201**, then left on to the **A2** for Limavady.*

🔟 Limavady, Co Londonderry

The Roe Valley was the territory of the O'Cahans, and O'Cahan's Rock is one of the landmarks of the nearby Roe Valley Country Park. One story says that it was here a dog made a mighty leap with a message to help relieve a besieged castle, giving this pleasant market its name, 'The Leap of the Dog'.

The *Londonderry Air* was first written down here by Jane Ross, when she heard it being played by a street fiddler. Limavady was the birthplace of

A trip back in time at Ballymoney's Leslie Hill historic farm, recalling a pre-technology agricultural age

William Massey (1856–1925), Prime Minister of New Zealand from 1912 to 1925.

📋 *Council Offices, Connell Street*

▶ *Take the **A37** for Coleraine, then turn right on to the **B66**; follow signs for the **B66** to Ballymoney.*

🔟 Ballymoney, Co Antrim

A bustling town, Ballymoney remembers its farming past at Leslie Hill historic farm, where visitors can travel through the park by horse and trap. At Drumaheglis Marina it is possible to reach the banks of the River Bann, elsewhere a fairly secluded river, and perhaps take a river cruise on a waterbus.

Three miles (5km) northeast, in Conagher, off the road to Dervock, is the birthplace of the 25th President of the US, William McKinley.

📋 *Council Offices, Charles Street*

▶ *Take the **A26** to Ballymena.*

🔟 Ballymena, Co Antrim

Ballymena, the county town of Antrim, boasts as one of its sons Timothy Eaton, who founded Eaton's Stores in Canada. To the east Slemish Mountain rises abruptly from the ground. It was here that St Patrick worked when he was brought to Ireland in slavery. In the south suburbs is the 40-foot (12m) Harryville motte and bailey – one of the finest surviving Anglo-Norman earthworks in Ulster.

Just to the west is 17th-century Galgorm Castle, a Plantation castle built by Sir Faithful Fortescue in 1618. Beyond is the charming village of Gracehill, founded by the Moravians in the 18th century.

📋 *Council Offices, Galgorm Road; Morrow's Shop*

▶ *Take the **A36** for 21 miles (34km) and return to Larne.*

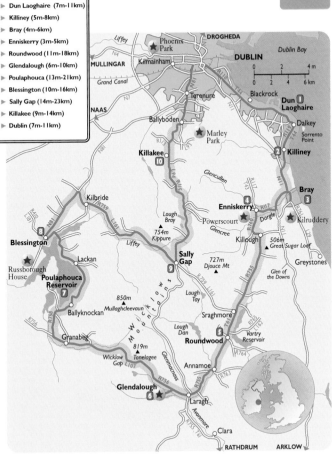

Dublin &
Wicklow

1/2 DAYS • 89 MILES • 143KM

There is plenty to do in Dublin. Take a walk around the fine Georgian squares; do a pub crawl or a church crawl; see Trinity College and Dean Swift's (author of *Gulliver's Travels*) St Patrick's. Then there's the Irish Museum of Modern Art, the Abbey Theatre and Phoenix Park, Europe's largest enclosed park, where you may even see the President on the way to her official residence.

Sitting at the feet of James Joyce

[i] 14 Upper O'Connell Street

▶ Take the **R118 (T44)** for 7 miles (11km) to Dun Laoghaire.

❶ Dun Laoghaire,
Co Dublin
This is a place to promenade, along the extensive harbour piers, or past the villas on the front, or through the parks. Savour the Victorian features of the place which was called Kingstown from the visit of George IV in 1821 until the establishment of the Irish Free State. When the piers were completed in 1859, the harbour was the world's biggest artificial haven. Large ships use the port and it is the home of several yacht clubs; the Royal St George and the Royal Irish are the oldest. There is also a fine Maritime Museum.

Near by, at Sandycove, a Martello tower, one of the squat round coastal defences erected in Napoleonic times, houses a James Joyce Museum (he stayed here briefly). This and the nearby 'Forty foot' gentlemen's bathing place are vividly described in his novel *Ulysses*.

[i] St Michael's Wharf

▶ Take the **R119 (T44)** coastal road to Dalkey and Killiney.

❷ Killiney, Co Dublin
With the broad sweep of a steeply dropping bay, elegant villas among tree-filled gardens and the two Sugar Loaf mountains to complete the vista, Killiney has been likened to the Bay of Naples. Indeed a good place to gain a full panorama is a place called Sorrento Point. Quite a way inland from the popular beach is Killiney Hill, where an attractive park gives superb views of the hills and sea from a height. Its 18th-century stone obelisk was built as a famine relief project.

▶ Continue on the **R119 (T44)**, then join the **N11** to Bray.

❸ Bray, Co Wicklow
A popular resort that retains much of its Victorian attraction, Bray's long beach stretches below the strong line of Bray Head, an extension of the Wicklow dome. From the promenade you can walk the outstanding cliff path for 3 miles (5km) to Greystones. Below the Head, fan-like fossils of the oldest known Irish animals have been found. In the town is an attractive Heritage Centre. Close by is Dargle Glen, a lovely wooded valley set in rugged mountains. Dargle Glen Gardens, which combine excellent planting with fine works of art, are occasionally opened to the public by their owner.

Kilruddery, by contrast, was one of the great set-piece landscape gardens of the 17th century. Very few of these early formal gardens, designed on a large scale with geometric patterns of water, avenues and plants, now survive.

▶ Return to and take the **N11** for Wicklow, then turn right for Enniskerry.

❹ Enniskerry, Co Wicklow
The first Irish Roman Catholic Gothic revival church was built in this pretty village in 1843. Its spire is an attractive feature in the lovely glen of Glencullen.

The superb mountain setting enhances Powerscourt, one of Ireland's great gardens, extravagantly created by the 6th and 7th Viscounts Powerscourt, and extensively altered between 1843 and 1875. A formal landscape of water, terraces, statues, ironwork, plants, flowers and ancient trees is stunningly contrasted with the natural beauty of Sugar Loaf Mountain, combining to form one of the most photographed vistas in the country. The house was a magnificent Palladian mansion, designed by Richard Castle, but was destroyed by fire in 1974. Also in the estate is Powerscourt Waterfall, where the Dargle river forms a torrential fall over a face 400 feet (120m) high.

▶ Take the **R760 (T43)** south, turning left to Killough. Take the **R755 (T61)** for 8 miles (13km) to Roundwood.

❺ Roundwood, Co Wicklow
The highest village in Ireland, Roundwood sits amid lovely scenery. The Vartry Reservoir, which helps to serve Dublin, lies close to the village.

To the northeast is the Glen of the Downs, a dry rocky gorge formed in the Ice Age, with an oak wood. The landscape gives an idea of what Ireland would have looked like in prehistoric times, before the clearance of the forests. Lough Dan and Lough Tay are dark loughs shadowed by granite.

Six miles (10km) southeast of Roundwood at Ashford is Mount Usher, one of the finest examples of the 'Wild Garden', an idea particularly suited to Irish gardens. In a sheltered valley, plants, which include many exotic species, grow naturally and in abundance in perfect harmony with the gentle landscape. They spread along the banks of a winding stream with cascades that are spanned by unusual suspension bridges.

▶ *Continue on the R755 (T61) to Laragh, then turn right on to the R756 (L107) to Glendalough.*

❻ Glendalough, Co Wicklow
Glendalough, the glen of two loughs, is the loveliest and most historic of all its Wicklow rivals. Two beautiful loughs lie deep in a valley of granite escarpments and rocky outcrops. On its green slopes are the gentle contours of native trees, on its ridges the jagged outline of pines. Add to this picturesque scene a soaring round tower and ruined stone churches spreading through the valley, and you have a combination which makes Glendalough one of the most beautiful and historic places in Ireland. St Kevin came to Glendalough in the 6th century to escape worldly pleasures. He lived as a hermit, in a cell on a little shelf above the lake, but the settlement he founded flourished and grew to become a monastic city whose influence spread

The formal elegance of Powerscourt gardens, framed by the Wicklow mountains

throughout Europe. The round tower was built when Viking raids troubled the serenity of Glendalough. Some of the little churches have fine stone carvings, and one has a good pitched stone roof. Guides will explain the full story of Glendalough, and a visitor centre skilfully illustrates the life of a monastery.

To the south near Rathdrum is Avondale, the home of the great Irish political leader Charles Stewart Parnell. The 18th-century house, which now houses a museum, is scenically set in a large and beautiful forest park on the banks of the Avonmore river.

▶ *Follow the R756 (L107) through the Wicklow Gap, then turn right on to the R758 for Poulaphouca.*

7 Poulaphouca, Co Wicklow
At Poulaphouca there is a series of large lakes, which have now been dammed to supply Dublin's water system and also form part of the Liffey hydroelectric scheme. The proximity to the city and the abundance of lakeside roads make it a popular venue for Dubliners.

▶ *Follow the lakeside road by Lackan to Blessington.*

8 Blessington, Co Wicklow
An attractive village with a long main street, Blessington was an important coaching stop on the main road south from Dublin.

Just south is Russborough House, serenely placed in a beautiful landscape before a fine lake. It was built in the middle of the 18th century, the work of architect Richard Castle, for Joseph Leeson, the Earl of Milltown. A Palladian house constructed of granite, it sweeps out elegantly along curving colonnades to flanking wings and pavilions. Decorative features include superb plaster-work by the Francini brothers, and the house now contains the famous Beit Art Collection.

▶ *Take the N81 for Dublin. After 4½ miles (7km) turn right on to the R759 (L161) to the Sally Gap.*

The Poulaphouca reservoir, backed by the Wicklow mountains

9 The Sally Gap, Co Wicklow
The most complete stretch of blanket bog on the east of the country is the beautiful Sally Gap. There are many pools and streams here, and the character-istic bog plant, the bog rose-mary.

▶ *Turn sharp left on to the R115 (L94) to Killakee.*

10 Killakee, Co Dublin
The view from Killakee gives an outstanding picture of Dublin, as George Moore put it, 'wandering between the hills and the sea'. It shows the impressive crescent of Dublin Bay, bounded by the twin bastions of Howth Head to the north and Killiney Head to the south. The River Liffey is clearly defined, and you can identify the green landmark of Phoenix Park.

South of Killakee is a tower, the eerie remains of a retreat of the Hell Fire Club, formed by a group of rakes in 1735. Tales of their wickedness included a game of cards with the devil.

North of Killakee, towards Dublin, is Marlay Park, an attractive parkland combining river, wood, miniature railway and craft centre. In the same area is St Enda's Park. Here, the house where Patrick Pearse, one of the revolutionary leaders in 1916, had his school is now a Pearse Museum.

▶ *Follow the R115 (L94) for 7 miles (11km) back to Dublin.*

Glendalough, once a monastic city

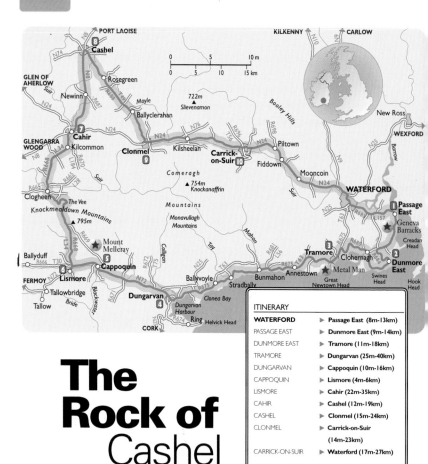

ITINERARY

The Rock of Cashel

Waterford, the most important seaport of the southeast, still has traces of its long history. Reginald's Tower, built by Reginald McIvor in 1003 on The Quay, is now a museum; parts of the Viking city walls remain, and Christ Church Cathedral was first established in 1050 by the same Reginald McIvor. Modern Waterford has its own appeal, too, with summer river cruises and guided walks.

2 DAYS • 147 MILES • 235KM

i *41 The Quay*

▶ *From Waterford take the R683 (L157) east to Passage East.*

❶ Passage East, Co Waterford

This quaint riverside village with its whitewashed cottages, narrow, winding streets and a car-ferry service to Ballyhack, County Wexford, was the landing point for Henry II, who arrived in 1171 with 4,000 men in 400 ships to receive oaths of loyalty from Irish chieftains who wished to hold on to their lands. The hill just above the village provides splendid views of the head of Waterford harbour.

On the road to Dunmore East are the ruins of Geneva Barracks, relics of a colony of goldsmiths and silversmiths from Switzerland who sought refuge from religious persecution and settled here in 1782. Their planned town of New Geneva was a failure, and by 1785 the site was abandoned. The barracks were used as a prison for insurgents (or 'croppies') of the 1798 rising, subjects of the ballad *The Croppy Boy.*

▶ *Follow an unclassified coastal road south, join the R684 (L158) and turn left for Dunmore East.*

❷ Dunmore East, Co Waterford

Neat thatched cottages perch on steep hills above the harbour in this pretty little village that is a popular summer resort and sea-angling centre. Pleasure boats and fishing vessels fill the picturesque harbour. The bay is divided by projecting headlands broken into cliffs and coves, with good walks to Creadan Head to the north, Black Knob promontory to the south, and Swines Head at the southern end of the peninsula. There are also several safe sandy beaches in the area.

▶ *Take an unclassified coastal road to the junction with the R685, turn left, then left again at the junction with the R675 (T63) and continue to Tramore.*

Boats in Dunmore East harbour

❸ Tramore Co Waterford

This lively seaside town is one of the southeast coast's most popular resorts, with a wide, 3-mile-long (5km) beach, its waters warmed by the Gulf Stream. Attractions include a 50-acre (20-hectare) amusement park, a race course, miniature golf, and an 18-hole golf course. Surfing is a popular water sport here, and there is good swimming at the pier, Guillameen Cove and Newton Cove.

The giant clifftop 'Metal Man' statue at Great Newtown Head, south of town, was erected as a navigational landmark for sailors, and legend has it that any unmarried female who hops around it three times will hop down the aisle within 12 months.

On the coastal drive to Dungarvan, the little fishing village of Bunmahon has a good sandy beach surrounded by jagged cliffs that rise to about 200 feet (60m), with interesting rock formations at their base.

Rugged coastal scenery between Tramore and Dungarvan

▶ *From Tramore, follow the R675 coastal drive via Stradbally southwest to Dungarvan.*

4 Dungarvan, Co Waterford
A busy market town, Dungarvan sits on the broad, natural harbour where the Colligan river meets the sea. Along the quays can be seen remnants of Dungarvan Castle, dating from 1186, surrounded by fortified walls. At the top of Main Street an excellent small museum, with prints, documents and artefacts of Dungarvan's turbulent history through colonial and revolutionary eras, is located in the Old Market House, which dates from 1642. Five miles (8km) south of town on the R674 is the

village of Ring, where Irish is the daily language and is taught in an acclaimed language college. Further east beyond Ring, Helvick Head rises to 230 feet (70m) and shelters a picturesque small harbour.

▶ *Take the R672 (T75), then the N72 west to Cappoquin.*

5 Cappoquin, Co Waterford
The broad Blackwater river makes a 90-degree turn to the west at Cappoquin, and

provides scenic riverside drives and some of the best salmon fishing, trout angling and coarse fishing in Ireland.

Four miles (6km) north of Cappoquin, via the R669, in the foothills of the Knockmealdown Mountains, Mount Melleray is a monastic centre for the Cistercian Order of the Strict Observance, built well over a century ago by monks who had been banished from France. The Order erected an impressive stone church and outbuildings and has transformed a bare mountainside into productive fields and pastures.

▶ *Follow the N72 for 4 miles (6km) to Lismore.*

6 Lismore, Co Waterford
Set on the Blackwater river, Lismore's most prominent feature is Lismore Castle,

which looms over town and river, looking for all the world like a fairy-tale castle. It was built by King John in 1185 on the site of a 7th-century monastery that became one of Europe's most renowned seats of learning. After surviving attacks by Viking raiders, the monastic university finally succumbed to the assaults of Raymond le Gros in 1173. The castle was presented to Sir Walter Raleigh, who sold it to Richard Boyle, Earl of Cork, in 1602. His son, Robert, the noted chemist and author of Boyle's Law, was born here. Since 1753 it has been the Irish seat of the Dukes of Devonshire, and the gardens are open to the public. The medieval Protestant cathedral dates from 1633, although it was largely rebuilt around 1680. It has soaring Gothic vaulting and still retains in its west wall 9th- and 11th-century grave slabs from an earlier church. The modern (1888) Catholic cathedral is Romanesque.

Five miles (8km) south of Lismore, via the N72, the little

less than 1 mile (1.5km) north-east of town, and there are ruins of an ancient fortified Fitzgerald keep ½ mile (1km) west of Tallowbridge.

Six miles (10km) west of Lismore, via the R666 (T30), the quiet village of Ballyduff is an angling centre and also holds the ruins of Mocollop Castle, another Fitzgerald fortress.

▶ *At the eastern end of the bridge in Lismore take the **R668 (L34)** which follows the Blackwater river, then climbs to the pass in the Knockmealdown Mountains known as The Vee and descends to Clogheen, then on to Cahir.*

7 Cahir, Co Tipperary
Cahir Castle, with its massive great hall, grim dungeon, and thick enclosing walls, is a superb restoration of the 1142 castle set on a rocky islet in the River Suir. It is also one of Ireland's best-preserved castles. Furnishings in the residential apartments are authentic

reproductions of the period. The Articles ending the long Cromwellian wars were signed here, and in modern times it has served as the setting for such films as *Excalibur* and *Barry Lyndon*. Cahir is a centre for walking and climbing.

A few miles northwest of Cahir, the N24 (the road to Tipperary town) leads to a left turnoff heading to the lush Glen of Aherlow, a secluded glen that was once a major route between the counties of Tipperary and Limerick and the scene of ancient battles. Later, Irish insurgents and outlaws took refuge in the thickly wooded valley that runs between the Galtee Mountains and Slievenamuck Hills.

BACK TO NATURE

The 1-mile (1.5km) nature trail in Glengarra Wood is a delight for nature lovers interested in rare and exotic trees and plants. To reach the wood, drive 8 miles (13km) southwest of Cahir via the N8, and turn right on to the sign-posted and unclassified road, then continue 2 miles (3km) to the car-park. There are nature walks along the Burncourt river and through forest groves, where Douglas fir, several types of fern and native heathers, Western hemlock, rowan, holly, birch, arboreal rhododendron, Bhutan pine from the Inner Himalayas of eastern India, and many other unusual plants and trees can be seen. Native birds such as the treecreeper, the tiny goldcrest, wren, robin, chaffinch, magpie, jay and the introduced pheasant make this their home, as do fallow deer.

town of Tallow was the birth-place of famed 19th-century sculptor John Hogan. Splendid panoramic views open up from 592-foot (180m) Tallow Hill,

Lismore Castle, one of the best-preserved in Ireland, towers above the treetops on its high crag over-looking the town of Lismore and the Blackwater river

▶ *From Cahir, follow the **N8** due north to Cashel.*

8 Cashel, Co Tipperary
Dominating the landscape for miles around is the awe-inspiring Rock of Cashel which soars 200 feet (60m) above the

surrounding plains. Since ancient Celtic times, its 2-acre (0.8-hectare) summit has been connected with royalty and mysticism. Cormac's Chapel, the Round Tower, St Patrick's Cathedral, and a replica of St Patrick's Cross, (whose base may actually have been a pre-Christian sacrificial altar), are among the impressive ruins, all in remarkably good condition. At the foot of the Rock, a visitors' centre of stylised Celtic design presents traditional Irish entertainment.

▶ *Take the R688 (T49) south-east to Clonmel.*

Note also the well-preserved old West Town Wall in Mary Street. The town's streets are lined with restored shopfronts.

▶ *Take the N25 east for 14 miles (23km) to Carrick-on-Suir.*

Clonmel, Co Tipperary

9 **Clonmel,** Co Tipperary
Set on the banks of the River Suir, Clonmel is the main town of County Tipperary, where the world's first public transport system was established by Charles Bianconi in 1815, based at Hearn's Hotel in Parnell Street. Parts of the 19th-century Franciscan church in Abbey Street go back to the 13th century. The 19th-century St Mary's Church near by is notable for its fine high altar. The gallery in the Library has good coin and military displays and features paintings by 20th-century Irish artists.

10 **Carrick-on-Suir,** Co Tipperary
This scenic little town is set on the River Suir, and its Ormonde Castle is the only Elizabethan fortified mansion of its kind in Ireland. One of the principal seats of the Butlers, the earls and dukes of Ormonde, it is

The Rock of Cashel is a place with royal and mystic links

said to have been built by the legendary 'Black Tom', Earl of Ormonde, to host Queen Elizabeth I, who proceeded to cancel her visit.

Despite their power and influence with the Crown, however, the Ormondes were not able to prevent the arrest of the Archbishop of Cashel, who was taken prisoner here and martyred in Dublin in 1584.

▶ *Take the N24 back to Waterford.*

on the road

FRANCE

The picturesque fishing villages of Normandy and Brittany; the impressive châteaux of the Loire; the rolling countryside of the Dordogne; and the Mediterranean coast with its beautiful beaches and deep blue skies.

Tour 16

Normandy is a region of cheerful seaside resorts, with good seafood restaurants in the fishing ports, archetypal rustic villages and attractive wooded farmlands which create some of the most beautiful landscapes in northern France.

Dieppe's harbour area includes ferry, freight, fishing and pleasure ports. Morning fish stalls are set up by the roadside. The best view of Dieppe is from the 15th-century hillside château. It houses a fine museum and art gallery with extensive maritime rooms and a fine collection of ivories, including a full-rigged ship with billowing sails.

Timber-framed house in Rennes

Tour 17

Brittany becomes more Breton as you move further west, noticeable by the place and family names. A wonderful coastline and a high-level interior are linked by central woodlands. Bretons tend to retain a feeling of 'apartness' from the rest of France, with something Celtic in the air. Traditional costumes and religious precessions underline the differences in culture and background.

Rennes is the historic and flourishing provincial capital

Page 97: top – a brilliant flash of colour on the landscape; bottom – view of Eze, from the gardens

of Brittany with the River Vilaine running through it. The Musée des Beaux-Arts has a rich display of paintings, drawings, engravings and sculptures, many confiscated from religious houses during the Revolution. In the southern suburbs, the Écomusée de la Bintinais illustrates the old style of agricultural life by concentrating on the fortunes of the farm in which it is set.

Tour 18

This area illustrates the great variety of landscape in France. Wines are yours for the tasting in individual growers' caves. Cuisine changes with the landscape and the weather.

Very much a river city, Nantes includes two channels of the Loire, three of its tributaries and, for good measure, a canal. Look for the moated castle of the dukes of Brittany, the cathedral and the half-dozen parks, including a riverside Japanese garden. A planetarium complements the nearby museum devoted to the life of the science fiction pioneer Jules Verne.

Tour 19

The Dordogne, in southwest France, features towering river cliffs and the winding valleys of the Vézère where you will find the greatest cluster of prehistoric sites in Europe, many of them troglodytic dwellings quarried thousands of years ago. Some of France's most

glorious towns and villages are here, among them the stunningly located Rocamadour, Domme, Sarlat and La Bastide d'Armagnac.

Périgueux is a handsome town whose beautiful old quarter includes many fine Renaissance and medieval buildings. The perhaps overrestored cathedral, Saint-Front, is a fascinating sight, all domes and cupolas, giving the town an almost Ottoman-Empire skyline. The Musée du Périgord in Cours Tourny has expanded well beyond its original brief to exhibit the results of excavated Roman sites. The Musée Militaire shows uniforms and weapons from several centuries and tells the story of the district's war-ravaged past.

There are pleasant gardens, and you can stroll along the rue des Gladiateurs to the site of the Roman arena. This is a cool place in summer, its fragmentary Roman archways within sight and sound of a modern mosaic-tiled fountain.

Tour 20

The South of France, the Côte d'Azur, the Riviera – under whatever name – offers not only a world-famous coastline, but also attractive hinterland. Half an hour inland you will find yourself in a dramatically different world of hills and mountains, forests and river valleys. where time slows down in delightful hilltop villages drowsing beneath a dazzling southern sky.

In Cannes, the great boulevard de la Croisette stretches eastwards from the casino and the Palais des Festivals. The finest viewpoint is the observatory at Super-Cannes, at 1,065 feet (325m) above sea-level and 2 miles (3km) to the northeast east, from which the town is seen in its wider landscape context between the Alps and the sea.

Sail to the Îles des Lérins: St-Honorat is a monastery island and on Ste-Marguerite,

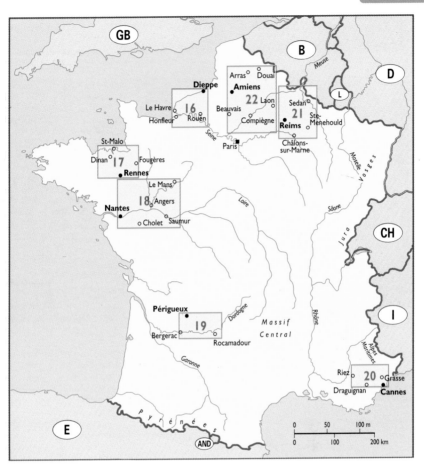

which offers scented forest walks, was the prison of the real-life Man in the Iron Mask.

Tour 21

Many visitors to France arrive at Calais, the busiest of all Channel ports. This area of northern France, travelling south, offers plenty to see and do. Hugh areas of arable land combine with magnificent forests. You can hardly miss the vineyards in the foothills of the Côte d'Or and the great champagne estates round Reims, where visitors may sample the local produce.

Reims is not just outwardly the city of champagne. Millions of francs' worth lies in cellars underground.

Visitors are welcome at the champagne houses which even commissioned stained-glass panels of the different vineyard areas for the cathedral. Two of the old city abbeys have been turned into museums. You can see where the German capitulation order was signed in 1945. And Reims has a major motor museum devoted entirely to French marques.

Tour 22

Near the border that France shares with Belgium are the lovely winding, wooded river valleys of the Ardennes. On the plateaux of Picardy you will find historic battlefields such as those from the World War I Somme campaign.

whose British and Commonwealth victims are remembered in dignified parkland memorials such as Vimy Ridge. Pierrefonds is one of the lavish state residences to be seen in the area.

Amiens, capital of Picardy, is centred on the Cathédrale Notre-Dame, largest of all the Gothic churches in France. Even its grubby exterior cannot hide the wonder fretted upper reaches. Inside are beautifully carved oakwood choir stalls. Museums and galleries concentrate on local art and history. Quaysides and inlets of the Somme thread through the northern suburbs, and there is an eastern quarter of market gardens first cultivated in medieval times.

PRACTICAL INFORMATION

Château d'Ussé, a classic fairy-tale castle in the Loire

BANKS
Normal banking hours are 9am–noon and 2– 4.30pm weekdays. Banks are closed either Mondays or Saturdays, and on Sundays and public holidays. Banks close at noon on the day before a national holiday, and all day on Monday if the holiday falls on a Tuesday.

CREDIT CARDS
International credit cards are accepted widely throughout France, though not so much in rural areas. They are not accepted at some petrol stations.

CURRENCY
The unit of currency is the franc, divided into 100 centimes. Coins are in denominations of 10, 20 and 50 centimes, and 1, 2, 5, 10 and 20 francs; notes in 20, 50, 100, 200 and 500 francs.

CUSTOMS REGULATIONS
See **Austria** (page 10).

ELECTRICITY
See **Austria** (page 10).

EMBASSIES
British Embassy: 35 rue du Faubourg St Honoré, 75008 Paris Cedex 08 tel: (1) 42 66 91 42.
Canadian Embassy: 35 avenue Montaigne, 75008 Paris tel: (1) 44 33 29 00.
US Embassy: 2 avenue Gabriel, 75008 Paris Cedex 08 tel: (1) 42 96 12 02.

EMERGENCY TELEPHONE NUMBERS
Police tel: 17
Fire tel: 18
Ambulance tel: 15.

ENTRY REGULATIONS
See **Austria** (page 10).

HEALTH MATTERS
See **Austria** (page 10).

MOTORING
Speed limits
Built-up areas 50kph (31mph). Outside built-up areas on normal roads 90kph (56mph); on dual carriageways separated by a central reservation 110kph (68mph); also motorways without tolls. Toll motorways 130kph (80mph).

The beginning of a built-up area is indicated by a sign with the place-name in blue letters on a light background; the end is signified by a thin red line diagonally across the place-name sign. Unless otherwise signposted, follow the above speed limits.

Breakdowns
If your car breaks down, try to move it to the side of the road so it obstructs the traffic flow as little as possible. You are advised to seek local assistance as, at present, there is no nationwide road assistance service in France. On autoroutes, ring from emergency phones located every 2km (1 mile) to contact breakdown service.

The use of a warning triangle or hazard warning lights is compulsory in the event of an accident or breakdown.

Accidents
If you are involved in an accident you must complete a *constat l'amiable* before the vehicle is moved. It must be signed by the other party, and in the event of a dispute or a refusal to complete the form, you should immediately obtain a *constat d'huissier*. This is a written report

from a bailiff (*huissier*). The police are only called out to accidents when someone is injured, a driver is under the influence of alcohol or the accident impedes traffic flow.

Documents

A valid full driver's licence is required. The minimum driving age is 18. An international licence is not required for visitors from the US, UK or Western Europe. You also require the vehicle's registration document, plus a letter of authorisation from the owner, if not accompanying the vehicle, and the current insurance certificate (a green card is not mandatory but remains internationally recognised and is strongly recommended). Also, a nationality plate or sticker is required.

Car hire and fly/drive

Many package holidays include car hire as an option. The main car hire companies are represented in France.

Driving conditions

Keep to the right (*serrez à droite*). Though main roads have priority (*passage protégé*), right of way is otherwise given to vehicles coming in from the right (*priorité à droite*).

The *priorité* rule no longer applies at roundabouts, which means you give way to cars already on the roundabout. Mountain tours, including the ones in the South of France, call for a properly serviced and not overladen car. Especially in these areas, petrol stations may be far apart. Unleaded fuel is now widely available all over France.

On the Clermont-Ferrand, Pau and Grenoble tours, roadside notices displaying either *Ouvert* (open) or *Fermé* (closed) will show the road conditions ahead. Do not make for a road notified as being closed.

The wearing of seat belts in both the front and·back is compulsory and children under 10 years of age may not travel as front seat passengers.

Route directions

Throughout this section the following abbreviations are used for French roads:
A – Autoroute
N – Route Nationale
D – Route Départementale
C and V – smaller roads.

POST OFFICES

Normal opening times for main post offices are 8am–5pm on weekdays, and 8am–noon on Saturdays, though some small offices may close for lunch weekdays.

Stamps (*timbres de poste*) may also be bought in tobacco shops (*tabacs*) or cafés marked with a red cigar sign. Letter boxes (*boîtes aux lettres*) are yellow.

PUBLIC HOLIDAYS

1 January – New Year's Day
Easter Monday
1 May – Labour Day
8 May – VE Day
6th Thursday after Easter – Ascension Day
2nd Monday after Ascension – Whitsun
14 July – Bastille Day
15 August – Assumption Day
1 November – All Saints' Day
11 November – Remembrance Day
25 December – Christmas Day

TELEPHONES

Insert coin after lifting the receiver; the dialling tone is a continuous tone.

To make a local call use a 1 franc coin. Most telephone booths now take phonecards (*télécartes*). Buy them for 50FF or 120FF from post offices, tobacconists and newsagents.

For international calls out of France dial 00, wait for a new tone, then dial the national code, followed by the local code, omitting the initial 0, and then the number.

TIME

France follows Greenwich Mean Time (GMT) plus one hour, with clocks put forward for a further hour from late March to late September.

TOURIST OFFICES

Where no address is given for a separate tourist information office, enquire at the Mairie (mayor's office) in a village or small town, the Hôtel de Ville (town hall) in a larger place, or perhaps the Syndicat d'Initiative office. In some places the tourist offices open only seasonally, and the Mairie or Town Hall will handle enquiries out of season.

USEFUL WORDS

The most useful phrase in French is *s'il vous plaît* or please. You will get a lot further using it after every request than if you leave it out. The following words and phrases are helpful in finding your way about.

English French
bridge pont
bus autobus
car park un parking
I need petrol j'ai besoin d'essence
my car has broken down ma voiture est en panne
oil huile
petrol essence
the road for la route pour
traffic lights les feux
tyres les pneus
underground Métro
after après
behind derrière
before avant
here ici
left à gauche
near près
opposite en face
right à droite
straight on tout droit
there là
where? où?
where is? où est?
at what time? à quelle heure?
I do not understand je ne comprends pas
do you speak English? parlez-vous Anglais?
help! au secours!
how much is it? ça coute combien?
I'm sorry pardon
thank you very much merci beaucoup
do you accept credit cards? acceptez-vous des cartes de credit?
money argent

Green &
Pleasant Normandy

West of the cross-Channel port and fishing town of Dieppe, the white cliffs and deep valleys which slice into them are hidden from the main roads, but this tour twists along the coast to some very attractive holiday resorts whose sweeping curves border the Forêt de Brotonne and the Marais Vernier.

3 DAYS • 434KM • 270 MILES

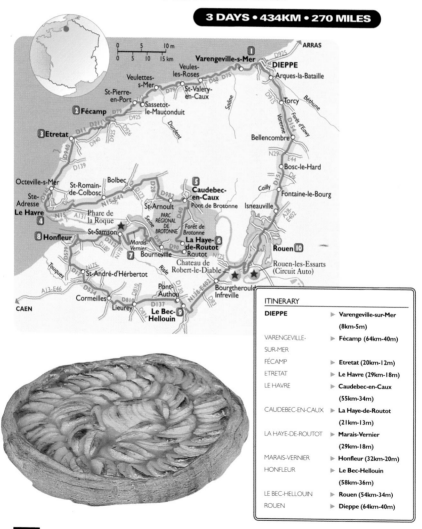

ITINERARY

DIEPPE	▶	**Varengeville-sur-Mer (8km-5m)**
VARENGEVILLE-SUR-MER	▶	**Fécamp (64km-40m)**
FÉCAMP	▶	**Etretat (20km-12m)**
ETRETAT	▶	**Le Havre (29km-18m)**
LE HAVRE	▶	**Caudebec-en-Caux (55km-34m)**
CAUDEBEC-EN-CAUX	▶	**La Haye-de-Routot (21km-13m)**
LA HAYE-DE-ROUTOT	▶	**Marais-Vernier (29km-18m)**
MARAIS-VERNIER	▶	**Honfleur (32km-20m)**
HONFLEUR	▶	**Le Bec-Hellouin (58km-36m)**
LE BEC-HELLOUIN	▶	**Rouen (54km-34m)**
ROUEN	▶	**Dieppe (64km-40m)**

ⓘ *Pont Jehan Ango, Dieppe*

FOR HISTORY BUFFS

On Dieppe seafront, look for the memorial to the disastrous raid of August 1942, by a force of mostly Canadian and Scottish troops.
The bitter lessons learned from its failure were put into practice on D-Day.
Appropriately, Canadians liberated Dieppe in 1944.

▶ *Leave Dieppe on the D75 to Varengeville-sur-Mer.*

❶ Varengeville-sur-Mer,
Normandy
You might be deep in the heart of an English county here, with villas and cottages in discreetly private grounds, wooded and grass-banked lanes, and half-timbered farms fitted like jigsaw pieces in between. There is a wonderful English-style landscape garden at the Parc Floral des Moutiers, the garden of the house called Bois des Moutiers created by the archi-tect Sir Edwin Lutyens and landscape gardener Gertrude Jekyll. Up on the farmland plateau, the Manoir d'Ango is a Renaissance manor house with a beautiful dovecote.

At the foot of the Petit Ailly gorge you can wander along the stony shore under the towering cliffs. The artist Georges Braque, a founder of Cubism, is buried beside Varengeville's parish church, for which he designed one of the stained-glass windows.

RECOMMENDED WALKS

At Varengeville, three very attractive colour-coded walks follow pleasant country lanes and footpaths behind the great chalk cliffs of the coast. They all meet up close to the Parc Floral des Moutiers.

▶ *Continue on the D75, then go into St-Aubin and follow signs to St-Valery-en-Caux, leaving it on the D925. Turn right to Veulettes-sur-Mer on the D79 then follow the signs to Fécamp.*

❷ Fécamp, Normandy
A fishing, freight and pleasure port at a dip in the cliffs, Fécamp has a shingle-bank beach and some remarkable places to visit. The Palais Bénédictine is the home of the liqueur of the same name, a distillation first carried out by monks of the Benedictine order, of 27 aromatic plants and spices whose precise recipe is a very closely guarded secret. There is a museum in the palace – a glorious 19th-century architec-tural confection of Gothic and Renaissance styles – which traces the history of Benedictine and also displays items of reli-

The painter Georges Braque (1882–1963) is buried in the churchyard at Varengeville-sur-Mer

gious art, furnishings and, in the Gothic hall, a magnificent oak and chestnut ceiling built by Fécamp shipwrights. The early Gothic abbey church, La Trinité, is enormous, its nave one of the longest in France.

As well as a fine art museum, the town also has the Musée des Terre-Neuves. While going back to the Vikings, who colonised this coast, it concen-trates on the years when the local fishing fleet used to spend months among the great cod banks of Newfoundland.

ⓘ *Rue Alexandre le Grand*

▶ *Leave Fécamp on the D940 as for Etretat, then go right on the D211 through Yport and follow the D11 to Etretat.*

Malraux, shows works by Renoir, Pissarro, Sisley and Dufy among others. The Musée de l'Ancien Havre illustrates the history of the town. Perhaps the best view of Le Havre is from the high-set fort at Ste-Adresse, a suburb to the northwest, which housed the Belgian government in exile during World War I.

ⓘ *Place de l'Hôtel de Ville*

FOR HISTORY BUFFS

In June 1940, while most of the British troops in France were being evacuated from Dunkirque, the 51st Highland Division was ordered to pull back to Le Havre. In this sacrificial manoeuvre, which helped to divert 10 German divisions, the Highlanders fought until their ammunition was exhausted, and thousands had to surrender at St-Valéry-en-Caux. A granite memorial on a hillside at St-Valéry commemorates the event, and the town is twinned with Inverness, the Highland capital.

🔞 Etretat, Normandy

Nowhere on this coast matches Etretat for location. It lies behind a beach at the foot of a wooded valley. To north and south rise tall white cliffs with weathered natural arches and a great isolated needle rock a little way off shore.

Paths climb to the cliffs called Falaise d'Amont north of the town and the Falaise d'Aval to the south. Amont probably has the finer overall view, as well as a seafarers' chapel with fish carved in the stonework, and a museum to the aviators Nungesser and Coli, whose plane was last seen over Etretat before disappearing during the first attempt in 1927 to fly the Atlantic from east to west. There is also a dramatic memorial to them, with a mosaic tricolour of France.

ⓘ *Place Maurice-Guillard*

▶ *Leave Etretat on the **D940** to Le Havre.*

Guy de Maupassant compared the Falaise d'Aval to 'a carved elephant dipping its trunk in the sea'

FOR CHILDREN

By the beach at Etretat, look for the playground with games, a roller-skating rink, a model boat pond and an aquarium.

🔞 Le Havre, Normandy

Parts of Le Havre look curiously all of a piece with their postwar reinforced concrete buildings. The explanation for this is that the town was reduced to rubble in 1944, and had to be largely rebuilt after World War II.

Now it is once again a major freight and ferry port – the second busiest in France, occupying not only the traditional harbour area but also miles of riverside along the Seine. You can take a harbour cruise.

A splendid fine arts museum, Musée des Beaux-Arts André-

▶ *Leave Le Havre on the **N15** as for Rouen. Turn right for Trouville on the **D40**, then go straight on along the **D29** and **D28**. Follow the **D28** left as for Anquetierville, but bear right to avoid the village. Turn left at the T-junction for Caudebec-en-Caux.*

🔞 Caudebec-en-Caux, Normandy

Just downstream from the Pont de Brotonne suspension bridge which soars over the Seine, Caudebec is ideally situated to show off the commercial life of the river, to and from the container port at Rouen. The Musée de la Marine de Seine covers the history of river boats and river traffic.

Look for the remarkable Church of Notre Dame in 15th- and 16th-century Flamboyant Gothic style. It has a lovely fretted roof and a west frontage like lacework in stone, with 300 now heavily weathered figures of saints, prophets, musicians and gentlefolk of the town.

A stunning memorial beside the main road commemorates the Caudebec-built Latham seaplane which was lost in 1928 during a rescue mission in the Arctic. Roald Amundsen, discoverer of the South Pole, was one of the crew.

i *Quai Guilbaud*

▶ *Leave Caudebec-en-Caux on the **D982** then turn left to cross the Pont de Brotonne. Go right on the **D65**, left on the **D40**, then bear left to La Haye-de-Routot.*

6 La Haye-de-Routot,
Normandy
This fascinating village lies in farmland on the edge of the Fôret de Brotonne. La Haye's Four à Pain is a restored 19th-century brick-built bakehouse, run as a working museum. The Musée du Sabotier is a work-shop museum devoted to clogs (*sabots*). In early summer, look for the 15m (50-foot) pyramid of wood which, on the morning of 16 July, is set alight to create the Feu de St Clair, an old pagan ritual taken over by the

Christian church. Opposite the Four à Pain, a half-timbered cottage features a wall-niche model of the Feu de St Clair.

From the Café des Ifs (Yew-tree Café), marked walking routes radiate through the village and the forest.

▶ *Leave La Haye for Routot. Go left, then right, at stops signs, then continue through Bourneville as for Quillebeuf-sur-Seine. Go left on the **D95** to Ste-Opportune and straight on at crossroads following the 'Réserve de Faune' sign. Hairpin right at the T-junction. Turn left at the 3.5t sign, then left at the T-junction. Follow Honfleur signs uphill to the view indicator.*

7 Marais-Vernier,
Normandy
Bounded by an amphitheatre of wooded hills, this area was once marshland flooded by the Seine (*marais* means marsh). After vague earlier reclamation efforts, it was at the beginning of the 17th century that Dutch workers dug channels to drain the southern part of the marsh. They are still recalled in the name of the Digue des Hollandais (the Dutchmen's Dyke) alongside the D103.

North of that road, the work was tackled only in 1947.

Now the Marais-Vernier is mostly lush grazing land for Camargue horses and Highland cattle. Some pockets of boggy ground remain, and there are central scrubby woodlands. In spring, pink and white blossom embellishes the surrounding farmland. La Grande Mare is the lake to which most of the drainage water flows on its way eventually to the Seine.

BACK TO NATURE

Where the main route turns sharp right after Ste-Opportune, bear left and after about 0.8km (½-mile) watch for the 'Reserve de Faune' car park. A steeply stepped viewing tower overlooks the nature reserve around the Grande Mare. You will often see mallards, coots, grebes, teal, pochard and tufted duck on the lake itself or in the reed beds and drainage channels round it. Grey herons and Cetti's warblers are present, but more secretive.

Fifteenth-century Notre-Dame Church at Caudebec-en-Caux

SPECIAL TO...

Upper Normandy is famed for apples and cider. Where the route goes straight on at Ste-Opportune, turn left for the Maison de la Pomme ('house of the apple') at Bourneville. Displays and a video presentation illustrate the cultivation of the apple and its use in cider and the famous Calvados brandy.

RECOMMENDED WALKS

Two walks, waymarked in green and red, head out from the centre of St-Samson along the wooded ridgetop overlooking the Marais-Vernier. For a different view, make for the Phare de la Roque, where an old river lighthouse provides a splendid viewpoint over the Seine.

▶ *After the view indicator, go right on the D100 to St-Samson then left past the church on the D39. Bear right to the give-way sign then left at the T-junction on the N178. Go first right and follow the signs to Honfleur.*

8 Honfleur, Normandy

To all its other attractions, Honfleur adds the lovely old slate-roofed houses overlooking the sheltered harbour of the Vieux Bassin and, near by, some splendid survivals like the Grenier à Sel (salt stores) in the Rue de la Ville.

Erik Satie, the composer, was born in this fishing town. So was the artist Eugène Boudin, still admired for his skyscapes and his ability to 'paint the wind'. His work is featured in the museum which bears his name. Another museum has 12 rooms richly furnished in traditional Norman style and offers visits to the old town prison. The Musée de la Marine is lavishly stocked with ship models and other memorabilia of the sea.

Honfleur commemorates Samuel de Champlain. It was from here, on eight great voyages between 1603 and 1620, that he explored Canada, claimed it for France and founded the city of Quebec.

i Place Boudin

▶ *Leave Honfleur by the Rue de la République as for Pont-l'Evêque, then go left as for Tancarville on the D17. Turn right on to the N175 then left on the D534 to Cormeilles. Leave Cormeilles on the D810, continue into Lieurey and follow the D137 to Pont-Authou. Go right on the D130 then left on the D39 to Le Bec-Hellouin.*

9 Le Bec-Hellouin, Normandy

This is a lovely hillside village, massed with flowers, including rosebeds by the timbered houses on the square. Many old buildings survive here, from the tiny red-tiled wash-house by a fast-flowing stream to the stalwart ruins of what was once a powerful abbey dating back to 1040. It has a great reputation as a centre of theological learning, and three of its 'sons' became archbishops of Canterbury – Lanfranc in 1070, Anselm in 1093 and Theobald in 1138. A motor museum occupies the parkland of the old abbey church. It displays luxury, sports

The calm of Honfleur harbour belies the town's turbulent past

and racing cars from 1920 onwards, including seven Bugattis.

16th centuries – contributed to the appearance of the cathedral in its doorways, towers, tombs, side chapels and stained-glass windows. From a distance, though, the most remarkable feature of the building is the tall, slim, tapering steeple added in the 19th century. Built entirely of fretted cast iron, it arrows towards the sky. There are museums here devoted to wrought ironwork (Musée Le-Seq-des-Tournelles), and the novelist Gustave Flaubert (in the suburb of Croisset). And

Richard the Lionheart's tomb in Rouen Cathedral

▶ Continue on the **D39** then go left on the **N138**. At the stop sign, go straight ahead on the **D3** as for Rouen, through Moulineaux. Turn right at traffic lights as for Elbeuf, and right over the level crossing. Go sharp left on the **N238** and follow the signs to Rouen.

10 **Rouen,** Normandy
The glory of the historic capital of Normandy is the magnificent Gothic Cathedral of Notre-Dame in the midst of a splendid 'old town' carefully restored after the devastation of World War II. Rouen's tourist office, for instance, occupies a very attractive Renaissance building, once the headquarters of the tax collector.

Architects and artists of many different eras – mainly 13th to

there is also a wax museum devoted to Jeanne d'Arc (Joan of Arc). After Rouen was lost to the English in the Hundred Years' War, it was here than Joan was brought as a prisoner and subjected to a shameful trial. Its aftermath was even more despicable when, her life having been previously spared, she was burned at the stake in the old marketplace. She was canonised in 1920. The Musée des Beaux-Arts has a good collection of 17th- to 20th-century French paintings.

ⓘ *Place de la Cathédrale*

▶ Leave Rouen on the **N28** then go left on the **D928**, left on the **D151** to Bellencombre and left again on the **D154** to Dieppe.

The Emerald
Country

Starting from Rennes, the capital of Brittany, this tour is drawn briefly into Normandy to visit Mont-St-Michel on its fortified tidal island. Along the Brittany coastline there are headlands offering magnificent views, then it's inland to historic towns such as Vitré, Fougères and Dinan, and St-Malo, on the coast.

3 DAYS • 392KM • 243 MILES

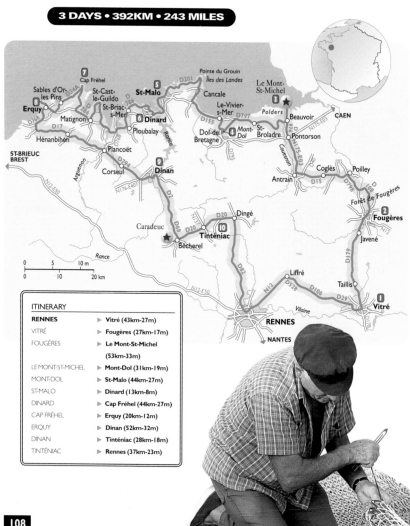

ITINERARY	
RENNES	▶ **Vitré (43km-27m)**
VITRÉ	▶ **Fougères (27km-17m)**
FOUGÈRES	▶ **Le Mont-St-Michel**
	(53km-33m)
LE MONT-ST-MICHEL	▶ **Mont-Dol (31km-19m)**
MONT-DOL	▶ **St-Malo (44km-27m)**
ST-MALO	▶ **Dinard (13km-8m)**
DINARD	▶ **Cap Fréhel (44km-27m)**
CAP FRÉHEL	▶ **Erquy (20km-12m)**
ERQUY	▶ **Dinan (52km-32m)**
DINAN	▶ **Tinténiac (28km-18m)**
TINTÉNIAC	▶ **Rennes (37km-23m)**

ⓘ *Quai Chateaubriand, Rennes*

▶ *Leave Rennes as for Fougères on the N12. Go right on the D528 to Liffré and in the town centre turn right for Vitré via La Bouëxière. Enter Vitré on the D857.*

❶ **Vitré,** Brittany

In the days when Brittany was separate from France, Vitré was a frontier fortress. Its triangular-plan castle, high above the River Vilaine, houses the town museum in three of its towers. A fourth provides an all-encompassing viewpoint. Many medieval and Renaissance buildings are still in use. The Centre Social, for instance, occupies a splendid 16th-century mansion with elaborate windows, doors and rooflines. Beautifully restored, the Rue de la Beaudrairie was the leather-workers' quarter.

Walks lead down into the pleasant valley of the Vilaine. On the southern outskirts, in the unlikely setting of an industrial estate, look for the Musée de l'Abeille Vivante (Museum of the Living Bee). Here you can see not only displays on all aspects of bee-keeping but also five colonies working in glass-sided hives.

ⓘ *Place St Yves*

▶ *Leave Vitré for 'Fougères par Taillis' on the D179.*

❷ **Fougères,** Brittany

The most important feature of this second medieval fortress town is the huge and superb castle on a peninsula site all but encircled by the Nançon river. But delay going to the castle itself until you have looked at it from the attractive Jardin Public in the high town. Its situation and layout are seen to best effect from the garden (despite the background scar of a modern quarry). Below the castle, the low town retains many fine buildings, such as the Flamboyant Gothic Church of St-Sulpice and the 17th-century houses round the Place du Marchaix. In the high town, one 16th-century house is now the Musée Emmanuel de la Villéon, devoted to the locally-born artist who was one of the last Impressionists.

ⓘ *Place Aristide-Briand*

Traditional-style half-timbered houses in Rennes

> *i* *Corps de Garde des Bourgeois*

▶ *Return to Beauvoir. Turn right for Les Polders, over the bridge and immediately left. Turn left at the first stop sign and right at the second stop sign. Go right on the D797 through St-Broladre, left on the D82 then right on the V5 to the village of Mont-Dol. Watch for a right turn before the Hôtel du Tertre up a steep and narrow road to Sommet du Mont-Dol.*

FOR CHILDREN

On the way back from Le Mont-St-Michel, call in at the Reptilarium in Beauvoir and let the children see the crocodiles, iguanas, lizards, pythons and boa-constrictors.

4 Mont-Dol, Brittany

From this hilltop with its marvellous 360-degree view, the first thing to notice is the great area of rich, reclaimed marshland of the 'polders' – as in the Netherlands – that you crossed after Beauvoir. Beyond them, across the bay, lies Mont-St-Michel.

A good display map shows the features of Mont-Dol itself – which include the scenes of the legendary struggle between St Michael and the Devil. There is also a chapel, an old seaward signalling tower, two 19th-century windmills and other features that add interest to a stroll among the pines, gorse and rock outcrops of a very popular excursion site.

▶ *Return from the summit. Go right to pass the Hôtel du Tertre. Leave Mont-Dol village on the D123. Turn right on the D155 and follow the signs towards Cancale on the D76. Go right on the VC15 signed 'Cancale le Port'. Leave Cancale following 'St-Malo par la Côte' and 'Pointe du Grouin' signs along the D201. Go straight on along*

▶ *Leave Fougères as for St-Hilaire on the D177. Immediately after leaving Fougères bear right along a 'route forestière'. Go left at Carrefour du Père Tacot then straight on across the main road. At Carrefour des Serfilières bear left, taking the fourth exit. Turn right at the stop sign (this is the D108) to Parigné. Leave Parigné on the D108 as for Mellé. At the crossroads go straight on, avoiding the right turn to Mellé. Go right at the stop sign along the D798. Turn left on the D15 through Coglès, left briefly on the D296 then right on the D15 again. In Antrain, turn right at the stop sign to Pontorson and continue via Beauvoir to Le Mont-St-Michel.*

3 Le Mont-St-Michel, Normandy

From whatever angle, and from however far away, a first sight of this isolated tidal rock is a stunning experience. It rises from

Fougères Castle – a fine example of medieval military architecture

rampart walls and a clustered village to a magnificent abbey whose highest steeple spears the sky. Reached by a causeway once served by an engaging steam tramway, Mont-St-Michel lies among the mazy channels of a vast encircling bay. The lowest towers and medieval sea-wall protect a village of lanes and stairways, where the Musée Grevin tells the story of the abbey and the island community in a series of tableaux, and the Archéoscope elaborates it with sound and lighting effects. More prosaically, the Musée de la Mer places the island in its marine and tidal context.

Crowning the granite summit, the abbey dedicated to the Archangel Michael is a triumph of Romanesque and then Gothic design. Finest of all the architecture are the 13th-century buildings which include the refectory and cloisters.

the C6 to Pointe du Grouin then return to the D201 for St-Malo.

8 St-Malo, Brittany

An extensive area of sheltered harbours continues the long maritime tradition of a town which was the historic base for privateers, explorers and the 16th-century Newfoundland fishing fleets. The heart of St-Malo is the granite-built district known as Intra Muros, inside the coastal rampart walls. It is almost entirely a reconstruction from the rubble of World War II. Look here for the historical Musée de la Ville in the 15th-century castle whose great keep and towers command impressive views of the harbour. Quic-en-Groigne is a waxwork museum recalling famous St-Malo characters and events. There is a well-stocked aquarium as well as a museum of dolls and old-time toys.

Ferries sail to destinations along the coast, and there is a hydrofoil service to Jersey. But the Château de Solidor recalls much grander voyages: it houses displays on the Cape Horners.

i Esplanade St-Vincent

▶ *Leave St-Malo as for Dinard. Go right on the D114 and right on the D266 into Dinard.*

St-Malo was named after a Welsh monk called Maclow

❻ **Dinard,** Brittany

To a beautiful seafront of bays, promontories, sandy beaches and offshore rocky islets, Dinard adds hotels, restaurants, a casino, a golf club, an equestrian centre and other sporting facilities to maintain its reputation as the premier resort of Brittany's Emerald Coast. The weather is mild, some of the vegetation Mediterranean along the footpaths which wander by the coast.

Fine villas stand in lovely wooded grounds, many of them dating from the turn of the century when British high society favoured Dinard – Edward VII and George V are remembered in street names today.

Dinard attracts many musical, film and artistic events. Every summer evening at dusk there is a *son et lumière* presentation on the seafront Promenade du Clair de Lune.

ⓘ   *Boulevard Féart*

▶ *Leave Dinard on the **D786** through St-Briac-sur-Mer and continue as for St-Brieuc. After Port-à-la-Duc turn right to Cap Fréhel on the **D16**.*

❼ **Cap Fréhel,** Brittany

In the 1920s a company tried to sell off building plots on this dramatic cliff-ringed headland. Fortunately, the misbegotten scheme failed. From the approach road, you may think that the cape ends at the lighthouse – completed in 1847, immense care having been paid to the design and the masonry work (visits can be arranged most afternoons) – and the 18th-century fortification known as the Tour Vauban. In fact, Fréhel extends much further out to sea.

A stroll around the cape, whose majestic rock stacks are a nature reserve, opens up views into precipitous wave-lashed inlets as well as southeastwards to the spectacularly located Fort la Latte, a medieval fortress situated on a headland some 4km (2½ miles) away.

ⓘ   *Tour Vauban*

BACK TO NATURE

Cap Fréhel and its offshore rock stacks are busy with gulls, fulmars, cormorants and guillemots, for whom this is France's premier nesting area. In summer the approach to the cape is purple with heather and gold with the flowers of gorse and bird's-foot trefoil.

FOR CHILDREN

Sables-d'Or-les-Pins, after Cap Fréhel, caters well for children, with sandy beaches, pony rides, 'bouncy castles' and pedal cars for hire. Look for the little battery-powered electric cars. Kids love to drive these 'grown-up' vehicles on their own.

▶ *Return from Cap Fréhel and turn right on the **D34a** as for St-Brieuc. Rejoin the **D786** for Erquy.*

❽ **Erquy,** Brittany

Built round a west-facing bay well sheltered from the northerly wind, Erquy is a pleasant and unpretentious little resort with no trace of obtrusive modern building. The bay is busy with courses in canoeing and windsurfing, and there is a local shellfish fleet.

Take the road to the Cap d'Erquy and you will climb to an exhilarating headland where the heath and low-lying scrub are criss-crossed by wandering footpaths. There are cliff edges to be carefully explored, views to the broken water over dangerous offshore reefs, and a splendid if unexpected east-

The medieval town of Dinan on the River Rance, where boats depart for St-Malo and Dinard

facing beach. There are also ditches and other signs of prehistoric fortifications dated as early as 4,500 years ago.

☐ *Boulevard de la Mer*

▶ *Leave Erquy on the D786 as for St-Brieuc, then go left for Dinan via Plancoët. Enter Dinan on the N176.*

❾ Dinan, Brittany

Since its appearance in the Bayeux Tapestry, in the 11th century, Dinan has had a clear line of history, each era marked by its own architectural styles in ramparts, towers, gateways and attractive houses. Streets in the old town bear the names of medieval trade guilds. The castle is a fortress of mellow stonework whose unusual 14th-century oval keep houses the local museum. You can admire Dinan from the upper viewing gallery of the 15th-century belfry, the Tour de l'Horloge

(Clock Tower). Another good viewpoint, although disappointing as an actual garden, is the Jardin Anglais (English Garden). It overlooks the valley of the Rance, in which enticing footpaths lead under the stately viaduct over which you approached the town, towards the downstream quays.

In the Church of St Saveur is buried the heart of Bertrand du Guesclin, who fought in single combat in the Place du Champ Clos in 1359 to free his brother from his English captors.

☐ *Rue de l'Horloge*

▶ *Leave Dinan from Lanvallay and turn right through Évran on the D2, which becomes the D68 as for Bécherel. In La Barre turn left for Tinténiac on the D20.*

❿ Tinténiac, Brittany

The church here, with its cupolas and sturdy but ornate

stonework, looks slightly puzzling. In fact it is a complete turn-of-the-century rebuilding of an old ecclesiastical site, and well worth a visit.

Tinténiac lies on the Canal d'Ille et Rance. At the Quai de la Donac, a redundant grain store is now the Musée de l'Outil et des Métiers (Museum of Tools and Trades), displaying tools and machinery from half-forgotten rural trades.

East of Tinténiac, the Musée International de la Faune is a spacious zoo park which also features a scented rose garden and a well-equipped children's playground.

FOR HISTORY BUFFS

Before Tinténiac, turn right in La Barre, through Bécherel to the Parc de Caradeuc and its château. The 18th-century lawyer Caradeuc de la Chalotais was devoted to the independence of the Breton parliament. Louis XV imprisoned him without trial. A message he smuggled out of jail, written with a toothpick in ink made from soot, vinegar and sugar, caused a sensation.

▶ *Continue on the D20 to Dingé. Watch for a right turn on the D82 before the Confiserie/Épicerie shop. Return to Rennes.*

SCENIC ROUTES

Approaching Vitré, the D22 runs through a pleasant rural landscape, which continues along the D179 to Fougères, with long eastern views. Even at times of hectic traffic, the approach to stately Mont-St-Michel has a magic all its own. The coastal stretch of the D155 looks over salt marshes and oyster beds to the rocky islets off Cancale. A succession of cliffs and sandy bays follows the D34a after Cap Fréhel.

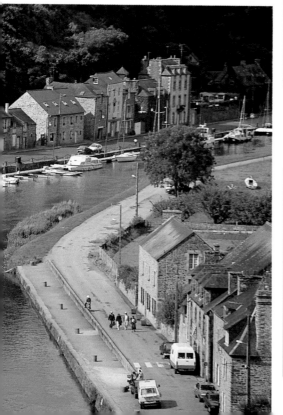

The Western
Loire Valley

Starting in Nantes, this tour soon leaves all Breton influences behind as it heads for the valleys of the Loire and the Sarthe. You will find some of France's finest *son et lumière* presentations here, one of the world's most famous motor-racing circuits, and the Pays Nantais and Anjou are packed with vineyards.

5 DAYS • 512KM • 319 MILES

i Place du Commerce, Nantes

▶ *Leave Nantes for Clisson on the **D59** through St-Fiacre. In Gorges go left of the **D113** then take the **D59** again into Clisson.*

❶ Clisson, Loire Valley West
The Vendée Wars and the savage reprisals of the Revolutionary government army all but obliterated this little riverside town. Then it was completely rebuilt, but not as it had been before. Present-day Clisson is mostly a tribute to Palladian Italy, with colonnades, loggias and belltowers of a style seen nowhere else in western France.

Look for the stabilised but unfurnished ruin of the 13th- to 15th-century castle, the 15th-century market hall, the two medieval bridges contrasting with the soaring 19th-century road viaduct, and Italianate creations such as the Temple d'Amitié and the Church of Notre-Dame.

There are beautiful walks in the valleys of the Sèvre Nantaise and the Moine. Local wines may be tasted. But

Clisson itself is the great attraction, especially as an Italianate skyline to a leafy riverside view.

i Place de la Trinité

▶ *Leave Clisson on the **N149**. Turn left as for Beaupréau on the **D762** then go along the **N249** and follow signs to Cholet.*

❷ Cholet, Loire Valley West
The Musée des Guerres de Vendée, here in a town where only 20 buildings were left standing in their brutal aftermath, is the place to learn about the Vendée Wars of 1793–96. It explains how the Vendée rising against the Revolutionary government's policies of mass conscription and the overthrow of all previous loyalties, was at first successful, then viciously crushed.

Other exhibitions are at the Musée des Arts, the Musée Paysan with its old-style dairy and country house interiors in the leisure park by the Ribou lake, and the Maison des Sciences, Lettres et Arts whose many attractions include a planetarium.

Clisson's impressive ruined 13th- to 15th-century castle sits atop a rocky outcrop

This is a famous textile town with many splendid modern buildings. Its trademark is the red-and-white handkerchief – the *mouchoir de Cholet* – whose design, as you will learn locally, is rooted in another incident of the Vendée Wars.

i Place de Rougé

▶ *Leave Cholet on the **D20** as for Poitiers. In Maulévrier turn left and right as for Vihiers, then left on the **D196** through Chanteloup to Coron. Go right on the **D960** to Doué-la-Fontaine.*

SPECIAL TO...

In Maulévrier, after Cholet, go straight on past the turn as for Vihiers to visit the Parc Oriental. Created early this century, abandoned in 1940 and completely restored in 1987, this is probably Europe's finest Japanese garden.

FOR HISTORY BUFFS

In a forest clearing beside the D196 after Maulévrier (on the way from Cholet to Doué-la-Fontaine), the chapel at the Cimetière des Martyrs commemorates victims of the Revolutionary fury in the Vendée Wars. Virtually alone in France, the Vendée region saw little to celebrate at the bicentenary of the Revolution in 1989.

3 Doué-la-Fontaine, Loire Valley West

If you arrived in the middle of Doué without paying attention to its outskirts, you might shrug it off as an ordinary little town. It is far from that. The zoo, adapted from the cliffs, caverns and ditches of an old quarry site, houses lions, tigers, lemurs, birds of prey, deer, emus, rarities such as snow panthers, and 15 separate monkey enclosures. Its Naturoscope explains the problems of threatened species and the destruction of their habitats.

The Musée des Vieux Commerces features seven old-style shops and a rose-water distillery, in part-restored 18th-century stables. The Maison Carolingienne is the substantial ruin of a fortress built before 1050.

Nobody is certain about the origins of Doué's arena, Roman in style but much later in date. However, there is no doubt about the Moulin Cartier. Built in 1910, it was the last windmill raised in Anjou.

BACK TO NATURE

Doué-la-Fontaine is France's great rose-growing centre. The Jardin des Roses displays dozens of different varieties, coloured crimson, scarlet and yellow – *Caroline de Monaco*, *Sarabande* and *Moulin Rouge* among them. Every July, an exhibition of 100,000 roses is held in the arena.

i *Place du Champ de Foire*

▶ *Leave Doué on the D69 to Gennes. Go right as for Saumur on the D751 through La Mimerolle and into St-Hilaire.*

FOR HISTORY BUFFS

After Doué-la-Fontaine, turn left off the D69 for Rochemenier and its strange troglodytic farms. You can visit furnished underground dwelling houses – with their cowsheds, barns, wine-cellars and even a chapel – still inhabited early this century.

4 St-Hilaire, Loire Valley West

Just before this village suburb of Saumur, the Musée du Champignon, in a cave system cut into the roadside cliffs, is more than simply an exhibition about mushrooms and how they are grown. The underground galleries were dug in medieval times, part of a network of more than 480km (300 miles) throughout the district, which produces 75 per cent of France's cultivated mushrooms. Turn right in St-Hilaire for the École National d'Équitation. This is France's national riding academy, excellently housed and staffed. In the practice arena, in front of high wall mirrors, you may see members of the acadamy's Cadre Noire put their horses through the intricate, disciplined and stylish movements for which they are famous all over Europe. They also perform summer season shows.

▶ *Continue on the D751 into Saumur.*

5 Saumur, Loire Valley West

Straddling the Loire, this very appealing town is passionate about horses and the cavalry, wines, museums and exuberant outdoor displays. The Château de Saumur, overlooking the river, houses three separate collections. The Musée des Arts

Décoratifs concentrates on the decorative arts – ceramics, enamelware, carvings in wood and alabaster. Another, Musée du Cheval, celebrates centuries of horsemanship; the third, Musée de la Figurine-Jouet has more than 20,000 models and figurines.

The cavalry has two separate exhibitions, one recalling its mounted days, the other taking the story to more recent times with a comprehensive display of tanks and armoured cars.

Second only to Champagne, Saumur is famous for its sparkling wines. Several firms welcome visitors to their cellars. Notre-Dame de Nantilly, dating from the 12th-century, houses a valuable collection of medieval and Renaissance tapestries. And the old quarter of Saumur with its restored 17th-century houses adds to the attractions of a justi-fiably self-confident town.

[i] *Place de la Bilange*

▶ *Leave Saumur on the N147 as for Le Mans. At the round-*

SPECIAL TO...

In Saumur, numerous wine cellars offer tastings of the region's wines.

about take the second exit to Vernantes on the D767. In Vernantes, turn sharp left at the traffic lights as for Baugé, then right on the D58 as for Baugé through Mouliherne. In Le Guédéniau go right in the D186 as for Lasse. Turn left following 'Les Caves de Chanzelles' sign. At the round-about in the forest take the fifth exit for Baugé. Rejoin the D58 and continue to Baugé.

6 Baugé, Loire Valley West
Plenty of space has been left around Baugé's 15th-century castle, originally a hunting lodge of Good King René, Duke of Anjou. Holding displays of weapons, coins and ceramics,

The château at Saumur has been dubbed 'the castle of love'

---

it stands before public gardens dipping to an attractive river-side. The Convent of La Girouardière houses a venerated relic – a jewelled cross believed to contain a piece of the True Cross brought to France by a crusader knight. Its unusual design was adopted as the Cross of Lorraine. Look also for Baugé's charming 17th-century Hospice-St-Joseph (pharmacy) with its beautiful array of apothecaries' jars.

Sometimes an unfamiliar language may be seen or spoken here, describing Baugé, for instance, as 'bela kaj malmova urbeto': the Château de Grésillon, on your exit route from 'this fine old town', is an international Esperanto centre.

[i] *Place de l'Europe*

BACK TO NATURE

Before Baugé, pause in the Forêt de Chandelais. Three-quarters of its trees are oak, most of the rest beech. Roe deer, wild boars and foxes live in the forest, and the beechwoods are alive with birdsong, including the liquid, fluty song of the golden oriole.

▶ *Leave Baugé on the D817, which becomes the D305, then go right on the D306 to Le Lude.*

7 Le Lude, Loire Valley West
Pride of this little town is the richly furnished château, rebuilt in Renaissance style after an English garrison was driven out – with heavy damage to the fabric – in 1427. Its situation is most attractive, above balustraded gardens rising from the River Loir, whose waters eventually feed the larger Loire. One of France's most dramatic *son et lumière* presentations takes place here. It recalls five centuries of events and person-alities, from the English occupa-tion to the Second Empire. This outstanding show is enhanced

by fountains and a lively firework display reflected in the river. In the town itself, La Sentinelle is an unusual museum with a huge collection of military uniforms and flags from all over the world.

[i] *Place Nicolay*

▶ *Leave Le Lude on the **D307** to Pontvallain. Go right on the **D13** through Mayet and across the **N138** to Le Grand-Lucé. Turn left at the give way sign and left on the **D304** as for Le Mans. Go under the bridge, then left following the 'Angers' sign, under another bridge and follow the 'Tours' signs along the **N138**. Go right at the roundabout on the **D140** as for Arnage, then right on the **D139** to the grandstands of the racing circuit.*

At the first right-hand bend after crossing the N138 between Le Lude and Le Grand-Lucé, bear left and follow signs to the Fontaine de la Coubre. A map opposite this woodland pool shows the way-marked footpaths in the Forêt de Bercé. They explore the beautiful deciduous woodland split by murmuring streams in the unexploited part of the forest, and the conifer plantations beyond. As the Musée du Bois in Jupilles shows, this was once a great centre for ships' timbers and, later, wooden clogs. When you continue from Fontaine de la Coubre, turn right at the first crossroads then left to rejoin the D13 through Jupilles.

at over 320kph (200mph).

There is a smaller but linked Bugatti Circuit. The two tracks play host to five major car and motor-cycle events, plus a 24-hour truck race! You can watch test sessions from the main grandstands, which are informally open on non-competition days.

An excellent motor museum also recalls that this was where Wilbur Wright, over from the United States, made the first powered flight in Europe in 1908.

[i] *Acceuil Reception*

▶ *Continue on the **D139** into Le Mans.*

9 Le Mans, Loire Valley West
Apart from some handsome churches, the busy, modern town offers little to the visitor,

To the left of the D13 in Mayet, after Le Lude, Le Petit Monde presents a junior version of *son et lumière* in a model town. Here, the whole thing is miniaturised and all the buildings are scale models.

8 Le Mans Circuit, Loire Valley West
Prosaically, they may be the N138, D140 and D139, but these roads are also part of the great motor-racing circuit where the Le Mans 24-Hour Race is held every June.

The N138 is the Mulsanne Straight, along which Jaguars, Porsches and Mercedes howl

Fascinating exhibits in Le Mans' automobile museum

but Le Mans has strong links with the Plantagenets. Henry II of England, for instance, was born here. Long before his time there was a Gallo-Roman settlement on the great rock-ridge in the heart of the modern sprawl. The old walled town – Vieux

Mans – retains its high-level medieval street plan. Split by the rue Wilbur Wright, which lies at the foot of a ravine cut through the heart of the rock, it features finely detailed Renaissance houses and later town mansions, leading to the majestic Cathédrale St Julien.

i Rue de l'Étoile

▶ *Leave Le Mans on the **D309** as for Sablé. In Parcé cross the river then go first right at the crossroads, left to Solesmes then continue to Sablé-sur-Sarthe. Go straight across the **D306** for Centre-Ville. At the roundabout take the last exit, then a side road right for Pincé. This is the **D159**. Bear right on the **C15** for 'Pincé par la Forêt'. Rejoin the **D159** then follow the **D18** and **D52** through Morannes. Continue through Etriché and Tiercé. Go straight on along the **N160** then right on the **N23** to Angers.*

10 Angers, Loire Valley West
Here in the heart of Anjou lies a university town of parks, gardens and colourful floral decorations, with a grand Plantagenet castle rising in towers of banded stonework, and a cathedral, Cathédrale Saint Maurice, best approached by the Montée St-Maurice, a stairway climbing from the River Maine.

The longest tapestry in France, *La Tenture de l'Apocalypse*, completed in the late 14th century to show the Apocalypse, is on display in the castle. Angers is a tapestry town. Many others, ancient and modern, are on show in the castle itself and in individual museums and galleries.

Fine Renaissance buildings survive, both around the cathedral and elsewhere. River cruises follow the Maine, and for the adventurous there are hot-air balloon flights to waft you high above the castles, vineyards and villages of Anjou.

i Place Kennedy

▶ *Leave Angers through Les-Ponts-de-Cé on the **N160**. In Mûrs-Érigné, turn right to go through Chalonnes-sur-Loire and Champtoceaux on the **D751** and return on the **N249** to Nantes.*

SPECIAL TO...

Angers is the home of Cointreau, which has been produced here since 1849. Guided one-hour tours of the distillery (La Distillerie Cointreau) show off the processes, production methods and famous advertising posters of this much-exported liqueur, but the recipe remains a secret.

Detail of Catedrale St-Maurice's tympanum above the 12th-century west front door in Angers

FOR CHILDREN

On the return route to Nantes, turn left instead of right in Mûrs-Érigné to visit the Aquarium Tropical. It shows a brilliantly coloured collection of exotic fish from Asia, Africa and America swimming in tanks which have unexpected décors, such as the Grand Canyon or craters of the moon.

SCENIC ROUTES

From Nantes to Clisson the route runs through the attractive Muscadet vineyards. Around the D13, the Forêt de Bercé is one of the most beautiful areas in the district. The D751 after Angers runs along the lovely Corniche Angevine above the Loire. The Layon vineyards are impressive, but the route is at its best near the 'panorama' viewpoint at La Haie Longue ('the long hedge'). A roadside memorial commemorates the pioneer aviator René Gasnier, whose first flights were from the level fields across the river.

Journey into
Prehistory

Although there are remains of old Roman buildings in the heart of Périgueux, this tour, featuring two of France's loveliest rivers, the Dordogne and the Vézère, takes you much further back into the history of man. Here, limestone provides the huge cliffs, the amazing caves and underground rivers, and the golden building stone of beautiful towns like Sarlat and Domme.

4 DAYS • 383KM • 238 MILES

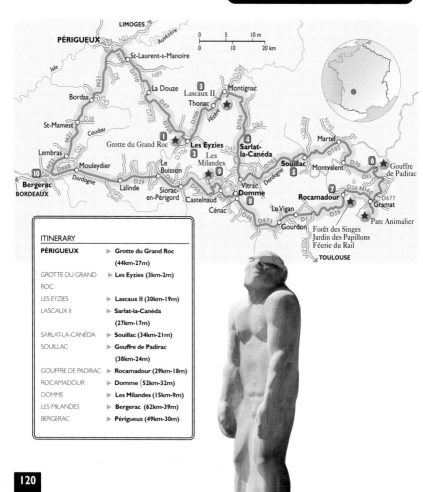

ⓘ *Place Francheville, Périgueux*

▶ *Leave Périgueux on the N89 as for Brive. Go right on the D710, left on the D45 then right on the D47 to Grotte du Grand Roc.*

SCENIC ROUTES

The approach to the Grotto du Grand Roc on the D47 introduces the stunning limestone cliffs which characterise this tour.

❶ Grotte du Grand Roc, Aquitaine

The great natural limestone wall here, facing the Vézère, with its overhangs forming the pitched roof lines of some bizarrely located houses, is honeycombed with ancient dwellings and caverns. In the Grotte du Grand Roc you will find an underground wonderland whose cave floors and hanging gardens of fretted limestone look like a spiky coral reef (wire grills protect some of the formations). In the same magnificent cliff, the prehistoric rock shelters of Laugerie Haute

and Laugerie Basse, which yielded countless objects left behind by their Ice Age inhabitants, are open to visitors.

Less forbidding than its name, the Gorge d'Enfer (Gorge of Hell) is set in a little wooded, grassy side valley whose caves display 25,000-year-old wall carvings. There is also an animal reserve, a fishing lake and a picnic site. Further on, the Musée de Spéléologie, entered by a stairway up a colossal overhanging cliff, illustrates the daring work of the modern cave explorers.

▶ *Continue on the D47 into Les Eyzies.*

❷ Les Eyzies, Aquitaine

If the Vézère is the 'valley of mankind', the village of Les Eyzies, spectacularly located between a northern limestone cliff and the river, is at the heart of the greatest concentration of prehistoric sites. The Musée National de la Préhistoire, built into the cliff face, is devoted in particular to the palaeolithic era, starting perhaps 2½–3 million years ago with the first traces of primitive man. Near by, the Abri Pataud is a cliff shelter of

more than 20,000 years ago. As a complete contrast, Les Eyzies also offers a botanical garden of medicinal plants; other displays here explain the culture of the crayfish and the bee.

ⓘ *Place de la Mairie*

▶ *Leave Les Eyzies on the D706 to Montignac. Turn right on the D704, then right again for Lascaux II.*

❸ Lascaux II, Aquitaine

Discovered in 1940, the caves at Lascaux are decorated with the most celebrated prehistoric paintings in the world – lively representations of bulls, deer and horses created nearly 18,000 years ago. The caves have had to be closed to the public to prevent deterioration of the original paintings, but painstakingly exact replicas are on display at the neighbouring site called Lascaux II. A visit here cures visitors of any notion that our ancestors of 800 generations ago were nothing more than primitive louts. Much older than Lascaux, the nearby cave

Périgueux has a rich historical mixture of architectural styles

Replicas of Lascaux' original cave paintings on show at Lascaux II

site of Régourdou is also open to visitors. The brown bears in its park match displays in the museum there about the prehistoric cult of the bear.

[i] *Place Léo-Magne, Montignac*

FOR HISTORY BUFFS

Off the D706, after Les Eyzies, several sites illustrate the everyday life of our very remote ancestors. Préhisto-Parc features outdoor tableaux of Neanderthal and Cro-Magnon (a type of 'modern' man), hunting expeditions and household scenes of 15,000 years ago. La Roque-St-Christophe is an amazing troglodytic fortress town, lived in from prehistoric days to the 18th century, with five great terraces overlooking the River Vézère. At Le Thot, a modern museum and gallery explain the environment and art of prehistoric times. In the parkland, present-day animals such as red and fallow deer, bison, tarpan and Przewalkski's horses can be compared with life-size replicas of mammoths and aurochs (an extinct type of ox).

▶ *Return to Montignac and turn right on the **D704** to Sarlat-la-Canéda.*

❹ **Sarlat-la-Canéda,** Aquitaine

The golden stone of Sarlat and the effortless grace of its Gothic and Renaissance buildings make this one of the loveliest towns in the Dordogne region. Even the tourist information office is housed in a 15th-century mansion near the handsome cathedral of the 16th and 17th centuries. Shaded alleys and courtyards in the old town are busy with a craftsmen's market and shops at which every third or fourth seems to specialise in *foie gras*. L'Homo Sapiens is a little museum of archaeological discoveries, prehistoric art forms, stone and flint tools. There is an imaginative Aquarium concentrating on the 30 or more species of fish found in the River Dordogne. On a wooded hillside above the square, pleasant public gardens can be found.

SCENIC ROUTES

The first ridge-top road on the tour is the D704 to Sarlat, giving wide-ranging views over rolling wooded hills.

---

[i] *Place de la Liberté*

▶ *Leave Sarlat-la-Canéda on the **D46** for Vitrac. In Vitrac-Port watch for a left turn on to the **D703** to Carsac and Souillac. Turn left on to the **N20** in Souillac.*

❺ **Souillac,** Midi-Pyrénées

The glory of this busy centre in the Dordogne valley is the restored 12th-century Romanesque church called Abbatiale Sainte Marie, whose red-and-white tiled roofs culminate in a series of cupolas, as in the cathedral at Périgueux. The carvings in the church are particularly fine. Behind the church you may hear the incongruous music of a 1920s jazz band. This is just one of the lifelike exhibits in the Musée de l'Automate. Tableaux of moving life-size figures also include a glamorous lady snake-charmer, a clown and a splendid animated 19th-century Passion Play.

FOR CHILDREN

Quercyland is a fun park on the outskirts of Souillac, where children subdued by all the prehistory can work off some energy.

ℹ️ *Boulevard Louis-Jean Malvy*

▶ *Leave Souillac on the **D703** to Martel. Turn right on the **N140**, left on the **D70** then right on the **D11** to Miers and left on the **D91**. Go left on the **D60**, right at the Y-junction at the stone cross, then right at the T-junction to Gouffre de Padirac.*

SCENIC ROUTES

After Montvalent, on the way from Souillac to Padirac, there is a landscape change as the D70 and D11 run through the parcels of sheep-grazed land on the limestone plateau known as the *causse*.

6 Gouffre de Padirac, Midi-Pyrénées

Open since the late 19th century when it was discovered, the Padirac chasm is one of the greatest underground sights in Europe. Lifts and stairways descend to the otherworldly cavern of a subterranean river where, by boat and pathway, you can visit glorious floodlit limestone chambers like the Great Dome Gallery, walls of stalagmites and a petrified waterfall. Cafés and restaurants, a picnic area and a small zoo are clustered above ground.

▶ *Continue on the **D90** to Padirac, turn left and follow signs to Gramat. Leave Gramat on the **N140** northwards, then turn left on the **D36**. Turn left on the **D32** into Rocamadour.*

7 Rocamadour, Midi-Pyrénées

Words and pictures rarely do justice to the reality of Rocamadour, the magnificent fortified pilgrimage town whose historic houses, sanctuary churches, bishops' palace, museums and – at the highest level – skyline castle cascade down a terraced limestone cliff. It became a place of pilgrimage in the 12th century, visited by the great and the good of Christendom. Lifts and staircases, including the long and tiring pilgrims' Holy Way, are threaded through the town. Once you have turned on to the D32 you should pause to admire the stunning situation of the place, from the viewpoint beside the Hotel Belvedere. In Rocamadour itself, the finest view is from the castle ramparts. The D32 road avoids the town centre often crammed with visitors. There are parking places in the valley.

RECOMMENDED WALKS

At busy times, you may appreciate leaving the narrow streets of Rocamadour for a walk, steep in places, based on old sheep tracks in the Alzou Valley. It starts from the bridge on the D32 below the town and heads up-river.

FOR CHILDREN

Just after the Jardin des Papillons on the D36 before Rocamadour, La Féerie du Rail (The Enchanted Railway) is a huge model layout with 60 trains hauling coaches and freight wagons past mountain villages, farms, a castle, a fairground and a windmill, and over a viaduct menaced by the ice cliffs of a glacier.

The ancient town of Rocamadour, situated above the Gorge of Alzou

▶ *Continue on the **D32** to Couzou, go right on the **D39** through St Projet, right on the **D1** then join the **D673** to Gourdon. Turn left as for Sarlat then left as for Salviac, leaving Gourdon on the **D763**. Go right on the **D6**, which becomes the **D46** to Cénac. Go right on the **D49** to Domme.*

8 Domme, Aquitaine
This lovely, mellow hilltop town, founded with defensive ramparts and gateways around 1280, provides one of the finest viewpoints in France. The River Dordogne curves below the town, giving way to fields, farmhouses and lines of poplars on the riverside plain.

Limestone cliffs, woods and hill villages march to the horizon. In Domme itself there are beautiful townscape views round every corner. A good museum illustrates local domestic life in the past. Shops sell local honey, jams, truffles and *foie gras*. In the central square, an old covered market hall is now the entrance to a marvellous series of underground caverns with mirror lakes and floodlit limestone columns.

🛈   *Place de la Halle*

▶ *Return to Cénac and go straight on along the **D50**, through St-Cybranet, then continue as for Siorac-en-Périgord. In Pont-de-Cause bear right for Castelnaud. In Castelnaud, go straight ahead for Fayrac and Les Milandes. Turn left on the **D53** as for Siorac then after a 'virages' sign watch for a sharp right uphill signed 'Château des Milandes'.*

9 Les Milandes, Aquitaine
Perched on a terrace giving spreading views over the Dordogne valley, the restored 15th-century castle in the attractive and tucked-away hamlet of Les Milandes was owned from

Domme's spectacular hilltop position has made it a coveted prize throughout France's turbulent history

1949 to 1969 by the American singer Josephine Baker, star of the Paris cabarets between the wars. It was here that she founded a philanthropic foundation to look after children from all over the world.

Beyond the castle, the white courtyard of the farm which was also part of Josephine Baker's estate houses a rural museum explaining the improvements in agricultural techniques through the years.

Medieval houses grace the revived old town in Bergerac

FOR HISTORY BUFFS

On the way from Domme to Les Milandes, on a glorious viewpoint site above the village of the same name, Castelnaud is a restored medieval castle which houses displays on artillery and siege warfare. During much of the Hundred Years' War, the castle was held by the English.

▶ *Continue from the farm museum and bear left as for Veyrines-de-Vergt. Turn right on the D53 then take the D50 to Siorac and the D25 to le Buisson-de-Cadouin. Follow signs to Lalinde, then Bergerac.*

10 Bergerac, Aquitaine
A cobbled car park which slopes down towards the River Dordogne is a convenient base for a stroll round the restored old town at the heart of present-day Bergerac. There are narrow lanes of part-timbered houses, and tiny squares, one of them shaded by chestnut trees where a statue of Rostand's hero Cyrano de Bergerac, the 17th-century nobleman and soldier famous for his large nose, stands, nobly cloaked.

The impressive Musée du Tabac in the town hall (Maison Peyrarède) illustrates the discovery of tobacco, its sources, and the local tobacco trade, as well as displaying beautifully worked pipes, cigarette holders, snuffboxes and tobacco jars. Its curious second-floor exit leads back down to street level through the town museum (history and regional ethnography).

Near by, the Musée du Vin et de la Batellerie combines several long-standing Bergerac interests – wine, barrel-making and river traffic. There are also guided visits to the old monastery housing the wine council on which all the Bergerac growers are represented.

ℹ *Rue Neuve d'Argenson*

▶ *Leave Bergerac on the N21 and return to Périgueux.*

SPECIAL TO...

Two great gourmet specialities of the Dordogne are truffles and foie gras. Truffles are rare edible fungi which grow underground, often in oak woods, and are dug out by truffle-hunting dogs – and even pigs. These trained animals are weaned on truffles from an early age and are trusted not to eat the precious quarry. The production of *pâté de foie gras* – goose or sometimes duck-liver pâté – involves grotesque force-feeding of the birds with huge quantities of maize. The pâté is preserved, often with a minute portion of truffle included, and sold at a luxury price.

The Riviera &
its Hinterland

From Cannes and other coastal resorts, by way of artists' and craft-workers' villages, this tour climbs into the glorious mountain scenery that forms the backdrop to the Côte d'Azur. Limestone cliffs and ridges, spectacular valleys and ranges of faraway mountains reach a landscape climax in the magnificent Gorges du Verdon.

4/5 DAYS • 440KM • 273 MILES

ITINERARY		
CANNES	▶	**Cap d'Antibes (14km-9m)**
CAP D'ANTIBES	▶	**Antibes (5km-3m)**
ANTIBES	▶	**Biot (7km-4m)**
BIOT	▶	**Grasse (20km-12m)**
GRASSE	▶	**Gourdon (12km-8m)**
GOURDON	▶	**Plateau de Caussols (14km-9m)**
PLATEAU DE CAUSSOLS	▶	**Castellane (52km-32m)**
CASTELLANE	▶	**St-André-les-Alpes (22km-14m)**
ST-ANDRÉ-LES-ALPES	▶	**Riez (60km-37m)**
RIEZ	▶	**Moustiers-Ste-Marie (15km-9m)**
MOUSTIERS-STE-MARIE	▶	**Gorges du Verdon (42km-26m)**
GORGES DU VERDON	▶	**Draguignan (72km-45m)**
DRAGUIGNAN	▶	**Fayence (38km-24m)**
FAYENCE	▶	**Mons (15km-9m)**
MONS	▶	**Cannes (52km-32m)**

| *i* | Boulevard de la Croisette, Cannes

▶ *Leave Cannes on the **N7** towards Golfe-Juan, then bear right on the **N98** signed 'Antibes par Bord de Mer'. In Juan-les-Pins watch carefully for all the 'Cap d'Antibes' signs and join the Cap d'Antibes coast road, **D2559**.*

❶ Cap d'Antibes, Côte d'Azur

There are tiny family-style beaches and boat moorings on the east side of the Cape, which also includes security-guarded millionaires' retreats and, at the Hôtel du Cap and the Eden Roc restaurant, two of the most exclusive establishments of their kind on the coast. A fine museum devoted to Napoleonic and naval history – Musée Naval et Napoléonien – occupies an old gun battery, perhaps surprising visitors from the United Kingdom with contemporary cartoons showing the British as the enemy. Around the Villa Thuret there is a botanical garden, and right on the summit of the Cape the Sanctuaire de la Garoupe, a seafarers' chapel beside the lighthouse tower, which is a marvellous viewpoint, houses a collection of simple but affecting thanks-offerings, often for a safe return from a voyage.

American writers and artists were attracted to the Cape from the 1920s onwards. Scott Fitzgerald's novel *Tender is the Night* had its real-life setting here. It is possible to trace the exact course of the disastrous car journey described in James Thurber's *A Ride with Olympy*. And Orson Welles once arrived in a hurry for a cash-raising meeting in the Hôtel du Cap, having come by taxi all the way from Rome!

▶ *Continue on the **D2559** into Antibes.*

❷ Antibes, Côte d'Azur

The old town here, with its narrow streets, cafés and restau-

Paintings in Notre Dame de Bon Port, Cap d'Antibes

rants, is one of the most attractive and least pretentious on the coast. Antibes' connection with the ancient Greeks – it was founded as *Antipolis* by Greek colonists from Marseille in the 4th century BC – attracted the Cretan writer Nikos Kazantzakis, author of *Zorba the Greek*, to settle here, as did the British novelist Graham Greene. While the archaeological museum in the old fortification of the Bastion St André may look gloomy from the outside, it has a wonderful collection of thousands of exhibits going back to Etruscan, Greek and Roman times, many recovered from the sea. The old castle was a stronghold of the powerful Genoese Grimaldi family. With the little 'cathedral', it watches over the bustling market place, and was long since turned into the Musée Picasso. The artist used part of it as a studio for six amazingly fruitful months in 1946, and now it contains many of his – and other artists' – paintings and ceramics, making it one of the most important Picasso collections anywhere. The so-called cathedral is, in fact, a church, with a Romanesque tower and east end and 17th-century façade.

| *i* | Place de Gaulle

RECOMMENDED WALKS

On the south side of the Cap d'Antibes, turn off the Boulevard J F Kennedy for the Sentiers des Douaniers – the Excisemen's Path. Starting alongside the wall of a private estate, it leads to a beautiful little park set among rocks above the sea, with a lovely bay stretching to the west.

▶ *Leave Antibes on the **N98** as for 'Nice par Bord de Mer'. Take the left-hand lane, turn left at the traffic lights for Biot, then right and left on the **D4** to Biot.*

FOR CHILDREN

Marineland, to the right of the D4 on the way to Biot, has penguins, seals, sea lions and a dolphin show. Near by are a butterfly jungle, a little Provençal farm, water chutes and an assault-course style of mini-golf layout. This was Europe's first marine park.

❸ Biot, Côte d'Azur

On the approach road to Biot, a road to the right leads to the Musée National Fernand Léger, unmistakable thanks to the huge abstract in multi-coloured

tiling which decorates its frontage. With more than 300 works on display, it celebrates the life of one of France's major 20th-century artists, and was opened in 1960 with fellow-artists Picasso, Braque and Chagall as its honorary presidents. The charming little town of Biot is largely given over to the shops and studios of painters, potters, woodworkers, embroiderers and craftworkers of many other kinds. Even the town maps are on painted ceramic tiles. Glassmaking is important here nowadays and it can be observed at the Verrerie de Biot near the southeast exit from the town. Gates and ramparts of the medieval town survive, and away from the tourist bustle there is a pleasant arcaded square beside a 15th-century parish church. The museum features mementoes of the days when the Romans and, later, the Knights Templar, were established here, and has a dazzling pottery display.

[i] *Place de la Chapelle*

▶ *Continue on the D4 via Valbonne to Grasse, turning right at a T-junction on the outskirts to follow the D4 towards the town centre.*

4 Grasse, Côte d'Azur
Spread over a south-facing hillside with splendid views over a lovely plain towards the sea, Grasse enjoys a year-long calendar of concerts, drama, dance and exhibitions of every kind. The old town, crammed with 14th- to 18th-century buildings, is Italian in appearance and atmosphere. Around it, Grasse expanded with exuberant 19th-century architecture in typical French Riviera style.

Grasse has the most famous perfume industry in the world, and one museum, Musée International de la Parfumerie, traces its history as well as the processes by which huge amounts of flower petals are distilled down to tiny volumes of the ultimate essence. The Maison Fragonard, named after the rococo painter who was born in the town, is a perfume factory open to the public. The Musée d'Art et d'Histoire de Provence, housed in an 18th-century mansion, celebrates the art and history of Provence.

Another museum, the Musée de la Marine, has gathered an intriguing collection of ship models to illustrate the career of the 18th-century Admiral de Grasse, an ally of George Washington in the American

Biot is set attractively on a small hill rising in the centre of a valley

War of Independence. A statue on one of the town's outlook terraces recalls Washington's gratitude to him.

[i] *Place de la Foux*

FOR CHILDREN

In Grasse, the Musée des Trains Miniatures on the Routes de Cannes has a fascinating model railway collection. The layout includes locomotives and rolling stock from many European countries and from many different eras, right up to the TGV – France's high-speed Train de Grande Vitesse.

▶ *Leave Grasse on the D2085 as for Nice. At Pré-du-Lac turn left at the roundabout and immediately bear left on the D3 to Gourdon. Turn right for the car park at the entrance to the village.*

5 Gourdon, Côte d'Azur
Some writers sneer at Gourdon for being a tourist trap. You will probably disagree, because this old Saracen stronghold, set on

the edge of a cliff which gives it tremendous views down into the valley of the Loup, goes about its business quietly. In the narrow lanes of restored and impeccably kept buildings, shops sell lavender, honey, herbs, perfumes, pottery, wines, basketwork and glassware, many of these goods being produced in the district.

The historic Château de Gourdon, with terraced gardens on the edge of the cliff, has architectural details from the 12th century onwards. Here you will see valuable furnishings, as well as collections of arms and armour, and 'naive' paintings by European and American artists.

▶ *Leave Gourdon on the D12 as for Caussols. In about 8km (5 miles) watch for a junction sign and then go sharp left under a sign giving advice to 'Visiteurs'.*

❻ Plateau de Caussols,
Côte d'Azur
A notice at the turn-off of the D12 warns that gathering stones, mushrooms and snails is forbidden. Do not worry about the mild potholes on the early stretch of the road; the surface never deteriorates too badly. Here on the high limestone plain is a countryside not many casual tourists know: clumps of pines and rock outcrops, occasional sheep farms, isolated holiday homes, groups of beehives and, here and there, a survivor from the days of the *bories*, the stone-built shepherds' huts. There are mountain ridges to

---

north and south, with the remote white buildings of the CERGA observatory high on the northern rim. The scenery may be faintly familiar to film buffs: this was the setting of the Charles Bronson thriller *Cold Sweat*.

▶ *Turn right at a T-junction beside a postbox, following an old sign 'St-Lambert'. This is the D12 again. Turn sharp left as for Thorenc on the D112, then follow 'Thorenc' signs on the D5. Go left on the D2, left on the D2211, then right on the N85 to Castellane.*

❼ Castellane, Côte d'Azur
A modest little town on the Route Napoléon, Castellane lies in a constricted location where the River Verdon elbows its way through the hills. Directly overlooking the square is a massive

---

cliff, 184m (604 feet) high, on which the original settlement, dating from Gallo-Roman times, was built.

When the population decided, eventually, to settle in the valley, plague, floods and occupation in the time of the religious wars in the 16th century was their reward. Now the classic outing at Castellane is a walk up the steep and occasionally rough pathway to the 18th-century Chapel of Notre Dame du Roc, a magnificent clifftop viewpoint.

ℹ️ *Boulevard St Michel*

▶ *Continue on the N85, go right on the D955. Then left on the N202 to St-André-les-Alpes.*

Perched high above the River Loup, Gourdon has stunning views of the coast

FOR HISTORY BUFFS

From near a car park on the D5 just before the summit of the Col de Castellaras, a steep footpath climbs to the hilltop ruins of Castellaras itself, a magnificently sited medieval fortress town. You will be able to make out the old castle, the barracks and the humble quarter where the peasants and their flocks took refuge in times of war. The whole town dominated the upper valley of the Loup.

8 St-André-les-Alpes, Côte d'Azur

This is a quiet little inland resort a world away from the hustle of the coast. But St-André was once a busy enough place. The village had four cloth mills, but all that remains of the industry is the canal which supplied their water-power. In the latter part of the 19th century it became the railhead of a line from Nice, and the place from which stagecoaches took passengers further on. This railway, now extended to Digne, is the last survivor of the old inland lines. St-André station is a halt on the year-round railcar service, and there are summer excursions on the steam-hauled Train des Pignes (the Pine Cone Train).

St-André lies in an attractive valley that has helped it achieve its present-day renown as a centre for hang-gliding and free-fall parachuting.

i   *Place Paslorelli*

RECOMMENDED WALKS

One walk from the centre of St-André-les-Alpes heads briefly south on the N202 before turning right for the steep climb to the 'lost' village of Courchons. Orange markers show where the footpath cuts out the hairpin bends of the Courchons road. Another route heads southeast up to the chapel of Méouilles overlooking the mountain-ridged reservoir of the Lac de Castillon.

▶ *Continue on the **N202** to Barrême, then turn right on to the **N85** and left on the **D907**, then in La Bégude-Blanche take the **D953** to Riez.*

SPECIAL TO...

On the way to Riez you will pass through one of France's biggest lavender-growing areas. Naturally, this is fine country for bees, and a great deal of honey is also produced here. Maison de l'Abeille, on the approach to the town, houses a fascinating exhibition, explained by an enthusiastic owner, of modern and historic bee-keeping and honey-making.

9 Riez, Provence-Alpes

Two structures show how old the settlement of Riez is. A group of columns now standing isolated at the edge of the field was once part of a 1st-century Roman temple; and there is an early Christian baptistery (dating from some time in the 4th to 7th centuries), complete with the original font, inside a 19th-century building set up to preserve it.

The old town may have a faded look, but its streets

Surely one of nature's most delightful harvests – fields of perfumed lavender at Riez

Moustiers has been famous for its pottery since the 17th century

contain medieval doorways and Renaissance frontages, some in the course of restoration. In pre-Roman times, the settlement stood on the summit of the St Maxime hill overlooking the present-day town in the valley below. St Maxime, which is the site of an attractive chapel, is a pleasant place for a stroll. A popular Riez industry is the production of *santons*, characteristic Provençal painted clay figurines, originally made for the traditional Christmas crib, but now sold as souvenirs.

[i] *Allées Louis Gadiol*

BACK TO NATURE

After Riez, the Lapidaire Pierres de Provence on the D952 displays beautiful examples of rose quartz, agates, amethysts and other semi-precious stones. This is a fine area for minerals and gemstones, but much of it is protected as a geological reserve.

▶ *Leave on the **D952** to Moustiers-Ste-Marie.*

10 Moustiers-Ste-Marie, Provence-Alpes

Any history of Moustiers pales before its amazing situation, clustered round the banks of a tumbling mountain stream at the foot of a huge gash in towering limestone cliffs. Footpaths climb to a spectacularly located church, Notre Dame de Beauvoir, set on a high rocky terrace. Across the break in the cliffs, and silhouetted against the sky, a chain supporting a gilded star was, according to tradition, first placed there by a crusader knight, who had sworn to do it when released from weary years of imprisonment.

The town is famous for its glazed pottery, or faienceware. The industry established in the 17th century died out for a generation or two, and restarted in the 1920s, but without equalling the delicacy of the

early designs, many of which are on show in the local museum, Musée des Faïences.

[i] *Rue du Seigneur de la Clue*

▶ *Continue on the **D952** to La Palud. Go straight on through La Palud, then bear right on the **D23**, the Route des Crêtes. If you enjoy exposed and narrow roads with steep, unguarded drops, follow the **D23** all the way back to La Palud and turn right to rejoin the **D952**. If you do not enjoy this kind of road, go along the **D23** to the first two or three belvederes, then retrace your route and turn right again on to the **D952**. Only the later part of the **D23** is difficult.*

11 Gorges du Verdon, Provence-Alpes

Landscape superlatives are needed here, because this is France's equivalent, on a smaller scale, to the Grand Canyon in Colorado. The River Verdon, on its way to Castellane, runs through a huge ravine in the limestone mountains, with colossal drops, vertigo-inducing views, exciting low-level footpaths and the possibility of organised expeditions on foot and by canoe, raft or rubber dinghy, right through the heart of the gorge. There are magnificent, high-level roadside views from railed-off belvederes (look-out points), some of which, on the Routes

des Crêtes, have warnings not to throw stones off the edge – they might fall on walkers 715m (2,350 feet) below!

▶ *Continue eastwards on the **D952**. After a stretch of overhanging cliffs, turn right on the **D955** to Comps-sur-Artuby and Draguignan.*

12 Draguignan, Provence-Alpes

Down from the mountains, and the vast military training area of Canjeurs which occupies the scrubland plateau south of the River Verdon, Draguignan marks a return to the milder landscapes of mid-Provence. There is a dignified old town here, and a fine museum, housed in the one-time palace of the Bishop of Fréjus, with thousands of exhibits connected with local industries, including a reconstructed olive oil mill. Shaded squares and gardens fend off the sun. On the boulevard John Kennedy, the American military cemetery commemorates the mostly Franco-American Provençal landings of August 1944. In front of the memorial there is an imaginative tribute in the form of a massive relief map, in bronze and copper, illustrating the campaign.

[i] *Boulevard Clemenceau*

FOR HISTORY BUFFS

After Mons, Roche Taillée, to the left of the D56, is a fine example of Roman civil engineering, a deep cutting in a limestone outcrop to take part of the 40km (25-mile) aqueduct which supplied the town of Fréjus near the coast. The aqueduct is still in use today.

▶ Leave Mons on the *D56* as for Callian, then go left on the *D37*. Follow the *D37* to the left for Montauroux at a T-junction where the right turn is signed 'Callian 0.5km'. Follow the 'Grasse' sign in Montauroux, still on the *D37*, cross the *D562*, then go left on the *D38* through Tanneron. At a five-road junction after Tanneron bear right for Mandelieu-la-Napoule, then watch for an abrupt left turn avoiding a road straight ahead signed 'Poney Club'. Take the *D92* to Mandelieu. Turn right on the *N7* then take the fourth exit at a roundabout signed 'Les Plages'. Go right at the T-junction as for Napoule, then keep in the right lane and return to Cannes.

▶ Leave Draguignan on the *D562* as for Grasse. Go left on the *D563* to Fayence.

13 Fayence, Provence-Alpes
Here is a classic back-from-the-coast village, facing southwards into the sun as its red-roofed houses climb a hillside from the plain. Fayence has a very well-cared-for 18th-century church, a good selection of craft studios and galleries, and terraces which act as splendid viewpoints. You may find it pleasant to laze around them, look out over the plain and watch the gliders soaring from one of France's most important launching fields far below.

ⓘ *Place Léon Roux*

▶ Continue on the *D563* to Mons.

14 Mons, Provence-Alpes
The colonists from Ventimiglia in what is now Italy, who founded this little hilltop village in the 13th century, picked the location well. The spacious square, in fact a semi-circle, looks out over an extensive

The Gorges du Verdon offers a range of activities and natural beauty to take your breath away

view from the islands off Cannes to the Italian Alps, with suggestions that, on a really clear day, Corsica appears as a smudge on the horizon. Mons survived two outbreaks of plague and the desertion of all its citizens after a brigands' raid in 1468, to doze in the sun for centuries before it recently decided to emphasise its situation as one of the 'belvederes of the Côte d'Azur'. There is a maze of cool, narrow alleyways. The historic ramparts are still partly in place. Local arts and crafts are displayed in a gallery. And the streets usually bear two names – one in French and one in Provençal.

ⓘ *Centre Culturel*

FOR CHILDREN

In Mons, ask them to find the electricity meter for the house at 22 Su Lou Coustihoun.

SPECIAL TO...

From the Lac de St-Cassien to Mandelieu, the beautiful Tanneron massif is planted out with mimosa. In summer there is no trace of the brilliant yellow blooms which light up the winter hillsides.

SCENIC ROUTES

Approaching Gourdon, the D3 looks deep into the valley of the Loup, then reveals a stunning view of the village in the eagle's-eyrie location on the summit of a plummeting cliff.

A Taste of
Champagne

Although Reims itself is the heart of champagne country, in the early part of the tour you will find many vineyards occupying sloping fields on the edge of the Montagne de Reims, south of the city. Arable plains stretch north to the hill and river country which France shares with Belgium in the Ardennes.

3/4 DAYS • 386KM • 240 MILES

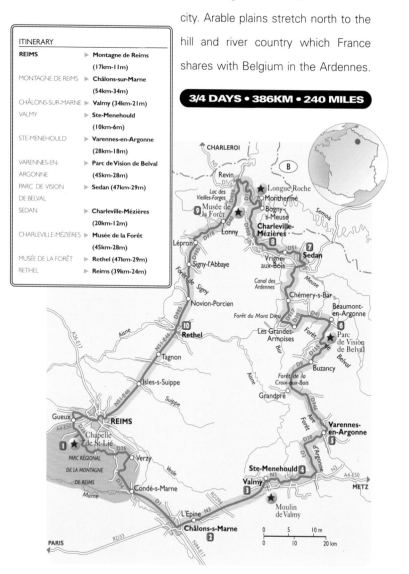

i *Place Guillaume de Machault, Reims*

▶ *Leave Reims on the N31 as for Soissons. Turn left on the D27 to Gueux, then left on the D26 through Vrigny. Turn right into Ville-Dommange, follow 'Courmas' sign, then go right to the Chapelle de St-Lié.*

❶ Montagne de Reims,
Champagne-Ardenne

From the viewpoint below the Chapelle St-Lié there is a glorious outlook down over the vineyards on the lowest slope of the wooded hills south of Reims, and of the city itself, separate on the plain. Many of the villages are the home of champagnes little known abroad – Rilly for *Vilmart*, Ludes for *Blondel*, Villedommange immediately below for *Champagne de la Chapelle*. St-Lié, a church on the summit of a wooded hill sacred from pagan days, is being sympathetically restored.

The hilly woodlands and the villages are all included in the Parc Naturel Régional de Montagne de Reims. Many waymarked walks have been laid out in it. St-Lié is on the *sentier petite montagne* which meanders along the north-facing slopes.

▶ *Return to the D26 and turn right. Follow this road, not always numbered on signs, through Villers-Allerand, Ludes, Rilly-la-Montagne and Verzenay to Verzy. In Verzy, watch for a right turn on the D34 to Louvois and Condé. Go left on the D1 to Châlons-sur-Marne.*

BACK TO NATURE

On the way to Châlons, turn left off the D34 for Les Faux de Verzy. These are bizarrely mutated beeches, first mentioned in monastic writings of the 6th century, with thin corkscrewed trunks and umbrella-like foliage.

---

❷ Châlons-sur-Marne,
Champagne-Ardenne

An old-established town – the main street is on the line of the Romans' Via Agrippa from Milan to Boulogne – Châlons sometimes calls itself Châlons-en-Champagne. It does have extensive champagne cellars to be visited. The largely 13th-century cathedral (St Étienne) with lovely stained glass which you can easily admire, because it is at less than the usual neck-craning angle, has a march of flying buttresses and a later north front uncomfortably out of tune with the rest. You may find Notre-Dame-en-Vaux just as interesting. In a cloister museum reached by a lane beside this multi-towered church, more than 50 carved columns featuring saints, prophets and medieval personalities are on display. Châlons has many waterfronts along the River Marne and the canals connected with it. Look for the series of parks and formal gardens called the Jards.

---

i *Quai des Arts*

▶ *Leave Châlons on the N3 as for Metz. After Auve, watch for a left turn signed for Valmy. This is the D284. Turn right for Moulin de Valmy.*

FOR HISTORY BUFFS

In the village of L'Épine, on the N3 after Châlons, the pilgrimage church is an astonishing miniature cathedral in Flamboyant Gothic style. It houses a statue of the Virgin found miraculously unharmed in a burning thorn bush (*épine*).

---

❸ Valmy, Champagne-Ardenne

The reconstructed windmill (*moulin*) on the hilltop at Valmy, marks the site of the most significant engagement in the war which Revolutionary France fought against the Prussians and Austrians. Plaques show the line-up of troops on 20

September 1792, when General Kellermann's inexperienced French army faced the battle-hardened Prussians under the Duke of Brunswick. Expecting an easy victory, the Prussians were in fact repulsed, and the young Revolutionary forces proved they could defend the homeland. Within a few hours, the Republic was proclaimed. The French troops, and Kellermann himself (by a spirited statue) are commemorated near by. There is a museum of the battle on the D31 in the little village of Valmy.

☐ *Maison du Meunier*

▶ *Continue on the D284, follow signs to Braux-Ste-Cohiere, then follow sign 'Vers N3'. Go left on the N3 to Ste-Menehould.*

➍ Ste-Menehould,
Champagne-Ardenne
A statue of Dom Pérignon recalls the fact that this Benedictine monk, to whom we owe the modern method of blending different wines into champagne, was born here in the 17th century. Incongruously, perhaps, you will find many shops selling a quite different speciality – pigs' trotters. It was at the now-restored Maison de Poste that the ill-fated Louis XVI and Marie Antoinette were recognised, to be arrested later.

At Ste-Menehould you will see a river flowing in different directions. Thanks to canal works, the Aisne splits into two channels which encircle the town and join up again after it. Since the Auve joins the Aisne here, Ste-Menehould has many pleasant waterways.

Its plateau location and a woodland fringe keep the old upper town almost out of sight, but a good self-guided walk links it with the lower town, whose elegant public buildings were raised after a disastrous fire in 1719.

A picturesque windmill (moulin) still operates in Verzenay

☐ *Place Leclerc*

▶ *Continue on the N3. In Les Islettes turn left for Varennes, following the D2 and then the D38.*

➎ Varennes-en-Argonne,
Champagne-Ardenne
In June 1791, when Louis XVI and his family fled secretly from Paris to try to join loyal troops at Metz, it was in Varennes that their coaches were stopped. Arrest, trial and the guillotine followed. The Musée d'Argonne is an excellent local museum, which describes the drama, and gives a balanced account of a king who forcefully supported the Americans in the War of Independence but made many political blunders at home. It also has intriguing displays on the old crafts and industries of the Forest of Argonne, and on the devastating effect on the district of World War I.

French and American flags fly at the entrance to the little grassy park leading to the pillared Pennsylvania Monument. It was troops from that US state who liberated Varennes in 1918.

☐ *Musée d'Argonne*

▶ *Leave Varennes on the D946. Turn right on the D6 to Buzancy, left on the D947, then right and left on the D155 to Fossé, taking care on the bumpy roads. Go left on the D55, left on the D4 and follow it right as for Beaumont, to the Parc de Vision de Belval.*

➏ Parc de Vision de Belval,
Champagne-Ardenne
In 350 hectares (865 acres) of woodland and clearings, with a lake to accommodate its ducks and geese, this extensive wildlife park houses around 400 wild animals belonging to species which either still live in the northern forests or are known to have lived in them within the last 2,000 years.

Because the red, roe and fallow deer, the wild boars, the moufflons, the bison and the other animals all live in semi-freedom inside the boundary fence, visitors drive slowly along the viewing roads, follow a fenced-in walking route or travel on the little 'train', whose locomotive is a thinly-disguised tractor. The only animal kept in a separate secure enclosure is a brown bear, which might otherwise become testy if annoyed!

▶ *Continue on the **D4** through Beaumont, then go straight on to the **D30** as for Le Chesne. Beyond Les Grandes-Armoises, after the bend sign, take the first right to pass an '8t' sign. Turn right at the Give Way sign. This is the **D977**. Follow the signs to Sedan.*

RECOMMENDED WALKS

After joining the D977 for Sedan, turn right on the D230 into the Forêt de Mont-Dieu. The Circuit de la Chartreuse walk wanders through the forest and overlooks the historic monastery of Mont-Dieu.

Sedan, dominated by its fortress, has had a turbulent history

7 **Sedan,** Champagne-Ardenne

Some quarters of the town are fairly depressing, but Sedan can barely dispel the memories of its past. This is where Napoleon III capitulated to end the Franco-Prussian War of 1870. In World War I the huge Château-Fort, in area the biggest castle in the whole of Europe, was a brutal forced-labour camp. And in the next war, this was where the Germans burst through the French lines in the invasion of 1940. Now the castle houses a museum on Sedan's military history, and there is a guided tour.

Away from these melancholy recollections, Sedan is famous for its high-quality woollen rugs; the workshop where rugs are still made as they were a century ago is open to visitors. There are pleasant promenades by the River Meuse.

i *Rue Rousseau*

▶ *Leave Sedan for Floing on the D5 and continue on this road to Charleville-Mézières. Avoid the autoroute.*

8 **Charleville-Mézières,** Champagne-Ardenne

Two once-separate towns, around loops of the River Meuse, have merged here. Mézières to the south is virtually on two islands. Within its 16th-century ramparts, the Flamboyant Gothic Church of Notre-Dame d'Espérance will surprise you with its abstract and geometrical stained-glass windows by René Dürrbach, a collaborator of Picasso's.

At Charleville the elegant, arcaded Place Ducale remains virtually as it was completed in 1628 (pity about the faded and obsolete shop signs).

The grand watermill (Vieux Moulin) on the Meuse is a local museum (Musée Ardenne), partly dedicated to the poet Arthur Rimbaud, who was born at Charleville.

i *Place Ducale*

FOR CHILDREN

Charleville-Mézières is the world capital of puppetry. Its Institut International de la Marionette has details of the summer puppet festival.

▶ *Leave Charleville on the D988 and follow signs to Monthermé along the D989. In Monthermé watch for a sharp left turn on the D1 to Revin. Go left on the D988 as for Les Mazures, then join the D40 as for Renwez and turn left at the junction with the D140 into the Musée de la Forêt.*

⑨ Musée de la Forêt,
Champagne-Ardenne
As much a museum 'in' the forest as 'of' the forest, this 5-hectare (12-acre) area of woodland is devoted to showing – partly with the aid of cheery wooden sculptures – the traditional crafts and harvesting methods of a few unmechanised generations ago.

Strolling round, you will see how birchwood brushes were made, how oak bark was peeled, how charcoal burners went about their trade, the kind of huts woodcutters lived in, and a selection of axes and single- and two-man saws.

The museum holds occasional wood-chopping contests, where competitors test their speed and accuracy as they axe their way through felled logs.

▶ *Continue on the D40. Go straight through Lonny. Turn right into Sormonne and left on the D978 as for Laon. Go left on the D985 and continue to Rethel.*

FOR CHILDREN

Before Rethel turn left off the D978 after Lonny for a neat little karting centre with two circuits for children of different ages. Low-powered karts are available for the real youngsters, and first-time drivers are patiently shown how to go about it.

⑩ Rethel, Champagne-Ardenne
An inscription at the bridge over the River Aisne here is a simple list of seven years between 1411 and 1940 – the years when war came to Rethel. In the 1930s the town hall was proudly re-created in Renaissance style; then in May 1940 more than three-quarters of the buildings in Rethel were flattened. But the town bobbed up again, as it always has.

The fine old Church of St-Nicholas was restored. The local museum was restocked, although it has very restricted opening times. Walks along the river and the nearby canal were opened up, including the tree-lined Promenade des Isles.

There are sports facilities here for everything from tennis and rugby to show-jumping and archery, and the modern swimming pool is partly under cover, partly in the open air.

Rethel is famous for its *boudin blanc*, a white sausage made from pork, eggs, shallots and seasoning.

SCENIC ROUTES

From the beautifully kept village of Gueux, the D26 runs along the foothills of the Montagne de Reims, through vineyards below the forest ridge.
Beyond Varennes the route follows a pleasant rural landscape, sometimes on the shallow valley floor. The D6 gives long views over fields and wooded hills.
After Monthermé the deep, sinuous and thickly wooded valley of the Meuse gives the finest scenery in the French Ardennes.

ⓘ *Avenue Gambetta*

▶ *Leave Rethel on the N51 to Reims.*

Monthermé is a popular resort in the Meuse valley

Towns of
Picardy

Centred on the cathedral city of Amiens, this tour is through districts often missed by visitors to France. It features wide rural landscapes in areas such as the Picardy plateau, goes through the fringes of the northern industrial belt and takes in elegant towns.

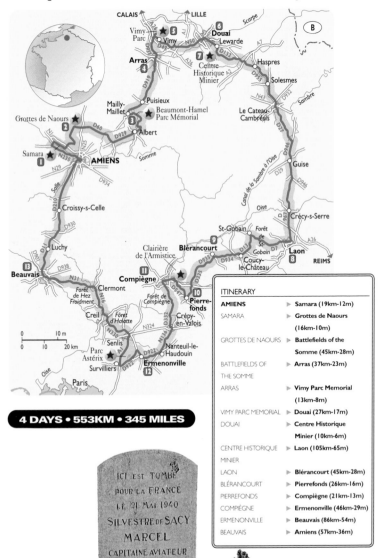

4 DAYS • 553KM • 345 MILES

ITINERARY

AMIENS	▶ Samara (19km-12m)
SAMARA	▶ Grottes de Naours (16km-10m)
GROTTES DE NAOURS	▶ Battlefields of the Somme (45km-28m)
BATTLEFIELDS OF THE SOMME	▶ Arras (37km-23m)
ARRAS	▶ Vimy Parc Memorial (13km-8m)
VIMY PARC MEMORIAL	▶ Douai (27km-17m)
DOUAI	▶ Centre Historique Minier (10km-6m)
CENTRE HISTORIQUE MINIER	▶ Laon (105km-65m)
LAON	▶ Blérancourt (45km-28m)
BLÉRANCOURT	▶ Pierrefonds (26km-16m)
PIERREFONDS	▶ Compiègne (21km-13m)
COMPIÈGNE	▶ Ermenonville (46km-29m)
ERMENONVILLE	▶ Beauvais (86km-54m)
BEAUVAIS	▶ Amiens (57km-36m)

ICI EST TOMBÉ
POUR LA FRANCE
LE 21 MAI 1940
SILVESTRE DE SACY
MARCEL
CAPITAINE AVIATEUR

[i] *Rue Catelas, Amiens*

▶ *Leave Amiens on the N235 through Picquigny, then go right on the D191 to Samara.*

❶ Samara, Picardy
Laid out among scrubland, marsh and ponds, Samara is a fascinating historical park which looks at thousands of years of human life and activity in the valley of the River Somme. There are accurate representations of ancient dwellings and demonstrations of prehistoric trades such as flint cutting. There is a botanical garden and arboretum. Along the pathways is an excavated Celtic town and a modern pavilion whose exhibits look not only into the distant past but also at what life may be like in the future.

[i] *la Chaussée Tirancourt, Picquigny*

▶ *Continue on the D191 to St-Sauveur, go left on the D97 at 'Grottes de Naours' sign, left on to the D933 to Flesselles, straight on along the D117 to Naours, right on the D60,*

Amiens, a pleasing mixture of ancient riverside streets and modern development

then sharp left to the Grottes de Naours.

❷ Grottes de Naours, Picardy
Burrowed into a wooded hillside above the village, the Underground City of Naours (Grottes de Naours) is one of the most amazing places in France. About 30 tunnels and 300 separate rooms – including chapels and stables – have been used as refuges in times of danger and invasion from the Gallo-Roman era to the 18th century. They were the haunt of salt smugglers and used as stores for the British Army in World War II.

▶ *Return from the car park, go left at the Stop sign and follow the D60 to Contay. Turn right on the D919, immediately left on the D23 to Franvillers and left on the D929 through Albert. Go left on the D20, right on the D151 to Thiepval, left on the D73 and follow signs to Beaumont-Hamel memorial park.*

❸ Battlefields of the Somme, Picardy
The countryside hereabouts is scattered with war graves and monuments recalling the first

day of July 1916, the opening of the Battle of the Somme. Among the most impressive are Sir Edward Lutyens's massive brick-and-stone memorial at Thiepval; the Ulster Tower also near Thiepval; and the Newfoundland Memorial Park at Beaumont-Hamel, where almost the whole of the 1st Newfoundland Regiment were mown down by enemy machine-gun fire and shrapnel.

▶ *Continue on the D53 to Mailly-Maillet. Turn right on the D129, then right on the D919 to Arras.*

❹ Arras, Picardy
Arras, the capital of Artois, would be a finer place if its two most spectacular squares – la Grand Place and la Place de Héros – had gleaming stonework to match the elegance of their arcaded buildings. The Hôtel de Ville (town hall) is a handsome affair, and there is a good view from its belfry. Part of the former Benedictine Abbaye de St-Vaast is now a cathedral (18th- to 19th-century); in the south wing of the abbey is a well-stocked fine arts museum with extensive collections of French and Flemish paintings, medieval

wood carvings and a superb display of local porcelain and tapestry.

i Place des Héros

▷ *Leave Arras on the N425, then take the D937 as for Béthune. Turn right on the D55 following the 'Memorial Canadien' sign to Vimy Parc.*

5 Vimy Parc Memorial, Picardy
One of the largest war memorial areas in France, Vimy Parc commemorates, in particular, the tremendous assault of 9 April 1917 when all four divisions of the Canadian Corps stormed the German defences on Vimy Ridge. Keep to the paths, as there is still a chance of encountering unexploded shells and ammunition. Guided tours explore the underground galleries. On the crown of the ridge, the Mémorial et Parc Canadien, whose soaring pillars bear the maple leaf of Canada and the fleur-de-lys of France, is the most majestic of all the monuments raised after the Great War.

▷ *From the memorial, return down the D55 as for Arras, then go left at the first junction following the 'Gendarmerie' sign. Turn right on the N17 to Thélus, left on the D49, right on the D33, go under a bridge, then turn left and join the N50 dual carriageway to Douai.*

The Vimy Parc Memorial honours the 75,000 Canadians who died in 1917

6 Douai, Picardy
An industrial town brightened by judiciously placed gardens, flowery roundabouts and avenues of trees, Douai is, at its heart, an island bounded by the River Scarpe and its associated canals, lined with old quaysides. The most impressive building is the ornate Gothic belltower, completed in 1410. Escorted tours show visitors the view from the top, over the town, and also the fine interior of the historic Hôtel de Ville (town hall). In the old Carthusian convent (Chartreuse) – a mixture of three centuries of architectural ideas – more than a dozen exhibition halls show off French, Flemish and Italian Renaissance paintings as well as sculptures, earthenware and ivories. There is a splendid antique map of Douai, drawn in 1709 to Louis XIV's command.

i Place des Armes

SPECIAL TO...

The belfry at Douai houses the largest carillon in France, using no fewer than 62 individual bells. Douai's official carillonist is the 34th in a line which started in 1391. Douai also owns the first mobile carillon in France, with 50 bells.

▷ *Leave Douai on the N45. In Lewarde turn right on the D135 and follow 'Centre Historique Minier' signs on to the D132.*

7 Centre Historique Minier, Picardy
On the site of the old Delloye pit (Fosse Delloye) near Lewarde, you will find an extensive indoor, outdoor and underground museum dedicated to coal-mining in the north of France. Former miners guide visitors round displays about the geology and exploitation of the coal-seams, the machinery and processing plant used in the mines, and the working conditions of miners through the centuries.

Finally, you can descend into one of the original pits where 450m (490 yards) of galleries have been reconstructed as they would have been in their heyday.

▷ *Continue on the D132 to Bouchain. Go right on the D943, left on the N30, then right to Haspres. Go left for Saulzoir and right before the FINA station, leaving Haspres on the D955 to Solesmes. Then follow signs to Le Cateau-Cambrésis. Leave Le Cateau on the D12, which becomes the D27, then follow the D946 and the D967 to Laon.*

8 Laon, Picardy
The attractions of Laon are partly in its situation, partly in the architecture of the old city (Ville Haute) surrounded by medieval ramparts and imposing entrance gates. Laon lies on a long narrow ridge which dominates the surrounding plain and is an excellent natural viewpoint. The many-towered 12th-to 14th-century cathedral, one of the great Gothic edifices of France, has a nave of immense grandeur and some beautiful medieval stained-glass windows. Beside an old garden chapel of the Knights Templar (Chapelle des Templiers), the museum holds extensive

archaeological and arts collections.

ⓘ *Place de la Cathédrale*

▶ *Leave Laon on the **D7** for St-Gobain. Go left on the **D13**, then right on the **D5** to Coucy. Join the **D937** as for Folembray, then turn left on the **D934** to Blérancourt.*

❾ Blérancourt, Picardy
Headquarters during World War I of the American volunteer ambulance corps, the pavilions, restored ground floor and gardens of the largely dismantled Château de Blérancourt are now the national Museum of Franco-American Co-operation. Notable Americans such as George Washington, Benjamin Franklin, John Paul Jones and Thomas Jefferson are honoured. There is a substantial library, as well as many documents and souvenirs of battles in which the two nations fought side by side, notably in the two World Wars.

▶ *Leave Blérancourt on the **D935**, which becomes the **D335**, to Pierrefonds.*

❿ Pierrefonds, Picardy
Drive slowly down the hill into Pierrefonds, so as not to miss the first stunning glimpse of the massive castle which towers over this engaging island resort. Handsome villas in discreet wooded grounds overlook a lake, which rowing boats and pedaloes share with the coots and mallards. The Parc Rainette is home to a herd of stately fallow deer. However, it is the château which dominates the town. Napoleon I bought it in ruins, but it was Napoleon II who commissioned the great architect Viollet-le-Duc to oversee its transformation into a grand imperial residence. Guided tours show off the whole lavish project; one room is dedicated to the architect himself, but the château itself is his memorial.

ⓘ *Place de l'Hôtel-de-Ville*

▶ *Leave Pierrefonds on the **D973** as for Compiègne. Go right on the **D547** to Vieux Moulin, then left on the **N31** and right on the **V4** to Clairière de l'Armistice. Then follow signs to Compiègne.*

⓫ Compiègne, Picardy
Here is a dignified and spacious town with a fine riverside frontage on the River Oise, spreading parkland and suburbs to south and west where villa gardens drift into the glorious Forêt de Compiègne. Louis XV and Louis XVI commissioned the building of a palace here, facing a wide cobbled square. It was completed in the fateful year of 1789. After the Revolution, Napoleon I had it rebuilt, and later still it was the favourite residence of Napoleon III and Empress Eugénie.

Open to the public, the royal and imperial apartments recall all these personages, and there is a separate Musée du Second Empire. Elsewhere in the complex of buildings a first-class motor and carriage museum (Musée National de la Voiture et du Tourisme) includes splendid exhibits of vehicles from the horse-drawn age, and cars which are a reminder that, although Germany was the birthplace of the automobile, the French were livelier designers and experimenters.

Another memorable museum in Compiègne is the Musée Vivenel, which includes exceptional collections of archaeological items and classical ceramics.

For 200 years until AD987, Laon was actually capital of France

and white 'A1' signs. Join the A1 autoroute as for Lille. Parc Astérix is reached by the first exit. After Parc Astérix take the next autoroute exit as for Senlis. After the toll booths follow the 'Creil' sign on the **N330**, then the Beauvais signs via Clermont into Beauvais itself.

FOR CHILDREN

Parc Astérix, off the A1, on the way from Ermenonville to Beauvais, is an expensive but massive theme park based on the adventures of the ancient Gauls – Astérix, Obélix and Toutafix – made famous by Goscinny and Underzo.

13 Beauvais, Picardy

One victim of World War II was the tapestry industry at Beauvais, removed elsewhere and never brought back here. The Galérie Nationale de la Tapisserie, a gallery of French tapestries from the 15th century onwards, is one of the sights of the town. Stained glass was another Beauvais interest, and much of it survives, both in the Church of St-Etienne and as a feature of the superb interior of the cathedral (St Pierre), which has a tremendous height for the area of its base. The cathedral's astronomical clock, gilded and astonishingly complicated, was completely restored in 1989.

Beside the cathedral, the old bishop's palace houses the Musée Départementale de l'Oise, the principal museum in the *département* of the Oise region. There are wide-ranging displays of classical and contemporary art, art nouveau and art deco, as well as a glorious exhibition of ceramics.

📍 *Rue Beauregard*

▶ Leave Beauvais on the **D901** as for Abbeville, then take the **D149** as for Crèvecoeur-le-Grand and the **D11/D210** back to Amiens.

📍 *Place de l'Hôtel de Ville*

▶ Leave Compiègne on the **D332** as for Meaux. In Crépy-en-Valois follow 'Paris' signs and take the **D136** into Nanteuil, ignoring the bypass. Watch the navigation here. About 55m (60 yards) after a Fiat garage, turn right following the sign 'Ermenonville Tourisme'. Go left on the **D922**, then right on the **N330** through Ermenonville.

RECOMMENDED WALKS

Ask at the tourist office in Pierrefonds for the *Itinéraires circuits pédestres* booklet describing four waymarked walks in the eastern part of the Forêt de Compiègne. One follows an ancient Roman road, another goes past the Empress Eugénie's hunting pavilion.

The elegant town of Compiègne

12 Ermenonville, Picardy

Ermenonville has been done no favours by the planners, who have signposted the road here as being a convenient way to bypass other towns. Traffic is usually heavy. However, the town itself has one haven of tranquillity. To the left of the main road is a park, introduced by a carved stone which says 'here begins the course of a sweet and rustic leisure' with woodland paths, ponds and streams.

Beyond Ermenonville is a small zoo (Zoo Jean-Richard). The Abbey of Chaalis, just north of the town, in a gracious parkland which contains one of France's finest rose gardens, is a classical 18th-century château on the site of an old Cistercian monastery.

▶ Turn sharp left for Mortefontaine. Join the **D922** and in Plailly follow the blue

on the road

GERMANY

As well as a diversity of cultures, Germany offers a contrast of scenery – spectacular Alpine peaks, castles perched high above the valleys, half-timbered medieval towns and villages, and terraced vineyards along the banks of the mighty Rhine.

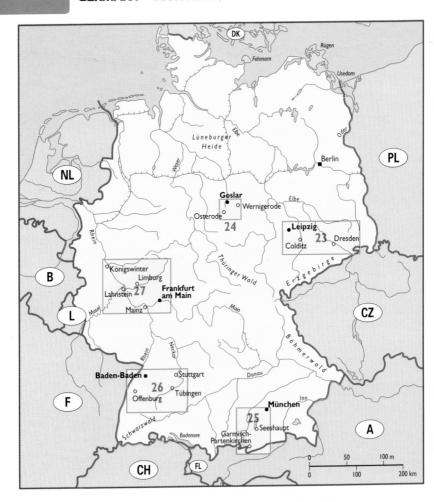

Tour 23

Strong associations with business dominate this tour; the world famous trade fair at Leipzig and the likewise famous porcelain factory at Meissen. Dresden, although nearly totally destroyed by Allied bombing at the end of World War II, is rapidly gaining its rightful place as one of the most fascinating towns in Germany.

Strong rulers of Saxony amassed enormous wealth

Page 143: top – fine detail of a doorway in the old town of Goslar; bottom – view of Cochem along the Moselle, with its romantic castle overlooking the town

during their reign at the end of the 17th and beginning of the 18th centuries and wisely invested it in works of the Old Master painters and promoting Dresden's magnificent baroque architecture. One of the great highlights here is the Zwinger collections of art treasures and porcelain displayed in a baroque palace. Further on there are startling natural wonders in the form of bizarre rock formations; and the tour ends with a visit to the famous World War II POW camp, Colditz.

The Elbe river provides a useful link right through Germany with the port of Hamburg and the North Sea.

Tour 24

Having been divided between East and West Germany during the cold war era, the division of the Harz region is now hardly noticeable. Old medieval market towns are scattered around the area and motorists beware: weekly markets are still held regularly and empty squares in the evening, appearing to be ideal parking places, can become filled with market stalls in the early morning of the following day.

The Harz region is called the Heart of Germany, and the Harz Mountains were exploited for their valuable ore deposits from as early as the 10th century. Forestry and the creation of hydro-electric power are two of the major industries to be found here, with tourists adding a human dimension.

This is one of the best areas for recreational pursuits and holiday-making in Germany – not too far from the capital Berlin, and within quite easy reach of the Ruhr, Bremen and Hannover. Although this is a mountainous region, it is not too strenuous for gentle strolls or hikes, and visitors to the area will find the many lakes and rivers provide a wealth of beautiful scenery to just sit and enjoy. There is plenty of history, too, and a great number of superb medieval buildings, many of which are classified as national treasures.

Tour 25

Travelling south of München (Munich) towards the Alps, a series of lakes stretches from west to east, before one is suddenly confronted by those mighty mountains, reaching heights of nearly 3,000m (9,840 feet). This district is called Oberbayern and tourism is playing a big part there. The skiing resort of Garmisch-Partenkirchen hosted the 1936 Olympic Winter Games and an excursion up the Zugspitze, Germany's highest mountain provides magnificent views over the area. One is reminded of the former Bavarian kingdom at Schloss Linderhof and on the Starnberger Lake, where King Ludwig II met his tragic death. Strong religious beliefs are documented at Oberammergau, where the famous Passion Play takes place every 10 years.

This tour starts by a lake at

Starnberg, the favourite weekend destination of visitors for the nearby capital of Bavaria. This is followed by resorts famous for their sports and their religious affiliations. A charming mountain retreat fit for a king provides an unforgettable experience.

Tour 26

The Romans discovered the joy of spa life centuries ago, but the Black Forest's natural

Colourful, highly decorated façades like this are typical of many of Germany's old buildings

hot springs suffered a long period of neglect when the Roman culture and civilisation was followed by an incursion of primitive tribes from the north and east. Only at the end of the last century were the facilities restored and the spas became fashionable again. Europe's ruling monarchs and the aristocracy enjoyed their summer vacations in these spas. Now they are open to all and are very popular. Scenic beauty blends in well with the provincial capital of Stuttgart, whose

name shows its development from a stud in a garden to an important industrial city without losing its beautiful natural surroundings.

From Baden-Baden, the tour follows a most attractive route through the Black Forest to the Mummelsee, near the Hornisgrinde mountain, a popular stopping point about halfway along the outward journey. Traffic around Stuttgart is heavy, but the centre of the city has achieved a very pleasant atmosphere with its pedestrian precincts. From here the tour takes in two extraordinary castles, and picks up the popular Badische Weinstrasse (Wine Road) at Gengenbach, before returning to Baden-Baden.

Tour 27

History runs along the rivers Main and Rhine and remnants of the great northern border of the Roman Empire can still be seen near Frankfurt. The city has become one of the world's leading financial centres. Two famous spas, Bad Homburg and Wiesbaden, afford the area more prominence and the busy rivers are lined by vineyards. Many castles, some now in ruins, are to be found on the hills overlooking the Rhine – witnesses to medieval warlords who had to build their own protective defences.

From Frankfurt, the route skirts along the 'Limes', the Roman border against the Germanic tribes. It then passes a famous spa and historic town in a beautiful setting, before the river is met again, further north. Ruins, castles and vineyards abound, and there are always ships passing up and down the Rhine.

BANKS

Banks are open Monday to Friday 8.30am–1pm; 2.30–4pm (5.30pm on Thursdays). Exchange offices of the Deutsche-Verkehrs-Kredit-Bank are located at main railway stations and road and rail frontier crossing points and are usually open from early morning until late at night.

CREDIT CARDS

Credit cards can be used in hotels, shops, restaurants and petrol stations displaying the appropriate signs. Cash can be obtained at banks and some cash dispensers.

CURRENCY

There are 100 pfennigs (Pf) in 1 Deutsche Mark (DM). Coins: 1, 2, 5, 10, 50Pf and DM1, 2, 5. Notes: DM5, 10, 20, 50, 100, 500, 1000.

CUSTOMS REGULA-TIONS

See **Austria** (page 10).

ELECTRICITY

See **Austria** (page 10).

EMBASSIES & CONSULATES

Australia
(embassy) Godesberger Allee 105–7, 53175 Bonn 2 (tel: 0228 81030)
(consulate) 4th floor, Kempinski Plaza, Uhlandstrasse 181–3, D10623 Berlin (tel: 030 8800880)
Canada
(embassy) Friedrichstrasse 95, 10117 Berlin (tel: 030 261 1161)
(consulate) Tal 29, 80331 München (tel: 089 29 06 50)
UK
Friedrich-Ebert-Allee 77, 5300 Bonn 1 (tel: 0228 344061)
US
(embassy) Deichmanns Aue 29, 53170 Bonn (tel: 0228 3391)
(consulate) Neuestädtische Kirchstrasse 4–5, 10117 Berlin (tel: 030 238 5174).

EMERGENCY TELE-PHONE NUMBERS

Police and Ambulance 110
Fire 112

ENTRY REGULATIONS

See **Austria** (page 10).

HEALTH MATTERS

See **Austria** (page 10).

MOTORING

Accidents

As a general rule you are required to call the police when individuals have been injured or considerable damage has been caused. Failure to give aid to anyone injured will render you liable to a fine.

Documents

You must have a valid driving licence, passport, third-party insurance (Green Card), and vehicle registration document. Anyone remaining in Germany for more than a year must have a German driving licence. Presentation of the foreign driving licence is usually sufficient for the issue of a German permit.

Car hire

Car hire is available at most airports, main railway stations and in larger towns. You must be over 21 and have driven for at least a year.

Breakdowns

If your car breaks down, try to move it to the side of the road so that it does not obstruct traffic flow. A warning triangle and hazard lights, if fitted, must be used.

The motoring club ADAC operates a breakdown service. Assistance is given free of charge; only the cost of materials has to be reimbursed. In the event of a breakdown on a motorway a patrol can be summoned from an emergency telephone. A small arrow on the marker posts on the verges indi-

cates the direction of the nearest one. When calling, ask specifically for Strassenwachthilfe (road service assistance).

Driving conditions

Drive on the right, pass on the left. There are on-the-spot fines for speeding and other offences.

Speed limits

No limit on motorways – recommended 130kph (81mph); outside built-up areas 100kph (62mph); and in built-up areas 50kph (31mph).

Traffic regulations are strictly enforced, particularly in relation to speeding and use of alcohol.

Route directions

Throughout this section the following abbreviations are used for German roads:
A – Autobahn
B – Bundesstrasse (federal/national roads*
* on tour maps B roads are indicated by number only.

POST OFFICES

Post offices are generally open Monday–Friday from 8am–6pm, Saturdays till noon. *Poste restante* mail is issued on presentation of an identity card or passport.

Money orders telegraphed from abroad are cashed in DM. Post boxes are bright yellow.

PUBLIC HOLIDAYS

1 January – New Year's Day
Good Friday, Easter, Whit Monday and Ascension Day – variable dates
1 May – Labour Day
3 October – Day of Unity
3rd Wednesday in November – Day of Prayer and Repentance
24 December (pm), 25 and 26 December – Christmas

TELEPHONES

International calls can be made from public telephone kiosks showing a black receiver in a green square. They take DM1, 2 and 5 coins. Cheap rates operate

during the weekend and Monday to Friday 8pm–8am. Phonecards can also be used for telephoning abroad.

TIME
Germany is one hour ahead of Greenwich Mean Time in winter and two hours ahead in summer.

TOURIST OFFICES
Australia – Lufthansa House, 9th Floor, 143 Macquarie Street, Sydney NSW 2000 (tel: (00 612) 367 3890).
Canada – 175 Bloor Street East, North Tower, Suite 604, Toronto, Ontario M4W 3R8 (tel: (001 416) 968 1570).
UK – Nightingale House, 65 Curzon Street, London W1Y 7PE (tel: (0044 171) 495 0081).
US – 122 East 42nd Street, Chanin Building, 52nd Floor, New York, NY 10168–0072 (tel: (00 1212) 661 7200); 401 N Michigan Avenue, Suite 2525, Chicago, Il 60611–4212 (tel: (00 1312) 644 0723); 11766 Wilshire Boulevard, Suite 750, Los Angeles, CA 90025 (tel: (00 1310) 575 9799).

USEFUL WORDS
The following is a list of useful words and phrases.
English German
yes ja
no nein
please bitte
good morning/day guten Morgen/Tag
goodbye auf Wiedersehen
excuse me entschuldigen Sie bitte
how are you? wie geht es Ihnen?
very well, thanks; and you? danke, gut; und Ihnen?
do you speak English? sprechen Sie Englisch?
I don't understand Ich verstehe nicht

View of the Danube river as it winds its way through Bavaria

my name is ... Ich heisse ...
where? wo?
when? wann?
where is ...? wo ist ..?
today heute
yesterday gestern
open offen
closed geschlossen
good gut
bad schlecht
big gross
small klein
expensive teuer
cheap billig
how much does it cost? wieviel kostet es?
Monday, Tuesday, Wednesday, Thursday, Friday, Saturday, Sunday Montag, Dienstag, Mittwoch, Donnerstag, Freitag, Samstag, Sonntag
1 to 10 eins, zwei, drei, vier, funf, sechs, sieben, acht, neun, zehn

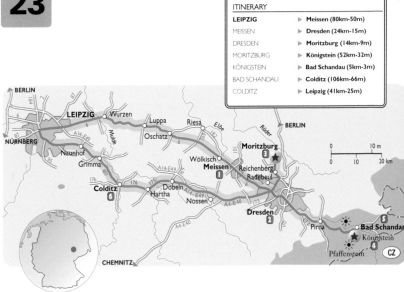

ITINERARY		
LEIPZIG	▶	**Meissen (80km-50m)**
MEISSEN	▶	**Dresden (24km-15m)**
DRESDEN	▶	**Moritzburg (14km-9m)**
MORITZBURG	▶	**Königstein (52km-32m)**
KÖNIGSTEIN	▶	**Bad Schandau (5km-3m)**
BAD SCHANDAU	▶	**Colditz (106km-66m)**
COLDITZ	▶	**Leipzig (41km-25m)**

The Upper Elbe,
Rocks & Castles

1/2 DAYS • 322KM • 200 MILES

Leipzig is famous for its literary and musical associations. Poet and dramatist Friedrich von Schiller studied at Leipzig University; Bach, Mendelssohn, Schumann and Wagner all lived here. The focus of civic life in Leipzig is the mid-16th-century Altes Rathaus (Old Town Hall). Behind it lies the Naschmarkt square and the 17th-century Alte Handelsbörse (Old Trading Exchange). Next to the university stands the cubist-inspired Neue Gewandhaus, and close by is the Kaffeebaum, Leipzig's famous coffeehouse, which opened in 1694 and later became the meeting point of literary and music circles, frequented by Goethe, Liszt, Wagner and Schumann.

ⓘ *Sachsenplatz 1*

▶ *From Leipzig take the B6 for 80km (50 miles) east to Meissen.*

❶ Meissen, Sachsen

The 1,000-year-old town of Meissen lies on the River Elbe, a short distance northwest of Dresden. Meissen is, of course, known the world over for its beautiful porcelain – identified by the distinctive trademark featuring two crossed swords.

The town's history begins with Heinrich I, who founded Misni Castle in 929. Forty years later it became the seat of a

and Albrecht who ruled over Saxony and Thuringia. The adjoining Dom (cathedral) was started in 1260. Its early Gothic origins have almost disappeared under many extensions and annexes, such as two western towers which were partly destroyed by lightning in 1547, and rebuilt between 1903 and 1908. St Afra's Church and the former Fürstenschule (Duke's School) are interesting.

South of the Nikolaikirche (St Nicholas's) the head office of the nationalised porcelain manufacturing company is open to visitors, who can inspect a wide selection of porcelain

Reflections of a restored city: Dresden, on the banks of the Elbe, rebuilt after wartime devastation

bishop, an important step in those days for a growing town. Around ad1000, Meissen was granted *Marktrecht*, a decree permitting the settlement to hold its own markets; and in 1150 it was first officially documented as a *Stadt* (town). Further development was hampered by the wars of the Middle Ages, but in 1719 Friedrich August der Starke (The Strong) founded the Königliche Porzellan-manufaktur (Royal Porcelain Works) in the Albrechtsburg. The institution was transferred to the valley of the Triebisch river during the 19th century.

The best views of the Albrechtsburg are from the opposite bank of the Elbe. Founded in 929, the castle is a good example of late Gothic architecture, and was intended to be the seat of Dukes Ernst

objects, and there are live demonstrations of the various processes involved in the manufacture of porcelain.

On a more relaxing note, Meissen is the centre of a wine-growing district. There are plenty of traditional old wine cellars in the town where thirsty travellers are welcome to sample the product.

ⓘ *An der Frauenkirche 3*

▶ *From Meissen continue on the B6 for a further 24km (15 miles) to Dresden.*

❷ Dresden, Sachsen

On a bend of the Elbe, Dresden is now a thriving centre of half a million inhabitants, a far cry from the smoking ruins of a city almost totally destroyed by massive British and American bombing in February 1945.

Countless cultural treasures built and acquired over the centuries were lost in a single night, and many thousands of lives. Historically, the driving force behind the city's development was the Saxon ruler Friedrich August der Starke (The Strong) and his son, August II. The latter initiated the golden age of Dresden baroque architecture by bringing in Matthäus Daniel Pöppelmann as chief designer, and Balthasar Permoser, the sculptor, to build the Zwinger Palace. Originally planned as an Orangery, the building grew and grew between 1709 and 1732. Later it was decided to house a gallery there, and Gottfried Semper, another well-known architect/builder, was commissioned to design a wing which would close the river end of the garden which had previously remained open. The central view from the gardens to the Wall Pavilion or the Glockenspiel Pavillon (Carillon) on the opposite side, amply demonstrates Semper's genius. The design of the square, with its elegant highly ornate buildings, gives an impression of openness and space. The carillon itself is of Meissen porcelain and was added at the beginning of the century. The Wall Pavilion displays the joint coat of arms of Saxony and Poland, reflecting August the Strong's additional role as King of Poland. Art lovers are in for an enormous treat in the palace Picture Gallery – the emphasis is on Old Masters.

The porcelain collection is equally magnificent – the Zwinger Collection is said to be the second largest in the world, featuring early Chinese ceramics and porcelain together with a unique display of Meissen products. The adjoining Carillon Pavilion houses an unusual Meissen carillon with 40 bells, all made of porcelain. Although the Zwinger complex was totally destroyed during the bombing raids of 1945, the structure was carefully rebuilt and completed in 1964, a symbol of Germany's determination to maintain her cultural heritage.

Bordering the Zwinger, Theaterplatz (Theatre Square) makes sightseeing easy, as nearly all Dresden's buildings are there. The Semperoper (Opera House), built to plans by Gottfried Semper, was one of the most beautiful theatres in Europe, erected between 1871 and 1878. Ruined in 1945, it was rebuilt between 1977 and 1985, keeping as close as possible to the original designs. On 13 February 1985, exactly 40 years after its destruction, it reopened with the Weber opera *Der Freischütz*.

Opposite the Opera House stands the Hofkirche (cathedral), designed by Italian architect Chiaveri and founded in 1738. Chiaveri never finished

the baroque-style building, which was subsequently consecrated in 1751 and completed in 1755. The Blitz destroyed the interior and sections of the walls, but the tower remained upright and was restored after the war. Notable features of the interior are Permoser's pulpit, carved in 1722; the altar painting, the *Ascension of Christ*; and the magnificent Silbermannorgel (organ). Down in the catacombs, a number of tombs contain the remains of the kings and princes of Saxony, and August the Strong's heart in its own urn.

Plans are being prepared to rebuild a number of the destroyed buildings in the city, including the Residenzschloss. The city gate, the Georgentor, has already been restored and can now be seen on the Schlossplatz (Castle Square), next to the Hofkirche.

[i] *Pragerstrasse 10/11*

▷ *From Dresden head northwest for 14km (9 miles) to Moritzburg.*

FOR HISTORY BUFFS

In Dresden, do not miss the impressive golden equestrian statue of Friedrich August II, Der Starke (The Strong), Elector of Saxony and King of Poland. Erected in 1736, it was designed by French Court sculptor Vinache, cast in copper and gilded by Wiedeman.
In the centre of the town, near the Augustusstrasse, the Fürstenzug (Train of Princes) decorates the wall of the Langer Gang (Long Gangway). Twenty-four thousand porcelain tiles from the Meissen factory were used to create images of the rulers of the House of Wettin, including a few eminent artists and scientists. It was erected between 1870 and 1876 using a sgraffito technique.

---

3 **Moritzburg,** Sachsen
Surrounded by a nature reserve, Moritzburg Castle was once a hunting lodge. It escaped war damage, and its well-preserved interior houses a good museum. At present the stables are being used to breed race horses. The Hengstdepot (stud farm) was founded in 1828 to rear race and cart horses. Now mainly race horses are bred there and during the summer horse shows are staged for buyers and visitors, attracting some 50,000 people to the Parade of the Stallions.

▷ *Return to Dresden, then take the B172 to Königstein, 52km (32 miles).*

4 **Königstein,** Sachsen
The massive and impregnable Königstein Castle squats on a rocky hill above the Elbe. Although there was mention of a fortress here as early as 1241, the present buildings were erected between 1589 and 1631 by the Elector Christian I. From the 17th century, the castle cellars were used to store huge barrels of wine, the largest holding some 250,000 litres (55,000 gallons). Königstein was also used as a secure prison by various rulers. Christian I locked up his chancellor Krell here; Böttger, the European discoverer of porcelain, spent some time incarcerated at Königstein; then it was the turn of the 1849 revolutionaries. During World War II, several important Allied prisoners were kept here, and many pitted their wits against the castle's security. The French General Giraud succeeded in making a daring escape during 1942.

There are particularly fine views from the castle over the Elbe Valley, which is also known as *Sächsiche Schweiz* (Saxon Switzerland).

[i] *Goethestrasse*

▷ *Continue on the B172 for a futher 5km (3 miles) to Bad Schandau.*

The wide curve of the Elbe seen from the Bastei, Bad Schandau

6 Colditz, Sachsen
On the return to Leipzig, a short detour leads to Colditz, a small town in the shadow of its castle. Popularised by a dozen or more films and books, Colditz Castle is best known for daring escapes by its Allied prisoners of war; tours show one of the escape tunnels. Most of those sent to Colditz were considered particularly troublesome due to earlier escape attempts, but stories of the castle's impregnability only spurred them on. Statistics record that of 460 prisoners who tried to escape, 300 were caught at the outset, 130 got out but were captured while still in Germany, and just 30 actually reached their final destination. Souvenirs of the period are displayed in the nearby Escape Museum. Since the end of the war, the castle, which used to be the seat of the Dukes of Saxony, has been used to house a hospital. There are now plans to convert it into a hotel and museum.

▶ *From Colditz take the **B107** to Grimma. Head northwest back to Leipzig via Naunhof.*

---

5 Bad Schandau, Sachsen
A favourite base for many excursions, Bad Schandau also has a sanatorium offering the Kneipp cure, based on physiotherapy, with the objective of developing resistance to common ailments. Hydrotherapy is also a part of the Kneipp cure.

The favourite local beauty spot is the Bastei, a high stone bridge linking a chain of sandstone peaks above the Elbe. From the bridge, there are fine views over the rocky landscape, which is also ideal terrain for rock-climbing schools. Walkers can explore some 1,200km (745 miles) of footpaths around the area. Popular hiking destinations further afield include the Lichtenhainer Waterfall, the Kuhstall and the Obere Schleuse. For more relaxed sight-seeing, pleasure steamers ply up and down the Elbe.

i *Markt 8*

RECOMMENDED WALKS

Cross the Elbe, then continue on foot to the Lilienstein mountain on a bend in the river. There are beautiful views from the 414m (1,360-foot) plateau, and the ruins of a fortress. Or head south to the 427m (1,400-foot) Pfaffenstein, with its interesting rock formations, particularly one called Barbarine.

▶ *Take the **B172** back to Dresden, then the **A4/E40** to Abzweigung Nossen and turn right for the **A14/E49** to Döbeln. Turn south for the **B175** and right after Hartha on the **B176** to Colditz, 106km (66 miles).*

BACK TO NATURE

For something a little out of the ordinary, check out the strangely shaped Schrammstein rocks south of Bad Schandau. The Bastei is another bizarre rock formation to the north of the town. The rock formations in this area are unique to Europe and were created by the Elbe river which eroded the sandstone mountains. The most outstanding have been given names and are a favourite spot for rock climbers.

The Harz
Mountains & Forests

Goslar's architectural treasures include the monumental 11th-century Kaiserpfalz (Emperor's Residence), the 15th-century Rathaus (Town Hall), and many burghers' houses, including the Brusttuch (Shawl), named for its steep roof. Of Goslar's original 47 churches, 23 remain. The largest – the Frankenbergkirche, Jacobkirche and Marktkirche – were all founded in around 1200 as Romanesque basilicas.

2 DAYS • 176KM • 109 MILES

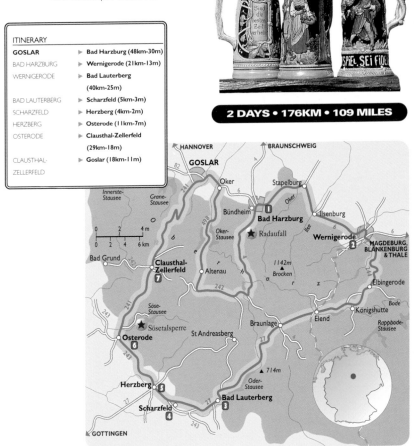

ℹ️ *Markt 7*

▶ *From Goslar take a short drive east to Oker, turn south on to the B498, then turn sharp east past Altenau for the B242. Turn north on to the B4 for Bad Harzburg.*

Eating out in style in Goslar's historic market square, lined with medieval burghers' buildings

❶ Bad Harzburg,
Niedersachsen

Away from the big towns, skimming the northern end of the Harz Mountain range, Bad Harzburg is a spa town with all the facilities for a relaxing and healthy stay. A natural spring delivers water at a constant 32°C (89°F) to the Hallenbad (covered pool), and there is an open-air annexe where the water temperature drops to a mere 29°C (84°F).

The only historical remains here are the ruins of the Harzburg, an 11th-century fortress founded by Heinrich IV, destroyed by the Saxons, then rebuilt by Emperor Friedrich Barbarossa, only to be demolished again in the 17th century.

A cable-car climbs the 500m (1,640-foot) Burgberg. The commanding view from the top explains the positioning of the fortress, and there are several strolls around the area which make this a pleasant excursion.

ℹ️ *Herzog Wilhelmstrasse 86*

▶ *Take the B6 east to Wernigerode.*

❷ Wernigerode, Sachsen-Anhalt

Located in what was formerly East Germany, Wernigerode is a beautifully preserved town with a medieval centre that is listed as a monument. The focus is the Marktplatz (Market Place) with its unique Rathaus (Town Hall), which looks as if it has been lifted straight from the pages of a fairy tale. This little jewel of medieval architecture has a raised ground-floor entrance which is reached by two staircases, flanked by a pair of oriel spires, and all its façades are painted and decorated. First documented in 1277 as a Spelhus, from the word for a play house or theatre (Spielhaus), this was not only a place for entertainment, it also served as a law court administered by the ruling Counts. After a fire in 1543 its function changed to that of a town hall, and weddings still take place there today. Other interesting buildings include the Waaghaus, whose scales date back to the 16th century, which adjoins the rear of the Rathaus; and there are a number of beautiful timbered houses all around the town centre bearing witness to an era of great and stylish architecture. On Breite Strasse, the Krummelhaus, at No 72, was built in 1674 and decorated with carved ornaments which conceal the timber-framed façade. The smallest house in town is found on Kochstrasse, just 4.2m (13½ feet) up to the eaves and less than 3m (10 feet) wide. Then there is the Schiefe Haus (Leaning House), formerly a mill which started to lean when water from the stream beneath attacked the foundations.

A few remnants of the old town fortifications can still be seen, including the moat and one of the city gates, the Westerntor. A tour of Schloss Adalbert gives several interesting insights into the changing demand for creature comforts through the ages.

About 7km (4 miles) from Wernigerode, towards the mountains, is the Steinerne Renne with a waterfall and Ottofelsen (Otto's Rock). The rock can be climbed with the aid of fixed steel ladders and offers some beautiful views from the top.

[i] *Nikolaiplatz*

FOR HISTORY BUFFS

When walking round Wernigerode, do not miss the house at No 95 Breite Strasse. Built in 1678, it is called Krell's Schmiede (Smithy), and above the door a horse's head juts out and horseshoes denote the nature of the occupant's trade. There has been a smithy here since the house was built.

SPECIAL TO...

The Harzquerbahn is a real old-time steam train which runs on narrow-gauge tracks from Wernigerode to Nordhausen, a distance of 60km (37 miles). The line was first opened on 27 March 1899, and it was hoped it would eventually run as far as Hamburg in the north and Vienna in the south.

▶ Take the **B244** south to Elbingerode and continue on the **B27** via Braunlage to Bad Lauterberg, 40km (25 miles).

❸ Bad Lauterberg,
Niedersachsen
It is worth considering a stop in Braunlage, before going on to Bad Lauterberg. This resort is one of the most developed in the Harz mountains. It is officially classified as a climatic health resort and offers a great variety of entertainment for all tastes. The sports-minded can take their pick of tennis, bowling, swimming, water gymnastics and skiing in winter, to name a few. The body conscious can visit the beauty studio or undergo a course of the Scarsdale diet, while the children can enjoy their favourite activities, and competitions are arranged for them in the Maritim Kinder Club (Maritime Children's Club). You can take a trip by cable-car to the top of the 971m (3,185-foot) Wurmberg (Worm Mountain) for fine views and to see the excavations of an ancient place of worship dating back to about 100BC. The Grosse Wurmbergstrasse (Great Wurmberg Road) can also be taken from Braunlage and leads along hairpin bends up to the mountain.

Bad Lauterberg is an officially classified health resort. There is no shortage of things to do here as the spa town is at the centre of an extensive network of nature walks, and its other great attraction is the Oderstausee, an artificial lake which offers a wide range of watersports facilities. Canoeing, rowing and sailing are all available on the 310m (1,016-foot) long stretch of water. On a more relaxed note, a chair lift operates rides up to the Hausberg, with views over Bad Lauterberg from the Burg-Restaurant.

[i] *Haus des Kurgastes*

▶ From Bad Lauterberg take the **B27/B243** west to Scharzfeld.

❹ Scharzfeld, Niedersachsen
The Steinkirche (Stone Church) in Scharzfeld is really a cave once used by prehistoric people as living quarters and then by early Germanic tribes for religious ceremonies. Later transformed into a church, the cave was still used as a place of worship well into the 16th century. Its former church bell is now housed in the local village church.

Another interesting cave near by is the 400m (1,310-foot) long Einhornhöhle (Unicorn Cave), noted for the skeleton of a prehistoric animal which was found here.

▶ Continue on the **B27/B243** for 4km (2 miles) to Herzberg.

❺ Herzberg, Niedersachsen
Herzberg's claim to fame is its timber-framed castle, formerly a hunting lodge and then seat of the local rulers. Built in 1510, it was the birthplace of Ernst August of Hannover, who later founded what was to become the English-Hanoverian royal dynasty.

[i] *Kurverwalthung, Marktplatz 30*

▶ Continue on the **B243** for 11km (7 miles) to Osterode.

❻ Osterode, Niedersachsen
The River Söse flows out of the Harz Mountains past the picturesque medieval town of Osterode. The main square, Kornmarkt (Grain Market), is edged with a collection of splendid historic buildings, including the Renaissance-style Englischer Hof dating from 1610. Near by is the renovated 16th-century Church of St Agidii; behind that the old Rathaus, built in 1552, stands together with the richly ornamented Ratswaage building, which once housed the official weights and measures office erected one year later.

The Heimatmuseum is located in the historical Ritterhaus (Knight's Hall), while the baroque Kornmagazin (Grain Warehouse) was built between 1719 and 1722. Since 1987 it has been used as the town council chambers. The nearby Sösetalsperre (Söse Dam) makes an interesting excursion. Drinking water from the dam is piped as far as Bremen, some 200km (124 miles) away. There is a very pleasant footpath that runs around the lake, with traffic restricted to the northern shore.

☐ *Eisensteinstrasse*

▶ *Take the B241 north for 29km (18 miles) to Clausthal-Zellerfeld.*

❼ Clausthal-Zellerfeld,
Niedersachsen

There are two towns rolled into one here, and each boasts its own particular highlight: the Oberharzer Museum at Zellerfeld, and the Protestant Marktkirche zum Heiligen Geist (Market Church of the Holy Ghost) in Clausthal.

After a serious fire in 1672, Zellerfeld was rebuilt along the lines of a chessboard. The Oberharzer Museum provides a historical overview of mining activities in the Harz region up until the 1930s. Most appropriately, there is a technical university located here with a noted traditional mining faculty.

Clausthal's Marktkirche has several unusual features. The building is totally constructed from timber, while inside, daylight is filtered through windows set at an angle, so creating an unusual perspective and a unique atmosphere. The altar dates back to 1641.

Side trips from Clausthal-Zellerfeld include the old silver mines which lie 8km (5 miles) to the north and date back to 1551. Also, a trip to nearby Bad Grund presents the opportunity to visit the Iberger Tropfstein-höhle (Iberger Caves). Discovered in 1874, the main cave is 150m (490 feet) long, and made up of a number of smaller caves, with the stalag-mites and stalactites mainly found in the upper sections.

☐ *Bahnhofstrasse 5a*

▶ *Continue north on the B241 for 18km (11 miles) back to Goslar.*

Immaculately renovated buildings in Osterode's main square

RECOMMENDED WALKS

The Harz region has more than 8,000km (5,000 miles) of hiking trails. The distinctly picturesque local term for them is Wanderwege, literally 'Wander Ways'. Drive from Wernigerode via Blankenburg to Thale. From Thale climb up to the Rosstrappe, which can also be reached by chair-lift. It is also possible to walk to the opposite side of the Bode Valley and scale the Hexentanzplatz (Dancing Place of the Witches) for another splendid view.

SCENIC ROUTES

The Harz Mountain region offers an abundance of scenic routes. The drive between Braunlage and Bad Lauterberg is particularly lovely. It is always useful to map out a circular drive, and there is a good circuit from Bad Lauterberg to St Andreasberg and back via Herzberg.
From Osterode you can take the scenic Deutsche Ferienstrasse (German Holiday Road) to Clausthal-Zellerfeld.

The Alps South
of München

The München (Munich) museums cover a dazzling range of displays: ancient Greek and Roman sculpture at the Glyptothek; vast international art collections at the Alte and Neue Pinakothek; and, at the Deutsches Museum, one of the most comprehensive science displays in the world.

2 DAYS • 288KM • 178 MILES

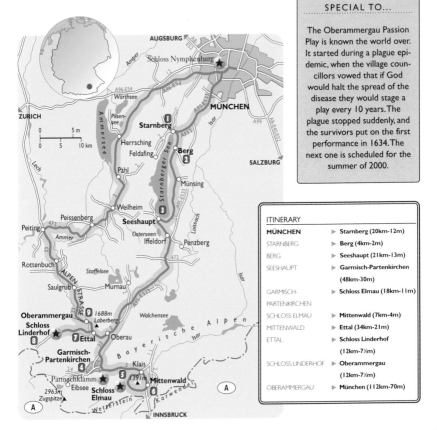

SPECIAL TO...

The Oberammergau Passion Play is known the world over. It started during a plague epidemic, when the village councillors vowed that if God would halt the spread of the disease they would stage a play every 10 years. The plague stopped suddenly, and the survivors put on the first performance in 1634. The next one is scheduled for the summer of 2000.

Ornately decorated façades grace the buildings in Mittenwald, set between two mountain ranges

⚊i⚊ *Sendlingerstrasse 1*

SPECIAL TO...

Munich's annual beer festival has to be mentioned, although it is very well advertised all around the world. The official title is Oktoberfest, but it takes place in the second half of September and ends at the beginning of October. Basically it is a popular carnival devoted to the consumption of large quantities of beer. Obviously, it is necessary to be in the right mood to enjoy this festival, and participants also need a good stomach!

▶ *From München take the A95 south, then take the exit for the A952 to Starnberg, 20km (12 miles).*

❶ **Starnberg,** Bayern

This is a very popular holiday resort, partly due to the excellent connections to and from München, and offers many leisure activities such as sailing, windsurfing, boating and diving. The adjoining villas, with their beautiful gardens, enhance the general holiday atmosphere around the lake.

The parish church of St Josef was built between 1764 and 1766 in the rococo style. The high altar built by Ignaz Günther is flanked by statues in white marble, and altogether the interior seems filled with light, no doubt enhanced by its position on top of a hill.

During the 16th and 17th centuries several 'playgrounds of the rich' developed in Europe, and Lake Starnberg claims to be one of the first. In 1663, the Elector Ferdinand invited 500 guests to attend a gondola party on the lake, with 100 oarsmen in charge of the boats. Nowadays there is a yacht harbour here, and more modest

---

FOR CHILDREN

A round trip by steamer on Lake Starnberg makes a pleasant outing for the whole family.

FOR HISTORY BUFFS

The former Austrian Empress Elisabeth, being Bavarian born, chose Feldafing on the western side of Lake Starnberg as her favourite summer retreat. Her former villa is now a luxury hotel bearing her name, and a commemorative statue stands in the hotel park.

---

sailing regattas take place during the summer. A Heimatmuseum (local museum) advises on local activities during the past and present, and a notable picture gallery features a selection of works by painters of the Romantic period.

⚊i⚊ *Kirchplatz 3*

▶ *Continue along the east side of the lake for 4km (2 miles) to the village of Berg.*

---

❷ **Berg,** Bayern

Berg is famous as the place where King Ludwig II met his tragic death. Having been certified insane and deprived of the throne, Ludwig was ordered to be taken to Schloss Berg and kept under medical supervision. An outing in a small rowing boat proved fatal for him and his doctor: both bodies were found by a search party, next to their boat, in shallow water. The exact circumstances of their deaths remain a mystery to this day. Ludwig had drained Bavaria's coffers in order to build the extravagant castles which are a monument to him. A cross in the Starnberg lake denotes the spot where the bodies were found, and a Memorial Chapel was built on the shores near by.

⚊i⚊ *Ratsgasse 1*

FOR HISTORY BUFFS

Every year on 13 June a service is held at the Votivkapelle in Berg in memory of the tragic death on that day of King Ludwig II in the lake near by.

▶ *Continue south along the lake for 21km (13 miles) to Seeshaupt.*

3 Seeshaupt, Bayern

Seeshaupt, on the southern end of the lake, is less crowded than the northern shores and is a good centre for exploring Osterseen, a group of tiny Ice Age lakes. It is of special interest to ornithologists because of the ideal nesting conditions in the tall reeds for many birds. Geologists will find the soil and rock formations of interest.

i *Weilheimerstrasse 1*

▶ *Turning south for 8km (5 miles), rejoin the A95 at Penzberg/Iffeldorf and proceed to Garmisch-Partenkirchen.*

The massive, snow-capped Zugspitze dwarfs the twin towns of Garmisch-Partenkirchen

4 Garmisch-Partenkirchen, Bayern

Two adjoining towns, united in a double name, are best known as the major German winter sports resort and host to the Winter Olympics of 1936. One of Germany's busiest resorts, it offers magnificent views of the surrounding mountain ranges, especially the massive Zugspitze, Germany's highest mountain – 2,963m (9,718 feet). King Ludwig's lodge is now a museum of local history. The German composer Richard Strauss lived here and met American troops when they occupied Garmisch-Partenkirchen at the end of World War II.

An excursion to the top of the Zugspitze should not be missed – first by cogwheel train to Eibsee, then by cable-car, or by a more leisurely route, continuing by train to Schneefernerhaus, followed by a short ride by cable-car to the top. The latter route avoids the very sudden change in altitude of about 2,000m (6,600 feet) in 10 minutes.

Glacier skiing is practised on the top all year round, and if you wish to venture into Austria, there is a tunnel link between the two countries, with windows cut into the rocks so that passengers are able to enjoy the views over the mountains on the way.

i *Dr Richard Strauss-Platz*

> From Garmisch turn east on the **B2** to Klais, 12km (7 miles) and then southwest on a toll road to Schloss Elmau.

5 Schloss Elmau, Bayern
Still owned by the family who built it during World War I, this stately home offers a sort of English house-party atmosphere with a mixture of cultural and intellectual pursuits on a residential basis for paying guests. Meals are taken communally, many of the staff are highly educated and guests can enjoy painting, music and dancing classes, concerts and music weeks, sometimes attended by famous musicians. A visit to the Schloss is worthwhile, even for day visitors who do not wish to stay. The feeling of space in the big halls and corridors, and the elegance of days gone by, are combined with modern comforts.

[i] Schlosshotel

> From Elmau drive about 7km (4 miles) southeast along the Lautersee to Mittenwald (toll road).

6 Mittenwald, Bayern
This name, which means 'in the middle of the woods', describes the beautiful surroundings of this health and winter sports resort, situated in a valley between two massive mountain ranges, the Karwendel and the Wetterstein.

The town flourished in the Middle Ages, when it was a staging point for trade between Venice and northern Europe, and reminders of this boom-time can still be found in the market-place. In 1684, Mathias Klotz founded the town's unique industry, which continues to this day: violins, violas, cellos, zithers and guitars are all made here, often using local wood. The descendants of Mathias Klotz continue the family business. The Geigenbau Museum and the Heimatmuseum offer more insights into local history and crafts. At the Geigenbau, it may even be a descendant of Mathias Klotz who demonstrates the art of violin-making.

Numerous excursions can be taken from Mittenwald. The western peak of the Karwendel Mountains can be reached by cable-car and offers a panorama of the Bavarian and Austrian Alps. Chair- and cabin-lifts take you to other peaks in the region.

[i] Kurdirektion, Dammkarstrasse 3

> From Mittenwald drive northwest to Klais, take the **B2** west to Garmisch, 12km (7 miles) and north to Oberau, 8km (5 miles), then turn left on the **B23** to Ettal.

7 Ettal, Bayern
Visitors are attracted to the Benedictine Abbey, a monastery founded in 1330 by the Holy Roman Emperor for his knights and monks. It is called 'Kloster', which means convent, although only monks live here. The Gothic building took 50 years to complete, and contains an enormous fresco 25m (82 feet) wide. Today, the abbey houses a school and the monks distil a special liqueur, called Klosterlikör, which is made from health-giving herbs in accordance with a centuries-old recipe, which is, of course, kept strictly secret.

[i] Ammergauerstrasse 8

> From Ettal continue west 12km (7 miles) to Schloss Linderhof.

Left: instrument-maker Mathias Klotz commemorated in Mittenwald
Below: Ettal Abbey

8 Schloss Linderhof,
Bayern

A charming, comparatively small castle built for Ludwig II, this is idyllically set, surrounded by woods, mountains and a small lake. The lavish interiors reflect the King's desire to emulate the grandeur of Louis XIV of France. The Hall of Mirrors is said to represent Ludwig's dream world. There is a collection of paintings portraying French celebrities during the reigns of Louis XIV and Louis XV. The extensive gardens are in harmony with the landscape, with waterfalls tumbling down rocks, fed by water from mountain streams. There is also a grotto dedicated to the goddess Venus and many fountains, dominated by the Neptune Fountain. This spouts out great jets of water into the air, rising higher than the top of the castle itself.

A Moorish pavilion was brought here straight from the Paris Exhibition of 1867.

▶ *From Schloss Linderhof return east for about 7km (4 miles), then take a left turn to Oberammergau.*

Schloss Linderhof, one of the castles built for Ludwig II

Detail of a decorated house in Oberammergau

9 Oberammergau, Bayern

Oberammergau is famous the world over for its Passion Plays, which have been performed since 1634, and in 10-year cycles since 1680. The houses in the main streets are decorated with colourful frescos showing that woodcarving is the local industry here. The Passion Play Theatre should be visited, even when no plays are taking place. The auditorium seats around 5,000 and the open-air stage has remarkable acoustics. Woodcarvers are at work at all times, and the variety of their products, mainly religious objects, can be seen in shop windows all over the town. The parish church was built by the famous Josef Schmuzer and the frescos are by Mathäus Günther.

Oberammergau also offers a variety of recreational facilities, including tennis, swimming, keep-fit, hang-gliding, canoeing and, of course, walks through the countryside. Or take the chair-lift to the Kolbensattel or the cable-lift to the Laberberg: both offer panoramic views over the countryside.

ℹ️ *Eugen Pabst Strasse 9a*

▶ *Take the B23 northwest to Peiting, and turn due east on the B472 to Peissenberg. After Peissenberg, take the left fork to Weilheim. Continue north on the B2 for about 8km (5 miles), then turn left for Pähl and the Ammersee. Drive along the eastern shore to Herrsching, then northeast along the Pilsensee for the A96 to München.*

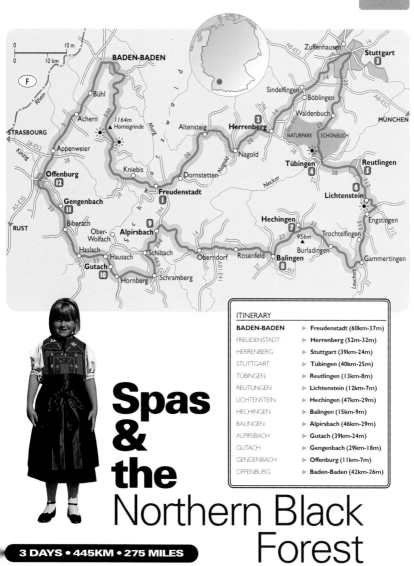

ITINERARY

BADEN-BADEN	▶ Freudenstadt (60km-37m)
FREUDENSTADT	▶ Herrenberg (52km-32m)
HERRENBERG	▶ Stuttgart (39km-24m)
STUTTGART	▶ Tübingen (40km-25m)
TÜBINGEN	▶ Reutlingen (13km-8m)
REUTLINGEN	▶ Lichtenstein (12km-7m)
LICHTENSTEIN	▶ Hechingen (47km-29m)
HECHINGEN	▶ Balingen (15km-9m)
BALINGEN	▶ Alpirsbach (46km-29m)
ALPIRSBACH	▶ Gutach (39km-24m)
GUTACH	▶ Gengenbach (29km-18m)
GENGENBACH	▶ Offenburg (11km-7m)
OFFENBURG	▶ Baden-Baden (42km-26m)

Spas & the
Northern Black
Forest

3 DAYS • 445KM • 275 MILES

Baden-Baden is one of Europe's top spas, its name denoting it as
the Baden (spa) of the province of Baden. The actual spa, the
Caracalla Therme, is today a luxurious complex. There is plenty to
do here if you like art and music. The Kunsthalle (Art Gallery) in the
Lichtentaler Allee, the Stadtmuseum and Brahmsmuseum in the
centre of the town speak for themselves, and there are seasonal
concerts and ballet performances as well as horse racing.

ⓘ Augustaplatz 8

▶ *From Baden-Baden take the **B500/B28** (Schwarzwald Hochstrasse) south for 60km (37 miles) to Freudenstadt.*

❶ Freudenstadt, Baden-Württemberg

Founded by Duke Friedrich von Württemberg as a silver-mining town in 1599, Freudenstadt was flattened by Allied bombs in 1945. The large square in the centre of town was part of the original plans drawn up by the duke, whose chess-board layout allowed all the houses around it and those in adjoining streets behind to be interconnected by passages.

The Stadthaus and Post Office are situated in the Marktplatz (Market Square), and the Protestant parish church takes up one corner. An interesting feature is the L-shaped nave which segregates men and women attending the same service.

On the opposite corner of the square, the Rathaus (Town Hall) tower affords superb views over the unique layout of the town and the surrounding country. Back at street level, take the time for a stroll through the charming shopping arcades built into the houses surrounding the square.

ⓘ Promenadenplatz 1

▶ *Take the **B28** northeast for 52km (32 miles) to Herrenberg.*

❷ Herrenberg, Baden-Württemberg

Herrenberg lies on the western border of the Naturpark Schönbuch and the 750-year-old Schlossbergturm (Castle Tower) gives a good view of the town, dominated by the Stiftskirche's mighty tower. The Gothic church, built between 1275 and 1294, features a 16th-century carved pulpit and a decorated choir section dating from 1517.

ⓘ Marktplatz 5

▶ *Follow the **B14** northeast for 39km (24 miles) to Stuttgart.*

❸ Stuttgart, Baden-Württemberg

Capital of the province of Baden-Württemberg, Stuttgart is situated at the bottom of a wide valley surrounded by hills, bordered to the northeast by the River Neckar and the adjoining town of Cannstatt.

Duke Liutolf set up a stud here in around 950. The town's name is derived from *Stute*, the German word for mare, and *Garten*, literally 'mare's garden'. The city's coat of arms bears a black horse.

The most impressive and important square in town is the Schlossplatz (Castle Square), across which the Altes Schloss (Old Castle) and the Neues Schloss (New Castle) face each other. The old castle is a massive Renaissance building, erected in the second half of the 16th century. The arcaded

The imposing castle buildings of Stuttgart, ranged around Schlossplatz (Castle Square)

SPECIAL TO...

A visit to the Daimler Benz Museum in Stuttgart-Untertürkheim is a must for motoring enthusiasts. Like Rolls and Royce, Daimler and Benz were – and the companies still are – pioneers in the development of motor vehicles. Exhibits range from the early days of motor transport right through to the most recent models, and modern demonstration techniques make this a fascinating visit. Another famous manufacturer, Porsche, is based at Zuffenhausen, just north of Stuttgart. The business was started here in 1931, and all Porsche models are pure sports and high-performance cars.

castle yard is particularly attractive and the castle houses the Landesmuseum collections of medieval artworks, Württemberg's crown jewels, examples of historic costumes and archaeological finds.

Adjoining the castle, Schillerplatz is notable for the historic buildings that surround it. There is the oldest church in Stuttgart, the Stiftskirche, which was founded in the 12th century; the Fruchtkasten, a wonderful medieval building of 1393; and the Prinzenbau (Dukes' Building), which was designed to contain the living quarters of the Erbprinz Friedrich Ludwig. At the centre of the square stands a monument to the poet Schiller.

Back on the Schlossplatz, the Neues Schloss was built along the lines of a French baroque castle between 1746 and 1807; it was all but destroyed in World War II. The façade was restored between 1959 and 1962, and the interior converted to house governmental offices as well as to host receptions.

The west side of the Schlossplatz borders Stuttgart's main thoroughfare. A pedestrian zone, it is lined with all the best shops and businesses.

ⓘ *Königstrasse 1a*

▶ *From Stuttgart take the **B27** south, via Waldenbuch, to Tübingen, 40km (25 miles).*

❹ **Tübingen,** Baden-Württemberg
There is a very good view of Tübingen's Altstadt (Old Town) from the Platanenallee on the right bank of the River Neckar. The Old Town rises steeply from the Neckar, sandwiched between the castle hill and the Osterberg's tower.

In Holzmarkt (Timber Market) the late Gothic Stiftskirche is a Protestant church dating from the 15th century. It houses several beautifully decorated tombs created for members of the House of Württemberg. When Goethe

visited the church, he was so impressed by the stained-glass windows, he described them as 'items of supreme glory'.

The 15th-century Rathaus (Town Hall) is a really magnificent building on the market square. Its astronomical clock was added in 1511. The Neptune market fountain in front of the 15th-century Rathaus was erected in 1615 and the whole market square is surrounded by marvellous medieval houses.

ⓘ *Neckarbrücke (Ebershardsbrücke)*

▶ *Take the **B28** east for 13km (8 miles) to Reutlingen.*

❺ **Reutlingen,** Baden-Württemberg
Reutlingen's Tübinger Tor (gate) is one of the old city gateways built in the 13th century. Its timber-framed upper storey was added in the 16th century to provide a better lookout and it somehow survived the great fire of 1726. Another architectural landmark is the Marienkirche, a particularly beautiful example of early Gothic style. The Holy

Sepulchre in the choir section is late Gothic.

The main artery of the town is Wilhelmstrasse, a pedestrian precinct, ideal for strolling along and admiring the interesting architecture. The Nikolaikirche overlooks a charming fountain erected by the tanners' and dyers' guild, while the mighty Spendhaus, built in 1518, now houses the town library and natural history museum.

ⓘ *Lisztplatz 1*

▶ *From Reutlingen take the **B312** south to Lichtenstein.*

An impressive view of Tübingen, its fine old houses ranged along the bank of the River Neckar

---

FOR HISTORY BUFFS

Three beautiful 16th-century fountains can be admired in Reutlingen: the Lindenbrunnen, erected in 1544; the Kirchbrunnen, with a statue of Emperor Friedrich II, built in 1561; and the 1570 Marktbrunnen, adorned by a statue of Maximilian II.

A Black Forest house in the Freilichtmuseum Vogtsbauernhof

6 Lichtenstein, Baden-Württemberg

In the heart of the mountainous Swabian Jura, three villages joined together to form the town of Lichtenstein. In 1826, author Wilhelm Hauff published *Lichtenstein*, a novel about the town's old fortress which had been demolished in 1802. This novel inspired Count Wilhelm von Württemberg to make plans for a new castle to be built on the same spot, and so the present edifice took shape from 1840 to 1842. It looks like an image from a fairy-tale and the design must have been influenced by Hauff's works.

Following a scramble up to the belvederes above the castle, there is an excellent detour to be made to the Nebelhöhle cave in nearby Unterhausen. The main part of the cave complex was discovered in 1920 and a 380m (1,246-foot) long walkway has been constructed for easy access. The view of the stalagmites and stalactites is superb and brilliantly enhanced by clever illuminations.

ⓘ *Bürgermeisteramt, Rathausplatz 17*

▶ *From Lichtenstein take the B313 south for 21km (13 miles) to Gammertingen, then the B32 for 26km (16 miles) to Hechingen.*

7 Hechingen, Baden-Württemberg

From fairy-tale castle to historic fortress, the imposing Burg Hohenzollern, seat of the kings of Prussia, perches on an 856m (2,808-foot) rocky outcrop. Plans for the old fortress were used for the new building, constructed between 1850 and 1867, but only the 15th-century Catholic Chapel of St Michael remains from the original site. The fortress treasury contains memorabilia of Friedrich der Grosse (the Great), decorations and insignia belonging to Wilhelm II, the crown of the Prussian kings and many works of art. On the Schlossplatz (Castle Square), the Altes Schloss (Old Castle), former seat of the dukes of Hechingen, now houses the local Heimatmuseum.

In 1976 the ruins of a Roman villa were discovered about 3km (1¾ miles) northwest of Hechingen. The excavated remains date back to the 1st to 3rd centuries AD and parts of the villa have been reconstructed.

ⓘ *Marktplatz 1*

▶ *From Hechingen take the B27 for 15km (9 miles) to Balingen.*

8 Balingen, Baden-Württemberg

Balingen's Protestant parish church is found in the market square. It was erected between 1443 and 1516, and the ceiling of the pulpit and the crucifix are the work of local sculptor Simon Schweitzer. Also of interest is the chapel in the cemetery which is decorated with late Gothic wall paintings. An attractive corner of town is the 'Little Venice' district, so named for the millstream which flows down past the old tanneries and remnants of the city wall.

The Waagenmuseum (Scales Museum) pays tribute to local priest M P Hahn, who invented a simple scale that could be used in the home, a precursor of the more modern appliances.

ⓘ *Neue Strasse 33*

▶ *From Balingen continue due west via Oberndorf to Alpirsbach.*

9 Alpirsbach, Baden-Württemberg

The abbey church of the former Benedictine Kloster Alpirsbach dates back to the 12th century. The basilica, with its three naves, has undergone several enlargements and attempts at restoration, but has remained largely intact. South of the church are the cloister buildings where international orchestras perform in summer. The candlelit surroundings and excellent acoustics create an unforgettable atmosphere.

i *Kurverwalthung Hauptstrasse 20*

▶ *Take the B294 south to Schiltach and continue on the B462 to Schramberg. Turn right to Hornberg, then right again on the B33 to Gutach.*

10 Gutach, Baden-Württemberg

North of Gutach, sited on the Hausach road, the Freilicht-museum Vogtsbauernhof is a fascinating open-air museum illustrating life in the Black Forest. Typical 16th- and 17th-century houses have been re-created with original furnishings and traditional artefacts and utensils to give the visitor a real insight into local lifestyles in former times. There are even old water-powered saw-mills shown in full working order. A monument to the 'Mourning

Lady of Gutach' is a popular subject for snapshots. It portrays a grieving girl in front of a small rock, crying for those lost in the wars.

i *Bahnhof Bleibach*

▶ *Take the B33 north, then west via Hausach for 29km (18 miles) to Gengenbach.*

11 Gengenbach, Baden-Württemberg

Gengenbach fulfils all one's expectations of a small, romantic German town. It has been placed under a preservation order and its timber-framed houses, gates and towers linked by sections of the old walls exude a timeless charm. There is a remarkable market-place edged by the Rathaus (Town Hall) built in 1784, the Kauf-und Kornhaus of 1696 and numerous well-preserved 17th-to 18th-century patrician houses.

i *Winzerhof*

▶ *From Gengenbach continue northwest for 11km (7 miles) to Offenburg.*

12 Offenburg, Baden-Württemberg

Offenburg lies on the outskirts of the Black Forest, between sloping vineyards and the plains of the Rhine Valley. The Marktplatz is the centre of the town, bordered by the Rathaus (Town Hall), which was built in 1741. Northwest of Marktplatz, the interior of the Heilige Kreuzkirche (Church of the Holy Cross) is dominated by an imposing high altar. Other historic sights include the Fischmarkt (Fish Market), St Andreas' Kirche, the Löwen-brunnen (Lion Fountain) and the Hirschapotheke (Pharmacy).

i *Gärtnerstrasse 6 (west of Marktplatz)*

▶ *Return to Baden-Baden on the B3, 42km (26 miles).*

BACK TO NATURE

Almost anywhere in the Schwarzwald is a good habitat for birds. Look for wood-peckers, collared flycatchers, Bonelli's warblers and red kites. Plants include coralroot orchids and yellow wood violets.

RECOMMENDED WALKS

The Black Forest region is well-organised and provides a staggering number of suggestions for walks, plus maps and information including the approximate duration of each route. Local information offices usually provide village maps and many offer to introduce visitors to the innovative Wandern Ohne Gepäck (hiking without luggage) concept. Certain villages and small hotels co-operate in the scheme by transporting your luggage from one stop to the next.

FOR CHILDREN

The Europa Park at Rust is one of the largest and most successful amusement parks in Europe. To get there, drive south from Offenburg on the A5 in the direction of Lahr, then take the Ettenheim exit, or the B3, the Badische Weinstrasse, through the vine-yards south to Ringshein and turn west to Rust. A trip on the suspended monorail around the grounds gives a good overall view of what is in store. Children will enjoy Chocoland, a so-called 'choco-late laboratory', where they can make their own chocolates. Other attractions include wild torrent rides, trips on the Swiss Bobsleigh, Acapulco 'death divers', high-wire acts and dolphin and sea-lion performances.

SCENIC ROUTES

The Schwarzwald Hochstrasse (Black Forest High Road) from Baden-Baden to Freudenstadt skirts the rim of the hills and mountains and runs through magnificent scenery. There are numerous opportunities for scenic drives in the Black Forest region, not just on the Hochstrasse, but remember when planning a trip it can take rather longer to drive these winding roads than the actual distances would suggest.

The River Main
& East of the Rhine

Heavily bombed during the war, Frankfurt re-created itself as an ultra-modern city. The centre does, however, feature a restored baroque-style building, the Hauptwache, and other old buildings include the Römer (1405), the 15th-century Eschenheimer Turm (tower) and the Dom (cathedral) of St Bartholomaus (1290).

2 DAYS • 393KM • 245 MILES

ITINERARY	
FRANKFURT	▶ **Hanau** (21km-13m)
HANAU	▶ **Bad Homburg** (35km-22m)
BAD HOMBURG	▶ **Kronberg** (8km-5m)
KRONBERG	▶ **Limburg** (40km-25m)
LIMBURG	▶ **Königswinter** (95km-58m)
KÖNIGSWINTER	▶ **Bad Honnef** (4km-2m)
BAD HONNEF	▶ **Lahnstein** (51km-32m)
LAHNSTEIN	▶ **St Goarshausen** (28km-17m)
ST GOARSHAUSEN	▶ **Assmannshausen** (25km-16m)
ASSMANNSHAUSEN	▶ **Rüdesheim** (6km-4m)
RÜDESHEIM	▶ **Mainz** (29km-18m)
MAINZ	▶ **Wiesbaden** (13km-8m)
WIESBADEN	▶ **Frankfurt** (40km-25m)

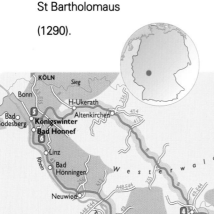

BACK TO NATURE

The Enkheimer Marsh near Frankfurt is an excellent spot for wildfowl, herons and waders, as are Westerwald and Vogelsberg lakes. In particular, look for greylag geese, black terns, bitterns, grey herons, redskank and pochard.

▶ *From Frankfurt take the A66 east for 21km (13 miles) to Hanau.*

❶ Hanau, Hessen

Hanau is the beginning of the German 'Fairy Tale Road', and the birthplace of the Brothers Grimm. Apart from their universally known stories, the chief trade is gold – master goldsmiths have worked here for centuries. The Goldschmiedehaus (House of the Goldsmiths) is an unsual timber-framed structure with a large gabled roof typical of this architectural style. The entrance is through an outside staircase to a raised ground floor, for security reasons. Inside, there are international exhibi-

tions of jewellery from the past and present. It also houses the oldest German college for metalworking.

The Schloss Phillipsruhe (castle) near Hanau functions as a museum for works of art, and the entrance gate is a creation in wrought iron from Paris. There are many objects relating to Hanau porcelain manufacture, brought here by Dutch refugees from religious persecution.

Schloss Steinheim, built between the 13th and the 16th centuries with a mighty belfry, houses a museum exhibiting objects of pre- and early history, from the Stone Age up to Roman times.

ⓘ *Markt 14*

▶ *Take the A66 west back towards Frankfurt and turn right for the A661 north to Bad Homburg, 35km (22 miles).*

❷ Bad Homburg, Hessen

Bad Homburg is a modern spa with a Roman history in the Taunus mountain range. The restored Römerkastell (Roman Fort) at Saalburg is about 5km (3 miles) north and has been restored to its original design. It was part of the Roman Limes

The Brömserburg, a 10th-century castle-turned-wine museum overlooking the Rhine in Rüdesheim

fortification line, and formed the northern frontier of the Roman Empire. The museum inside allows an interesting glimpse back to Roman times. The original fort was built in AD120, and could accommodate a contingent of 500 soldiers. The inside looks as though the Romans had just left it: catapults, armouries, shops, houses, temples and baths are all there.

The Schloss (castle) in its present form was built between 1680 and 1685 on the same spot as an older fortress. The medieval fortress is remembered only by one surviving tower, called the Weisse Turm (White Tower). The castle was the residence of the Counts of Hesse-Homburg and later the summer residence of the Prussian Emperor Wilhelm II. The Schloss is open to the public, with valuable paintings and furniture from the 17th and 18th centuries. The Schlosspark is well cared for and has some exotic plants.

A curiosity to visit in the centre of Bad Homburg is the Siamtemple, donated by a Siamese king in gratitude for a successful cure at the spa. There is also a Russian chapel, and no less than seven health-giving springs in the attractively named Brunnenallee (Alley of the Springs).

[i] *Louisenstrasse 58*

FOR HISTORY BUFFS

In Bad Homburg there are mementoes of the famous men and women who visited this spa in its heyday. These include King Edward VII, Emperor Wilhelm II of Prussia, the Russian writer Dostoevsky and the last Tsarina of Russia, who, before her marriage, had been a Princess of Hessen.

▶ *Turn south to Oberursel and west to Kronberg on the* **B455**.

3 Kronberg, Hessen
On a rock in the middle of the town stands the fortress of the Knights of Kronberg, which dates from 1220. The town has been popular with painters because of its picturesque winding streets and timber-framed houses. In the 19th century the town became the home of the Kronberger school of artists, thus making its contribution to German art.

[i] *Katharinenstrasse 7*

▶ *From Kronburg drive west to Königstein, and turn right for the* **B8** *to Limburg, 40km (25 miles).*

FOR CHILDREN

The Opel Zoo, near Kronberg, has elephants, apes, giraffes, zebras and camels, with other exotic and indigenous animals. Altogether over 950 species are kept here. Play areas and a special petting zoo attract children. Camel riding is also on offer.

---

4 Limburg, Hessen
On the way to Limburg, the ruins of Falkenstein and Königstein make good stopping places. Königstein is also an interesting old town, with the Altes Rathaus (Old Town Hall) now housing the museum.

In the valley of the River Lahn, Limburg is an attractive medieval town with a cathedral dating from the 13th century, a masterpiece in late Romanesque style with seven towers. Inside, its original colours have been restored, and 13th-century frescos revealed. This restoration work was completed in 1973, and the visitor is given a unique flavour of a real medieval cathedral.

The Domschatz (Treasury) is located in the bishop's residence and exhibits sacred works of art which also have great historic value. Special mention should be made of the Staurothek, a cross created by Byzantine craftsmen in the second half of the 10th century and the gem of the collection.

In the centre of the old town, around the fish market, are many timber-framed houses, among them the Rathaus (Town Hall). Another building from 1296, claimed to be the oldest timber-framed house in Germany, is still lived in.

[i] *Hospitalstrasse 2*

▶ *Head northwest on the* **A8** *for 68km (42 miles), then take the road leading west to Königswinter.*

5 Königswinter, Nordrhein-Westfalen
Königswinter lies on the banks of the Rhine, and one of the most popular ruins in this area is the fortress Drachenfels, which was destroyed in 1634. There are several ways of getting up there to enjoy the wide view over the Rhine Valley and the countryside around: on foot, by donkey, by horse-drawn carriage or by cogwheel railway. The walk takes about half an hour, the railway eight minutes.

[i] *Drachenfelsstrasse 11*

▶ *Take the* **B42** *south for 4km (2 miles) to reach Bad Honnef.*

6 Bad Honnef, Nordrhein-Westfalen
Bad Honnef is a spa town offering mineral springs, a 30°C (86°F) swimming pool and a modern therapeutic institution. A visit is also recommended to the parish church of St Johann, which dates from the 12th century. In the section of town known as Rhöndorf there stands a memorial to Konrad Adenauer, the well-known German statesman.

[i] *Hauptstrasse 28a*

▶ *Continue on the* **B42** *for 51km (32 miles) to Lahnstein.*

7 Lahnstein, Rheinland-Pfalz
Lahnstein lies on twin sites at the meeting of the rivers Lahn and Rhine. The left bank is called the Oberlahnstein, with Niederslahnstein opposite. Near Oberlahnstein, on a hill above the Rhine stands the fortified castle of Burg Lahneck, erected in the 13th century and typifying the charm of the Rhine Valley. The interior furnishings and decorations are remarkable. There are attractive views from the castle down to the Rhine, but the best view of the castle and its setting can be obtained down below from the Alte Lahnbrucke.

In Niederlahnstein, there remain a few of the old manor houses which belonged to the aristocracy, as well as the Wirthaus an der Lahn (Inn on the Lahn), which features in many German songs.

The colourful riverside town of St Goarshausen, guarded by its brooding fortress, Katz

i Stadthallenpassage

▶ *From Lahnstein continue on the B42 south for 28km (17 miles) to St Goarshausen.*

8 St Goarshausen,
Rheinland-Pfalz
This is also known as Loreleystadt (town of Lorelei) because of its proximity to the famous rock known as the Loreley Rock.

Above the town stands the fortress Katz, crowning the rock on which it was built by the Counts of Katzenelnbogen. They controlled this area and the traffic on the Rhine through strategically sited fortresses, exacting what they believed to

be their 'dues' from the passing ships. The fortress was constructed around the end of the 14th century and following its destruction rebuilt in 1806. It is not open to the public.

i Bahnhofstrasse 8

▶ *Continue on the B42 south for 25km (16 miles) to Assmannshausen.*

9 Assmannshausen, Hessen
The route passes the Loreley Rock, 132m (433 feet) high. In German legend, various stories are told about the attractive Rhine maiden, the Loreley, who sits on her rock and lures passing ships to disaster.

There are not many districts in Germany which produce red wine, but Assmannshausen is known for its blue Burgundy grapes, which produce an excel-

Taverns jostle for space in Drosselgasse, a busy gathering place in Rüdesheim

lent red. East of the town, in Niederwald, stands a monument to German unity. The figure of *Germania* which stands on top of the monument is 10m (33 feet) high and brandishes a 7m (22-foot) long sword in one of her hands.

▶ Continue on the **B42** south for 6km (4 miles) to Rüdesheim.

RECOMMENDED WALKS

Take the cable-car from Rüdesheim and ride over the vineyards to the hilltop. Very pleasant walks through the vineyards lead down to the valley and the town.

---

10 Rüdesheim, Hessen

In this wine centre on the banks of the Rhine, Drosselgasse, in the heart of town, is a popular meeting place with one tavern after another, and entertainment and music which go on until the early hours of the morning. The Brömserburg, a castle dating back to the 10th century, is now an important wine museum. The Adlerturm (Eagle's Tower) is a remnant of the town's 15th-century fortifications. It is only 20m (66 feet) high, but the walls are 1m (3 feet) thick. A cable-car travels to the Niederwald monument.

ℹ️ Rheinstrasse 16

▶ Continue on the **B42** towards Wiesbaden, turn right at Schierstein Kreuz for the **A643** and left for Mainz over the Rhine.

11 Mainz, Rheinland-Pfalz

The cathedral of Mainz is not far from the banks of the Rhine. The St Martins Dom, as it is called, belongs to a group of Romanesque cathedrals which show the mastery of German religious architecture in the Middle Ages. This enormous building project began in AD975. The western part of the cathedral is meant to symbolise the spiritual world. After several fires the cathedral was finished in 1239. Throughout the centuries it has been used for coronations and banquets, to house soldiers during the Thirty Years' War, and as a hospital for Napoleon's troops.

The Kurfürstliche Schloss (Electoral Palace) was finished in 1678 and now houses collections of the Römisch-Germanisches Zentralmuseum (Romano-German Central Museum). The history of Mainz

goes back to a Roman stronghold called *Monguntiacum*, near a former Celtic settlement.

ℹ️ Bahnhofstrasse 15

▶ From Mainz proceed to the ring road and drive north across the Rhine to Wiesbaden, 13km (8 miles).

12 Wiesbaden, Hessen

On the right bank of the Rhine, between the foothills of the Taunus mountain range and the river, lies Wiesbaden, capital of the province of Hessen. The Romans first discovered the healing spring here, and called it *Aquae Mattiacorum*, after the Germanic tribe resident here. It probably became a Roman fort between AD41 and 50, was abandoned in 406 and taken over by the Franconians, who made it a local capital. The name of Wiesbaden is first recorded as Wisbada in AD829, German for 'bath in the meadows'.

Its real prosperity grew in the 19th century, when the rich and famous of Europe rediscovered the hot springs and their healthful properties. The English had a special liking for the spa, even building their own church here in 1863. Wiesbaden was also the summer home of Emperor Wilhelm II, and its popularity peaked around the turn of the century. The Wilhelmstrasse, the town's elegant main street, recalls those affluent days.

ℹ️ Ecke Wilhelm/Rheinstrasse 15

▶ From Wiesbaden take the **A66** for 40km (25 miles) back to Frankfurt-am-Main.

SCENIC ROUTES

The route from Bad Homburg to Königswinter is particularly beautiful, while the delightful scenery from St Goarshausen along the Rhine is enhanced by the numerous castles and ruins on the hills, and the more graceful traffic of the river.

on the road

ITALY

Italy is at the heart of Europe's culture. From the canals of Venice and the splendours of Rome to the whitewashed hilltowns of Umbria and glorious art treasures of Florence, the cradle of the Renaissance, Italy offers an embarrassment of riches.

Tour 28

This region covers one of the most popular parts of the Italian Peninsula. From the flat plain of the Po river to the alpine region of the Dolomites and the marshy lagoons around Venice, the Veneto is a varied region. But its reputation has more to do with art and architecture, particularly of the Renaissance, than culi-

Page 171: top – typical tiled roof and window detail; bottom – delightful vineyard in the Chianti region of Tuscany

nary activities and geography. Its hills and southern plain are filled with towns and villages whose past affinities with Venice are acknowledged usually by an ancient stone-carved lion of St Mark – the Venetian symbol – placed conspicuously in the centre of town.

Even the cultural activities of this great city spread to the remotest corners of the Veneto: the churches and museums of the province are filled with masterpieces of Venetian art.

Tour 29

North of the industrial centre of Milan lie a number of great lakes, all long and narrow, amidst the foothills of the Alps. The inhabitants are the industrious descendants of former invaders from northern Europe, who were attracted by the gentle and fertile countryside and its wealth. Olive oil and wine are amongst the agricultural produce of the region and count amongst Italy's best. Many old palaces and villas on the lakesides contain famous works of art in ideal medieval surroundings. An abundance of museums witnesses the region's glorious past.

Milan, the capital of Lombardy, is also the economic capital of Italy, and is unquestionably northwest Italy's major art centre. The duomo (cathedral) is the most srtiking example of northern Italian Gothic architecture that you will see anywhere.

Tour 30

As the mountain range called the Appenines sweeps down towards Firenze (Florence), much of the countryside is folded into hills and valleys which hide villages and castles, known only to a few. This area is part of the northeast of Toscana. By contrast, the Chianti region, which produces Italy's most famous wine, and located between Fireneze and Siena, is imensely popular and is a fixture on most traveller's itineraries. Here the lie of the land is gentler with more rounded hills covered with olive groves and vineyards. Here trails of cypresses can be found climbing the hills, or running along their spines towards ancient terracotta-coloured farmhouses and Renaissance castles.

Firenze is Tuscany's capital and the undisputed centre of the art of the Renaissance. In its heart, the Piazza del Duomo, is the great duomo (cathedral), crammed with paintings, sculptures and frescos by early masters, and the baptistery, a strange little building in green-and-white marble with its famous and much-imitated 15th-century sculpted bronze doors by Ghiberti. From the art in the Galleria degli Uffizi (Uffizi Gallery) to the numerous notable churches and palaces and the antique shops, boutiques, markets and restaurants, Florence's reputation rests on the fact that it can offer everything that is best about Italy.

A face from the past: the Museo Capitolino in Rome

Tour 31

Umbria is remarkably undervisited. It is green and fertile, a land of saints and artists, a gentle region whose towns have on the whole been left alone by the march of progress. It is the Appenines, the mountainous backbone of Italy, that are responsible for the region's varied scenery. They continue their southward march from Firenze towards Perugia, the capital of Umbria, becoming more and more rugged as they approach the region of the Marches.

Perugia was a flourishing commercial centre in the Middle Ages, and the major buildings in its centre – the duomo, the Palazzo dei Priori and the Corso Vannucci lined with fortified palaces (now shops and cafés) – date from this period or shortly after. The narrow cavernous back streets contribute to this old world character. In addition, Perugia has the region's finest paintings in the Galleria Nazionale dell'Umbria in the Palazzo dei Priori.

Tour 32

Since the early days the wealthy Romans have had the desire to leave the city, especially in summer, when the heat becomes unbearable. Fortunately not far away to the east is the Abruzzo region, where Roman Emperor

Hadrian selected his country retreat at Tivoli. Later, in medieval times, the powerful clergy also favoured the area and constructed villas which could be more accurately called palaces. The Popes developed their retreat out of a ducal palace dating back to the 12th century at Gandalfo, southeast of Rome. The port of Ostia on the shores of the Mediterranean Sea now provides relaxation for the masses at the Lido di Ostia. Many buildings there document connections with ancient Rome.

The ancient capital of the Roman Empire (and now the capital of Italy) was built on seven hills – the Palatine, Capitoline, Esquiline, Viminal, Caelian, Aventine and Quirinal. Much of its ancient structure survives; you could easily spend a week just visiting the ruins of such imperial splendours as the Colosseum, the Forum and the Baths of Caracallà.

Tour 33

Puglia forms the spur and heel of the boot of Italy and the terrain is mostly gentle and flat, with greater areas of cultivation (wheat, tobacco, vegetables, grapes and olives are all grown). Some of the region's ports are the busiest in Italy, with regular ferries to Greece and the Dalmatian coast. It bustles with life, and while the southern Italian coastline is attractive, with sheer cliffs plunging into the sea, it is still little geared to tourism.

Bari, Puglia's capital, consists of an old quarter – the Città Vecchia – which lies nearest the sea and has medieval buildings in its labyrinth of streets. The city contains some of the most magnificent buildings in the region, most notably the Romanesque cathedral, the castle and the great basilica of San Nicola, founded in the 11th century by the Normans.

173

BANKS

Usual banking hours are 8.30am–1.30pm and 3/3.30pm–4/4.30pm Monday to Friday. Check locally as times vary in the afternoon from bank to bank. All banks are closed at weekends and on national holidays. On weekdays, evenings and holidays money can be changed at main railway stations and airports.

CREDIT CARDS

All principal credit cards are accepted by most establishments, but not petrol stations.

CURRENCY

The unit of currency is the lira (plural lire). Notes are issued in denominations of 1,000, 2,000, 5,000, 10,000, 20,000, 50,000 and 100,000 lire. Coins are issued in denominations of 5, 10, 20, 50, 100, 200 and 500 lire. You will find lire is abbreviated to 'L' in shops.

CUSTOMS

See **Austria** (page 10).

ELECTRICITY

See **Austria** (page 10).

EMERGENCY TELEPHONE NUMBERS

Fire, police and ambulance tel: 113.

ENTRY REGULATIONS

See **Austria** (page 10).

HEALTH MATTERS

See **Austria** (page 10).

MOTORING
Documents

Visitors must be at least 18 years of age, and in possession of the vehicle's registration document, an international green card or other insurance, and a valid, full driving licence. A green UK or red Republic of Ireland licence is acceptable in Italy provided it is accompanied by an official Italian translation, available free from ACI affiliated motoring clubs or from agents of the Italian State Tourist Office. The translation is not required for holders of the pink EU-type UK or Republic of Ireland licence.

Route directions

Throughout this section the following abbreviations are used for Italian roads:
A – Autostrada (motorway)
SS – Strada Statale (state road)
Dir, ter, bis, q, qu – suffixes to state roads (SS) relating to links and extensions of major roads minor roads – unnumbered roads.

Breakdowns

In case of breakdown dial 116 at the nearest telephone box. Tell the operator where you are, the registration number and type of car; the nearest ACI office will be informed for immediate assistance. The use of a warning triangle is compulsory in the event of an accident or breakdown. It must be placed on the road not less than 50m (55 yards) behind the vehicle. Motorists who fail to do this are liable to an administrative fine.

Accidents

In the event of an accident, a report must be made to the insurance company. If the accident involves personal injury, medical assistance must be sought for the injured party, and the incident reported to the police. On some autostrada there are emergency telephones as well as emergency push-button call boxes.

Speed limits

In built-up areas 50kph (31mph); outside built-up areas 90kph (56mph); on motorways 130kph (81mph). For cars towing a caravan or trailer the speed limits are 50kph (31mph), 80kph (49mph) and 100kph (62mph) respectively.

Driving conditions

Vehicles must keep to the right-hand side of the road or street and close to the nearside kerb, even when the road is clear. Side mirrors are compulsory on the left-hand side of the car, also for right-hand drive vehicles. The wearing of seat belts is compulsory.

Car hire

Car hire is available in most cities and resorts. Rates generally include breakdown service, maintenance and oil, but not petrol. Basic insurance is also included but additional cover is available at fixed rates. Most firms require a deposit equal to the estimated cost of hire. Some firms restrict hire to drivers over 21 years of age. Generally you must have had a valid driving licence for at least one year before applying for car hire.

POST OFFICES

Post offices are open 8.15am–12.30pm Monday to Friday and 8.15am–noon on Saturday. On the last day of the month offices close at noon. Times vary from place to place.

PUBLIC HOLIDAYS

1 January – New Year's Day
6 January – Epiphany
Easter Monday
25 April – Liberation Day (1945)
1 May – Labour Day
2 June – Proclamation of Republic (celebrated on following Saturday)
15 August – Ferragosto (Assumption)
1 November – All Saints
8 December – Immaculate Conception
25–26 December – Christmas

TELEPHONES

Some phones still take tokens called *gettone* which cost 200 lire each and can be purchased at post offices, tobacconists, some bars or slot machines. It is much

Boats at rest in Sorrento harbour

easier to use a *carta telefonica* (a pre-paid telephone card) which you buy at the same outlets. They have a value of either 5,000 or 10,000 lire and can be used for international calls. Call boxes also take 200 and 500 lire coins which you insert before lifting the receiver. The dialling tone is short and long tones. To call abroad, first dial 00, then the country code, followed by the city code and the number itself. The prefix for the UK is 0044; Eire 00353; US and Canada 001; and Australia 00 61. If you wish to make a reverse charge or person-to-person call you will need to go through the operator – dial 15 for European countries or 170 for elsewhere.

TIME

Local standard time is one hour ahead of Greenwich Mean Time (GMT). Italian Summer Time (when clocks go forward an hour) is in operation from the last weekend of March to the last weekend of September. The time is one hour ahead of Britain except for a few weeks from late September to late October when the time is the same.

TOURIST OFFICES

The Italian State Tourist Office (ENIT) is represented in the following countries:

Australia and New Zealand: c/o Alitalia, AGC House, 124 Phillip Street, Sydney, New South Wales (tel: 02 221 3620)

Canada: 1 Place Ville Marie, Suite 2414, Montreal 113, Quebec H3B 3M9 (tel: 514 866 7667)

UK: 1 Princes Street, London W1R 8AY (tel: 0171 408 1254)

US: 630 Fifth Avenue, Suite 1565, New York 10111 (tel: 212–397 5294).

USEFUL WORDS

The following is a list of useful words and phrases.

English	Italian
yes	si
no	no
please	per favore
thank you	grazie
good morning	buon giorno
good afternoon or evening	buona sera
small	piccolo
large	grande
quickly	presto
hot	caldo
cold	freddo
good	buono
do you speak English?	parla Inglese?
open	aperto
closed	chiuso
near	vicino
far	lontano
on the left	a sinistra
on the right	a destra
straight ahead	diritto
how much?	quanto?
expensive	caro

The Gentle
Veneto

This tour takes you through one of the most popular parts of the Italian peninsula. If travellers are not chasing the memory of a famous writer or painter, they are in search of the sublime beauty of Venice and its islands. Asolo, where the tour begins, claims Robert Browning as its most famous inhabitant. From Asolo you can visit the Renaissance villas among the vineyards that produce some of Italy's most characteristic white wines.

3 DAYS • 274KM • 170 MILES

ITINERARY		
ASOLO	▶	**Possagno (12km-7m)**
POSSAGNO	▶	**Feltre (31km-19m)**
FELTRE	▶	**Conegliano (56km-35m)**
CONEGLIANO	▶	**Treviso (28km-17m)**
TREVISO	▶	**Venézia (31km-19m)**
VENÉZIA	▶	**Murano (4km-2m)**
MURANO	▶	**Burano (6km-4m)**
BURANO	▶	**Torcello (3km-2m)**
TORCELLO	▶	**Venézia (return)**
		(13km-8m)
VENÉZIA	▶	**Castelfranco Véneto**
		(66km-41m)
CASTELFRANCO	▶	**Asolo (24km-15m)**
VÉNETO		

▶ *From Asolo going north, follow the signs to Possagno.*

FOR HISTORY BUFFS

You cannot go on this tour and not visit at least one villa designed by the great architect Andrea Palladio. His designs, based on the architectural principles of the ancient world, were immensely influential throughout Europe and in the United States. Indeed, this influence is apparent in neo-classical buildings built even in the present century.
The Villa Barbaro at Maser, about 10km (6 miles) east of Asolo, is the very best of his houses. Still a private residence, it has fabulous frescos by Veronese, as well as original furnishings and lovely gardens. There are other villas; in fact you could go on a special villa route, seeing most of them.

❶ Possagno, Veneto
The first thing you will notice about Possagno is the huge mausoleum, the Tempio, of the sculptor Canova, who died here in 1822. You can see this building for miles around. It sits on a hill overlooking the town with the snow-covered heights of Mount Grappa looming behind it. Designed by Canova himself, the Tempio is based on the Pantheon in Rome. Canova's house is not far away, at the bottom of a wide straight road leading down from the Tempio. His rooms are preserved in the pretty courtyard house, now partly an art gallery, and there is a Gipsoteca (gallery of casts) where examples of his work, as well as full-scale plaster models for pieces now in museums at home or abroad, can be seen, including the *Three Graces*.

▶ *From Possagno, follow the signs for about 9km (6 miles) to the **SS348**, then branch north on this, along the River Piave, to Feltre, about 22km (13 miles).*

❷ Feltre, Veneto
You enter old Feltre, squatting on a low incline, through the Imperial Gate. From here, a road rises gradually to the Piazza Maggiore, passing on the way a series of palaces some of which, like the Casa Franceschini, have frescos by Morto da Feltre painted on their external façades. The Piazza Maggiore itself is full of old buildings, mainly from the 16th century. Apart from the Church of San Rocco and a lovely central fountain by Tullo Lombardo there are the remains of the town's old castle with its clocktower. Surveying the entire scene is an enormous column on top of which stands

Grand Canal, Venice's main thoroughfare, runs for two miles (3km) through the city

the Lion of St Mark, the symbol of Venice.
A large ornate palace to one side is the Palazzo Municipale, which has a striking Palladian portico of a type fairly common in this part of Italy. Beyond the piazza is the Palazzo Villabuono in which is the Museo Civico (Civic Museum). Here you will see paintings representative of the region's famous art history, in particular works by Cima da Conegliano and Gentile Bellini. The Museo Rizzarda contains a collection of wrought-iron work, much of it locally made

by Carlo Rizzarda. Just below the spur on which Feltre is situated, and close to the site of the weekly market, is the Duomo (cathedral) with a 15th-century façade. Make a point of seeing the Byzantine cross of AD524 housed here. It is carved with 52 scenes from the New Testament.

ℹ️　*Largo Castaldi 7*

▶ *Go back to the SS348 and follow it south to Funer, at which turn left on to the Strada del Vino Bianco to Conegliano, a total of 56km (35 miles).*

❸ Conegliano, Veneto
Conegliano is the centre for a wine-producing region. It was also the birthplace of the painter Cima da Conegliano, the great rival of Bellini. Preserved here is Cima's home, restored and filled with copies of his greatest work. In the Gothic Duomo (cathedral) is one of Cima's greatest works – an altarpiece dated 1493. Near by is the important Sala dei Battuti, a guildhall whose walls are covered in 16th-century frescos by, among others, Francesco da Milano. The details are extraordinary and the countryside scenery recognisably Venetian.

Above the town, standing on a cypress-covered hillock, is the castle, which has been turned into an art gallery. This is full of interesting works of art, including paintings by Palma il Giovane, a late 16th-century painter who once worked in Titian's studio, and sculptures by the Florentine sculptor Giambologna.

▶ *From Conegliano, the SS13 goes straight down to Treviso, about 28km (17 miles).*

❹ Treviso, Veneto
Treviso is a bright, busy provincial capital, crossed by rapidly flowing canals that once fed the moat beneath the town's walls. There is plenty to see, although

None of Venice's grandeur on Burano, but plenty of colour

SPECIAL TO...

In Conegliano is the Strada del Vino Bianco (the Road of White Wine), a 42km (26-mile) wine route that encompasses some of the main vineyards between Conegliano and Valdobbiadene.
You can taste such wines as the *Prosecco di Treviso* and *Prosecco di Conegliano*, two delicious sparkling wines, at various stops along the way. There is also a Strada del Vino Rosso which starts at Conegliano.

---

the town suffered much damage during World War II. In the Duomo di San Pietro (St Peter's Cathedral), which has seven domes, is an *Annunciation* by the greatest Venetian painter, Titian, who died in 1576 at the age of 99. The 12th-century crypt is also interesting for its sea of ancient columns and its fragmentary mosaics. In the Museo Civico (Civic Museum) is the town's art gallery with works by Venetian artists such as Bellini, Guardi and Tiepolo.

Of Treviso's churches, perhaps the large Dominican Church of San Nicolò, with its fine apse and decorated columns, is the most interesting. In the restored 13th-century

Church of San Francesco you will see the tomb (1384) of Francesca, daughter of the poet Plutarch. Out in the streets of Treviso the arcades are full of cafés, and here and there you will see frescos painted on the walls of the older houses.

☐ *Via Toniolo 41*

▶ *From Treviso, take the SS13 towards Mestre, about 18km (11 miles), then via the SS14 and the SS11 to Venézia. At Venézia you must leave your car in a specially provided garage.*

5 Venézia, Veneto
Venézia (Venice) is one of the great 'art cities' of Italy, and its churches and galleries are still crammed with magnificent paintings. To see the city's many treasures, you must take to the water – the *vaporetto* (water bus) is the main means of transport through the canal system and the lagoon. In Piazza San Marco (St Mark's Square) is the Basilica di San Marco, the chief glory of Venice, which was built after the original burned down in 976. Mosaics, coloured marbles, ancient columns and the famed bronze horses of St Mark are its chief attraction. The latter are copies of the 3rd-century BC originals, kept in the Basilica's Museo Marciano. Next door is the Palazzo Ducale (Doge's Palace) which took on its present appearance in about 1309. It has a lovely façade of lacy Gothic tracery and decorative brickwork. Look for the two reddish pillars on the front said to have acquired their colour from the tortured corpses that used to hang there.

Behind the palace is the Ponte dei Sospiri (Bridge of Sighs) leading to the prison and just across the water of the Giudecca canal and standing on a separate little island, is the

Murano is known for its exceptional glassware which can be found all over the town

Church of San Giorgio Maggiore (1565), built by Palladio, one of Italy's most influential architects. Other great sights are the Ca' d'Oro, a former palace on the Grand Canal with a picture gallery, the Ponte di Rialto (Rialto Bridge) across the Grand Canal, and the Galleria dell' Accademia, the art gallery with some of the greatest masterpieces of Venetian art.

☐ *San Marco Ascensione 71c*

▶ *From Venézia take a vaporetto from Fondamenta Nuove to the island of Murano.*

6 Murano, Veneto
Murano has been famous for its glass-blowing workshops since the early 13th century. Many palaces in Venice contain elaborate multi-coloured chandeliers from this island and nowadays you can visit the descendants of the glass-blowers in their forges and workshops. In the Museo

Vetrario (Museum of Glass) are the best examples of the work of the Murano glass-blowers and the Modern and Contemporary Glass Museum contains more up-to-date pieces. There are even fine pieces from Roman times. Glass objects can be purchased here in a large variety of shops. In the Church of Santi Maria e Donato, built at roughly the same time as St Mark's in Venice itself, you can see fragments of Murano glass in the 12th-century mosaic floor.

▶ *Murano and Burano are connected by boat. You can do a round trip that includes both, or else you can visit either on a single trip from Venice. The distance from Murano to Burano.*

Attila's Chair, outside Torcello's Church of Santa Fosca

☑ **Burano,** Veneto
Lace-making is to Burano what glass-blowing is to Murano. All over the island you will find exquisite examples of it for sale. In the local Lacemaking School, the Scuola dei Merletti, you can watch women at work. This school was established late in the last century to rejuvenate the craft, which had all but died out. Burano is a very pretty island and its town, also called Burano, is like a miniature Venice. In the Church of San Martino, is a *Crucifixion* by Tiepolo, the last of the great Venetian painters. While here, you could visit the little island of San Francesco del Deserto, about 20 minutes by ferry to the south of Burano. Here you can visit the little monastery with beautiful gardens said to have been founded by St Francis of Assisi in 1220.

▶ *From Burano, the boat goes to the island of Torcello, a few miles further north.*

☑ **Torcello,** Veneto
All that remains of this once great city, the first settlement in the lagoon in the 5th century AD, and once a serious rival to Venice itself, are two beautiful churches. One, the Byzantine-style Duomo di Santa Maria dell'Assunta, founded in 639 but rebuilt in about 1008, has splendid mosaics covering the floor as well as the walls. The *Last Judgement*, done by Greek artists in the 11th century, is particularly noteworthy. In the apse, the mosaic of the Madonna on a stark gold background, is one of the finest examples of Byzantine art anywhere.

The other church, 11th-centruy Santa Fosca, is just as ancient. In the garden outside is a stone seat known as 'Attila's chair', the exact origins of which are unknown. Near the cathedral is the Museo dell'Estuario which contains finds from the ruins of the old city and is worth a visit. There is a silver altarpiece from the cathedral and some Roman remains from the ancient city of *Altinum*, which once stood near the present-day town of Mestre (seen on the way to Venice). Malaria virtually wiped out the population, bringing life in Torcello to an end.

▶ *From Torcello, return to Venice. Here take the **A4** to Padua (35km/22 miles), then go north on the **SS307** to Castelfranco Véneto, about 31km (19 miles).*

☑ **Castelfranco Véneto,** Veneto
This little town's claim to fame is that it was the home of Giorgione, one of the most mysterious and elsuive painters of the Venetian Renaissance. Little is known of him and few of his works survive (nobody knows why) and those whose authorship has been authenti-

cated are very precious. You can see one in the town's duomo (cathedral). The *Madonna and Child with Saints*, often called the *Castelfranco Madonna*, dated 1504, has a typically lyrical Venetian landscape in its background.

The old town of Castelfranco was once surrounded by a battlemented brick wall. One chunk of this – the Torre Civica – survives in the centre of town, and there is another length of moated wall to the west. Visit the Casa del Giorgione (Giorgione's house); also see if you can get inside the pretty 18th-century Teatro Accademia.

▶ *From Castelfranco, the SS307 leads northwards to Caerano di San Marco, about 15km (9 miles), where you turn left on the SS248 to Asolo, a further 9km (6 miles).*

RECOMMENDED WALKS

There are some good, pretty walks in the foothills of the Dolomites around the little town of Asiago – about 32km (20 miles) from Bassano del Grappa, a town within easy reach of both Possagno and Asolo.
If you have time, spend as long as you can walking around the islands of the Venetian Lagoon – Murano, Burano, Torcello. Torcello in particular has little paths leading through the ghostly remains of what was once a large and important city.

Torcello's cathedral of Santa Maria Assunta is noted for its magnificent 11th- and 12th-century Byzantine mosaics

SCENIC ROUTES

The countryside is fairly flat on this tour. However, it has its scenic parts:
– the exit from Conegliano on the SS13: the profile of the town and its little mountain is idyllic;
– the scenery looking out over the Trevisian Plain from the castle at Asolo;
– the boat trip from Venice, to the islands of Murano, Burano and Torcello, with views of the lagoon and back over Venice.

Of Lakes, Alps
& Plain

Lombardy is crossed by the huge River Po and studded with great lakes – Maggiore, Garda, Como, Iseo and Lugano. Since the Middle Ages it has been a prosperous commercial region. Milano (Milan) nowadays is the thriving economic capital of Italy but the traces of its cultural past are everywhere.

4 DAYS • 728KM • 452 MILES

ITINERARY		
MILANO	▶	**Sacro Monte Varese (65km-40m)**
SACRO MONTE VARESE	▶	**Lago Maggiore (32km-20m)**
LAGO MAGGIORE	▶	**Como (76km-47m)**
COMO	▶	**Lecco – around Lake Como (109km-68m)**
LECCO	▶	**Bellágio (22km-14m)**
BELLÁGIO	▶	**Bérgamo (61km-38m)**
BÉRGAMO	▶	**Lago di Garda (78km-48m)**
LAGO DI GARDA	▶	**Mantova (48km-30m)**
MANTOVA	▶	**Cremona (66km-41m)**
CREMONA	▶	**Pavia (136km-84m)**
PAVIA	▶	**Milano (35km-22m)**

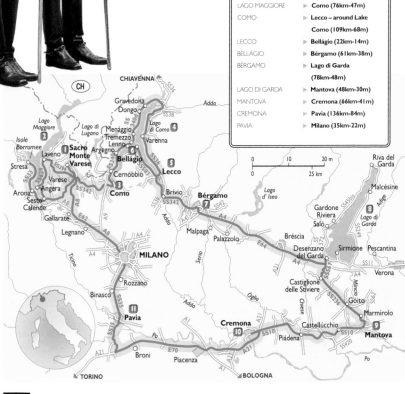

ⓘ *Via Marconi 1, Milano*

▶ *From Milano, take the **A8** going north (via Legnano and Gallarate) – the latter about 38km (24 miles) – to Varese, about another 17km (10 miles). About 10km (6 miles) north of Varese lies Sacro Monte Varese.*

❶ Sacro Monte Varese,
Lombardia

The 'Sacred Mountain of Varese', with its narrow passages and ancient covered alleys, is only the backdrop for a pilgrimage route more famous nowadays for its art than for its saintly connections. It is supposed to have been founded by St Ambrose in thanks for Lombardy's deliverance from the Arian heresy (the doctrine put forward by the 4th-century theologian Arius, that Christ is not one body with God).

From the bottom of the Sacro Monte to the top, about 800m (2,625 feet), is a cobbled route with 14 chapels at intervals along the Sacred Way, each one dedicated to the Mystery of the Rosary. The shrines are the work of Bernascone and each is filled with life-size terracotta figures, by Bussola, acting out some religious episode. At the top is the lavishly decorated Church of Santa Maria del Monte. The views from the Sacro Monte are wonderful and, to restore you after the climb, you will find cafés and restaurants in the town.

▶ *From Sacro Monte Varese, go back to Varese, then continue on the **SS394** to Lago Maggiore, about 22km (14 miles).*

❷ Lago Maggiore,
Lombardia

Only the eastern shore of Lago Maggiore (Lake Maggiore) is in Lombardia. Its western shore is in Piedmont and its northern part in Switzerland. It would take days to drive around the lake seeing all that there is to look at. The highlights are the towns of Angera, Arona, Stresa and Isole Borromee (the Borromean islands) in the middle of the lake opposite Stresa.

At Angera is the Visconti castle (open to the public), which contains well-preserved 14th- and 15th-century frescos. At Arona is another castle, this time ruined. Visit the Church of Santa Maria with, in the Borromeo Chapel, an altarpiece of 1511 by Ferrari.

Stresa is the largest resort on the lake. Full of Victorian-style hotels, it is also dotted with old-fashioned villas and luxurious gardens running down to the water's edge. Some gardens are open, including the Villa Pallavicino.

But the real gem of Maggiore is the Borromean islands. Isola Bella, perhaps the best known, is a huge private garden surrounding a palace (Palazzo Borromeo) – both open to the public. The gardens were laid out for Count Carlo III Borromeo in the 17th century by Angelo Crivelli. The elaborate complex includes white peacocks, grottoes, fountains and statuary. Isola Madre is another of the islands, famous for its large botanical garden which, with its palace, is well worth a visit. Boats to these islands leave from Stresa.

Lago (Lake) Maggiore, with its 'Beautiful Isle', Isola Bella

▶ Make for Varese from Stresa, take the **SS33** to Sesto Calende at the very foot of the lake, about 25km (16 miles) then follow the signs to Varese, about 23km (14 miles). From Varese, take the **SS342** to Como, about 28km (17 miles).

🔲 Como, Lombardia

Como was the birthplace of the Roman writer Pliny the Elder. In fact you will see signs dotted around Lago di Como (Lake Como) pointing to the sites of the various villas the Pliny family owned here. One of the most elegant towns on the lake, Como has, facing the water, a huge promenade which fills with people at dusk. There are busy cafés, palm trees and parks. The Duomo (cathedral) dates mainly from the 14th century. The rose window on the façade is Gothic in style and there is excellent carving by the Rodari brothers of Maroggia, about 1500.

Other relics of old Como include the churches of Sant'Abbondio, and San Fedele, which was once the cathedral, and the Porta Vittoria, the late 12th-century city gate. In the Museo Civico (Civic Museum) you will see objects dating from the neolithic period to World War II. See also the Museo Alessandro Volta which houses equipment used by the man who gave his name to the electric volt.

▶ From Como, drive around the lake, starting on the **SS340** up its left-hand side.

🔲 Lago di Como, Lombardia

All around the lake you will see vast villas and castles overlooking the water. Cernóbbio is a pretty town about 7km (4½ miles) from Como. Here is the grand Hotel Villa D'Este, once the home of the English Queen Caroline. At Tremezzo is the Villa Carlotta, once lived in by Princess Carlotta of Prussia, who laid out its gardens in the 1850s. You can visit this as well as the Villa Arconati, just a few kilometres outside Tremezzo, at Lenno. The parish Church of Lenno has an ancient crypt that is well worth a visit. Further on around the lake are Menaggio and Gravedona. The latter has the interesting Church of Santa Maria del Tiglio which contains early frescos of St John the Baptist.

At nearby Dongo, Mussolini was captured by the partisans in 1945. On the other side of the lake, at Varenna, visit the Villa Monastero with its formal gardens and the Romanesque Church of San Giorgio. One really good way to see the lake – and admire the towns from a distance – is to take a boat trip around it. It is possible to take one that stops at a number of places, using it like a bus. Begin at Como.

▶ *Lecco lies at the foot of the eastern arm of Lake Como, from Como itself, a direct distance of 29km (18 miles).*

6 Lecco, Lombardia

Lecco is in direct contrast to its illustrious neighbour Como. More industrial than prettier Como, Lecco's claim to fame is that it was the birthplace of Alessandro Manzoni, the great 19th-century Italian novelist. The Villa Manzoni, his former home, is now a museum – you will find it in Via Promessi Sposi, named after the writer's most famous novel which, translated, means 'The Betrothed' (the street is also known as Via Amendola). While you are in town, visit the Duomo (cathedral), with its 14th-century frescos in the style of Giotto, and the Ponte Azzone Visconti, a medieval bridge over the Adda river. Although much altered (it

Bellágio – sometimes called the prettiest town in Europe

no longer has any towers) and enlarged, it still has much of its early character.

▶ *From Lecco, take the SS583 up the western edge of Lecco's portion of Lake Como, called the Lake of Lecco, to Bellágio.*

6 Bellágio, Lombardia

Bellágio is one of the most beautiful points on Lake Como. Not only is it an interesting old town, but it is splendidly sited on a promontory overlooking the three arms of the lake. There is plenty to do here apart from just sitting in the sun enjoying the view. The 12th-century Church of San Giacomo has good carving in the apse and on its capitals. There is the Villa Serbelloni, with good gardens which can be visited, and the Villa Melzi d'Eril, which is open to the public and contains a collection of sculpture from Egypt. If time is short, the Villa Sebelloni gardens, supposed to

stand on the site of the younger Pliny's villa 'Tragedia', are the more interesting.

▶ *Return to Lecco, then take the SS36 going south for about 15km (9 miles) until it cuts the SS342. Take the latter to Bérgamo, about 24km (15 miles).*

FOR HISTORY BUFFS

Near Bérgamo, just off the SS573 south of the city, is Malpaga, in whose castle you can see frescos of Bartolomeo Colleoni hosting a banquet in honour of a visit by the King of Denmark in 1474. This is fascinating if you have already seen Colleoni's grandiose tomb in Bérgamo.

7 Bérgamo, Lombardia

Bérgamo is divided into the Città Alta and the Città Bassa, the Upper City and the Lower City. The former is the more interesting, as well as being the older. Its best monuments are in the Piazza Vecchia. In it is the Biblioteca Civica (Civic Library), a late 16th-century building modelled on Venice's great library building, designed by Sansovino. Across the square, past Contarini's fountain surrounded by stone lions, is the 12th-century Torre Civica with its 15th-century clock that still tolls the curfew hour (10pm). Behind the 12th-century Palazzo della Ragione are the Duomo and the ornate Colleoni Chapel. You can just see the base of the latter through the pointed arched loggia beneath the Palazzo della Ragione. Built in 1476, the façade of the Colleoni Chapel is a mass of sculptured decoration and coloured marble. Inside is the tomb and a statue of Bartolomeo Colleoni, who controlled Venice's armed forces in the 15th century. The ceiling fresco is by Tiepolo.

The Church of Santa Maria Maggiore, in Piazza Duomo, is a

fine Romanesque building. Also in the Upper City is the Cittadella (citadel), which contains the Natural History Museum, and the Museo Donizetti – this great composer was born in Bérgamo, and you can visit the Teatro Donizetti in

Bérgamo's splendid Piazza Vecchia is the town's historic centre

the Lower City. Between the Upper and Lower Cities is the Galleria dell'Accademia Carrara, a first-class collection of art, well worth taking in.

[i] *Via Paleocapa 2*

▶ *From Bérgamo, take the **A4** via Brescia to Lago di Garda, about 78km (48 miles) – at*

Desenzano del Garda at the foot of the lake.

8 Lago di Garda, Lombardia The most interesting ports of call around Lago (Lake) di Garda are Salò, Gardone Riviera, Riva del Garda, Malcesine and Sirmione. All are accessible by the steamer, and rather than drive around the

Castello Scaligero, Sirmione, built by the Della Scala family

archaeological finds from the area, housed in the Rocca.

Malcesine, halfway down the eastern edge of the lake, is the proud possessor of the magnificent Castello Scaligero (Scaliger Castle) dramatically situated at the water's edge. But the castle at Sirmione is more remarkable. Also from the 13th century and one of the Scaligeri castles, its battlements and its dramatic situation half in the water makes it possibly the most memorable sight on the Lago di Garda.

▶ *From Desenzano del Garda, take the SS567 for 11km (7 miles) to Castiglione delle Stiviere, at which branch on to the SS236 and continue on to Mantova, about 37km (23 miles).*

9 Mantova, Lombardia
Mantova (Mantua) sits on a swampy, marshy bend in the Mincio river. Its claim to fame is that it was the seat of one of the most intellectually active and refined courts of the Italian Renaissance. The Gonzaga family were the rulers and they embellished the town with a remarkable Palazzo Ducale (Ducal Palace) that still contains some of their art collection. The neo-classical rooms have a set of early 16th-century Flemish tapestries and the duke's apartments have a fine collection of classical statuary. Here you will see Rubens' vast portrait of the Gonzaga family. The Camera degli Sposi in the Castel di San Giorgio is world famous for its brilliant frescos by Mantegna, finished in 1472. Apart from a series of portraits of the family, there are others of their favourite dwarfs. In the Casetta dei Nani, the House of the Dwarfs, you can see the miniature rooms where the latter were once thought to have lived. The Palazzo del Té is another Gonzaga palace built by Giulio Romano in 1527 for Federico II Gonzaga's mistress. The Sala dei Giganti, the Room of the Giants, is its masterpiece:

lake, you could leave the car at Desenzano del Garda and go by boat. Salò has a fine Gothic Duomo (cathedral) with a noteworthy Renaissance portal. At Gardone Riviera, most things to visit have something to do with Gabriele d'Annunzio (1863–1938), one of the greatest writers and poets of his generation. His villa, Vittoriale degli Italiani was specially built for him and can be visited. The villa and grounds are filled with an extraordinary array of bits and pieces, like the great ornate organs in the music room, among which the writer chose to live. There is also a museum and a mausoleum in the villa's grounds.

At Riva del Garda, right at the northern tip of the lake, about 95 breathtaking kilometres (60 miles) away from Desenzano del Garda up the western edge of the lake, and actually in the Trentino region, is a 13th-century tower, the Torre Apponale, and a clutter of other ancient edifices of which the Palazzo Pretorio and the 12th-century Rocca (fortress) are the most interesting. The town's Museo Civico (Civic Museum) contains an interesting collection of armour and

huge frescoed fighting giants seem to bring down the ceiling. The Basilica of Sant'Andrea, designed by Leon Battista (1472), houses a chalice of Christ's blood, a relic once much venerated by the Gonzaga.

SPECIAL TO...

In Mantova is the Good Friday Procession on 1 April. Sacred vases which, according to tradition, contain earth soaked with the blood of Christ, are carried in a procession around the town.

ⓘ *Piazza Mantegna 6*

▶ *Take the SS10 for 66km (41 miles) to Cremona.*

⑩ Cremona, Lombardia
You cannot come to Cremona and not visit the Museo Stradivariano (Stradivarian Museum). The modern violin was developed in this city in 1566, and one of the great masters of violin-making here –

Pavia, capital of the Lombard kings for two centuries

though much later – was Antonio Stradivarius. There is also the Museo Civico (Civic Museum) in which much space is devoted to Roman Cremona. Here, too, are works of art from defunct local churches. The Duomo (cathedral) has five wonderful 17th-century Brussels tapestries as well as a series of frescos by local artists. Among the town's most interesting churches is Sant' Agostino with, in the fifth chapel on the south, a *Madonna and Saints* by Perugino, who was once Raphael's teacher.

ⓘ *Piazza del Commune 5*

▶ *From Cremona, take the A21 via Piacenza for 33km (20 miles) as far as the Casteggio turning, 82km (51 miles), for the SS35 to Pavia, a further 21km (13 miles).*

⑪ Pavia, Lombardia
Pavia was at one time an important Roman city (*Ticinum*). Not a lot remains from this period, though the Museo Civico (Civic Museum) does contain finds from Roman times and earlier Pavia. On an upper floor you will find the picture gallery with works by, among others,

Bellini and Van der Goes, the latter one of the most important of the Netherlandish Renaissance painters.

But in Pavia, the most noteworthy monument to visit is the Certosa di Pavia, a remarkable and highly decorative Renaissance monastery complex, situated just on the outskirts of town. A tour will take in the vestibule, the Little Cloister, the Great Cloister and the church with Gothic, Renaissance and baroque decoration. Back in the town once again, Leonardo was partially responsible for the design of the Duomo (cathedral), begun in 1488, and in addition to the cathedral, there are about six other churches worth seeing in the city.

ⓘ *Via Fabio Filzi 2*

▶ *Take the SS35 back to Milano, about 35km (22 miles).*

SCENIC ROUTES

The most scenic parts of this tour are the following:
– From Sacro Monte Varese, drive to Monte delle Tre Croci (the Mount of the Three Crosses) where you will have wonderful views of the surrounding countryside. Another 200m (220 yards) further up, at Campo dei Fiori – a long ridge – an even wider panorama can be enjoyed.
– From Stresa on Lago Maggiore, take a cable-car to Mount Mottarone and see the views to the Alps and to Lake Garda.
– On the west shore of Lago di Como, at Argegno, there are views to the northern snowy mountains.
– The SS45bis for the last 11km (7 miles) before you reach Riva del Garda on Lago di Garda, is one of the most spectacular stretches of road on the lake, should you elect to drive rather than take the steamer.

The Cradle of
the Renaissance

The city of Firenze (Florence), the cradle of the Renaissance, was the brilliant new world which succeeded the murk of the Dark Ages. Visiting Florence first gives a foretaste of the other great monuments of art and architecture to be seen in such places as Siena and Arezzo.

3 DAYS • 456KM • 282 MILES

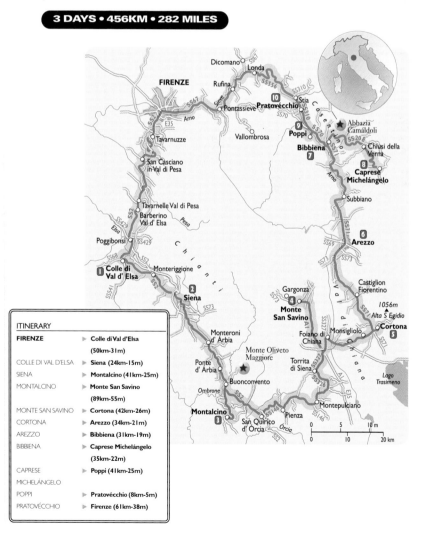

i *Via Manzoni 16, Firenze*

▶ *From Firenze, take the **SS2** going south for about 43km (27 miles) to Poggibonsi. Two kilometres (1 mile) further on, branch right to Colle di Val d'Elsa.*

❶ Colle di Val d'Elsa,
Toscana

Colle di Val d'Elsa is a small town sloping down the side of a steep ridge. There are two parts to it: the Colle Alto (upper town) was always the religious and administrative centre, while the Colle Basso (lower town) was home to artisans and their workshops. And today, while the buildings in the former are still almost uniformly Renaissance, the latter has changed with the times and today there are factories producing excellent glassware and crystal. In the upper town, the Castello is still walled by grim fortifications in which is a massive castellated gate called the Porta Volterrana (or Porta

16th-century bronze crucifix over the altar – and ancient administrative buildings, including the Palazzo dei Priori (now the Civic Museum) and the Palazzo Vescovile (the museum of religious art).
The most interesting museum is the little Antiquarium in the Piazza del Duomo, containing a collection of objects from the Casone Necropolis, in use from the late Iron Age to the last days of the Romans. Colle di Val d'Elsa was the birthplace of the architect Arnolfo di Cambio (died *c*1302), who designed the belltower – the Campanile – of the cathedral in Florence. His house is marked with a plaque.

FOR HISTORY BUFFS

From Colle di Val d'Elsa, go to Monteriggione (about 8km/5 miles), a fortified hamlet that survives with its walls and 11 of its huge stone towers intact. It has a little church and sits on its own like an island in a sea of olive groves.

Siena's main square, Piazza del Campo, is one of the finest in Italy

Nuova). Beyond, crammed in among dark stone alleyways lined with brooding medieval houses, are the Duomo (cathedral) – go inside and see the

▶ *From Colle di Val d'Elsa, the road leads in a southeast-wards direction towards Siena, a distance of about 24km (15 miles).*

❷ Siena, Toscana

After Florence, Siena is the most interesting city in Tuscany. Its most memorable characteristic is the Campo, a sloping semi-circular piazza dominated by the mighty Palazzo Pubblico. This late 13th-century Gothic building is topped by a 102m (335-foot) high tower, the Torre del Mangia, from the top of which there are amazing views of the surrounding countryside. Nearer at hand, it looks down over the Campo crammed with the tables of open-air cafés, and other important Sienese landmarks, including the Duomo (cathedral), sited at the city's highest point. This Romanesque building was added to over the centuries and restored in the 19th century. The most ambitious part of it is the polychrome marble façade designed in the 13th century by Giovanni Pisano. There is also a magnificent rose window in the upper façade, which was added in the next century, and the pinnacles of the gables are decorated with 19th-century mosaics. This remarkable decorative display is matched inside by black and white bands on the columns and walls. Before leaving the building look at Nicola Pisano's fantastic pulpit, 1265–8, with New Testament scenes in relief. One of Siena's greatest works of sculpture is in the Battistero San Giovanni (baptistery) under the cathedral. This is a baptismal font, the bronze relief panels of which are by some of the greatest exponents of Renaissance art – Ghiberti, Donatello and Della Quercia.
As with Florence, it would take days to explore Siena fully. Nearly any church you see is worth entering, though San Francesco, with 14th-century frescos by the Lorenzettis, is among the best. For a closer look at the original works from the cathedral go to the Museo dell'Opera del Duomo (cathedral museum). The Pinacoteca Nazionale (art gallery) is in the 14th-century Palazzo

The 'icing sugar' fantasy of Siena's magnificent cathedral

Buonsignori; here there is an excellent survey of Sienese art from its beginnings to the 17th century. Pre-eminent here are the works of Guido da Siena, the best of the earliest Sienese painters, and the work of Pietro and Ambrogio Lorenzetti. Others to look out for are the works of Beccafumi, born 1484, a High Renaissance artist and contemporary of Raphael, and the works of Il Sodoma, born in 1477, the leading mannerist painter in Siena. You can see other works by him in the nearby Church of Sant' Agostino.

While in Siena make sure you wander through the back streets, away from the main tourist spots, and see its medieval houses, ancient alleyways and little churches. The Church of San Domenico contains the head of Saint Catherine in a golden reliquary. She, like St Francis, received the *stigmata*. Not far away is Casa di Santa Caterina (Saint Catherine's house), now a museum and a shrine to this mystic reformer, one of the co-patrons of Italy. Also near by is the medieval Fonte Branda, a fountain which was once an important source of water for Siena's inhabitants.

If you have time, go out of Siena on the SS2, south, and after about 27km (16½ miles) branch right on the SS451 to the remote Abbey of Monte Oliveto Maggiore which is still inhabited by monks. Chief among its treasures is the huge cloister with a fresco cycle depicting the life of St Benedict, partially by Luca Signorelli (born *c*1441), and by Il Sodoma. There is a lovely early 15th-century church here, and the entrance gate is decorated by fine della Robbia terracottas. The abbey is set in a striking position and is considered one of the chief attractions of the Sienese locality (you could go here on the way to the next town, Montalcino).

[i] *Via di Città 43*

Taking a quiet moment from the daily chores in Cortona

▶ *From Siena, take the SS2 south as far as Buonconvento, about 27km (17 miles) then, about 2km (1 mile) further on, branch on to the smaller country road that leads to Montalcino.*

8 Montalcino, Toscana

The most memorable thing about Montalcino is the number of wine shops scattered around what is a rather small town. They make sight-seeing difficult because their attractions are hugely popular. Montalcino is the home of the famous *Brunello di Montalcino* and perhaps the best place to taste this wine is in the café housed in the old Rocca, the 14th-century castle at the top of the town.

Montalcino is a hilltown surrounded by medieval walls. Its precipitous streets straggle up to a lovely medieval Palazzo Comunale in the Piazza del Popolo, while higher up is the Romanesque Church of Sant'Agostino with a good rose window in its façade. There are two collections of Sienese paintings in the town, one in the Museo Civico (Civic Museum), the other in the Museo Diocesano (Diocesan Museum).

Montalcino is a good place from which to visit a collection of other lovely, typically Tuscan towns and villages. It should take an extra afternoon or morning. One of these, Castelnuovo dell'Abate, just 8km (5 miles) to the south, has the lovely 12th-century Benedictine Abbazia di Sant'Antimo which is supposed to have been founded by Charlemagne. Just to the north of Montalcino, also about 8km (5 miles), is the little town of Pienza, famous for having been the birthplace of one of the greatest popes of the early Renaissance, Pius II (Aeneas Sylvius Piccolomini). During the Pope's lifetime it became something of a centre for art – see the magnificent façade of Pius' family home, the Palazzo Piccolomini which was designed by Bernardo Rossellino in 1460, one of the great Renaissance architects, with significant works in Florence. He was also responsible for Pienza's cathedral. To the east of Montalcino is San Quirico d'Orcia, another well preserved town with a good Romanesque church.

▶ *Return to the SS2, turn right and continue southeast for about 14km (9 miles) on this road to San Quirico d'Orcia. From here, take the SS146 to Pienza and Montepulciano and then follow the signs to the A1 via the SS326 and the SS327. Go north on the A1 for 14km (9 miles) to the exit for Monte San Savino.*

4 Monte San Savino, Toscana

Monte San Savino is another of Tuscany's most characteristic hilltowns. It is a quiet, pretty place that comes alive early in the morning, the shopping hours, and late in the afternoon when everyone takes their evening stroll. The most interesting things to see here are the monuments that were either designed or restructured by Andrea Cantucci, a sculptor who was born here in 1496, and subsequently nicknamed Sansovino. His is the Loggia dei Mercanti in the Corso Sangallo and he was responsible for altering the 14th-century Church of Sant'Agostino. Some of his sculptural works can be seen in Santa Chiara. It was Antonio da Sangallo the elder, an architect who built some of the masterpieces of Renaissance architecture, who designed the Palazzo Comunale early in the 16th century.

Not far from Monte San Savino (take the SS73), is the little walled village of Gargonza. Turned by its owners into a hotel, it was once frequented by Dante and is an interesting and beautiful spot to stay. It has a little church dedicated to the saints Tiburzio and Susanna, and the whole clutch of buildings behind their north wall is dominated by a medieval tower.

▶ *Go back down the A1 for 14km (9 miles) as far as Val di Chiana, then follow the signs via Foiano di Chiana and Monsigliolo to Cortona.*

RECOMMENDED WALKS

A lovely walk is one that takes in the estate surrounding the castle of Gargonza, just outside Monte San Savino. It is even better if you stay in the castle hotel here. Routes are planned and laid out on paths through the woods and gardens and there are good views out over the plain to Monte San Savino.

---

5 Cortona, Toscana
Cortona, one of the oldest towns in Tuscany, is also one of the highest. The views from its ramparts are among the best in the region. There is a lot to see and do here but be prepared for your calf muscles to bear the brunt of your sightseeing. Cortona is perched on the side of Monte Egidio and all the streets, like the medieval Via del Gesù with its overhanging houses, and the steps leading to and from the central piazza, are immensely steep. The Duomo (cathedral), poised above a steep drop to the valley below, is perhaps the least interesting building in this lovely medieval town. Originally Romanesque, it underwent later alterations that left it leagues behind the 13th-century Church of Sant'Agostino and the 14th-century San Niccolò which contains a *Deposition* by Luca Signorelli. More works by Signorelli, who was born in Cortona, can be found in the Museo Diocesano (Diocesan Museum) alongside other precious Renaissance paintings, most notably those by Fra Angelico and Pietro Lorenzetti. Relics of the Etruscans can be seen in the museum in the Palazzo Pretorio, while the Etruscan walls, nearly obliterated by the Roman and medieval ones, can be seen around the Porta Colonia (the Colonia Gate).

At the top of the town is the forbidding Fortezza Medicea, not far from the Basilica di Santa Margherita da Cortona, which contains a fine Gothic tomb. Cortona is a lovely place to be in the late afternoon when the townsfolk emerge after their siesta. They loiter in the main square eating ice-creams and gossiping, or else indulge in the universal Italian pastime – *la passeggiata*. This is the leisurely evening stroll backwards and forwards up the piazza, down the other side, then along one of the side streets and back again. Overlooked by ancient buildings, this scene can not have changed much over the centuries.

▶ *From Cortona, return to the SS71, west of Cortona, which leads to Arezzo, about 29km (18 miles) further on.*

SCENIC ROUTES

The most scenic parts of the route are:
– the road from Montalcino to Montepulciano. This is the classic Tuscany that attracts visitors, richly agricultural with wheatfields, vineyards and distant hill villages and castles;
– the SS2 from Siena to Buonconvento, typical Chianti landscape with trails of cypresses following each other in a line up to the crest of a hill. Look out for the characteristic Tuscan farmhouses;
– the views from Cortona to the Lake of Trasimeno. These are among the highest and most far-reaching in this part of the region. Look first at the Renaissance landscapes in the art galleries, then look at the views from Cortona. The perspectives, the detail and colours are the same;
– the views from Stia across the Casentino to Poppi and Caprese Michelángelo. In this unspoilt landscape you can see each of these towns – over a distance of about 40km (25 miles).

---

6 Arezzo, Toscana
Arezzo, birthplace of the poet Petrarch, is another Tuscan city with a medieval air about it. Piazza Grande is its most magnificent square, lined with an assortment of medieval houses, some of which are attached to castellated towers. The piazza slopes downwards from Giorgio Vasari's 16th-century loggia – built in the style of an ancient Greek stoa or portico – of the Palazzo delle Logge on the right of which is the Palazzo della Fraternità dei Laici topped by a clocktower. Just below this building, also on the right, is the apse of the Romanesque Church of Santa Maria della Pieve. The entrance to this church is at the other

side, by way of a most extraordinary façade consisting of a three-tiered loggia. Inside is Pietro Lorenzetti's famous polyptych (1320) of the *Madonna and Saints*. The Gothic Duomo (cathedral) is further up the hill past the Palazzo Pretorio, whose façade is decked with the coats of arms of imperial and Florentine governors of the city. The best things about the cathedral, begun in 1277, are the 16th-century stained glass, by the Frenchman Guillaume de Marcillat, and the tomb of Bishop Guido Tarlati, who died in 1327, an enormous sculpted monument set with 16 relief panels.

Above all, do not miss the Church of San Francesco which contains one of the finest fresco cycles to have emerged from the Renaissance. The work of the great Piero della Francesca, it depicts the *Legend of the Cross*, and is generally accepted as one of the world's greatest paintings. Piero, a follower of the Florentine school of painting, produced his masterpiece between 1452 and 1466, but its drama, colour and light speak across the centuries. Other places to visit are the Casa del Vasari, the house of the painter and early art critic Giorgio Vasari (1511–74) which is now a museum; the remains of a Roman amphitheatre down near the station; and the Museo

Archeologico next door, containing the relics of the city's more ancient past, including good Etruscan items.

> ℹ️ *Piazza Risorgimento 116*

▶ *From Arezzo, take the SS71 going north to Bibbiena for 31km (19 miles).*

7 **Bibbiena,** Toscana

Bibbiena is in the heart of the Casentino area of Tuscany, the lovely wooded valley in which the River Arno rises. It is the biggest town in the area, a typical hilltown where the pace of life is slow and easy. Here is the 15th-century Church of San Lorenzo which contains terracottas attributed to the school of della Robbia.

The 12th-century Church of SS Ippolito e Donato has a triptych painted by Bicci di Lorenzo (1435) as well as the remains of some late medieval frescos. Most interesting of all is the 16th-century Palazzo Dovizi with a dramatic façade lining the main street in the centre of town. This was the home of Cardinal Bibbiena (1470–1520), friend of the painter Raphael.

From Bibbiena (take the SS208) it is easy to get to the Abbey of La Verna high above the town, the site of which was given to St Francis in 1213; it was here that he received the *stigmata* (Christ's wounds).

▶ *Take the SS208 to Chiusi della Verna from where follow signs to Caprese Michel-ángelo, a total of 35km (22 miles).*

BACK TO NATURE

A wide variety of wild orchids grace the countryside of Tuscany from March until May. Seemingly dry and barren areas are often surprisingly good, especially if the soil is undisturbed and the bedrock is limestone. Look for numerous members of the bee orchid family – the flowers resemble small, furry insects – as well as tongue orchids, lizard orchids and giant orchids.

8 **Caprese Michelángelo,** Toscana

This tiny hamlet, birthplace of Michelangelo, occupies a rock site with the source of the Tevere (Tiber) river that runs through Rome, just to the east, and the upper reaches of the Arno river to the west. Everything there is to see here has something to do with Michelagniolo di Lodovico Buonarroti – Michelangelo – perhaps the greatest artist that Italy ever produced. You can

Pieve di Romena church near Pratovécchio, a Romanesque gem

SPECIAL TO...

In Arezzo the antiques fair happens on the first Sunday of every month. This is one of the best in Italy and has items ranging from statues to old brass beds for sale. Arezzo also has an annual medieval festival called the Giostra del Saracino (the Joust of the Saracen), which takes place on the first Sunday in September. It happens in Piazza Grande with the contestants all dressed in 14th-century costume.

visit his birthplace among the chestnut trees; the Casa del Podestà, where his father was the Florentine governor, is now a museum. There are also the remains of a castle and the little Chapel of San Giovanni Battista where Michelangelo is said to have been baptised.

▶ *From Caprese Michelángelo, return to Bibbiena. Turn right on the SS70, which leads after 6km (4 miles) to the turning for Poppi.*

9 Poppi, Toscana
You can see Poppi from miles around. It stands high above the plain of Campaldino, where an important battle was fought in 1289 (at which the poet Dante was present). Dante's bust faces the piazza in front of the Palazzo Pretorio which dominates the town and the countryside. This was once home to the Guidi counts who, in the Middle Ages dominated the entire Casentino hill region. Today it houses some frescos from the 15th century and a chapel decorated a century earlier. Poppi is very pretty indeed. Its main street is arcaded and lined with medieval houses. Nothing stirs here, not even the cats lying in the sun when you walk past.

From Poppi cross over to the Abbey of Camaldoli, about 8km (5 miles) to the north. Its buildings date mostly from the 17th and 18th centuries – visit the monks' old pharmacy, and also the little baroque church about 2.5km (1½ miles) above the abbey. Here, housed in cells, lived (and still live) hermit monks in complete isolation.

ⓘ *Piazza Amerighi*

▶ *From Poppi, return to and turn left on to the SS70. Turn right within 2km (1 mile) on to the SS310 to Pratovécchio, a further 6km (4 miles).*

10 Pratovécchio, Toscana
Pratovécchio, like other places in the area, is associated with the poet Dante. It serves as a base from which to visit places of interest in the immediate vicinity. For example, a short way out of town is Stia, from whose lofty position you can see right over Casentino to Poppi and Caprese Michelangelo. In the centre of this village, and at its highest point, are the remains of a castle which also belonged to the Guidi counts and in which Dante was imprisoned for a while.

Near by, and just above Pratovécchio, is the Castello di

Enjoying a quiet moment in Montalcino's Piazza del Popolo

Romena, once a fortified village but now in ruins, and a country church called the Pieve di Romena, one of the most beautiful Romanesque buildings in the region. Ask for the key at the neighbouring farmhouse, go inside, and examine the carvings on the columns lining the nave.

▶ *From Pratovécchio continue north on the SS310. After 2km (1 mile), branch left on to, and follow, the SS556 via Stia until it cuts the SS67 which leads back into Firenze.*

FOR CHILDREN

Show the children true Tuscan cooking. Take them to a barbecue Tuscan style (by doing so you are following the real tradition of Tuscan cuisine) and eat juicy wild boar sausages or a steak *alla Fiorentina* grilled on the open flame. The latter is a steak on the bone with a drop of olive oil added once it is cooked. Fish, too, is delicious. Follow the whole lot with the best ice-cream in Italy – from Vivoli's in Florence.

The Green
Heart of Italy

Umbria is best observed from the ramparts of the ancient hill-towns crammed into its central valley. Its hills and lower slopes are covered with olive groves, pines and grapevines and the towns in this magical region are among the most evocative in Italy. Perúgia is an imposing city with a grand central square, Gothic cathedral and magnificent 13th-century fountain.

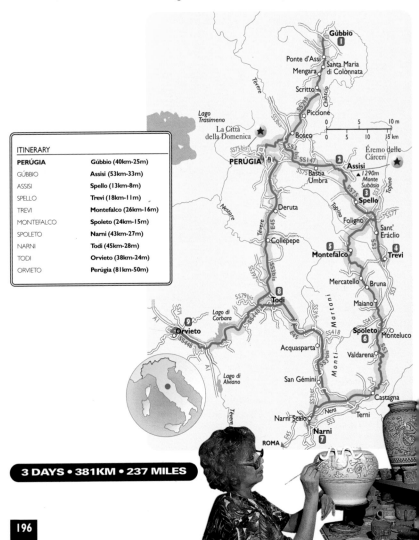

ITINERARY	
PERÚGIA	**Gúbbio (40km–25m)**
GÚBBIO	**Assisi (53km–33m)**
ASSISI	**Spello (13km–8m)**
SPELLO	**Trevi (18km–11m)**
TREVI	**Montefalco (26km–16m)**
MONTEFALCO	**Spoleto (24km–15m)**
SPOLETO	**Narni (43km–27m)**
NARNI	**Todi (45km–28m)**
TODI	**Orvieto (38km–24m)**
ORVIETO	**Perúgia (81km–50m)**

3 DAYS • 381KM • 237 MILES

ℹ *Via Mazzini 21, Perúgia*

FOR CHILDREN

La Città della Domenica is a Disney-style playground 8km (5 miles) west of Perúgia, just off the SS75bis. The 200-hectare (500-acre) park has a zoo, archaeological zone, games rooms, bumper cars and a variety of buildings based on fairy-tale themes, such as 'Snow White's House'.

▶ *Take the SS298 going north-east from Perúgia to Gúbbio.*

🄽 **Gúbbio,** Umbria

Beautifully situated at the mouth of a gorge and rising up the slopes of Mont'Ingino, Gúbbio has managed to preserve much of its medieval appearance. In the Middle Ages it was one of the fiercest and most warlike places in Umbria, and the 14th-century Palazzo dei Consoli, a massive Gothic battlemented structure of dressed stone, in Piazza della Signoria, still dominates the town. It now houses a museum and art gallery. Among its many exhibits are the famous *Tavole Eugubine* (Gúbbio Tablets), seven 2nd- to 1st-century BC bronze plaques with inscriptions in Umbrian and Latin, which are the most important evidence extant of the Umbrian language. The Palazzo Ducale, built in 1476 for Federico da

Steep winding streets in the hilltop town of Spello

Montefeltro, Duke of Urbino, by Luciano Laurano, has a delightful Renaissance court-yard and charming rooms with unusual architectural fashions, carved doors and 16th-century fireplaces.

As you wander through the town look out for the Porte del Morto (Doors of Death or Deadman's Gates). Many houses still have two doorways. The lower one, according to tradition, was where coffins were removed from the house after death. In the lower part of the town is the Gothic Church of San Francesco, whose simple façade is adorned with a great

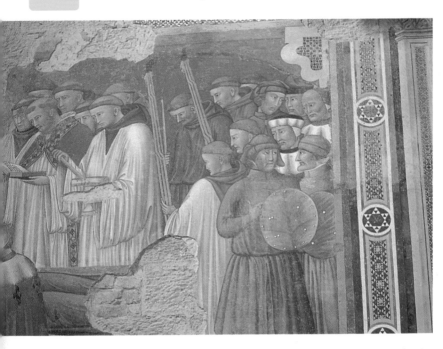

rose window, creating a striking effect. Inside is a notable fresco depicting the *Life of the Virgin*, painted by Ottaviano Nelli in the early 1400s.

Gúbbio's 1st-century AD Roman theatre is one of the largest surviving of its kind. It is in an excellent state of preservation, and in the summer provides dramatic performances.

Fine frescos in Todi's Romanesque and Gothic Duomo, Piazza del Popolo

i *Piazza Oderisi 6*

▶ *Return towards Perúgia on the SS298. Just before Perúgia turn south on the SS3bis, then on to the SS75 eastwards for a short distance before taking the SS147 to Assisi.*

2 Assisi, Umbria

Nestling on the slopes of Monte Subasio, Assisi has hardly changed since St Francis, born here in 1182, the son of a wealthy merchant, walked its streets, and its ancient character has helped to preserve his cult. Little winding, stone-paved streets, lined with old houses, lead from the base of the town to the various monuments. Almost everything worth seeing is in some way associated with the saint. Art-lovers should head for the Basilica di San Francesco, which consists of two fine 13th-century churches, one on top of the other. Here there are frescos celebrating the life of St Francis. Most important is the series of 28 by Giotto, the first major artist of the early Renaissance, in the basilica's upper church. More exquisite are the scenes from the life of St Martin by the Sienese painter Simone Martini (1322) in the Chapel of St Martin in the basilica's lower church. In addition, there are a number of relics belonging to the saint, among them his sandals and his patched grey cassock.

You cannot avoid the religious life in Assisi: the streets are full of nuns and monks and there are several other churches well worth visiting, including the 13th-century Santa Chiara which enshrines St Clare's body still intact. Even though she died nearly 750 years ago, her body, blackened by time, lies open to view in the crypt. One of St Francis' earliest and most enthusiastic supporters, St Clare founded the order of the

SPECIAL TO...

In Gúbbio is the Corsa dei Ceri (Feast of Candles), which takes place every year on 15 May and begins with a picturesque procession through the streets to the Abbey of Sant'Ubaldo on Mont'Ingino, just outside the town. The festival is centred round a dramatic race in which three teams of sturdy men each carry a huge, heavy, candle-shaped pillar up the hill to the abbey in honour of St Ubaldo, whose mortal remains are preserved in an urn beneath the main altar. Legend has it that the venerable saint intervened in a battle against Perugia, giving the victory to the outnumbered Gubbians. If you don't care to walk, the abbey can be reached by car or funicular.

Poor Clares. With your back to this church gaze out over the pinkish-brown rooftops to the Umbrian Plain below, one of the most stunning views you will ever see.

It is well worth the stiff walk up Via San Francesco to the Piazza del Comune. Here you can see the remains of the Temple of Minerva, a good example of Roman architecture dating from the 1st century AD and now the Church of Santa Maria della Minerva. There are also several fine medieval buildings: the Palazzo del Capitano del Popolo, and the Torre and Palazzo del Comune, the latter containing the Pinacoteca Civica (Civic Picture Gallery).

i *Piazza del Commune 12*

▶ *Take the road southeast from Assisi to the SS75, which runs for 3km (2 miles) before the turning to Spello, 13km (8 miles) from Assisi.*

FOR HISTORY BUFFS

For those interested in the life of St Francis, and who have the stamina, a walk up Monte Subasio, offering magnificent panoramas of the surrounding countryside, brings you to the Eremo delle Carceri, the saint's favourite retreat. The hermitage, cut out of the rock, is set in the dense woodland covering the mountain, 5km (3 miles) behind Assisi. Most of the miracles recounted in St Francis' *Fioretti* ('Little Flowers') took place in these woods.

---

❸ Spello, Umbria
Clinging to the southern slopes of Monte Subasio, Spello has changed little since the Middle Ages. History lies all around you here, as you will find if you pick your way through its streets: if not Roman, then it is bound to be medieval or, at the very latest, Renaissance. The town was under the influence of the Romans for much of its history.

Look for the Porta Venere, a fine old Roman gateway which survives in the town's walls. Near the station you will find another, the Porta Consolare, with three statues from the Roman theatre whose ruins can be seen just before entering the town.

Steep winding streets lead from it and up into the town, past higgledy-piggledy medieval shops and houses to the centre and the Church of Santa Maria Maggiore. The church's magnificent Cappella Baglioni (Baglioni Chapel) contains frescos (1501) by Pinturicchio, which tell the life of the Virgin in a fresh and lively way. An important Renaissance artist, whose work

can be seen in the Sistine Chapel in the Vatican, Pinturicchio was assistant to Perugino. The church itself is a hotch-potch of different periods – the front door is Renaissance, the carvings above it Roman and the interior is unexpectedly baroque.

▶ *Rejoin the SS75 heading southwest and turn right on to the SS3 round Foligno to Trevi, about 18km (11 miles) away.*

❹ Trevi, Umbria
Magnificently situated on the slopes of a steep hill, dominat-

Ancient Narni, on Umbria's border, was once a fortress-city

ing the Spoletino plain, Trevi is set so high that on approaching it you cannot see it from the car windows. It is a lovely, undiscovered place whose pavements are speckled with mosaic-like arrangements of cobbles, while a maze of winding streets and blind alleys is contained within two sets of medieval walls. The 14th-century Palazzo Comunale in Piazza Mazzini, the site of the town's Pinacoteca (art gallery), contains a mixture of Renaissance paintings by Pinturicchio and Lo Spagna, Roman remains, sculptures and ceramics. You can see Lo Spagna's fresco of the *Life of St Francis*, 1512, in the Church of San Martino in Via Augusto Ciufelli on the edge of town. This is thought to be his best painting and it has a contemporary view of Assisi in its background.

Also worth a visit is the 12th-century Church of Sant' Emiliano with its richly decorated altar by Rocca da Vicenza, and if you still have time, take a walk below the town to the Church of Santa Maria delle Lacrime, with its beautiful doorway and fine Umbrian

A modern sample of Gubbio's centuries-old pottery industry

School pictures, including one by Perugino.

▶ *Return to Foligno via the SS3, then follow signs to Montefalco.*

5 **Montefalco,** Umbria

The pretty little walled hilltown of Montefalco – 'Falcon's Mount' – once boasted more saints than any other town in the region, earning itself the title of 'a little strip of heaven fallen to earth'. With a population of only 6,000, this is quite a feat! The Church of San Francesco, founded in 1336, contains 15th-century frescos by Benozzo Gozzoli, and work by other Umbrian painters. These frescos are considered so important that the building is no longer used as a church but has become a museum.

Other churches to see are the Gothic Church of Sant'Agostino with its fine selection of Renaissance frescos by local artists, and the baroque Church of Santa Chiara di Montefalco. Here you can see the crumbling remains of Santa Chiara's heart. Montefalco is a tranquil, peaceful place, often called the 'Balcony of Italy'; you should sit in one of its cafés and sample the famed *Sagrantino* wine or

take in the delightful views of the surrounding countryside.

▶ *Head across country, via Mercatello and Bruna, to Spoleto.*

6 **Spoleto,** Umbria

Spoleto, shadowed by its 14th-century Rocca (castle), is a very old city, rich in evidence of a history that began centuries before the Roman occupation. It has survived sieges, earthquakes, plagues, a period of misrule by the notorious Lucrezia Borgia and World War II bombing. The Duomo (cathedral), built in 1067 but restored in the 12th century, with its splendid doorway and Renaissance porch surrounded with mosaics, is without doubt the most beautiful in Umbria, though the Spoleto churches of San Gregorio Maggiore, Sant'Eufemia and San Pietro come close. Be sure to visit them all, particularly the latter (just out of town), with its extremely early relief sculptures.

Among Spoleto's many Roman ruins is a partially restored theatre in the vicinity of Piazza della Libertà, which is still used for concerts, and the 1st-century AD Arch of Drusus, in an excellent state of preservation. The imposing Ponte delle Torri (Bridge of the Towers) was erected in the 13th century as an aqueduct over a river gorge (pedestrians only now), and links the town with neighbouring Monteluco. Built of stone, with 10 arches, it is 230m (755 feet) long and 81m (265 feet) high and was probably constructed on the foundations of an earlier Roman aqueduct.

Spoleto can get very busy at peak times, so it is best to plan your visit to avoid these. It is one of the liveliest towns in the region, helped by the annual Festival dei Due Mondi (Festival of the Two Worlds) that takes place here. The festival, in June and July, presents the latest trends in art, music,

The Duomo in Orvieto: detail from the much-admired carved façade

theatre, painting and sculpture against the magnificent setting of the ancient town.

i   *Piazza della Libertà 7*

RECOMMENDED WALKS

The countryside round Spoleto is particularly picturesque and quite accessible by foot. For spectacular views follow the road at the eastern end of the Ponte delle Torri for 1km (half a mile) to the Church of San Pietro (one of the finest achievements of Umbrian architecture and sculpture). A little further afield, for those who have the stamina, another road from the east end of the Ponte delle Torri winds its way up the hillside for 6km (3½ miles). Here, at the top of thickly wooded Monteluco, you will find a monastery founded by St Francis, with enchanting views of the valley.

▶ *Take the SS3 south. Bypass Terni, and head for Narni, entering on the SS3ter, 43km (27 miles).*

7 **Narni,** Umbria
Narni, crammed on its hilltop, is so constricted that it has hardly

expanded since Roman times. This solid, stone-built town has an interesting, though ruined, 14th-century Rocca (castle), with fine views in most directions, and the odd-looking Palazzo del Podestà, which was created by joining three fortified tower houses together. Now it houses the local art gallery whose greatest treasure is a *Coronation of the Virgin* by the 15th-century master Ghirlandaio. See the fine inlaid choir stalls and early marble screen in the Romanesque Duomo (cathedral), which, with the Podestà Palace, provides a splendid backdrop to the Corso dell'Anello, a spectacular costumed pageant enacted each May, when horsemen representing the town's rival quarters joust for a coveted prize.

Just below Narni, on the line of the ancient Via Flaminia, are the ruins of the Roman Ponte d'Augusto (Bridge of Augustus) which was originally 120m (400 feet) long and carried the road almost 30m (100 feet) up over the River Nera.

▶ *From Narni, head back towards Terni, turning north on SS3bis to Todi, about 45km (28 miles).*

SCENIC ROUTES

Most of the route along this tour of Umbria offers an outstanding range of scenery, but there are certain stretches of road where the views are particularly spectacular.
Perúgia to Gúbbio – along the SS298 between Piccione and Santa Maria di Colonnata;
Gúbbio to Assisi – the last 13km (8 miles) of the SS147 before Assisi;
the roads in and around Montefalco;
Todi to Orvieto – the SS448 round the south shore of Lake Corbara and in to Orvieto;
Orvieto to Perúgia – the SS3bis from Deruta to Perúgia.

8 **Todi,** Umbria
Todi occupies a triangular site, still partly surrounded by its rings of Etruscan, Roman and medieval walls, on a ridge above the Tevere (Tiber) valley. The Piazza del Popolo, at the centre of town, is the kind of place where you could sit all day in the sun at one of the cafés and do nothing but watch the world pass by. On one side of the piazza is the Romanesque Duomo (cathedral), on the site

of a former Roman temple to Apollo, while the remaining sides are bounded by a variety of other medieval buildings, in particular the 14th-century Palazzo del Capitano. The sleepy charm of this place is enlivened early in the evening when the residents pour into the piazza for the daily stroll and a chat: then it seems like a drawing room with a party in progress.

You should not leave Todi without visiting Santa Maria della Consolazione, inspired by Bramante's plan for St Peter's in Rome. This domed church on the plan of a Greek cross, is much admired as one of the finest creations of Renaissance architecture. Started in 1508, it took over 100 years to complete.

ℹ️ *Piazza del Popolo 38*

▶ *Leave Todi on the **SS448**, and head southwest, around the Lake of Corbara, to Orvieto.*

🅓 **Orvieto,** Umbria
Orvieto's commanding position on a great square rock makes it an amazing sight, visible from miles around. An ideal site for a fort, it was first settled by the Etruscans (who called it *Volsinii*), but they could not withstand the might of the rising new power, and eventually Orvieto fell to Rome. It is a dark, brooding town, dominated by its glorious Gothic-style Duomo (cathedral), which was started in the late 1200s, supposedly to the designs of Arnolfi di Cambio, famed for his Duomo and Palazzo Vecchio in Florence. It was built in alternate courses of black basalt and greyish-yellow limestone, and decorated by the finest artists of the day, to commemorate the Miracle of Bolsena (when the Host started to bleed during a celebration of Mass in the town of Bolsena). The façade, adorned with elaborate sculptures and coloured mosaics, was designed by Lorenzo Maitani of Siena. To appreciate fully, you should view it in bright

sunlight, when the effect is quite stunning. Inside, magnificent frescos in the lovely Cappella della Madonna de San Brigio are largely the work of Fra Angelico and, later, Luca Signorelli. The town abounds in interesting monuments: the 11th-century Palazzo Vescovile, an old papal residence; the 12th-century Palazzo del Capitano del Popolo; and the churches of San Domenico, San Lorenzo, Sant'Andrea and San Giovenale are among the best buildings.

Orvieto is famous for its wine, particularly the whites. Signorelli, when painting the Duomo, is said to have asked

On the east side of Orvieto, you can descend into Pozzo di San Patrizio (St Patrick's Well), a vast cylinder cut through the rock on which Orvieto stands. Built in the 16th century, this 61m (200-foot) deep well, with two separate spiral staircases winding round the shaft, one for the descent and the other for the ascent of the donkeys which brought up the water, was commissioned to ensure the town's water supply in times of siege. Near by are the remains of an Etruscan temple. Take a look at the Etruscan Museum and the various artefacts unearthed from tombs in the area – in particular, see the 4th-century sarcophagus found near the Torre San Severo in 1912.

that part of his contract be paid in wine, and the rock beneath the city is honeycombed with caves used to ferment the grapes for the Orvieto vintages.

ℹ️ *Piazza del Duomo 24*

▶ *Take the **SS448** back towards Todi, then turn left on to the **SS3bis** to Perúgia.*

While you are travelling in Umbria you will undoubtedly notice the kind of countryside which naturalists call *macchia* (*maquis*). This is the characteristic Mediterranean habitat of evergreen trees with a shrubby understorey.

As well as its distinctive wildflowers, including several species of orchid and the much more easily spotted, but no less pretty, rock-roses, this habitat contains such creatures as praying mantids, wall lizards and green lizards (look for them basking in the morning sunshine) and lots of snakes (don't worry, they are likely to see you a long time before you see them and beat a quiet retreat!). You probably will not see, but will almost certainly hear, Scop's owls. Their call, delivered for most of the night – usually from trees – is a quite uncanny and unnatural sound, likened by some to sonar bleeps.

View over the heart of Perúgia, capital of Umbria

Roman
Country Retreats

The upper echelons of Roman society have always relaxed in villas and secluded countryside retreats just outside Roma (Rome). There are all kinds of villas and castles from Emperor Hadrian's ruined country palace at Tivoli to Pope John Paul II's country house at Castèl Gandolfo. But there are also more 20th-century forms of relaxation available on the beaches at Ostia, Gaeta and Sperlonga. Rome itself has a variety of palaces and villas that can be visited.

4 DAYS • 483KM • 300 MILES

ITINERARY		
ROMA	►	Tivoli (32km-20m)
TIVOLI	►	Anticoli Corrado
		(28km-17m)
ANTÍCOLI CORRADO	►	Subiaco (21km-13m)
SUBIACO	►	Gaeta (201km-125m)
GAETA	►	Sperlonga (16km-10m)
SPERLONGA	►	Castèl Gandolfo
		(98km-61m)
CASTÈL GANDOLFO	►	Frascati (19km-12m)
FRASCATI	►	Ostia (40km-25m)
OSTIA	►	Roma (28km-17m)

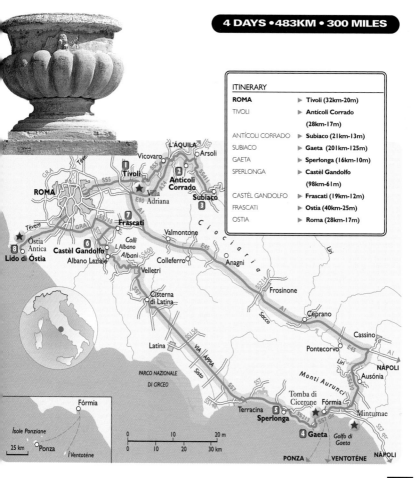

ⓘ *Via Parigi II, Roma*

▶ *From the centre of Roma, the SS5 goes east for 32km (20 miles) to Tivoli.*

BACK TO NATURE

The Parco Nazionale del Circeo is well worth a visit. This area lies less than 100km (60 miles) south of Rome on the Italian coast. It is a calcareous promontory with unspoilt beaches and dunes. The evergreen oak forests and *macchia* are good for flowers, insects and birds.

---

❶ Tivoli, Lazio

Tivoli sits on a wide spur of Monte Ripoli just before Lazio becomes really mountainous. The town grew up as a strategic point on an ancient route from the east to Rome. Today it is largely associated with the Villa Adriano (Hadrian's Villa), built by the Emperor Hadrian. Construction began at his accession to the imperial throne and continued until AD134. Here the Emperor set about reconstructing buildings he had seen on his foreign travels, such as the Canopic Temple at Alexandria and Plato's Academy in Athens. But this huge villa, the biggest ever in Italy, also contained libraries, baths, temples, theatres, and there was even a little private palace built on an island in a huge pool and surrounded by a colonnade. The richness of the complex is demonstrated by the enormous quantity and excellent quality of the sculpture which has been found on this site over the centuries. Most of it has ended up in the Vatican Museum in Rome.

During the Renaissance other villas were built at Tivoli by rich cardinals. The most sumptuous is the Villa d'Este, built by Ippolito d'Este. The gardens here are more elaborate than the actual buildings; a river was diverted to provide water for countless fountains and a huge variety of cascades and pools. The Villa Gregoriana is another place worth a visit, with a fine waterfall by the great architect and sculptor Bernini, formed by the diversion of the River Aniene.

ⓘ *Largo Garibaldi*

▶ *Continue along the SS5 from Tivoli for 23km (14 miles) until the turning on the right to Antícoli Corrado.*

❷ Antícoli Corrado, Lazio

This is a lovely hilltown poised dramatically on an eminence dominating the countryside all around. It has remained completely unspoilt by the passage of time and has for years been the destination of painters in search of sublime landscape scenes. Antícoli Corrado's houses are mostly medieval with small windows and outside staircases. The Church of San Pietro preserves fragments of its early mosaic floor.

▶ *From Antícoli Corrado return to the SS5 and turn right. Shortly after, branch right and follow the winding country road (SS411) southeast, past the hamlet of Agosta to Subiaco, a total of 21km (13 miles).*

Ceiling fresco from St Benedict's monastery church at Subiaco

The impressive Roman ruins of Ostia Antica

SCENIC ROUTES

The road from Anticoli to Subiaco goes through one of the most mountainous parts of Lazio. Look at the views, up to the left, to Monte Simbruini. Particularly fine is the approach to, and views from, Anticoli Corrado. From here you can see over the artists' landscape to the village of Saracinesco and Marano Equo.

3 Subiaco, Lazio

One of an isolated group of interesting little places on the edge of the Simbruini mountains, Subiaco has some very ancient buildings, most of which have something to do with St Benedict. This saint retired here late in the 5th century to write his *Rule* which was to heavily influence Christian monasticism. Subiaco originally had 12 monasteries organised by Benedict. Much later, in the atmosphere of piety and learning that these engendered, the first printed books in Italy were made (1464). While not much remains the early illustrious period of St Benedict himself, there is the Monastery of Santa Scolastica (Benedict's sister) which has three cloisters. Of St Benedict's own monastery, San Benedetto, high upon a rocky site, all that remains are two churches, one carved out of the rock, with frescos of varying ages.

Subiaco is a quiet, interesting place and well worth the visit. While you are there, you could visit the nearby gorge of the River Aniene, where there is a lake with a waterfall that might have been the work of the Emperor Nero who once had a villa at Subiaco (*Sublaqueum*).

▶ *Retrace the route via the SS411 to the SS5. Head for Roma, but after 9km (6 miles) join the A24 at the Vicovaro-Mandela junction,*

continuing towards Roma. About 22km (14 miles) along the autostrada, turn on to the A1 heading towards Naples. Continue on the A1 for 106km (66 miles) until the Cassino turning. Follow the signs to Gaeta via the SS630.

4 Gaeta, Lazio

The old town of Gaeta sits at the very end of a promontory jutting out into the Tyrrhenian Sea. This ancient centre still stands behind its old walls and remains largely medieval. There is plenty to see here, and it might be an idea to stay, as the beaches, the restaurants and the daily life of this seaside town are lively and varied. Apart from the Duomo (Sant'Erasmo), there is a 13th-century fortress and a maze of little ancient alleys and streets harbouring churches, old doorways and quirky little squares full of cats. The cathedral itself has been rebuilt at various times

Fountain in Tivoli's Villa d'Este

but its campanile (belltower), with its decorative upper parts, is of about 1148.

A great rock known as Torre d'Orlando (the Tower of Orlando) dominates Gaeta and on it is the circular mausoleum of the Roman consul Lucius Munatius Plancus, who died at Gaeta in 22BC. Mount Orlando divides ancient Gaeta, called *Sezione Erasmo*, from the newer part of town. This is the Porto Salvo, consisting of a series of narrow, straight streets of brightly painted houses and lots of wrought-iron balconies.

ℹ️ *Piazza Traniello*

FOR HISTORY BUFFS

Near Gaeta (20km/12 miles going south on the SS213) are the remains of *Minturnae*, a Roman town founded in 295BC. You can visit the excavations which include an aqueduct, theatre and forum, and the Antiquarium which contains memorable sculptures. Closer to Gaeta, just before Formia, is the so-called Tomb of Cicero. The great orator and writer was killed in 43BC near his villa at Formia. Both of these monuments have the added attraction of being very near to beaches.

▶ *Take the SS213 from Gaeta to Sperlonga, 16km (10 miles).*

5 Sperlonga, Lazio
The coastline from Gaeta to Sperlonga is beautiful, with many coves and promontories. Like Gaeta, Sperlonga sits on a spur of land that juts out into the Tyrrhenian Sea. Its centre is consistently medieval. Near by is the Grotta di Tiberio (Tiberius' Cave), where the emperor is said to have made merry in his own particular way. There is also the emperor's villa, and some good classical sculpture in the Museo

Archeologico Nazionale di Sperlonga.

▶ *From Sperlonga, continue along the SS213 to Terracina, then take the SS7 for 80km (50 miles) to Castèl Gandolfo, leaving the SS7 and following the signs from Albano Laziale.*

6 Castèl Gandolfo, Lazio
Castèl Gandolfo is where the Pope has his summer residence. Both town and papal palace are poised on a ridge above Lago (Lake) Albano and both come alive each year from July to September when the papal court transfers itself there from the Vatican City. All year round, however, the Swiss Guards are pacing up and down at the palace entrance, which faces a

large square full of cafés and little shops. Entry to Castèl Gandolfo, which takes its name from the castle built on the site of the present papal palace by the Gandolfi dukes in the 12th century, is via a magnificent 16th-century doorway. After resting in the square by the palace, visit the Church of San Tommaso di Villanova by Bernini, inside which are frescos by Pietro da Cortona. Both Bernini and da Cortona were among the founders of the Roman high baroque style.

From any number of points around the town you can look down over Lago Albano, a lake of volcanic origin that was chosen in the 1960s as the venue for the Olympic Games' rowing competitions. The

Frascati's landscape since ancient Republican times when wealthy Romans settled at nearby *Tusculo*, an even more ancient city, now ruined, some distance up the slope behind modern Frascati. The villas at Frascati date mostly from the 16th and 17th centuries. Most are still private and are not normally accessible, but some, like the Villa Falconieri, can be visited with prior permission. One of the greatest late baroque architects, Borromini, was responsible for parts of its design, though it was unfinished at the time of his death. The Villa Aldobrandini is the most spectacular here. Around 1,600 plans were made to bring water to the villa and a large cascade and water theatre were constructed. You can see the villa from the road and at odd times it is open to the public. The town itself has a pretty cathedral (San Pietro) built in 1598.

[i] *Piazza G Marconi 1*

RECOMMENDED WALKS

Take the boat from Formia to the Pontine Islands of which Ponza and Ventotène are the most interesting. Ponza has some lovely beaches. You could walk along these, visiting the little isolated coves on the way, and lunching perhaps in the main town there. Ventotène is much smaller. It has only a small beach but you can walk to the remains of the villa built by Augustus' daughter, Julia, in the 1st century AD.

---

installations built at the time are still in use and it is a lovely place to swim. All around are thick woodlands of oaks and chestnuts and there are also some ancient remains in the form of the Bagni di Diana (Baths of Diana) and the Villa dell'Imperatore Domiziano (Villa of the Emperor Domitian) – follow the yellow signs from the centre of town to find these.

[i] *Piazza Libertà 10*

▶ *From Castèl Gandolfo, rejoin and continue along the **SS7** to Frattócchie (about 4km/2½ miles) then branch right across country for about 9km (5½ miles), past the **SS511**, to the **SS215**, turning right for Frascati.*

SPECIAL TO...

The area around Frascati and Castèl Gandolfo has a favourite snack often consumed out in the piazza. This is *porchetta*, pig roast on a spit and eaten in huge chunks. It is very salty and delicious, especially the crackling. Wash this down with ice-cold, white Frascati wine.

---

7 **Frascati,** Lazio

This little country town is famous not for the buildings in its centre, but for the country retreats in the hills surrounding it. Although Frascati itself is medieval, the existing villas are much later. However, villa retreats have been a part of

▶ *From Frascati, return on the **SS215** to the GRA encircling Roma and continue clockwise on it for 18km (11 miles) until the turning left to the **SS8**, bound for Ostia and the sea.*

8 **Ostia,** Lazio

Ostia, the port of Roma, offers two contrasting attractions:

Gaeta's popular beach on the Tyrrhenian Sea

map of the city before you go and plan a route around it. The Museo Ostiense contains the portable artefacts from the site. The Lido di Ostia has a hugely long beach, very popular in the summer. Most people tend to rush past the old city in their haste to get to the sea. This is a mistake.

▶ *From Ostia, the **SS8** goes directly back to the centre of Roma.*

FOR CHILDREN

At Lido di Ostia, an extensive, well-organised resort, there are shallow beaches and some of the hotels have swimming pools. Also there are fine beaches east and west of Sperlonga.

Ostia Antica archaeological site and Lido di Ostia. The old port of Ostia Antica, now Italy's best preserved Roman town after Pompeii, was established in about 338BC when Rome needed to establish a settlement to supervise naval traffic and protect the mouth of the Tevere (Tiber) from raids by Tyrrhenian pirates. But old Ostia saw further construction right up to the 4th century AD, when it was abandoned. A visit should start perhaps at the Porta Romana (the Roman Gate), past the statue of Minerva Victoria and the forum. There are some re-erected columns of temples in the forum and a little further on are the Terme di Nettuno (Baths of Neptune) with their installations for heating. There is also a small restored theatre capable of holding 3,000 spectators. Some of the houses have lovely mosaic floors – see the Casa di Apuleio (House of Apuleius) – and there is one, the Casa di Diana (House of Diana), which still has its first floor intact, which is very unusual.

You could spend hours in Ostia Antica. There is a lot to see but make sure you pick up a

View over the quiet, medieval town of Subiaco

Ancient
Puglia

From towns with hefty, solid Norman cathedrals and castles, to villages with curious, prehistoric-looking, conical-roofed houses and farmsteads, central Puglia is packed with the evidence of a rich and diverse past. Bari is one of the biggest cities in Puglia, and the most cosmopolitan spot on this tour with a large variety of shops and restaurants as well as a medieval centre and a busy port.

3/4 DAYS • 314KM • 196 MILES

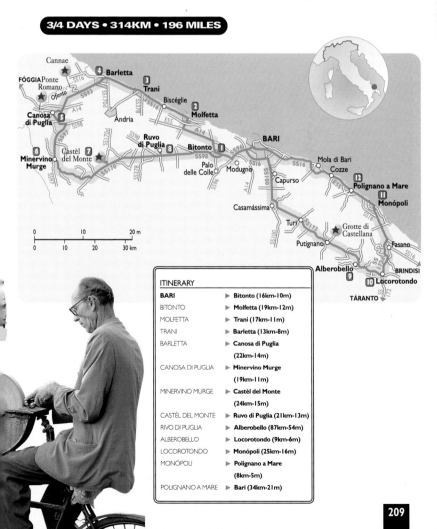

ITINERARY		
BARI	▶	**Bitonto (16km–10m)**
BITONTO	▶	**Molfetta (19km–12m)**
MOLFETTA	▶	**Trani (17km–11m)**
TRANI	▶	**Barletta (13km–8m)**
BARLETTA	▶	**Canosa di Puglia (22km–14m)**
CANOSA DI PUGLIA	▶	**Minervino Murge (19km–11m)**
MINERVINO MURGE	▶	**Castèl del Monte (24km–15m)**
CASTÈL DEL MONTE	▶	**Ruvo di Puglia (21km–13m)**
RÌVO DI PUGLIA	▶	**Alberobello (87km–54m)**
ALBEROBELLO	▶	**Locorotondo (9km–6m)**
LOCOROTONDO	▶	**Monópoli (25km–16m)**
MONÓPOLI	▶	**Polignano a Mare (8km–5m)**
POLIGNANO A MARE	▶	**Bari (34km–21m)**

SPECIAL TO...

Bari holds its Festa di San Nicola (Feast of St Nicholas) on 7 May. Recalling the arrival in Bari of the bones of the saint, brought from the Far East by sailors in 1087, an antique icon of the saint is carried in procession to the Basilica of St Nicholas. The following day the saint's statue is mounted on a boat which leads a water-borne procession.
The district around Bari has a particularly fine brand of olive oil. If the label says it comes from Bitonto in particular, then buy it.

i *Piazza Aldo Moro 33a, Bari*

▶ *Bitonto is 16km (10 miles) from Bari. Take the **SS96** from the city centre, then branch along the **SS98**.*

❶ **Bitonto,** Puglia
Right in the centre of Bitonto is the fine Puglian Romanesque 13th-century cathedral. Its best features are the women's gallery, the carvings of animals on the entrance portals, and the pulpit with its primitive bas-relief portraits of Emperor Frederick II and Isabella of England. Go down into the crypt and see the lovely column supports there. Other interesting churches are San Francesco with its late 13th-century façade, and the Church of the Purgatorio which has a sculptured relief of human skeletons just above the main entrance portal. Most of the centre of town is either Renaissance or baroque. See in particular the Palazzo Sylos-Labini and its Renaissance courtyard.

▶ *From Bitonto, travel north to the **A14**. Take the autostrada northwest for 11km (7 miles) until the Molfetta exit.*

❷ **Molfetta,** Puglia
Molfetta is an active fishing port – its fleet is one of the larger ones on the Adriatic. Predominantly medieval, it has

a lovely 12th- to 13th-century cathedral, the Duomo Vecchio, dominated by three domes – a Byzantine feature. There is also the Duomo Nuovo (new cathedral), though in this case 'new' means late 18th-century. This building has a baroque façade. The town has two museums. The Archaeological Museum contains the finds, including some Hellenistic ceramics, from local excavations. Still a large and prosperous port, it is The Museo Diocesano (Diocesan Museum) is housed in the bishop's palace.

▶ *Take the coastal road SS16 going northwest via Bisceglie to Trani, about 17km (11 miles).*

8 **Trani,** Puglia
Trani has always been an important port. Trade with the Orient in the 11th century drew into its orbit merchants from Genoa, Pisa and Amalfi and also created a large Jewish community. Still a large and prosperous port, it is full of little restaurants serving seafood.

The cathedral, which sits in an open-ended piazza facing the sea, is a fine building. Puglian Romanesque in style, it contains the remains of two other, earlier, structures on the same site. The oldest of these was an early Christian catacomb which you can still see with its marble columns and frescos; above that, though below the existing nave, are the remains of Santa Maria, the earlier Byzantine cathedral. The most noteworthy element of the present building is the pair of 12th-century bronze doors by a local master. Two other buildings that should not be missed are the Church of the Ognissanti, built by the Knights Templar as a hospice and, near the harbour, the Palazzo Caccetta, a 15th-century palace in the Gothic style – unusual in Puglia.

ℹ *Corso Cavour 140*

Castèl del Monte is one of the great medieval buildings of Europe

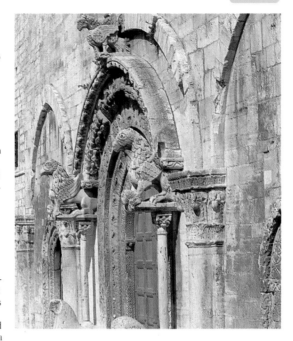

▶ *Continue up the coast on the SS16 to Barletta, 13km (8 miles).*

4 **Barletta,** Puglia
In Barletta is the largest known bronze statue in existence. Called the Colosso, it is 5m (15 feet) high and represents a Roman emperor, possibly Valentinian, who died in AD375. You can see it on its pedestal at the end of Corso Vittorio Emanuele. In the Middle Ages Barletta was an important and prosperous port. Like Trani it still retains much of its prosperity and has a pretty, if somewhat dilapidated medieval centre. As usual, the cathedral is the town's most interesting building. Built in the 12th century, the Duomo has a lovely rose window and there is an inscription above the left entrance portal which records how the English king Richard Coeur de Lion was involved in its construction (he came here on his way to the Crusades). Visit the 13th-century Church of San Sepolcro, the design of which recalls the Church of the Holy Sepulchre in Jerusalem, and the former

Ruvo di Puglia's fine Romanesque cathedral

convent building of San Domenico which now houses the Museo Civico (Civic Museum) and picture gallery. The castle is a massive structure, originally built by Emperor Frederick II and enlarged by Charles of Anjou.

ℹ *Via Gabbiani 4*

▶ *The SS93 branches inland from Barletta and goes to*

BACK TO NATURE

The Saline di Margherita is a large area of saltpans and wetlands just along the coast from the town of Margherita (a few kilometres west of Barletta). Birds such as black-winged stilts, Kentish plovers, pratincoles and short-toed larks breed in the area, and migrant waders, including curlew sandpipers, spotted redshanks, and wood sandpipers, pass through on passage.

Trani's cathedral is considered one of the best in Puglia

Canosa di Puglia, about 22km (14 miles).

FOR HISTORY BUFFS

The site of *Cannae*, where Hannibal gained his last great victory over the Romans, lies between Barletta and Canosa di Puglia on the Ofanto river. The remains of a huge necropolis can be seen and traces of the former city of *Cannae*. An Antiquarium houses finds from the site. On a hill above is the citadel which has yielded mainly medieval remains.

5 Canosa di Puglia, Puglia
Standing in the Tavoliere Plain, this town was an important Roman centre, called *Canusium*. Remains of Roman baths, amphitheatres and basilicas can be seen, and there is a Roman bridge over the Ofanto river which only survives because its arches were rebuilt in the Middle Ages. There are two later items of interest in the town's Romanesque cathedral: the marble 11th-century bishop's throne, which rests on the backs of two elephants, and the Tomb of Bohemund, Prince of Antioch, who was the son of Robert Guiscard and who died in 1111. The tomb's doors were made from a single slab of bronze. Other relics of the town's past are kept in the Museo Civico (Civic Museum).

▶ *From Canosa di Puglia, take the SS98 towards Andria, turning off right after 7km (4 miles) on the SS97 to Minervino Murge, a further 12km (7 miles).*

6 Minervino Murge, Puglia
Minervino Murge is known as the 'Balcony of Puglia' because of its wonderful position at the edge of the Murgia Alta, the rolling hills on Puglia's southern border. 'Minervo' derives from an ancient temple dedicated to the worship of Minerva on whose remains rises the present-day Church of the Madonna del Crocifisso. Apart

from the church and the panoramas of the countryside, this little town has a 12th-century castle, a Palazzo Comunale built in local style and a Norman cathedral, re-embellished in the Renaissance.

SCENIC ROUTES

The views from Minervino Murge to the surrounding countryside show a landscape that is most typically Puglian – gently rolling, almost flat.

▶ *Take the **SS170** eastwards for 22km (13½ miles) until the **SS170dir** branches off to the left. Follow the latter for 1km (½ mile) to the turning for Castèl del Monte on the left.*

7 Castèl del Monte, Puglia
This huge isolated castle is one of the most impressive monuments surviving from the reign of Emperor Frederick II and is well worth a special excursion to visit it. With its eight Gothic corner towers, you can see it from miles away, crowning an isolated peak way above the surrounding countryside. It was built around 1240 and in plan is a perfect octagon – the number eight being the symbol of the crown. You can wander through huge rooms, eight on each floor, that were once decorated with reliefs in Greek marble, porphyry and precious stones, now mostly disappeared. The castle may have been used originally as a centre for astronomy as its proportions are supposed to relate to the movements of the planets. But it was also the very grim prison of Frederick II's grandsons, who were incarcerated here for 30 years. Notice the beautiful carved entrance portal and, among what is left of its decoration, the signs of classical, Gothic, Persian and Arabic influences.

▶ *Return to the **SS170** and follow it eastwards. It joins the **SS98** 2km (1 mile) before Ruvo di Puglia.*

RECOMMENDED WALKS

On a visit to the Castèl del Monte, walk some way from the castle to appreciate the full impact of this extraordinary building.
All around is a pretty, agricultural and virtually empty landscape, called the Tavoliere, splendid for walks and also for picnics.

8 Ruvo di Puglia, Puglia
Ruvo di Puglia was a town celebrated in ancient times for its pottery. As long ago as the 5th century BC, its terracotta vases were highly sought after and some of these can be seen in the Palazzo Jatta. Here, too, is the magnificent red-figured Greek vase known as the 'Crater of Talos'. It is an important collection which you should not miss. Ruvo's cathedral is an important Puglian Romanesque building – one of the best in Puglia. Built in the 13th century, it has a richly decorated façade and a superb 16th-century rose window. In

particular, notice the griffins surmounting the columns on either side of the main entrance. Around the sides of the building are little sculpted figures of ancient, pagan gods, which it is thought may have been copied from classical pottery.

▶ *Return to Bari via the **SS98**. Skirt round the southern edge of the city on the **SS16** and turn right on to the **SS100**. Take the latter as far as Casamassima, 15km (9 miles), then branch left along the **SS172** to Alberobello, 35km (22 miles).*

9 Alberobello, Puglia
Alberobello is a very curious town. Clustered together in its centre is a collection of the prehistoric-looking local buildings called *trulli*. These small, circular, single-storey, stone buildings with cone-shaped tiled roofs look a bit like upside-down ice-cream cornets. There is nothing quite like them in any other part of Italy. Once such houses were common in Mediterranean countries – the beehive-shaped prehistoric Sardinian *nuraghi* are not dissimilar – but in Puglia, for some reason, they are a living tradition. Wander through the narrow streets of the Rione Monti and Aia Piccola quarters of Alberobello, where most of the *trulli* (there are over 1,000) are whitewashed and still inhabited. Even the style of the

Conical-roofed *trulli*, the traditional houses of Puglia

Church of Sant'Antonio seems to have derived its looks from the *trulli*. Most of Alberobello is a national monument, so that what has survived of its strange appearance is in very good

Molfetta's domed 'old cathedral' gazes benignly over the harbour

condition. One or two of the *trulli* are open to the public or have been turned into shops and restaurants.

FOR CHILDREN

Puglia is really not an area to bring children. However, they might enjoy looking into the *trulli* – built, it seems, more for hobbits than for humans. Everything in these igloo-like structures is in miniature. In both Alberobello and Locorotondo, one or two of them are open to the public. At Fasano, a developing holiday centre about 10km (6 miles) from both Alberobello and Locorotondo, there is a zoo/safari park, where animals of the African plains, such as giraffes, can be seen in the rough, dry terrain not far removed from their natural habitat.

▶ *The SS172 leads straight to Locorotondo.*

10 Locorotondo, Puglia
Locorotondo was laid out in concentric circles around the pinnacle of a low hill, and takes its name ('round place') from this plan. From the town there are wonderful views out over the Itria Valley in which you can see clumps of *trulli* scattered about – generally farmhouses and barns. In Locorotondo everything is covered with whitewash and gleams in the scorching Puglian summer sun. Small Greek-looking houses cluster around secret courtyards. There are geraniums in pots on the balconies, and the cobbled alleys and passages make this one of the more picturesque towns of Puglia. If you want to get out of the sun for a while, visit the churches of San Giorgio and San Marco della Greca, the former neo-classical, the latter a much earlier, possibly late Gothic, building.

▶ *The SS172dir leads via Fasano to the SS16. From Fasano, take the SS16 to Monópoli, about 12km (7½ miles).*

SCENIC ROUTES

The views from Locorotondo across the Trulli Zone of the Itria Valley make it easy to imagine yourself in a prehistoric landscape: the strange, *trulli* (beehive-like buildings) which dot the countryside are the kind of houses that the long-ago ancestors of present-day Puglians might have lived in. Nobody knows the real age or origins of these dwellings which are found solely in a small region round Alberobello and nowhere else in Europe.

11 Monópoli, Puglia
Monópoli is the most beautiful port on this strip of the Adriatic coastline. In the older quarter, tall medieval houses are built right up to the quay, overlooking the port and the little brightly painted fishing boats. The old centre is full of churches and other buildings which bear the traces of Byzantine and Venetian invaders. There is a castle, a Romanesque cathedral of 1107, with an impressive baroque façade and belltower, and the Church of San Domenico, perhaps the most magnificent building in the town. The Renaissance façade of San Domenico is split into three parts by columns and decorated

with statues, and there is a fine rose window. At various points beneath Monópoli, there are underground chambers and places of worship. One such is the Chiesa-Grotta, a natural cave, decorated in Byzantine times.

▶ *From Monópoli, take the coast road northwest to Polignano a Mare, about 8km (5 miles).*

12 Polignano a Mare, Puglia
Polignano a Mare is a delightful old city with little alleyways and flights of stepps. In the old quarter is the parish church dedicated to Our Lady of the Assumption. Although Romanesque in style, it was added to during the Renaissance period. Ask to see the painting by the 15th-century Venetian artists Vivarini, in the sacristy. Just outside town are the Grotte Palazzese (Palazzese Caves), set into the cliffsides. These are two huge sea caves, reached by climbing down precarious steps set into the rock just below the town.

▶ *The SS16 leads back to Bari, 34km (21 miles).*

SCENIC ROUTES

The coastline from Polignano a Mare to Molà di Bari, going along the SS16 is lovely unspoilt coastal scenery (though not suitable for swimming except from the rocks).

on the road
SCANDINAVIA

Linked by geography and a common heritage, Scandinavia sees itself as apart from the rest of Europe. Denmark, Finland, Norway and Sweden conjure up images of sparkling lakes, unspoiled countryside, magnificent forests and fiords slicing into craggy mountains and cliffs.

tal) and Gothenburg is the lake district of central Sweden.

Here, around Mälaren, the country's third biggest lake, is the heartland of Sweden. The lake provides easy access to the Baltic and was an important trading region as early as the Viking times.

Built on the mainland and islands at the point where Lake Mälaren meets the mighty Baltic Sea, Stockholm is very much a city of the water. It is the most beautiful and grand of the Scandinavian capitals. Wander round its waterfronts and the narrow lanes of Gamla Stan (Old Town). Visit the many museums on the neighbouring islands of Djurgården (including the 17th-century warship *Vasa* and the old buildings at Skansen) and Skeppsholmen with its Modern Art Museum. The old Town Hall overlooks Lake Mälaren at the point where there are boats to the royal palace of Drottningholm. One of the greatest pleasures in Stockholm is to catch a white ferry from outside the Grand Hotel and travel far out into the magnificent archipelago.

Tour 34

Although small in size, Denmark is rich in natural beauty. Verdant countryside, fine beaches and vast areas of woodlands characterise the island of Sjaelland, or Sealand. Here, Roskilde, København (Copenhagen), Helsingor and their surrounds offer a splendid climax to a journey through Denmark. The Danish Council of Tourist Trade have devised the excellent Marguerite Route for the motoring tourist. Winding its way through Denmark's most

Page 215: top – typical colourfully painted house in Denmark; bottom – dusk over the lake at Suomussalmi, Finland

picturesque countryside it links the main attractions and sights and can be followed here, by taking a trail well signposted by a daisy symbol on a brown background.

For the past 1,000 years the port of Korsør has been the entrance into Sealand for travellers from Funen. The history of this role as ferry terminus is related in the Museum of Korsør, housed in the old cannon hall of the castle. All that remains of the castle's original medieval structure is the 23m (75-foot) high tower, which is open to visitors.

Tour 35

Between the two major cities of Stockholm (Sweden's capi-

Tour 36

Norway is famed for its spectacular fiords, mountains and glaciers. You can easily enjoy yourself in unspoilt natural surroundings, with nature never far away. One of its main roads, Route 11, leads westwards from Oslo, along valleys and over mountain passes in the direction of Bergen. A highlight of the journey is the Hardanger fiord, which is at its most beautiful in June when the apple blossom is in bloom.

Founded in the 11th century by Harald Hardrade, Oslo was Norway's ecclesiastical base and later, around 1300, it became the country's capital.

the country, the Viking Ship Museum with Viking vessels from the 9th century, and the Farm and Ship Museums with boats used by Nansen and Amundsen on their Arctic expeditions; Thor Heyerdahl's *Kon-Tiki* and *Ra II* are also here.

Back in town there are many museums with notable art collections, the most celebrated being the Munch Museum with works by Norway's great artist Edvard Munch (1863–1944).

a territory now torn in two by an international border. Elias Lonnot travelled the region in the early part of the last century and came across bards who recounted old folk poetry to him. He compiled these into the epic poem *Kaleva*, which was heralded as the discovery of Finnish roots. At last the Finns could trace an identity of their own which was divorced from their intimate past with the Swedes.

Kuopio has a beautiful waterside location in Finland's

Fredericksborg Castle, Hillerød

The city suffered bleak periods over the following centuries with a horrific plague, occupation by the Danes and a disastrous fire. Today, the city is the busy commercial and industrial hub of Norway. The pleasantest part of the downtown area is the walk along the main Karl Johansgate, past the old university and towards the palace. Bear left by the National Theatre to the huge, brown-brick Town Hall and quayside where there are bars, restaurants, shops and ferries to the outlying islands. The nearest island is Bygdøy (also accessible by road) with its extensive Folk Museum and collection of old buildings from around

Tour 37

Most people approach Finland by sea from the southwest. The Swedes did, arriving in medieval times and occupying the country as a province, with the capital at Turku (Åbo). They were ousted by the Russians in 1808, who in 1809 made it a Grand Duchy and then shifted the seat of power to Helsinki. Finland declared itself independent in 1917 following the Russian revolution.

The central southern region is covered by an enormous and beautiful lakeland which is more water than land. The lakes stretch east into Karelia,

northern lakeland region. Its position is best appreciated from the watch tower on Puijo Hill, from where there is a splendid view over the spacious modern city and the lakes dotted with numerous islands. Kuopio has a large Finnish Orthodox community with St Nicolas church as the seat of its archbishop. North of the centre, at the archbishop's residence, is the Orthodox Church Museum, which includes priceless works of religious art salvaged from the original Valamo monastery. Kuopio's Lutheran cathedral is in the centre of this city, together with a university (1972), a modern concert hall and a fine regional museum.

PRACTICAL INFORMATION

BANKS
Weekdays only throughout.
Denmark: 9.30am–4pm
(often 6pm).
Sweden: 9.30am–3pm; in
larger towns banks may be
open until 5.30pm; in smaller
places they may close earlier.
Hours may be shortened on
the eve of a bank holiday.
Norway: 8.15am–3.30pm
(3pm from June to
September); Thursday, open
until 5pm.
Finland: 9.15am–4.15pm.

CREDIT CARDS
All principal credit cards are
fairly widely accepted.

CURRENCY
Denmark: the Danish crown
(krone; kr or DKK), is divided
into 100 øre. Notes are issued
in denominations of 50, 100, 500,
and 1,000 kr coins in denominations of 25 and 50 øre and 1, 2, 5,
10 and 20 kr.
Sweden: the Swedish crown
(krona; kr or SEK), is divided
into 100 øre. Notes are issued in
denominations of 20, 50, 100,
500,1,000 and 10,000 kr; coins in
denominations of 50 øre and 1, 5
and 10 kr.
Norway: the Norwegian crown
(krone; kr or NOK), is divided
into 100 øre. Notes are issued for
50, 100 and 1,000 kr; coins in
denominations of 50 øre and 1, 5
and 10 kr.
Finland: the Finnish mark
(markka, plural markkaa; mk or
Fmk), is divided into 100
penniar (singular penni; abbreviated to p). Notes are 20, 50, 100,
500 and 1,000 mk; coins in
denominations of 10 and 50p
and 1, 5 and 10 mk.

CUSTOMS REGULA-TIONS
Applicable to Denmark, Finland
and Sweden:
Visitors from EU countries are
governed by EU regulations and
can bring in items for their
personal use without paying

One of Sweden's pretty fishing
villages: Hällviksstrand

duty. Limits apply to goods
obtained at duty-free shops.
Visitors resident outside Europe
are entitled to higher allowances
and amounts should be verified
at the time of purchase.
  Different concessions apply to
Norway, which is not a member
of the EU. Duty-free limits for
Europeans: 1 litre wine, 1 litre
spirits (or 2 litres wine if no spirits); 2 litres beer; 200 cigarettes
or 250g tobacco. Visitors from
outside Europe can bring in the
same amount of wine and spirits;
400 cigarettes or 100 cigars or
500g tobacco. These duty-free
allowances apply only to persons
of 18 years or over for wine, beer
and tobacco products and 20
years or over for spirits.

ELECTRICITY
The current is generally 220
volts AC throughout
Scandinavia, with plugs of the
two round-pin type (an adaptor
will be needed). British,
Australian or New Zealand
appliances normally requiring a
slightly higher voltage will work.
Visitors from North America may
require a voltage transformer.

EMERGENCY NUMBERS
Denmark: tel: 112 for fire,
police or ambulance.
Sweden: tel: 9 00 00.
Norway: look under SOS in
the phone book for the local
number.
Finland: tel: 112 for fire,
police or ambulance.

ENTRY REGULATIONS
EU nationals need a valid
passport or identity card.
Australian, Canadian, Irish,
New Zealand and US nationals need only a valid passport.
For stays of over three
months, special regulations
apply to all visitors, check
with appropriate embassies or
consulates. Quarantine regulations are so strict that the
importation of animals into
Norway and Sweden is virtually
impossible.

FERRIES
The ferries to and around
Scandinavia are excellent and
are rather like mini-cruises on
the longer services.

Denmark to Norway
Copenhagen–Oslo (16 hours):
Scandinavian Seaways.
Hirtshals–Oslo (10–13 hours):
Color Line.
Hirtshals–Kristiansand (4–7
hours): Color Line.
Frederikshavn–Larvik (6–10
hours): Larvik Line.
Frederikshavn–Oslo (9–12
hours): Stena Line.
Frederikshavn–Moss (7 hours):
Stena Line.
Hanstholm–Egersund (7 hours):
Fjord Line.

Denmark to Sweden
Helsingør–Helsingborg (25
minutes): Scand Lines.
Dragør–Limhamn (55 minutes):
Limhamn–Dragør Line.
Frederikshavn–Göteborg (4
hours): Stena Line.
Grenå–Varberg (5 hours): Lion
Ferry.

Grenå–Halmstad (5 hours): Lion Ferry.
Frederikshavn–Göteborg (2 hours): Seacatamaran.
Rønne–Ystad (3 hours): Bornholmstrafikken.

Sweden to Finland
Stockholm–Helsinki (15 hours): Silja Line, Viking Line, Birka Line.
Stockholm–Turku (12 hours): Silja Line, Viking Line.
Sundsvall–Vaasa (7 hours): Silja Line.
Ornsköldsvik–Vaasa (5 hours): Skellefteå–Jakobstad (5 hours): Jakob Lines.
Skellefteå–Karleby (4 hours): Jakob Lines.
Umeå–Vaasa (3 hours): Wasa Line.

HEALTH MATTERS
See **Austria** (page 10).

MOTORING
Accidents
In the event of an accident, a report must be made to the insurance company. If the accident involves personal injury, medical assistance must be sought for the injured party and the incident reported to the police. There are special bureaux which deal with accidents involving foreign motor vehicles; local police will advise.

Elks are numerous in parts of Sweden, Norway and Finland and they often cross the roads (the same applies to reindeer in Lappland). Warning signs showing the approximate lengths of the danger zones are posted in these areas. These animals weigh anything up to 500–600kg and collisions involving them are usually serious. Elks are most active at dusk but may also be encountered at other times. If you are involved in a reindeer or elk collision, report this without delay to the local police.

Breakdowns
In case of breakdown:
In **Denmark** ask for the services of Dansk Autohjalp (tel: 31 31 21 44) or Falck (tel: 44 66 22 22).

In **Sweden** contact Alarm Centres (020) 91 00 40 (free phone).
In **Norway** contact Norges Automobil-Forbund (NAF) – Oslo, tel: (22) 34 14 00 or (22) 34 1600 (24-hour emergency service), Bergen, tel: (05) 29 24 62, Trondheim, tel: (07) 96 62 88, Tromso, tel: (083) 7 07 00.
In **Finland** contact Autolitto, tel: (97) 00 80 80.

Car hire
Car hire is available in most cities, resorts and main airports throughout Scandinavia. Many international firms operate this service; local rivals often offer better deals. Rates sometimes include breakdown services, maintenance and oil, but not petrol. Basic insurance is also included and additional cover can be bought. Costs fluctuate according to type of car, duration of rental and time of year. The minimum age of the hirer varies from 18 to 25 years; they should be in possession of an international driving licence.

Documents
Visitors taking their own (therefore foreign-registered) car to Scandinavia must be at least 18 years of age, and in possession of the vehicle's registration document, an international green card or other insurance, and a valid, full driving licence; it is also advisable to be in possession of an international licence. There should be a clearly visible sign attached to the vehicle showing the nationality.

Driving conditions
Vehicles must keep to the right-hand side of the road and close to the nearside kerb, even when the road is clear. Side mirrors should be fitted on the left-hand side of the car. The wearing of seat belts is compulsory in the front and rear of the car. Use dipped headlights at all times.

Route directions
Roads, except for the minor ones, are numbered. A road prefixed by an E denotes a main

Europa road; other roads are not prefixed by a letter.

Speed limits
Denmark: built-up areas 50kph (30mph); outside built-up areas 80kph (50mph); motorways 110kph (66mph).
Sweden: built-up areas 50kph (30mph); outside built-up areas 90kph (56mph); motorways 110kph (66mph).
Norway: built-up areas 50kph (30mph); outside built-up areas 80kph (50mph); motorways generally 90kph (56mph).
Finland: built up areas 50kph (30mph); outside built-up areas 80kph (50mph); motorways 120kph (75mph).

POST OFFICES
Denmark: mostly 9am–5pm Monday to Friday; 9am–noon Saturday.
Sweden: 9am–6pm Monday to Friday; 9am–noon Saturday.
Norway: 8 or 8.30am to 4 or 5pm Monday to Friday; 8am–1pm Saturday.
Finland: 9am–5pm Monday to Friday.

TELEPHONES
Telephone cards (from tobacconists and various other outlets) are becoming increasingly more common in Scandinavia; for the time being there are also coin boxes in most towns, using 1, 5 and 10 kr/mk coins.

To call abroad use the following international dialling codes:
Denmark to UK: 00 44
Denmark to US or Canada: 00 1
Sweden to UK: 009 44
Sweden to US or Canada: 009 1
Norway to UK: 095 44
Norway to US or Canada: 095 1
Finland to UK: 990 44
Finland to US or Canada: 990 1.

TIME
Denmark, Sweden and Norway follow Central European Time, (one hour ahead of GMT). Finland follows Eastern European Time (two hours ahead of GMT). Summer time – one hour ahead of normal time – is observed from the end of March to the end of September.

Sjælland
(Sealand)

The journey through Denmark has progressed eastwards to the isle of Sealand and continues to the northeast quarter to explore the cathedral city of Roskilde, the capital, Copenhagen, royal palaces, smart coastline (along Strandvejen) and Helsingør, the setting for Shakespeare's *Hamlet*, from where it is just a short hop to Sweden.

4 DAYS • 757KM • 456 MILES

▶ From Korsør follow road 265 through Skælskør to Borreby (19km/12 miles). From here it is a further 11km (7 miles) to Holsteinborg.

① Borreby and Holsteinborg, Sealand

Chancellor Johan Friis, the man responsible for Hesselagergård Manor on Funen, built on a grander and stronger scale at Borreby. Fearing he would be targeted by the peasants during their period of discontent in the mid-16th century, Friis constructed Borreby Castle with particularly solid fortifications. Hans Christian Andersen used to stay at Borreby; his story about *Valdemar Daae and his Daughters* is based on the Daae family who were later occupants of the castle. Andersen also enjoyed visiting the nearby 17th-century Holsteinborg Castle which stands amidst extensive parklands; the guest room where he lodged is unchanged since his time.

▶ From Holsteinborg drive to and turn right on to road 265 (not part of the Marguerite Route), before dipping on to the minor coast road before the approach to Næstved (27km/16 miles).

② Næstved, Sealand

The important market town of Næstved evolved around the Benedictine monastery of Skovkloster in the 12th century. Today its attractions are the churches of St Peter, Denmark's largest Gothic church with 14th-century murals and chancel, and St Morten, a 13th-century edifice with a richly decorated altarpiece. The modern town has rather overwhelmed other relics of the past, but the Næstved Museum provides an interesting picture of the rich local history; it is housed in the 15th-century Helligåndshuset, formerly a home for the sick and destitute. The well-heeled had their children looked after at Herlufsholm, an old and prestigious private boarding school which stood on the site of the original Skovkloster; the church is the only building that remains of the old abbey and is open to the public.

▶ From Næstved travel east via Fensmark to Gisselfeld (25km/15 miles) and Bregentved Castle (a further 6km/4 miles).

> ### SPECIAL TO...
>
> Gavnø Castle, on a small island linked by a bridge 6km (4 miles) south of Naestved, was a brigands' hideout in medieval times and later a royal nunnery before Otto Thott had the present grand manor built in the 18th century; he also accumulated a huge library and one of the largest privately owned art collections in Scandinavia, both of which are now on display.

Gisselfeld captured the imagination of Hans Christian Andersen

③ Gisselfeld and Bregentved, Sealand

The Gisselfeld Castle is another estate which apparently served as inspiration for Hans Christian Andersen. It was built in its present Renaissance style in 1545 by Peder Oxe, the man who succeeded Johan Friis as chancellor of Denmark. The extensive gardens are open to

> ### SPECIAL TO...
>
> On leaving Næstved you pass Fensmark in 10km (6 miles). Lying roughly 1km (½ mile) to the east of Fensmark, Holmegård is one of Denmark's most famous glass-works; visitors are welcome – glass-blowing is demonstrated and glassware can be bought at favourable prices.

the public, as are the grounds at the nearby late 19th-century Bregentved Castle.

▶ *From Bregentved continue to Fakse and Fakse Ladeplads, and keep along the coast, via Vemmetofte Manor and Rødvig, to Højerup (47km/29 miles).*

4 Højerup, Sealand

The stretches of sand beach on this southern coast give way to a headland cliff known as Stevns Klint, which reaches a height of 41m (134 feet). The cliffs are constantly being eroded by the sea and now Højerup's small medieval church stands precariously on the edge; part of it crashed into the sea in 1928.

▶ *From Højerup follow the road through Store Heddinge to Karise, and then north to Vallø Castle and Køge (31km/19 miles).*

Above: Vallø Castle, the imposing fortress built on one of the Rosenkrantz estates
Left: a half-timbered Køge house

5 Køge, Sealand

Køge was a thriving herring port during the Middle Ages and keeps the charm of an old town along streets such as Kirkestræde, Nørregade and Vestergade, where there are many fine half-timbered houses. The oldest house is 20 Kirkestræde (1527) and the smallest is around the corner from the church of St Nicholas,

famous for its splendid 17th-century altarpiece.

> ### SPECIAL TO...
>
> The old trams from Copenhagen, Århus and Odense are now on display at the Tram Museum at Skjoldenæsholm.

> ### SPECIAL TO...
>
> With its two great towers and surrounding moat, Vallø Castle – 8km (5 miles) south of Køge – is among the most imposing castles of Sealand. It was one of the estates of the Rosenkrantz family in the 16th century and later became home of Anna Sophie Reventlow – Frederik IV's morganatic wife. Most of the castle had to be restored after a terrible fire in 1893. For over 250 years Vallø has been a home for unmarried ladies of the more refined class.

▶ *From Køge head west past Ejby, Borup, Jystrup and Skjoldenæsholm, and then bear northwards for Kirke Hvalsø and Lejre to reach Roskilde (44km/26 miles).*

6 Roskilde, Sealand
The royal seat of Denmark shifted to Roskilde after Harald Bluetooth set up his quarters here at the end of the 10th century. Dominating the city is

> **SPECIAL TO…**
>
> One of Europe's top summertime rock festivals is staged annually at Roskilde.

> **SPECIAL TO…**
>
> At Lejre, 10km (6 miles) southwest of Roskilde, there is a preserved ship tumulus to mark the site of a 10th-century Viking settlement; nearby Oldtidsbyen is a reconstruction of an an Iron Age village where activities from that period are enacted. Also near Lejre is the 18th-century Ledreborg manor, which is reached by way of a 7km (4-mile) long avenue of lime trees. There is a rococo garden and rich woodland – 'visitors welcome when the forests are green', says the sign. Visitors are also welcome at the house – which has a good art collection – and the richly decorated chapel.

One of the Viking ships which sank while defending the Roskilde Fjord over 800 years ago

the huge twin-towered cathedral, built in the 1170s by Bishop Absalon on the site of Bluetooth's old wooden church. The towers were added some time after the original building programme and their sharp spires provided the finishing touch in 1636. All Danish monarchs since 1536 have been laid to rest here.

One of the most dramatic discoveries from the Viking era found anywhere in Scandinavia is the Viking ships of Roskilde. In the early 11th century five ships were sunk as they tried to defend the Roskilde Fjord at Skuldelev, 20km (12 miles) from Roskilde. They were discovered in 1962 and put on show at the Viking Ship Museum.

▶ *From Roskilde head eastwards towards Copenhagen. The capital can be avoided by passing through the suburbs and joining the coast road 152 at Charlottenlund, on the north side of the city (77km/48 miles). Continue north from Charlottenlund along the 152 (the famous Strandvejen) to Helsingør (38km/23 miles).*

7 Helsingør, Sealand
As Denmark's closest point to Sweden, Helsingør has long provided a ferry service across the narrow strait to Helsingborg; today a boat leaves every 20 minutes, with a 20-minute crossing time. Down by the waterfront is Kronborg, the large, austere Renaissance castle which served Shakespeare as a setting for *Hamlet*. Built in 1585 by Frederik II, it had to be extensively restored after a fire in 1629 destroyed all except the chapel. Rebuilt by Christian IV, the great halls, chambers and chapel are open to visitors. In contrast to the tragic Hamlet is Ogier the Viking, whom Danes call upon to fill them with fighting mettle in times of need; his statue is in the casements. The

> **SPECIAL TO…**
>
> Fredensborg Castle, between Helsingør and Hillerød, is often dubbed the favourite royal residence. Frederiks IV, V and VI each had a hand in its building during the 18th century. Fredensborg is open to the public in July, while the lovely gardens can be visited at any time. Royal guards stand rigidly to attention.

other principal sight is the splendidly preserved St Maria church and Carmelite monastery, dating from 1517. Much of the old town has been tastefully restored and provides an historic and pleasant backdrop for this busy thoroughfare between nations.

▶ *From Helsingør travel westwards, via Tikob, to Fredensborg and on to Hillerød (28km/17 miles).*

8 Hillerød, Sealand

Frederik II acquired the Hillerødsholm estate as a royal hunting ground in 1560. Not content with the modest manor then in existence, he set about building Frederiksborg Castle, which his son, Christian IV,

Frederiksborg Castle, a Renaissance masterpiece, built on the Hillerødsholm estate

completed with great flourish in the early 1600s. Huge, surrounded by a moat and adorned with carved façades and figures, Frederiksborg is probably the most spectacular Renaissance castle in Denmark – it is certainly the most ostentatious hunting lodge. The chapel and its extravagant decoration survived the very damaging fire of 1859 and still has its original Compenius organ of 1610. The town evolved because of the castle and Frederiksborg is now on the edge of Hillerød; the gardens and woods of the estate spread behind the castle.

▶ *From Hillerød head west on road 19 to join road 16. Bear right for Annisse and skirt Lake Arresø to Frederiksværk. Continue south on road 211 to Frederikssund and Jægerspris (61km/37 miles).*

9 Jægerspris, Sealand

Another royal hunting home, the castle of Jægerspris has been a popular estate among the Danish kings since medieval times, none more so than Frederik VII who enjoyed it as a family summer residence. On his death the Countess of Danner, his wife, handed the castle to a charity for abandoned young women. The apartments used by Frederik VII remain unchanged and are open to visitors in summer.

developed as a trading port around its medieval castle. The town reached its peak of prosperity between the 17th and 19th centuries when it became an important grain exporter. Some of the old merchants' houses still stand, and the one now occupied by the local museum dates from 1670. Holbæk remains the principal market town of the region; compared to the east, the countryside to the west is comprised of more sparsely populated farmlands. Four kilometres (2 miles) south of the town, the twin-towered Tveje Merlose church dates from the early 12th century.

▶ *From Holbæk take road* **57** *southwards, bearing right along the* **231** *at Ugerløse for Mørkøv. From Mørkøv travel west on road* **23** *to Jyderup, then north via Kundby for Asnæs and Høve, and then southwest for Ordrup and Dragsholm Castle (101km/63 miles).*

⑪ Dragsholm, Sealand
The original medieval castle of Dragsholm served as a strong refuge during the uprisings of the 1530s and then as a sound prison 40 years later for the Earl of Bothwell, the husband of Mary, Queen of Scots. The Scottish nobleman ended his days here and the cell where he was allegedly manacled to the wall can be visited. The castle proved an inadequate defence, however, against the Swedes who blew it apart during a battle in 1659. Most of the present castle dates from the late 17th century.

▶ *From Dragsholm continue along the coast and join road* **23** *for Kalundborg (30km/18 miles).*

⑫ Kalundborg, Sealand
Sheltered in its fiord at the western extreme of Sealand, the port of Kalundborg is a ferry point for Jutland (to Århus and Juelsminde) and the island of

Samsø. It was a substantial medieval fortification and capital of Denmark for a short time. Most remarkable of the present sights is the church built in 1170 by Esben Snare, the man also responsible for the original defences and the brother of Bishop Absalon who was behind the construction of Roskilde Cathedral. Lerchenborg Castle, the 18th-century baroque manor of General Christian Lerche, is 5km (3 miles) along the coast to the south; it – like so many others – boasts a visit by Hans Christian Andersen, and the room where the author stayed is on display.

▶ *From Kalundborg head for Lerchenborg, then east across country via Sæby and Tersløse to Fjenneslev and west to Sorø, 82km (51 miles).*

⑬ Sorø, Sealand
The 12th-century abbey at Sorø was converted into an academy for upper-class boys in the 17th century. The main building underwent reconstruction in the 1820s, but the old abbey chapel is medieval; the influential Bishop Absalon of Roskilde, who died in 1201, is buried here behind the altar. The academy – still a boarding school – has a lovely setting by the Sorø lake.

▶ *From Sorø head south and bear left to follow the shore of Tystrup Sø (Lake Tystrup); then continue to Bisserup, following the coast back to Korsør, 67km (40 miles).*

SPECIAL TO...

The granite church at Fjenneslev, 11km (7 miles) east of Sorø, dates from the early 12th century. A further 7km (4 miles) east is Ringsted, where medieval royalty – including Queen Dagmar (died 1212) of Dagmar Cross fame – were buried at St Bendt's church. There are interesting murals at both these churches.

SPECIAL TO...

The manor at Selsø which Jakob Ulfeldt built in the 1570s was greatly modified in 1734 by Christian Ludvig von Plessen. The interior is now a museum. Selsø Castle is 18km (11 miles) south of Jægerspris.

▶ *From Jægerspris turn southwards past Skuldelev, Sønderby, Selsø and Skibby, and continue through Sæby and Lyndby. Bear west to Holbæk, via Rye and Eriksholm (63km/39 miles).*

⑩ Holbæk, Sealand
Situated on the southern end of the large Isefjord, Holbæk

Lake
Mälaren

With its waters stretching from far inland to the Baltic, Lake Mälaren provides easy access to the open seas. Vikings and medieval merchants founded settlements on its shores and islands; modern Stockholm sits where the lake meets the sea. Surrounded by countryside dotted with castles, cathedrals and old towns, Mälaren is ideal for excursions from the capital.

3 DAYS • 333KM • 207 MILES

ℹ️ *Sverigehuset, Kungsträdgården*

▶ *From Stockholm take the E4
northwards and just before
reaching Märsta bear left on
to road 255 (34km/21
miles). After 6km (4 miles)
turn left again on to road 263
and continue for a further
6km (4 miles) to Sigtuna.*

SCENIC ROUTES

A wonderful change from driving is the 3½-hour journey
along Lake Mälaren on the old
steamboat SS *Mariefred* from
Stockholm to Mariefred (and
the castle of Gripsholm).

recounting the region's Viking-
medieval period, and
Lundströmska Gården, the old
burgher's house.

ℹ️ *Stora gatan 33*

▶ *From Sigtuna head north via
Haga to join road 255 for
Uppsala (31km/19 miles).*

Stockholm's glorious old town
buildings ranged proudly along
the shore of Lake Mälaren

1 **Sigtuna,** Uppland

Dating from 970, Sigtuna is
reputedly the oldest town in
Sweden. It thrived as a trading
port and attracted merchants
from Asia and the Middle East.
Coins were struck here by
English minters, and churches
and monasteries – each better
than the next – were commissioned by the wealthy. There
were setbacks, however;
notably when Uppsala stole the
limelight as the region's major
ecclesiastical centre and again
when the Estonians burnt down
the town in 1187. But Sigtuna
survived and remained a prosperous centre throughout the
Middle Ages.

Today it is a quaint, small
town pleasantly located on the
shores of Mälaren. Colourfully
painted wooden houses line the
main Stora gatan, built on the
ground plan of the original high
street. The remains of the 12th-

century churches of St Olof, St
Lars and St Per are notable,
though in best condition is St
Mary's, part of a monastery
dating from 1247. Other points
of interest include the old Town
Hall of 1744, the local museum,

SPECIAL TO...

The 13th-century Cistercian
monastery of Skokloster was
dismantled in 1574 and
replaced by the present
magnificent, white baroque
castle, which was
commissioned in the late 17th
century by Karl Gustav
Wrangel, Count of Salamis and
Grand Marshal and Grand
Admiral of Sweden. Exhibitions
of armour and paintings are on
display. About 14km (8 miles)
northwest of Sigtuna,
Skokloster can be incorporat-
ed into a day excursion to
Sigtuna and Uppsala, the
former of which can also be
reached by ferry from
Stockholm.

2 **Uppsala,** Uppland

The pre-Viking chiefs of Svea
had their seat in Gamla Uppsala
(Old Uppsala) and under three
huge burial mounds lie their
kings, Adil, Egil and Aun. The
nearby church is a remnant of
the cathedral built in 1125 on
the site of a Svea heathen
temple.

In 1273, however, the arch-
bishopric was moved 5km (3
miles) south to the port of Östra
Aros (present Uppsala), while
the kings transferred their residence to Stockholm. Work
began on a new cathedral,
which was eventually consecrated in 1435. The result was,
and still is, the largest Gothic
cathedral in Scandinavia,
measuring 119m (390 feet) in
both length and height; the
18th-century twin spires dominate the Uppsala skyline.
Sweden's patron saint, Saint
Erik, and its kings, archbishops
and heroes are all buried in the
cathedral.

The old quarter of Uppsala is
on the west bank of the Fyrisån,

and opposite the cathedral is the onion-domed, early 17th-century Gustavianum, originally an anatomical theatre and now a museum with ancient Nordic and Egyptian collections. Behind this, gardens dotted with runic stones and bronze statues lead to the main building of Uppsala University, constructed in lavish fashion in the late 1800s. Founded in the late 15th century, the university is one of Europe's great seats of learning. Like Oxford and Cambridge in England, Uppsala and Lund (in the south) are the two most famous university cities of Sweden. The university library, with over two million volumes and 30,000 manuscripts, is particularly impressive. On display is the famous 6th-century *Codex Argenteus*, a translation of the Gospels written in gold and silver on purple parchment.

It is a short walk southwards through the park and up the hill

One of the many runic stones that are scattered throughout Uppsala University gardens

to Uppsala Castle which was started – but never completed – by Gustav Vasa in 1548. One of Uppsala's many famous old boys was botanist Carl von Linné (Linnaeus), who worked as the curator of the gardens which now bear his name; the Linnéträdgården (Linnaean Garden) and its museum are on the east side of the river.

[i] *Fyristorg 8 (also in the castle during the summer months)*

▶ *From Uppsala take road **55** southwest to Enköping (45km/28 miles).*

8 Enköping, Uppland
Another of Mälaren's old trading towns, Enköping was the main spice and herb market. Originally endowed with a castle, churches and monasteries, the town lost much of its heritage in the great fire of 1799. Some old buildings have been restored, while others retain just small sections of the past. More recently Enköping has attracted industries and it is as an industrial city that it is best known.

Minor roads lead through the pleasant countryside to the south of Enköping and to the bathing spots at Harjarö, at the tip of the peninsula.

[i] *Torggatan 2 (also Kyrkogatan 29 during the summer months)*

▶ *From Enköping take the **E18** west to Västerås.*

9 Västerås, Västmanland
Västerås is a medieval city with an imposing, but much restored, Gothic cathedral of 1271; among those dignitaries enshrined within the building is King Erik XIV.

The city has boomed in recent years, thanks largely to ASEA Brown and Boveri (ABB) setting up their electrical plant here. Today the population is around 120,000, representing an increase of tenfold during the 20th century. The Kyrkbacken district, to the north of the cathedral, has preserved its old character well; the museum of local history is housed in the medieval castle, while the city's art collection, which features works ranging from the 17th century to the present, is displayed at the old Town Hall.

[i] *Stora gatan 40*

> ### SPECIAL TO...
>
> One of the country's largest burial mounds and ship tumuli from the Iron Age and Viking periods is at Anundshögen, 6km (4 miles) northeast of Västerås.

▶ *From Västerås continue west on the **E18** and then bear south on road **53** for Eskilstuna (42km/26 miles).*

> ### SPECIAL TO...
>
> Silver mined at Sala, about 40km (25 miles) north of Västerås, was of the finest quality and in the 16th century it significantly enriched the country's exchequer. The main mine was closed in 1908 but has now reopened to the public. A museum explains the mining process and the history of the site.

> ### BACK TO NATURE
>
> Better known as Linnaeus, the Swedish botanist Carl von Linné initiated the system of nomenclature using the Latin names of both the genus and the species to classify plants. Linnaeus (1707–78) spent his last years at Hammarby Farm, 12km (7 miles) southeast of Uppsala; the house and gardens can be visited. Near by are the stones of Mora where Swedish kings would be sworn in.

> ### FOR CHILDREN
>
> Located 15km (9 miles) southwest of Västerås, part of the 17th-century Tidö Castle has been converted into a toy museum with around 35,000 exhibits.

5 Eskilstuna, Södermanland

The town was named after the missionary bishop, St Eskil, who was stationed at Eskilstuna and martyred in nearby Strängnäs in 1080. Built along the banks of Eskilstunaån, the river which links Mälaren to Lake Hjälmaren, Eskilstuna emerged as an important iron-working town in the 16th century. Some of the large old foundries that date from the 1600s have been converted into museums and craft shops. Today, steelworking is the town's main industry and Sweden's finest cutlery bears Eskilstuna's name.

i Hamngatan 19

▶ From Eskilstuna take the *E20* eastwards for 30km (19 miles) to Strängnäs.

A traditional wooden windmill stands on the banks of Lake Mälaren at Strängnäs

6 Strängnäs, Södermanland

Set on the banks of Mälaren, Strängnäs is a small, pretty town with old wooden houses and a large historic cathedral of 1291. Olavus Petri introduced the Reformation into Sweden at Strängnäs in the 1520s, convincing the local archdeacon, Laurentius Andreae, of the virtues of this new trend of Christianity. And it was from the cathedral's outdoor pulpit that Andreae proclaimed Gustav Vasa King of Sweden in 1523; the great king then set about confiscating the riches of cathedrals and churches throughout the land, and Strängnäs was not exempt. Charles IX, son of Gustav Vasa,

is buried here and his gilded armour sits astride a model horse to the left of the splendid 15th-century high altar. Charles' funeral ensigns are displayed with other treasures in the Silver Chamber between the Lower and Old Vestries.

Various chapels skirt the nave; one of the most interesting houses the sarcophagus of Admiral Carl Carlsson Gyllenhjelm, the illegitimate son of Charles IX who was ennobled by his father. The cathedral has one of the finest ecclesiastic libraries in Sweden.

i By the harbour

▶ From Strängnäs continue on the *E20*, bearing left on the minor road for Stallarholmen and thereafter south for Mariefred (30km/19 miles).

Gripsholm, the rambling 500-year-old castle that overlooks the lake's waters at Mariefred

7 Mariefred, Södermanland
This is yet another quaint town of wooden houses and narrow lanes, pleasantly set on the shores of Mälaren. Mariefred's great attraction is its large castle, Gripsholm, which was originally a medieval fort but gradually gained its present shape over the succeeding centuries. New owners constantly embellished the castle, even going so far as knocking down the 14th-century monastery, Pax Marie, for further supplies of building blocks. (Echoes of the monastery's presence still rever-

berate, however, in the name of the town; Pax Marie, or Marie's Peace, translates in Swedish to Mariefred.) The castle also houses the Swedish State Portrait Collection, including some 3,500 paintings of royalty and nobility.

Local train enthusiasts have restored early steam locomotives and rolling stock and now use them to run a service between Mariefred and Läggesta (45 minutes).

[i] *Radhuset*

▶ *From Mariefred continue south to the E20 and turn left. Turn off the E20, then bear north before Turinge for*

Ekeby, returning to the main road at Södertälje (40km/25 miles). From Södertälje head northeastwards on the E4 for Stockholm (35km/22 miles).

SPECIAL TO...

Of all Mälaren's ancient trading centres it was Birka, on the island of Björkö, in eastern Mälaren, that flourished the earliest and the most successfully. Established between the 9th and 10th centuries, today the town-port is little more than an archaeological site, but it makes for an interesting visit all the same.

The Oslo
Circuit

4 DAYS • 757KM • 456 MILES

This tour goes west from Oslo, passing the silver mines of Kongsberg and the stave church of Heddal before reaching the empty high Haukelifjell and then swinging north-wards to give the first taste of the fiords. Ferries from Kinsarvik cross the beautiful Hardangerfjorden to join the road to Bergen. Then road 7 passes through dramatic fell lands, turning south at the ski resort of Gol to follow a gentler course along the Hallingdal Valley back down to Oslo.

[i] *Fylkeshuset, Oslo*

▶ *Take the road southwest out of Oslo for 40km (25 miles) to Drammen.*

❶ Drammen, Buskerud

The industrial and port town of Drammen, comprising the Bragernes and Stromso districts, is mainly of interest for the Spiral, a 1,700m (5,577 feet) toll road which coils up through six spirals of tunnel to a high vantage point at the top of Bragernesasen (293m/961 feet). The Drammen Museum, with its 18th-century manor farmhouse of Marienlyst, concentrates on local history. Drammen's Stromso church of 1667 underwent an Empire-style facelift in 1840, whereas the Town Hall of 1872 was awarded the prestigious Europa Nostra Prize in 1986 for its accurate restoration.

▶ *Continue west on road 11 to Kongsberg (41km/26 miles).*

❷ Kongsberg, Buskerud

On 2 May 1624 King Christian IV opened Kongsberg's silver mines. Discovered here the year before, the precious metal was to be the source of the town's fame and wealth for the next 300 years and the reason why it became Norway's second largest town (after Bergen) in the early 1800s. The mines closed in 1957 and sections are now open to visitors.

The Mining Museum is housed in an old smelting hut and displays a fine collection of silver, including coins minted in Kongsberg's Royal Mint. The rich baroque interior of the large 18th-century Kongsberg church is a vestige of that golden age. Lagdals open-air folk museum, offers memories of a more humble past.

The 13th-century stave church of Røldal, which used to attract crowds of pilgrims

---

▶ *From Kongsberg continue on road 11 to Heddal (37km/ 23 miles).*

❸ Heddal, Telemark

Built at the height of the settlement's importance, the splendid stave church at Heddal is one of the largest in Norway. Consecrated on the feast day of St Crispian (25 October) in 1147, its chancel was expanded and lavishly adorned with paintings over the next couple of centuries. The chair in the chancel is believed to be even older than the church itself and is carved with tales derived from the ancient sagas, while the altarpiece dates from the 17th century.

Sadly, Heddal's importance declined and today it is no more than a village. Although the church suffered neglect, a private donation in the 1950s enabled its restoration to the medieval style. Near by is an open-air museum with a traditional farmstead.

▶ *From Heddal continue west on road 11 to Røldal (201km/125 miles).*

❹ Røldal, Hordaland

Road 11 travels through magnificent scenery as it climbs the fells of western Telemark, crosses the border into Hordaland and descends to Røldal, a lakeside enclave surrounded by mountains. Its 13th-century stave church once drew pilgrims who believed its crucifix had miraculous powers.

SPECIAL TO...

In summer you can catch a ride on the old mining train at Saggrenda (6km/4 miles west of Kongsberg) and travel deep into the now defunct silver mine of Kongens Grube. The guided tour is conducted 2.5km (1½ miles) into the mountain and over 300m (980 feet) underground.

SCENIC ROUTES

At Odda you can follow the quieter road 550 for 45km (28 miles) along the west shore of Sørfjorden to the pretty village of Utne where there are short ferry rides to Kinsarvik.

▶ *From Røldal continue on road 11 through the Seljestad Gorge and then bear northwards on road 13 for Odda (44km/27 miles).*

⑤ Odda, Hordaland

With its lovely situation at the southern tip of Sørfjorden, Odda was a fashionable resort at the turn of the century but after it built up a chemical industry, visitors drifted elsewhere.

Energy for the chemical plants comes from the power stations at nearby Tyssedal. From Tyssedal a road leads to Skjeggedal on man-made Ringedalsvatn (Lake Ringedals) and the cableway up to Magelitoppen (930m /2,735 feet).

.... SPECIAL TO... ....

The region between Hardangar and Sogne is the heart of Norway's apple country and is at its most beautiful between May and June when the orchards on the slopes of the fiord's shores are in full blossom; magnificent snow-capped mountains serve as their backdrop.

South of Odda a minor road goes to Buar, from where there is an approach to the Buar glacier.

One of the powerful waterfalls where composer Edvard Grieg found inspiration for his music

▶ *From Odda continue north along road 13 to Kinsarvik (41km/26 miles).*

⑥ Kinsarvik, Hordaland

Kinsarvik is the ferry point for the service across Hardangerfjorden via Utne to Kvanndal (45 minutes). Near Kinsarvik are the Kinso falls, a group of waterfalls of which Nykkjesoyfossen and Sotefossen have particularly impressive drops. Edvard Grieg, who liked to visit the region's waterfalls, used to retire to a cottage in Lofthus, 10km (6 miles) to the south, to compose his music. At Bu, 15km (9 miles) beyond Kinsarvik, you can visit a museum of traditional costumes.

Opposite: a lone boat drifts as the sun sets over the calm waters of the Eidfjord
Right: Eidfjord village

▶ *From Kinsarvik continue alongside the fiord, before joining road 7 for Eidfjord (29km/18 miles).*

7 Eidfjord, Hordaland
A minor road leads north from the resort of Eidfjord to Sima, one of Norway's largest power stations (guided tours available). The road from the Sima Valley snakes through tunnels up to Kjeåsen with its traditional farmstead. This is an area of plunging waterfalls, and further up the valley the mighty Skykkjefoss drops 600m/1,973 feet (half of which is vertical) to make it one of the main suppliers of hydroelectric energy to the local power stations. Five kilometres (3 miles) along route 7 from Eidfjord, a road from Saebo leads up into the mountains to the south, heading towards Hjølmo and waterfalls such as Vedalsfoss, one of the longest falls in Norway – 650m (2,138 feet), with a vertical drop of 200m (657 feet).

Vøringsfossen, one of Norway's most spectacular falls, is further up road 7, and wonderful views of it plummeting 200m (656 feet) can be gained by ascending from Eidfjord to Isdola and then turning left for Fossli (19km/12 miles).

▶ *From Eidfjord continue on road 7 to reach Geilo (90km/56 miles).*

8 Geilo, Buskerud
Geilo is one of Scandinavia's top ski resorts, catering for both downhill and cross-country enthusiasts, and it remains the region's hub during the summer months. A cable-car can be taken up to the top of 1,200m (3,937 feet) Geilohogda from where a magnificent path can be taken back downhill. This is splendid walking country and many other more demanding treks are found throughout the region. Three kilometres (2 miles) west of Geilo is Fekjo, where there are 9th and 10th-century AD burial mounds.

▶ *From Geilo continue northwestwards for 50km (31 miles) on road 7 to Gol.*

9 Gol, Buskerud
Gol, another popular skiing and trekking resort, has an open-air museum and a hydroelectric power station constructed within a mountain. Its stave church caught the eye of King Oscar II, who bought it in 1885 and had it erected near his summer palace on Bygdøy in Oslo, where it still stands today.

There is a fine stave church at Torpo, 14km (9 miles) before Gol, which dates from the 12th century. It had its ceiling painted in the 13th century.

▶ *From Gol bear southeastwards on road 7, initially along the Hallingdal valley, to Hønefoss (138km/86 miles). From Hønefoss take the E16 for the final stretch to Oslo.*

The Kuopio Circuit

The tour encircles a lovely area of the northern central lakelands with the attractive 'lake town' of Kuopio in the west and the remote road along the Russian border to the west. The Karelian culture and the Orthodox church are evident throughout the region and most conspicuously at Ilomantsi, a centre for all things Karelian. Trees dominate the roadsides – as they do in most of Finland. As a pleasant break from driving, consider taking a boat trip across Lake Pielinen to Koli, from where there is a panoramic view across the forests and lakes towards Russia.

3 DAYS • 581KM • 361 MILES

ITINERARY	
KUOPIO	▶ Nurmes (127km-79m)
NURMES	▶ Lieksa (56km-35m)
LIEKSA	▶ Ilomantsi (134km-83m)
ILOMANTSI	▶ Joensuu (73km-45m)
JOENSUU	▶ Valamo (71km-44m)
VALAMO	▶ Kuopio (113km-70m)

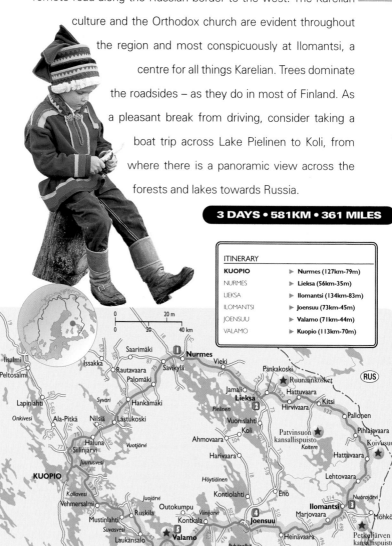

Taking advantage of the early morning calm near Kuopio

▶ From Kuopio travel north on road **5** to Siilinjarvi (22km/14 miles); turn right and follow road **75** northeast to Savikylä and continue to Nurmes (105km/65 miles).

❶ Nurmes

On the northern shore of Pielinen, Finland's fifth largest lake and one of its most beautiful (if that is possible to gauge) – Nurmes was founded by Tsar Alexander II as a point on the waterway route from St Petersburg north into deep Finland. The spirit of Karelia can be found at Bomba House, a Karelian village and tourist complex dating from 1978. There are handicrafts for sale, but the best reason for coming here is the lunch buffet of traditional Karelian food.

▶ From Nurmes take road **73** southeast to Lieksa (56km/35 miles).

❷ Lieksa

The Lutheran church, completed in 1982, was designed by Raila and Reima Pietila (the architects of the Reider Sarestoniemi studio near Kittila in Lapland); 70 older buildings are on display at the Pielinen Heritage Museum. Savotaranta is Finland's largest forestry museum.

▶ From Lieksa take road **73**; soon after, bear left on road 522 via Pankakoski and continue east, parallel to the Russian border, through remote Finnish Karelia to Ilomantsi (134km/83 miles).

❸ Ilomantsi

Ilomantsi, the country's most eastern town (further east than St Petersburg) is the spiritual and cultural centre for Karelians in Finland. This was where Elias Lönnrot met Mateli Kuivalatar, Karelian folk singer, shaman and provider of a substantial number of poems used in Lonrot's collection of *Kanteletar*. The old customs are still practised – the celebrating of *prazdniks* (religious festivals), the playing of the stringed *kantele*, the wearing of traditional costumes, the cooking of favourite Karelian food. Things Karelian are currently rather fashionable in Finland and

---

SCENIC ROUTE

From Lieksa head south on road 73, bearing right on the 5071 which leads down to Lake Pielinen and Vuonislahti, about 30km (19 miles). From here follow the signs to the studio and Forest Church of Eva Ryynanen (Paateri). Ryynanen is a wood sculptor from Lieksa who lives and works up in these hills. Her sculptures are highly acclaimed and she is particularly well known for her Forest Church, the wood and glass church next to her studio. Continue with this scenic lake route, rejoining the main 73 near Eno from where it is 32km (20 miles) south to Joensuu.

---

while some of what you see at Ilomantsi may seem to have been contrived for tourists, there is, none the less, a genuine pride in displaying the culture. For heritage and handicrafts visit Parppeinvaara Hill on the south side of town; the famous Karelian songs and traditional Kantele music is performed at the Runonlaulajan Pirtii (Bard's House).

Up until the 15th/16th century all Christians in Karelia were Orthodox; today, here in Ilomantsi, they account for less than 20 per cent of the population. On the north side of town is the Church of Elijah, the largest Orthodox church, dating from 1891; the nearby Lutheran church is 100 years older. To the east, about 25km (16 miles) down road 500 to Russia, are the 18th-century ironworks of Möhkö. Ore used to be brought from the region's '57 lakes' to feed the foundry; the museum relates the history. On the way you pass Petkeljärvi National Park (Petkeljärven Kansallispuisto).

▶ From Ilomantsi travel westwards on road **74** to Joensuu (73km/45 miles).

❹ Joensuu

Attractively situated with water on two sides, Joensuu has a young, modern feel to it. The university town, which is capital of the province of North Karelia, was founded in 1848 by Tsar Nicholas I, who was keen to use the network of natural waterways to probe far into the interior of the north. Joensuu's chief landmark is the huge red-brick towered Town Hall down on the River Pielisjoki which was built by Eliel Saarinen in 1914. Here a bridge crosses the river and provides access to the island of Ilosaari (from which people bathe) with its Museum of North Karelia, devoted to the land, history and culture of the peoples of this torn region. Joensuu has a grid network of streets: a block inland from the Town Hall is the Freedom Park, behind this is the busy market square and two blocks further along is the Art Museum specialising in Finnish art from the mid-19th century to the present. Here hangs Albert Edelfelt's *Virginie*, *La Parisienne*, one of Finland's most famous paintings. Follow the main Koulukatu (Lieksa–Nurmes road) northwards: four blocks up and one to the right is the church of St Nikolaos, the town's late 19th-century Orthodox church which has an icon from the St Alexander monastery in St Petersburg. Ten per cent of the population are Orthodox Christians, and though this seems a small fraction, it constitutes 5,000 people, the second largest community of this faith outside Helsinki.

▶ *Take road 17 west from Joensuu and after 26km (16 miles) turn left on road 23 and continue for Valamo (45km/28 miles).*

5 Valamo
Sergius, a Greek monk, arrived on the island of Valamo in Lake Ladoga in the 12th century. Here he and his disciple Herman, a Karelian, established a highly reputable Orthodox monastic community. During the Winter War of 1940, however, the monastery was abandoned as Karelians fled

A detail from the 19th-century Orthodox church, St Nikolaos, in the university town of Joensuu

Russia, and the monks settled in Heinävesi, where they founded the present Valamo, consecrated in 1977. Although this is still a 'living' monastery, members of the public are welcome. The church houses icons brought from old Valamo; an icon of special note is the *Mother of God of Konevitsa*, the greatest treasure of the Orthodox Church of Finland. Accommodation is available.

Glittering mosaics in the monastery of Valamo, still a working religious community

The canal boat *Sergei* ferries visitors to nearby Lintula convent.

▶ *Back on the main road (number 23) bear right to Karvio and right again, approaching Kuopio via Mustinlahti and Vehmersalmi.*

SCENIC ROUTE
Twice a week the steamer M/S *Vinkeri II* departs from the wharf by Joensuu's Town Hall and sails up the Pielisjoki through a series of locks into Lake Pielinen, continuing northwards to Koli; it is a 7-hour one-way journey (shorter are the ferry services from Lieksa and Nurmes). Alternatively, drive to Koli along the Nurmes road (number 18), bearing right at Ahmovaara as indicated. Koli National Park covers 11sq km (4 square miles) of predominantly spruce-covered rocky hills with its summit at 347m (1,138 feet). From here you can drive to within a short walk of a high point – the view over Lake Pielinen, dotted with its many islands, is magnificent. Folklore has it that Sibelius was so overwhelmed by the scene that he had his piano carted to the top. In the distance, far beyond the lake, is Russia.

on the road

SPAIN

Spain has absorbed many influences over the centuries but has retained a strong sense of its own identity. Its magical, palm-fringed beaches, Moorish towns and ancient citadels, timeless villages and sweeping plains are there to be discovered.

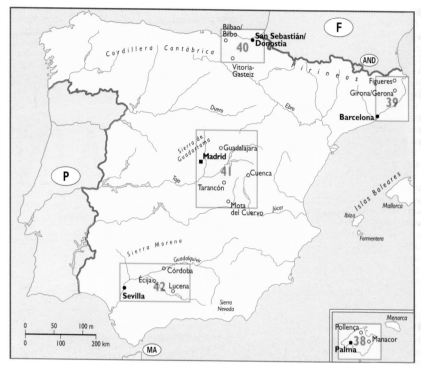

Tour 38

Opposite the coast of the Levante region lies Mallorca, the largest of the Balearic Islands. Between the rugged Sierra de Tramuntana in the northwest and the gentler slopes of the Sierra de Levante in the east is a vast plain of orchards, fields and windmills. Known for the beauty of its coastline, pinewoods and olive groves, the island is at its best in spring when the almond blossom is out.

There are two Mallorcas; the Mallorca of the mass tourism that invades parts of the island in the summer, and the Mallorca of magnificent unspoilt scenery.

This tour takes in some of its most outstanding features – old monasteries, Roman

Page 239: top – ceramic decorations on Plaza de España, Seville; bottom – traditional red-roofed, whitewashed townscape

remains, spectacular caves and picturesque fishing villages. There are beautiful stretches of coastline, with rocky coves and sandy beaches. Together with its blue waters, dense greenery and pine-scented air, they make up the essence of this very Mediterranean island.

Tour 39

The Costa Brava is a region which presents a variety of panoramas. In the north of the region are the eastern Pyrenees, which form a natural border with France and separate the Iberian peninsula from the rest of Europe. This is a sparsely populated area dominated by rugged mountains and green valleys, irrigated by the rivers Ter, Llobregat and Segre, together with tributaries of the Ebro. To the east of these mountains, the wild rugged coastline features high cliffs, rocky coves and sandy beaches.

The once desolate Costa Brava (Wild Coast) has long since become one of Spain's most popular holiday areas. Parts are still very attractive, however, with picturesque little fishing villages set in sandy coves surrounded by pine-clad hills. The tour offers stretches of stunning beauty, as steep cliffs plunge sharply down to the sea below.

The vivid blues and greens of the Mediterranean, and the purple shades of the mountains, coupled with the fragrance of the pines form a large part of its attraction. Visits to ancient Greek and Roman ruins, inland towns and a beautiful old monastery provide cultural interest.

Barcelona, the capital of Catalonia, is a thriving commercial centre, and is for many Spain's top city. The official language is Catalan and street names and places are usually written in Catalan.

Tour 40

The Basque mountains start where the western Pyrenees end and give way to the Cordillera Cantábrica, which sweeps across the north. Its northern regions consist of fresh green pastures, with maize-growing areas and plantations of fruit and walnut trees. Further south are vast plains with vineyards and fields of corn and dotted about are little stone farmhouses called *caseríos*. This tour is an exploration of the region, which includes beautiful drives along a rugged coastline with magnificent sandy beaches, and stops in picturesque little resorts. A visit to Spain's busiest northern port provides a contrast to some of the typical little Basque mountain villages you will encounter in the interior of the country. The people and customs of the Basque country give the region an unmistakable character, which you will discover on your travels.

Tour 41

La Mancha is a vast region of fields and plains, where windmills and castles serve as a reminder that it is Don Quixote land. Its fields are cultivated with cereals, olive groves and saffron, and it is also Spain's largest wine-growing region. To the east, this gives way to the wild and rugged landscapes of the Serranía de Cuenca.

This eastern section of Castile-La Mancha offers an unusual itinerary with terrific scenery. The route takes in some of the splendid old fortified towns that once protected the borders between warring kingdoms. A total contrast is provided by a visit to the fascinating 'hanging houses', and a drive through some spectacular scenery to an area of extraordinary rock formations. Old Roman ruins provide more cultural interest. The journey picks up the trail of the legendary Don Quixote, which leads down to the great plains and windmills of La Mancha.

Tour 42

To many people the image of Spain is the reality of Andalucia, a region which has tremendous appeal and offers a diversity of attractions. Dazzling white villages perched on mountain tops are silhouetted against brilliant blue skies. Present-day Andalucia is a result of traditions inherited from the past, which has included almost 800 years of Moorish occupation. This brought the region rich cultures and some unique monuments, of which the Mosque of Córdoba and the Alcázar in Sevilla are among the finest examples. Spain's Moorish past is more evident in Andalucia than in any other part of the country.

This tour passes through the basin of the River Guadalquivir, through golden cornfields and groves of old twisted olive trees with small farmhouses dotted about. There are wine-growing areas among the gentle hills and distant mountains. The delightful villages are Moorish in appearance – brilliant white houses, red-tiled roofs and picturesque old streets. The prize is the visit to Spain's glorious Moorish mosque, magnificent in all its entirety, and a unique attraction worldwide.

Relaxing on one of Spain's many attractive beaches

Olives for sale. Try a selection of green and black

BANKS

Most banks are open Monday to Friday 9am–2pm; Saturday 9am–1pm (except in summer), although times may vary. Money exchange facilities are available outside these hours at airports and other centres.

CREDIT CARDS

Major credit cards are widely accepted. Cash can be obtained from banks and certain cash dispensers. Make a note of your credit card numbers and emergency telephone numbers in case of loss. Tell the company immediately if one of your cards is stolen or lost.

CURRENCY

The peseta is available in the following denominations: notes – 1,000, 2,000, 5,000 and 10,000; coins – 1, 5, 10, 25, 50, 100, 200 and 500.

CUSTOMS REGULATIONS

See **Austria** (page 10).

ELECTRICITY

220 volts, 50 cycles AC (occasionally 110/125 in older establishments) on a continental two-pin plug. UK, Australian and New Zealand appliances will need an adaptor. US appliances will also need an adaptor and transformer if not fitted for dual voltage.

EMBASSIES

Australia: Paseo de la Castellana 143, 28046 Madrid (tel: 91 2798504).
Canada: Edificio Goya Calle Nuñez de Balboa 35, Madrid (tel: 91 4314300).
UK: Calle de Fernando el Santo 16, Madrid 4 (tel: 91 3190200).
US: Serrano 75, 28006 Madrid (tel: 91 5774000).

ENTRY REGULATIONS

See **Austria** (page 10).

EMERGENCY TELEPHONE NUMBERS

Policia Nacional 091
Policia Municipal 092
These 24-hour numbers will not necessarily connect you with the nearest station but will get your message relayed. State the nature of emergency, your location and the services required.
Bomberos (Fire) 080;
Medical Emergencies 061;
Madrid: Red Cross (Cruz Roja) 533 7777
Ambulances 522 222
Barcelona:
Ambulances 300 2020

HEALTH MATTERS

Residents of EU countries are entitled to medical treatment if they produce form E111 or the relevant form from their country (obtain this before departure). The best advice is to buy a travel insurance policy which provides comprehensive cover in case of accident or illness.

MOTORING
Documents

Licences issued by EU countries are acceptable (for UK and Republic of Ireland driver's licences should be of the pink EU-type). Visitors from other countries should have an international driving licence, obtainable from the motoring organisations in their home countries. Third-party insurance is compulsory in Spain. Travellers are advised to obtain a Green Card, together with a bail bond (in case of accident).

Breakdowns

Special arrangements may be provided by an insurance policy

bought from your motoring organisation. In the case of rental vehicles, contact the rental company. The Spanish motoring club (RACE) runs a 24-hour breakdown service from Madrid (English spoken), tel: 593 33 33.

Speed limits
For cars and motorcycles: Motorways 120kph/74mph; 80kph /50mph for vehicles with a trailer. Dual carriage roads or with overtaking lanes 100kph/62mph; 80kph/50mph for vehicles with a trailer. Other roads outside built-up areas 90kph/56mph; 70kph/43mph for vehicles with a trailer. Towns and built-up areas 50kph/31mph.

Car hire and fly/drive
The big international firms operate throughout Spain and you can make bookings with them in your home country. Holiday operators have car rental schemes, and airlines offer 'fly-drive' deals. Renting from a smaller local firm is usually cheaper.

Accidents
Road users involved in an accident should mark the presence of their vehicle on the road, try to move it to the hard shoulder or layby, then take the necessary steps to ensure it is retrieved by the rescue services as soon as possible.

Those witnessing an accident should tend to the victims and seek help. The police need only be contacted if the acident has resulted in serious casualties. SOS telephone posts are normally available on motorways only.

Driving conditions
Driving is on the right. The motorway system has both toll and toll-free sections. In the Basque area, local versions of the same place names appear on signposts together with the national version. Most roads across the Pyrenees are frequently closed by winter snowfalls.

Drinking and driving
The limit on drinking for drivers is 0.8g per 1,000cc. Drivers must submit to an alcohol test when requested by the authorities.

Seat belts
The use of seat belts is compulsory for the driver and front-seat passenger. Middle-and rear-seat passengers are also required to use seat belts if vehicles are fitted with them.

POST OFFICES
Post offices are generally open Monday to Saturday 9am–2pm. Mail can be sent addressed to you at Lista de Correos. Take personal identification when collecting. Post boxes are yellow. Some have different sections for different destinations. Stamps can be bought at tobacconists.

PUBLIC HOLIDAYS
1 January – Año Nuevo (New Year)
6 January – Día de los Reyes (Epiphany)
Good Friday – Viernes Santo
1 May – Día del Trabajo (May Day)
15 August – Asunción (Assumption)
12 October – Día de la Hispanidad
1 November – Todos los Santos (All Saints' Day)
6 December – Constitucíon
8 December – Immaculada Concepción (Immaculate Conception)
25 December – Navidad (Christmas Day)

ROUTE DIRECTIONS
Throughout this section the following abbreviations are used for Spanish roads:
A – Autopista
C – Comarcal
N – Nacional

TIME
Spain is two hours ahead of GMT in the summer and one hour ahead in the winter.

TELEPHONES
International access codes are as follows: to call Spain from Australia, dial 00 11; Canada 011; New Zealand 00; UK 00 44; US 011. Country codes are: Australia 61; Canada 1; New Zealand 64; Spain 34; UK 44; US 1. Public phone booths are plentiful. They take 500, 200, 100, 50, 25, 10 and 5 peseta coins and some accept credit cards.

TOURIST OFFICES
Spanish National Tourist Offices:
Australia: 203 Castlereagh Street, Suite 21a, PO BOX A-685, Sydney, NSW 2000.
Canada: 102 Bloor Street West, 14th Floor, Toronto.
UK: 57–8 St James's Street, London SW1A 1LD.
US: 665 Fifth Avenue, New York 10022: 8383 Wilshire Bvd, Suite 960, Beverly Hills, California 90211.

USEFUL WORDS
The following words and phrases may be helpful.
English Spanish
hello hola
goodbye adiós
good morning buenos días
good afternoon buenas tardes
good evening and goodnight buenas noches
do you speak English? ¿habla usted inglés?
yes/no sí/no
please por favor
excuse me, I don't understand perdón, no entiendo
could you please speak more slowly? ¿podría hablar más despacio, por favor?
thank you (very much) (muchas) gracias
I am/my name is ... soy/me llamo
what is your name? ¿como se llama usted?
how are you? ¿como está?
very well muy bien
where is ... ? ¿dónde está ...?
open/closed abierto/cerrado
what time is it? ¿qué hora es?
I would like ... me gustaría ...
do you have ... ? ¿tiene ... ?
how much is ... ? ¿cuánto es/vale/cuesta ... ?
I to 10 uno, dos, tres, cuatro, cinco, seis, siete, ocho, nueve, diez

The Magic
of Mallorca

Palma has great charm and is well worth exploring. The tree-lined Paseo Marítimo stretches along the seafront; the 13th- to 17th-century Catedral (La Seu) overlooks the harbour and near by is the 15th-century La Lonja (formerly the Stock Exchange). To the west of town, the Castillo de Bellver (Bellver Castle), built by Mallorcan kings in the 14th century, was first a palace, then a prison, and is now a fine museum.

4 DAYS • 757KM • 456 MILES

i *Avenida Jaime III, 10*

▶ *From Palma take the **C719** southwest to Port d'Andratx.*

0 Port d'Andratx, Mallorca
From a tiny fishing village, Port d'Andratx has become one of Mallorca's most prominent yachting centres, and sailing vessels of all shapes and sizes are moored in the harbour. The town is set in an attractive bay surrounded by hills and has a pleasant seafront promenade lined with bars and restaurants. The yachting set provides an international atmosphere during the season.

▶ *Take the **C710** and branch off to the right to Valldemossa.*

2 Valldemossa, Mallorca
To many, the name of Valldemossa conjures up visions of Chopin, music and romance. The Polish composer Frederich Chopin spent the winter of 1838 to 1839 here with the French authoress Georges Sand. The Real Cartuja (Charterhouse) where they stayed is the main feature of the village. After the monks who originally lived here had been expelled in 1835 the place served as lodgings for travellers.

Top: the Real Cartuja, where Frederich Chopin once stayed, in Valldemossa
Above: Port d'Andratx

The apartments, or rather cells, where the couple stayed are furnished in the style of the period, and include the piano on which the great master composed some of his best-known works. In the cloister is a very old pharmacy. First established by the monks as early as 1723, it looks much the same as in former times. It's worth taking a look, too, at the small museum which is now housed in the monks' library.

▶ *Rejoin the **C710** for 10km (6 miles) to Deià (Deyà).*

❸ **Deià,** Mallorca

Deià has long been a favourite haunt for writers and artists. Poet and writer Robert Graves spent some time here after World War II. The village consists of a cluster of red houses on top of a hill, among almond trees and groves of oranges, lemons and olives. Take a look at the small tile altars in the parish church, depicting scenes from Calvary. Behind the church is the cemetery where Graves is buried. There is a wonderful view from here of the surrounding mountains and rocky coves below. A somewhat precipitous climb down the hill leads to the sea.

▶ *Continue on the **C710**. Take a left turn to Port de Sóller.*

Santuario de Santa Catalina, by the old fishing quarter, provides a fine view of the resort. Five kilometres (3 miles) inland is Sóller town, linked to Port de Sóller by a narrow-gauge railway or by road, where the Convento de San Francisco (St Francis) is worth a visit, along with the handicrafts centre in the local museum.

▶ *Rejoin the **C710** and branch off to the left to the Monasterio de Lluc.*

❺ **Monasterio de Lluc,** Mallorca

Situated on one of the highest points of the island is Mallorca's principal monastery and pilgrimage centre. The entrance is lined with houses and doorways, which once provided shelter for pilgrims who arrived here to venerate

▶ *Continue on the **C710** for 21km (13 miles) to Pollença (Pollensa).*

❻ **Pollença,** Mallorca

Pollença's crowning glory is El Calvario (The Calvary), which stands at the top of a flight of 365 steps lined with cypress trees. Those who make it to the top will find a little white 18th-century chapel with an old crucifix and a good view over the bays of Alcúdía, Pollença and even as far as Cabo (Cape) Formentor. On Good Friday there is a service in the chapel followed by a torchlit procession down the steps.

Back in the town, monuments worth a visit are the Gothic chapel of Roser Vell, which has a fine altarpiece, the church of Montision (both 18th-century), and the baroque-style Convento de Santo Domingo. There is a Roman bridge just outside town.

Port de Pollença, some 6km (4 miles) away, is an attractive little fishing port set in a wide bay framed by the dramatic silhouette of the Sierra de Sant Vicenç (San Vicente mountains). It is a fast-developing resort and yachting centre.

If time permits you should not miss a side tour to the Formentor peninsula, one of the most scenic parts of the island. A drive to the lighthouse at the end of Cabo Formentor offers magnificent views of this superb coastline.

Despite tourist incursions, Port de Sóller is still a working harbour with a character of its own

❹ **Port de Sóller,** Mallorca

The route from Deià passes through the small hamlet of Lluc Alcari, where Pablo Picasso lived for a time. The picturesque old fishing port of Port de Sóller is now a popular tourist spot. It has an attractive harbour, framed by the pine-covered hills of the Sierra de Tramuntana and an excellent sandy beach. The

the Virgin of Lluc, patron saint of the island.

Inside the monastery is a wooden statue of the Virgin encrusted with jewels. There is also a 17th-century church, and a small museum with a collection of paintings, ceramics and religious items. Mass is celebrated each day, when you can hear the stirring singing of the famous boys choir of Lluc.

> ### RECOMMENDED WALKS
> ....
> A pleasant stroll can be taken in Port de Pollença along the seafront promenade, which starts from the end of town and follows the sea, well shaded by trees and lined with attractive residential villas and gardens.

► *From Port de Pollença take the coast road for 15km (9 miles) to Alcúdia.*

7 Alcúdia, Mallorca

The little medieval town of Alcúdia is encircled by old ramparts dating back to the 14th century. Inside are small narrow streets and handsome mansions, mainly from the 16th and 17th centuries. The town once had quite a large Roman population and the local museum has exhibits of items from prehistoric and Roman times. A colourful market takes place twice a week – every Tuesday and every Sunday – just outside the old city walls.

An old Roman theatre, about 1.5km (1 mile) south, is situated in some fields beyond the city. The theatre was carved from a rock, and items uncovered here are on public display in the museum in the Castillo de Bellver, Palma.

► *Take the C712 southeast to Artá. Continue southeast on a minor road to the Coves d'Artá (Caves of Artá), 45km (28 miles).*

The remains of the ancient Roman theatre carved into the rock outside Alcúdia

8 Coves d'Artá, Mallorca

On the beach of Canyamel are the caves of Artá. The largest known caves on the island, they are said to have provided the inspiration for Jules Verne's famous story, *Journey to the Centre of the Earth*.

The caves are reached by a huge opening in the cliff, standing some 35m (115 feet) high, overlooking the sea. They consist of a vast number of cavities and are noted for the extraordinary, sometimes grotesque shapes of the stalactites and stalagmites.

Artá itself features some attractive mansions, churches

and the Almudain, an old medieval fortress with a sanctuary inside. The Ermita de Betlem (Sanctuary of Betlem) is near by. It stands high on a hill with a fine view of the bay of Alcúdia.

► *Take the C715 southwest for 29km (18 miles) to Manacor.*

9 Manacor, Mallorca

Manacor has a long tradition of furniture-making dating back to the 17th century, when the place became a centre for wood craftsmen. Its real claim to fame, however, lies in its production of the famous Majorica pearls, an important industry in Mallorca and internationally known. You can visit the factory and see the pearls being produced in a simulated process that resembles the natural one. Guided tours are available at specific times of the day. Other places of interest include the Gothic Iglesia de San Vicente, the Museo Arqueológico and the remains of the old tower, which was once the summer residence of Jaime II, the conqueror of Mallorca in the 13th century.

► *Take the road southeast for 13km (8 miles) to Porto Cristo.*

10 Porto Cristo, Mallorca

The attractive little port of Porto Cristo is one of the oldest anchorages on the island,

Weird and wonderful stalagmites and stalactites: the Coves del Drac

confirmed by the discovery of a sunken Roman ship in the area. The port began to flourish in the Middle Ages when it was used to service the island with materials. As with so many other seaside locations, it has developed over recent years into a popular holiday destination, which has changed its character. Nevertheless it still remains a resort with considerable charm.

▶ Near Porto Cristo are the Coves del Drac (Caves of Drac).

11 Coves del Drac, Mallorca
The Caves of Drac are the best known in Mallorca, and no tourist trip is complete without a visit here. They stretch for some 2km (1½ miles) and the way leads through a superb setting over bridges and past a series of underground pools. Lago de Martell (Lake Martell) is the largest underground lake in Europe and its transparent waters reflect the weird rock formations. In summer, concerts are held aboard a small vessel which floats along the lake.

If you want to see more caves, the Coves del Hams (Caves of Hams) near by are also magnificent, noted for the pure white of the stalactites, and lovely underground lakes with names like Mar de Venezia (Sea of Venice) and Lago de las Columnas (Lake of Columns).

▶ Return to Manacor and take the **C714** south to Felanitx.

12 Felanitx, Mallorca
The old town of Felanitx dates back to the 13th century. Be sure to visit the Convento de San Augustín and the parish church, which has a fine Gothic façade. Felanitx is the birthplace of the contemporary artist, Miguel Barceló. He still keeps a studio here.

South of Felanitx is the old convent of Castillo de Santueri, perched on top of a huge rock mass.

▶ Continue for 16km (10 miles) on the **C714** south to Santanyi (Santani).

13 Santanyi, Mallorca
A solid gateway, known as Porta Murada, still remains from the town fortifications. This was built as a defence against piracy, which was once a recurring problem in this part of the island. The local parish church has an excellent rococo organ, and there is an excellent Romanesque-Gothic oratory in the Roser's chapel. Near by are the remains of some prehistoric sites and fortifications.

▶ Take the **C717** for 51km (32 miles) back to Palma.

The Costa
Brava

Barcelona's attractions include **2/3 DAYS • 378KM • 235 MILES**

the tree-lined Ramblas; unique architecture such as the Casa Milá (La Pedrera), with its curving façade, and the Temple of the Sagrada Familia (Holy Family), by Catalan architect Antonio Gaudí; and the redeveloped old port area, with marinas and beaches, created for the 1992 Olympics.

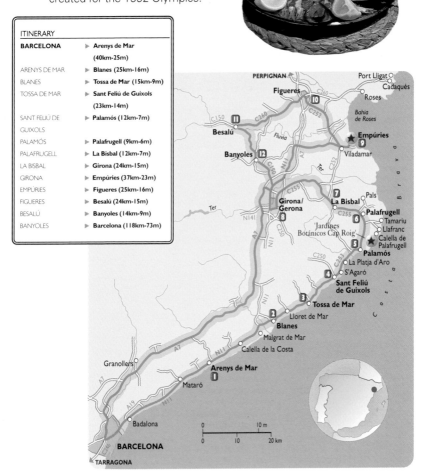

8 Tossa de Mar, Girona-Gerona

Tossa de Mar was called 'The Blue Paradise' by the famous French artist, Marc Chagall, who produced many paintings of the town in the 1930s. Some of his works are exhibited in the Museo Municipal, along with other paintings and an interesting mosaic from the Roman settlement here. This is located in the old town, which is worth a visit, with its narrow streets and medieval houses contained within massive walls, and turrets from the 12th century. There is a splendid view from the lighthouse, which is situated on the highest point of the town.

▶ *Continue northeast to Sant Feliú de Guixols.*

FOR CHILDREN

Near Malgrat de Mar (follow the road towards Blanes and take a left turn) is the splendid Marineland. This large leisure centre offers many amusements, including an aquarium, small zoo, boating pool and children's playground. A major attraction is the sea-lion and dolphin show. In Lloret de Mar is Water World, which offers numerous aquatic attractions and mini-golf in 60,000sq m (71,760 square yards) of leafy woods.

BACK TO NATURE

Just beyond the harbour of Blanes is the splendid Botanical Garden of Marimurtra (sea and myrtle), where you will find hundreds of species of exotic flowers and plants, largely from the Mediterranean area. The garden is beautifully laid out on an original design by the German, Karl Faust, whose bust stands near the entrance. There are stunning views of the coast from the gardens.

A stunning view of the Blue Paradise – Tossa de Mar and its beautiful curving bay

ℹ *Gran Vía de les Corts Catalanes 658*

▶ *Leave Barcelona from the Plaça Glòries Catalanes and take the A19 coast road east. Turn right at Badalona and join the NII through Mataró to Arenys de Mar.*

1 Arenys de Mar, Girona-Gerona

The main attractions in Arenys are its pretty little port and its reputation for excellent seafood. The fishing harbour is fun to explore and is full of activity when the catch comes in. The large marina is now an international regatta centre.

The Iglesia de Santa María (begun in 1584 by the French) is well worth a visit to see the magnificent 18th-century retablo by the renowned artist Pablo Costa.

Arenys has a long tradition of white bobbin lace-making and although this is gradually dying out, you may still see some of the local women, known as *puntaires*, sitting out on their doorsteps practising their ancient skills.

▶ *Continue on the NII coastal road. At Malgrat branch off northeast to Blanes.*

2 Blanes, Girona-Gerona

Blanes is a popular tourist resort which enjoys an attractive setting. After exploring the harbour you can stroll along the promenade to the old town which has a lovely Gothic fountain in the main square.

Further up, the Iglesia de Santa María looks down on the roof-tops. A climb up to the top of the Sa Palomera southwest of the harbour is rewarded with an excellent view of the fine sandy bay of Blanes.

ℹ *Plaça Catalunya*

▶ *Follow the road as it passes through Lloret de Mar to Tossa de Mar.*

4 Sant Feliú de Guixols,
Girona-Gerona

This large, cheerful town is considered to be the capital of the Costa Brava. Its busy port and lack of a good, sandy beach gives it a different ambience to some of its better-known neighbours. The 11th-century Porta Ferrada (iron gate) and the adjoining church near the promenade, are the remains of a former Benedictine monastery. The Museo Provincial has items from prehistoric, Greek and Roman times.

The Ermita de Sant Elm, on the outskirts of town, offers a splendid view of the coast.

▶ *Take the* **C253** *for 12km (7miles) to Palamós.*

5 Palamós, Girona-Gerona

Palamós's main attractions are its beautiful setting in a wide curved bay and its lively port and yacht harbour. A major fishing centre, it is one of the most important towns in the region. Fish auctions take place in a special hall called the Lonja and are colourful occasions.

In the old part of the town is the 14th-century Gothic Iglesia de Santa María with a Flemish altarpiece, surrounded by the narrow streets of the original fishing village.

ℹ *Passeig del Mar s/n*

▶ *Take the* **C255** *inland for 9km (6 miles) to Palafrugell.*

6 Palafrugell, Girona-Gerona

Palafrugell's main functions are commerce and shopping. A few remains of Moorish walls can be seen and a visit to the little Gothic Iglesia de San Martín is worthwhile. This is a good spot, however, for a detour to some of the Costa's most delightful resorts. A short drive through

pine woods leads to the resort of Tamariu and another road to the fishing resorts of Calella de Palafrugell and Llafranc. There is a stunning view of the bays from the lighthouse below the Ermita de San Sebastián, poised on top of the hill.

ℹ *Carrilet 2*

▶ *Continue northwest on the* **C255** *for 12km (7 miles) to La Bisbal.*

7 La Bisbal, Girona-Gerona

La Bisbal is renowned as a ceramic centre and is the location of the Escuela de Cerámica (School of Ceramics). The tradition goes back to the Middle Ages, and contemporary work has been influenced by the designs of the Arabs, French and Italians. The pottery is displayed all over the town and is recognisable by its dominant colours of green, brown and yellow. While here, take a look at the large 14th-century Romanesque castle, once the seat of the ruling Bishops of La Bisbal, the parish church and the old bridge.

▶ *Continue west on the same road for 24km (15miles) to Girona.*

Girona is a warren of little streets and squares, straddling the Onar

8 Girona, Girona-Gerona

Founded by the Iberians, Girona was occupied by the Romans, the Moors, and retaken by Charlemagne in 785, later to form part of the kingdom of Catalonia and Aragon. The River Onar separates the new town from the old, which is located on the east bank and best explored on foot. There are good views of the old town from either of the main bridges. Entry into the old town is a step right back into the Middle Ages. You will find yourself among dark, secretive streets, picturesque houses and hidden squares. The cathedral appears unexpectedly, rising majestically from a flight of steps. This impressive monument dates back to the 14th century, with later additions, and is considered one of the finest cathedrals in Catalonia. The huge 12th-century embroidered *Tapestry of the Creation* is a unique exhibit among many valuable treasures to be seen in the museum. The adjoining 12th-century cloister is noted for its finely carved capitals. Other buildings of special interest include the former Iglesia Colegiata de Sant Feliú (collegiate church), with its tall tower, the Art Museum in the old Palacio Episcopal (Episcopal

---

FOR HISTORY BUFFS

The name of the 'city of a thousand sieges' may be something of an exaggeration, but Girona did spend long periods under siege over the years. The most famous was the siege of 1809, when a large force of Napoleon's troops was kept at bay for some six months by the citizens of the town, including a battalion of women and a few English volunteers. Under the command of Alvarez de Castro, the city finally had to surrender because of lack of food and ammunition. A commemorative monument stands in the Plaça de la Independencia.

► *Take the* **NII** *north and after 21km (13 miles) make a right turn to Empúries (Ampurias).*

❷ Empúries, Girona-Gerona
This impressive archaeological site is one of the most important in Spain and has both Greek and Roman ruins. It was originally founded by the Greeks in the 6th century BC and known as '*Emporion*' which means market. The place flourished and produced coins which were used in the region.

In the 2nd century BC the Romans arrived to wage war against the Carthaginians, and built on to the existing town. Some of the most valuable pieces that have been excavated from the site can be seen

Palace) and the 12th-century Baños Arabes (Arab Baths). A short walk from the baths takes you to some pleasant gardens under the ramparts, where you will have a splendid view over the valley of the Ter. Although interesting by day, the old town is fascinating by night, when floodlighting creates a medieval effect.

Among the most pleasant areas in the new town are the

Roman ruins in Empúries, where a long, turbulent and glorious history is well documented

central square, the Plaça de la Independencia, which is surrounded by attractive arcades, and the Parque de la Dehesa, a large park with a tree-lined avenue, fountains and statues.

i *Rambla de la Libertad 1*

in the Archaeological Museum in Barcelona. It became an episcopal seat under the Visigoths, and was then destroyed during conflicts with the Moors. In the lower town is a museum, which has an interesting collection of archaeological finds from the area, along with reconstructions of everyday life in Greek and Roman times.

A detour northeast to the coast will take you to the

delightful white-washed village of Cadaqués and nearby Port Lligat, where the great eccentric Salvador Dalí lived and painted for many years.

▶ *Retrace the route to Viladamar and then take the* **C252** *northwest to Figueres (Figueras).*

⑩ Figueres,
Girona-Gerona

Figueres is a major town of the Ampurdán region and features a few buildings of historical interest, such as the 14th-century Iglesia de Sant Pere (St Peter), noted for its fine Romanesque tower, and the Castillo de San Fernando, an impressive 18th-century fortress. The Museo del Ampurdán (Museum of Ampurdán), located on the town's pleasant tree-lined Rambla, has a wide variety of exhibits, including items from the ruins of Empúries.

The real interest, however, is undoubtedly the great Salvador Dalí, surrealist artist and eccentric, who was born here in 1904. The Museo Dalí (Dalí Museum) is a feature of the town and can be seen from quite a distance, with its distinctive glass domes. Here you can see a vast selection of Dalí's works presented in the most exciting and imaginative way. Whatever your feelings about his work, you should not miss this museum.

ⓘ *Plaça del Sol*

▶ *Take the* **C260** *southwest for 24km (15 miles) to Besalú.*

⑪ Besalú, Girona-Gerona

A splendid old fortified bridge over the River Fluvia serves as the main entrance to the ancient town of Besalú. Once capital of the Garrotxa region, the town is a medieval treasure, with its narrow streets and old houses.

The eye-catching exterior of the Museo Dalí, a display of the surrealist's works in Figueres

Handsome buildings surround the Plaza Mayor, which is lined with attractive doorways. A

FOR CHILDREN

The Toy Museum in Figueres has a large collection of dolls from different countries and periods of history.

SPECIAL TO...

The *sardana* is an important part of the Catalan folklore. Although the dance's origins are not clear, it is believed to have deep roots in the Cerdanya region. It is danced all over Catalonia, at weekends or on festival days. Anyone may take part (although newcomers should try to learn some of the steps before joining in). The participants join hands and dance in a constantly moving circle, following some fairly intricate steps, to the accompaniment of the local *cobla* (band).

---

number of interesting monuments in the town include the massive 12th-century Romanesque Monasterio de San Pedro and the churches of San Vicente and Santa María, also from the 12th century.

ⓘ *Plaça Llibertat*

▶ *Take the* **C150** *southeast to Banyoles (Bañolas).*

⑫ Banyoles,
Girona-Gerona

The lakeside town of Banyoles is a popular summer resort. The lake, used as the 1992 Olympic rowing course, has a good beach, offering facilities for bathing and watersports. On the Plaça del Fuente (Fountain Square) is the Museo Arqueológico (Archaeological Museum) which displays antiquities from the area. In the Iglesia de Sant Esteve (St Stephen), dating back to the 10th century and rebuilt in the classical style, is a 15th-century retablo, the work of the stone mason, Joan Antigo.

ⓘ *Passeig Indústria 25*

▶ *Continue on the* **C150**, *then join the* **A7** *back to Barcelona.*

SCENIC ROUTES

The stretch between Tossa de Mar and Sant Feliú is particularly beautiful. Its tortuous bends take you high over mountain tops and down among the pine forests, with magnificent views of cliffs that plunge sharply down to the sea, forming rocky coves and bays.
The stretch between Besalú and Banyoles on the C150 also offers some splendid mountain scenery.

Exploring the
Basque Country

San Sebastián (Donostia in Basque) is the capital of the Basque province of Guipúzcoa. The elegant buildings lining the seafront are a reminder of the 19th century, when San Sebastián was Spain's most fashionable resort. The lovely Paseo de la Concha promenade skirts the bay, lined with handsome buildings, and the old town sprawls up Monte Urgull, where the Castillo de la Mota and a figure of Christ overlook the bay.

2 DAYS • 359KM • 222 MILES

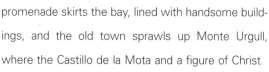

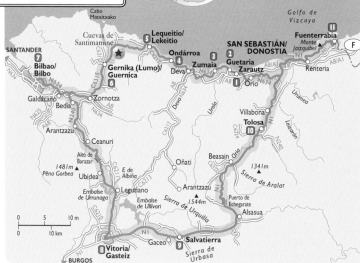

The elegant seaside city of San Sebastián, with the island of Santa Clara in the middle of its bay

☐ *Miromar Calle Andria*

▶ *From San Sebastián take the N1 south. Turn right on to the N634 to Zarautz, 26km (16 miles).*

SCENIC ROUTES

The Cornisa Cantábrica (Cantabrian Corniche) is a magnificent stretch between Zarautz, Guetaria and Zumaia on the N634. A zigzagging road follows the coast, offering magnificent views.
From Zumaia the drive continues along the coast, on the C6212, with beautiful views, to Lequeitio. The N1 offers some scenic parts after Alsasua, with excellent views over the Puerto de Echegarate, and again passes through beautiful scenery between Tolosa and San Sebastián.

❶ Zarautz, Guipúzcoa

You may like to make a quick stop en route in the picturesque little fishing port of Orio, which lies along the bank of an estuary.

The stately summer resort of Zarautz is situated in an old harbour backed by the tall Monte de Santa Barbara. Once popular with the élite of Madrid in the 19th century, it has a splendid beach. Monuments of major interest are the Gothic/baroque Iglesia de Santa María, the Iglesia de San Francisco and the hermitages of San Pelayo and San Pedro. The Torre Lucea (Lucea Tower) and the Palacio del Marqués de Narros (Narros Palace) from the 15th century, are also impressive. The place was once an important shipyard. It was here, between 1519 and 1522, that the *Victoria*, which carried Juan Sebastián Elcano, companion of Magellan, around the world, was built.

▶ *Continue on the N634 for 4km (2 miles) to Guetaria.*

SPECIAL TO...

The national sport of the Basque country is *pelota* (also known as *jai-alai*). There are variations, but it is a type of handball played between four men in a court called a *frontón*, using scoop rackets and a small, hard ball that travels at tremendous speed. The sport is supposed to be the fastest in the world. Each town and village has a court and a team.
The Basque has its own folklore, including the unusual *aurresku*, a war-like dance, and the *ezpata dantza*, a sword dance, accompanied by flutes and a drum.

❷ Guetaria, Guipúzcoa

There is some magnificent scenery as you approach Guetaria, and a fine view down over the pretty little fishing village which stands on a promontory. The Gothic parish church of San Salvador overlooks the harbour, and has

The picturesque little fishing port of Guetaria

underground tunnels linking it to the harbour. Over the breakwater is the little fortified Isla San Anton (island of San Antonio – known as the 'Ratón de Guetaria', Mouse of Guetaria, for reasons unknown), which rises up steeply to a lighthouse.

A drive or walk up here offers a rewarding view of the area. The Ayuntamiento (Town Hall) contains some interesting frescos describing the voyage around the world of the famous navigator, Juan Sebastián Elcano, who was born here.

▶ *Continue west for 6km (4 miles) to Zumaia (Zumaya).*

3 Zumaia, Guipúzcoa
Nestling at the foot of the Monte Santa Clara hill is Zumaia, another delightful little resort with a charming harbour and attractive houses. The Villa Zuloaga, formerly an old monastery, is now a museum founded by the great painter Ignacio Zuloaga, and has a fine collection of paintings by Zuloaga, El Greco, Goya and many of Spain's most famous

painters. The Iglesia de San Pedro is an attractive little Gothic church.

▶ *Follow the coast road, the N634, west. At Deva, turn right on to the C6212 to Ondárroa.*

4 Ondárroa, Vizcaya
You are now in the neighbouring province of Vizcaya, where the resort of Ondárroa is set in a bay protected by low hills. The town is a pleasing combination of attractive old cottages and more modern blocks. Glass balconies and half-timbered houses abound. It has a sandy beach and a pleasant harbour, where there is a lively fisherman's quarters. An old Roman bridge, the Puente Romano, spans the river.

▶ *Continue on the coast road C6212, northwest to Lequeitio (Lekeitio).*

5 Lequeitio, Vizcaya
Lequeitio is another popular seaside resort, where there are attractive houses and a good beach, which separates the

resort area from the fishing port. The 16th-century Iglesia de Santa María is a fine example of Vizcaya Gothic architecture. Narrow cobbled streets lead down to the old part of town. The palaces of Abaróa and Uribarren are particularly elegant buildings.

▶ *Take the C6212 west for 23km (14 miles) to Guernika-Lumo.*

6 Guernika-Lumo, Vizcaya
The famous painting, *Guernica*, by Pablo Picasso serves as a reminder of the terrible event that took place here in 1937 during the Spanish Civil War, when German aircraft bombed the town, killing a large number of the population. The town was devastated, and has been rebuilt in the traditional style. Originally displayed in the Museum of Modern Art in New York, Picasso's painting now hangs in the Centro de Arte Reina Sofía, in Madrid, together with the preliminary sketches.

The Casa de Juntas (Assembly Hall) contains an interesting library and archives. The Sala de Juntas (Council Chamber) is the venue of the General Assembly of officials of the provinces of Biscay. It also serves as a chapel, which is known by the rather grand title of 'la Iglesia Juradera de Santa María de la Antigua'. Near by is a monument commemorating the 1937 attack on the town. Some 5km (3 miles) north are the Cuevas de Santimamine, where wall paintings believed to date back some 13,000 years were discovered in 1917.

[i] *Ayuntamiento (town hall) Plaza Fuero 3*

▶ *Take the **C6315** south and join the **N634** west to Bilbao (Bilbo).*

7 **Bilbao,** Vizcaya
Bilbao (Bilbo) is the capital of the Basque province of Vizcaya (Uizcaya) and its largest port. It is essentially a busy industrial town, which may be off-putting to the visitor at first glance, but does have its attractions and is well worth a visit. Along the right bank of the river is the Paseo del Arenal, a pleasant esplanade that leads to the old quarters, known as Las Siete Calles (Seven Streets).

The Plaza Nueva is a charming square built in the neo-clas-sical style and the Gothic Catedral de Santiago (14th–16th century) near by is noted for its modern west front, large bell tower and Gothic cloister. The Ayuntamiento (late 19th-century) has an imposing tower and a Moorish-style ceremonial hall. The Museo Arqueológico, Etnográfico e Historico Vasco (Basque Archaeological, Ethnographical and Historical Museum) has a collection of tombs, arms and carvings.

In the new town, the Palacio de la Diputación del Señorío de Vizcaya (Palace of the Regional Government) has a modest picture gallery and museum of provincial history. Near by is the Museo de Bellas Artes (fine arts museum), which contains a good collection of works by famous Dutch and Spanish painters of the 15th and 16th centuries. The Museo Moderno contains works by contemporary Spanish painters.

[i] *Plaza Arriaga*

▶ *Return east along the **N634** and take the **N240** southeast for 66km (41 miles) to Vitoria.*

8 **Vitoria,** Alava
Vitoria is the capital of Alava, the largest of the Basque provinces, and the seat of a bishop. A focal point of the old town is the Plaza de la Virgen Blanca, which is surrounded by houses and balconies typical of Vitoria. In the centre is an imposing monument commemorating Wellington's victory over the French at the battle of Vitoria in 1813. Overlooking the square is the 14th-century Iglesia de San Miguel. A stone image of the Virgen Blanca (White Virgin), patron saint of the city, can be seen in a niche on the outside portal. Inside is a fine 17th-century altarpiece by Juan de Velázquez and Gregorio Hernández. The Catedral de Santa María was built between the 14th and 15th centuries in the shape of a Latin cross and is noted for its richly decorated triple-arched tympanums. An impressive Assumption can be seen in the side chapels. Look out also for a bullfighting scene carved on one of the pillar's capitals.

In the Plaza Santo Domingo near by is the Museo de Arqueología (Archaeological Museum), which displays objects from the Celtiberian and Roman times, among other items. The 14th-century parish church of San Pedro features a fine doorway and impressive sculpted tombs of the Alava family. Vitoria was a centre for craftsmen since the middle of the 15th century who worked predominantly in the wool and iron trades. The Portalon, built in wood and brick, is a remaining example of one of the many trading houses of the medieval and Renaissance times. Other attractive areas are the Plaza del Machete and the Cuchillería (Street of Cutlery), where you will find the 16th-century Casa del Cordón (House of Cordons), noted for a fine Gothic ceiling, and the Bedaña Palace, a fine 16th-century mansion with a magnificent façade. The new cathedral of María Inmaculada, which was consecrated only in 1969, shows a rather unusual neo-Gothic style.

i *Oficina de Informacion de Turismo, Pasea de Ribes Rogers*

▶ *Take the NI to Salvatierra.*

A quiet street in the attractive town of Fuenterrabía

9 Salvatierra, Alava
The little town of Salvatierra was founded by Alfonso X in 1256. It still preserves its medieval streets and parts of the old defensive walls. Its two main churches, those of San Juan and Santa María, have a somewhat fortress-like appearance.

▶ *Follow the NI east and then north for 6km (38 miles) to Tolosa.*

10 Tolosa, Guipúzcoa
Tolosa was capital of the province of Guipúzcoa for a period in the middle of the 19th century and is now a thriving industrial town (known for the *boinas*, or Basque beret). There are Roman antiquities and ancient buildings of the Templars. The Iglesia de Santa

María has the appearance of a cathedral.

i *Centro de Iniciativas Turísticas, Calle San Juan*

▶ *Continue on the NI north, bypassing the centre of San Sebastián, and then east. Turn off north for Fuenterrabía.*

11 Fuenterrabía, Guipúzcoa
The little town of Fuenterrabía was a stronghold over a long period of time and the scene of many battles. It is now a popular seaside resort. The remains of its ancient walls are preserved as a national monument and the 12th-century Palacio del Rey Carlos V (now a *parador*) was built as a defence against pirate raids. There are good views from here. Other buildings worth a look are the 16th-century Iglesia de Santa María (mainly Gothic with Renaissance influences), and the 17th-century Ayuntamiento. A short drive up to the ridge of Jaizquíbel leads to the Santuario de Nuestra Señora de Guadalupe and offers fine views.

▶ *Rejoin the NI back to San Sebastián, 25km (16 miles).*

BACK TO NATURE

There is an area of great natural beauty in the province of Alava, north of Vitoria, around three artificial lakes. Embalse de Urrunaga (Lake Santa Engracia) is situated along the road from Bilbao to Vitoria. On the slopes of the mountain are the Cuevas de Mairelegorreta, which are well worth a visit.

Embalse de Albiña (Lake Albina), east of the N240, lies at the entrance to the Aramayona valley. Further south is Embalse de Ullívari (Lake Ullívari), which stores water in the Gamboa canyon. The lake offers water sports and fishing.

Traces of
Don Quixote

Madrid's history can be seen in its buildings: the Casa del Ayuntamiento, the Capillo del Obispo and the Convento de las Descalzas Reales, for instance, recalling Habsburg rule. And from the Bourbon period, the Palacio Real is one of the finest examples of neo-classical architecture.

3 DAYS • 668KM • 416 MILES

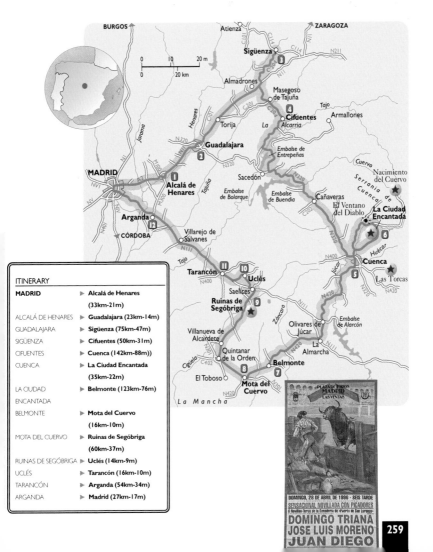

ⓘ *Plaza Mayor 3*

▶ *From Madrid take the **A2**, which becomes the **NII**, northeast to Alcalá de Henares*

Tiling on a Madrid shopfront

🄾 **Alcalá de Henares,** Madrid

Alcalá is known as the birthplace of Miguel Cervantes, author of *Don Quixote de La Mancha*, and for the founding of the famous Ildefonso University in 1508. The university developed into one of the most famous centres of culture and science in western Europe. When it was transferred to Madrid in 1837 the town lost its status and subsequently went into a decline.

The old headquarters of the university were rebuilt between 1543 and 1583 by the great Rodrigo Gil de Hontañón and is the present Colegio Mayor de San Ildefonso (College of St Ildefonso). This is an elegant Renaissance building with an impressive Plateresque façade,

decorated with the founder's coat of arms. It was badly damaged during the Spanish Civil War, but has been well restored. Inside are three graceful patios decorated in different styles. In the Central Hall is the seating area for the public. The walls are decorated with tablets bearing the names of the intellectuals who were here in the 16th and 17th centuries.

The town's main square is called Plaza de Cervantes, after the author. The Calle Mayor, where Cervantes was born in 1547, leads off the square. The Casa de Cervantes (House of Cervantes) was built very near his birthplace and houses a small museum with interesting items and relics relating to his life.

Cervantes had already written a number of works before he received instant acclaim with the publishing of the first part of *Don Quixote de La Mancha* in 1605. The second part was completed in 1615.

FOR CHILDREN

Alcalá de Henares is renowned for its wide variety of sweets and cakes. It is especially known for its *almendras garrapiñadas* (caramelised almonds), which are produced by the nuns of the Convento de San Diego and can be bought from the revolving hatchway in the door of the convent. Many different types of cakes, special to Alcalá, can also be found here, such as *rosquillas de Alcalá* (cakes in the form of a ring), *pestiños* (honey cakes) and *canutillos rellenos* (filled cakes in a tubular shape).

ⓘ *Callejón de Santa María*

▶ *Continue on the **NII** to Guadalajara.*

🄱 **Guadalajara,** Guadalajara

The finest feature of Guadalajara is the Palacio del Infantado (Palace of the Infant). Built between 1461 and 1492 by Mendoza, second Duke of Infantado, the palace was severely damaged by bombs in 1936 during the Spanish Civil War, but has been restored. Its main attraction is the pale façade, with diamond stonework decorations and an intricately carved gallery on top. Inside is a lovely two-storey patio with notable Isabelline arching (a type of ornate decoration used in the 15th century during the reign of Queen Isabella the Catholic). A small fine arts museum is housed here. Among the churches in the town, the 15th-century Iglesia de María features a fine Mudejar tower and the 16th-century Iglesia de San Ginés contains the tombs of various important personalities. Take a look, also, at the old Roman bridge over the River Henares.

ⓘ *Plaza Mayor 7*

▶ *Take the **NII** northeast then turn left on the **C204** to Sigüenza.*

🄲 **Sigüenza,** Guadalajara

The Castle was founded by the Romans and rebuilt between the 12th and 15th centuries to become the residence of the bishops until the middle of the 19th century. The castle has a somewhat formidable fortress-like appearance and is a recognisable landmark in the vicinity. It has now been converted into a *parador*, with magnificent views of the surrounding landscapes. The Plaza Mayor is overlooked by the cathedral, a solid structure of great towers and buttresses, built between the 12th and 14th centuries. It has an impressive interior, with

several fine chapels. In the Capilla de Santa Librada is the tomb of the town's patron saint. Adjoining the cathedral is the Museo Episcopal, where you can see some fine paintings by El Greco and Zurbarán and other works of art.

i *Cardenal Mendoza 2*

▶ *Return to the **NII**, turn right for a little way, then left to take the **C204** 50km (31m) southeast to Cifuentes.*

4 Cifuentes, Guadalajara
The name of Cifuentes means 'a hundred fountains', and indeed there are springs all over the area. Around La Provincia square is the 12th- to 13th-century Iglesia de El Salvador, with a late Romanesque portal and a Gothic rose window, and the Convento de Santo Domingo, which features an impressive 16th-century coat of arms on its façade. The ruins of a large 14th-century castle can be seen on top of the hill.

▶ *Continue south on the **C204** and just east of Sacedon turn left on to the **N320**, travelling southeast to Cuenca, 142km (88 miles).*

5 Cuenca, Cuenca
The little main square is dominated by the cathedral, an imposing structure with an attractive pale-coloured façade. Built between the 12th and 13th centuries, it shows a mixture of Gothic and Renaissance styles. The high arches bear influences of Anglo-Norman architecture. Features of special note are the 18th-century high altar and elaborate 16th-century grille before the choir. The Knight's Chapel contains a number of tombs and panels by the celebrated artist Yañez de la Almedina. Around

The imposing former university building at Alcalá de Henares

the corner is the Museo Episcopal, which contains two fine El Greco paintings, some beautiful tapestries and a collection of rich gold religious crosses.

A road from the main square leads to the Museum of Sacred Art, which displays some beautiful treasures, principally from the 13th and 15th centuries. The Iglesia de San Miguel, situ-

> ### RECOMMENDED WALKS
>
> From Cifuentes you can walk in several directions, such as Villanueva or Armallones. South of Cifuentes are the three large reservoirs of Entrepeñas, Bolarque and Buendia.

Cuenca's Casas Colgadas, or Hanging Houses, originally built as a palace and still clinging to the cliff

ated high above a gorge, has a fine Mudejar ceiling and is especially renowned for its Holy Week concerts.

A path along the southern wall of the cathedral leads down to the spectacular 'Casas Colgadas', or Hanging Houses, for which Cuenca is famous. The buildings cling to the side of the cliff with balconies that protrude over the precipice. Originally built in the 14th century as a palace, they were later used as a town hall. By the 19th century they had fallen into decay but were restored in the early part of this century. One of the houses has been converted into a Museum of Modern Art and shows large, mainly abstract canvases hanging to striking effect against pure white walls.

i *Glorieta González Palencia 2–3°*

▶ *Take the regional road to the north. Soon after El Ventana del Diablo lookout point, take a right turn on to the minor road which takes you to La Ciudad Encantada (the Enchanted City).*

'The Mayor's Parlour', part of the strange world created by nature at La Ciudad Encantada

BACK TO NATURE

The Parque Cenegético del Hosquillo (Game Reserve) lies in the Serranía de Cuenca and is used as a breeding sanctuary for deer. It is home to moufflon (wild sheep), red and roe deer, ibex and wild boar. There may still even be a few bears in the area. Eagles and vultures are also seen here. Permission to visit the park must be obtained from the Spanish Nature Conservancy Institute (ICONA).

⑥ **La Ciudad Encantada,** Cuenca

By the car park is the entrance to this extraordinary fantasy world of gigantic rock formations, the result of thousands of years of erosion. Nature really has had a go here, and the imagination runs riot with the sheer size and incredible shapes of the rocks, which resemble here a Roman bridge, there a giant mushroom or a tortoise, or a human profile or even the 'lovers of Teruel'. A route is

indicated by arrows marked high up on the stones (it is quite easy to miss them) and leads through a labyrinth of lost worlds.

▶ *Return to Cuenca by the alternative route, taking the regional road to the south, through Valdecabras. At Cuenca, take the N420 south to Belmonte (via La Almarcha).*

RECOMMENDED WALKS

Walkers will love the rocky landscapes of the Serranía de Cuenca. Northeast of La Ciudad Encantada is an area of rich vegetation and pine forests, offering gentle walks and the source of the River Cuervo (Nacimiento del Cuervo), which emerges from a cave in rippling cascades.

⑦ **Belmonte,** Cuenca

Make a brief stop here to take a look at the old castle that stands on top of the hill. It has circular towers and was built by Juan Fernández Pacheco, Marquis of Villena, in the 15th century as a means of defending his extensive territories. It was later abandoned, and was restored in the 19th century. The main features of interest are the splendid Mudejar ceilings, especially in the audience chamber. There is a good view of the landscape of La Mancha. If possible, take a look inside the old Colegiata (Collegiate Church), which has impressive altarpieces from the 15th to 17th centuries and choir-stalls carved with religious scenes.

9 Ruinas de Segóbriga, Cuenca

These ruins were once part of an important, bustling Roman town, the capital of Celtic Iberia. Here you can see the remains of an old Roman amphitheatre and thermal baths. Traces can also be seen of

10 Uclés, Cuenca

The main attraction here is the monastery, which once belonged to the knightly Order of Santiago (St James), lords of the village from the 12th century. It has a magnificent Plateresque façade and an elegant 16th-century cloister.

▶ *Return to the NIII and continue north-west to Tarancón.*

11 Tarancón, Cuenca

Stop here to see the church, which has a fine Gothic façade, the Palacio del Duque de Riansares and the mansion built by Queen María Christina after she married a guardsman, whom she gave the title of Duque de Riansares.

▶ *Continue on the NIII to Arganda.*

▶ *Continue for 16km (10m) on the N420 southwest to Mota del Cuervo.*

8 Mota del Cuervo, Cuenca

Right in the heartland of La Mancha country is the little village of Mota del Cuervo, which offers the familiar sight of white windmills silhouetted against deep blue skies, with the parched plains of La Mancha stretching away into the far distance. Now you are well and truly on the Route of Don Quixote, and a fleeting look at the windmills, some of which have now been restored to working order, soon makes it clear why the gallant old knight saw them as huge giants and attacked them.

▶ *Take the N301 to Quintanar de la Orden. Turn right on to the regional road which heads northeast to the Ruinas de Segóbriga, just before the NIII, on the right.*

The round towers of the restored 15th-century castle of Belmonte, guarding the surrounding lands

an old wall and of the Hispano-Visigothic basilica. A museum on the site provides an interesting insight into the ancient history of the area.

▶ *Continue on the regional road to join the NIII. Take a left turning and after 2km (1 mile) branch off to the right to reach Uclés.*

SPECIAL TO...

Mota del Cuervo produces some interesting pottery and is the only place in the region where 'turntable moulding' is done exclusively by women. It is known for its small jugs, called *tinajas*, which have a slim shape and flat handle, and are polished.

12 Arganda, Madrid

The Renaissance church, the Iglesia de San Juan Bautista, was built in 1525 and has altars in the Churrigueresque style. The Casa del Rey, a former country house, was once the property of the Spanish royal family, and there is a castle dating from 1400.

▶ *Return to Madrid on the NIII.*

FOR HISTORY BUFFS

South of Quintanar de la Orden is the small village of El Toboso, claimed as the home of Dulcinea, legendary heroine of Cervantes' *Don Quixote*. A so-called Casa de Dulcinea (Dulcinea's House) contains a library relating to Cervantes. The village itself has one wind-mill and is charming, with little streets and patios, evoking scenes described in the book.

The Great
Mosque &
Moorish Towns

Capital of Andalucia, Sevilla stands on the banks of the
Guadalquivir, with the Torre del Oro (Golden Tower) as a landmark.
Its wonderful architecture includes the 12th-century Giralda, built
as the minaret of the Great Mosque; a Gothic cathedral containing
the tombs of Christopher Columbus and St Ferdinand of Spain;
and the Palace of the Alcázar.

2/3 DAYS • 428KM • 267 MILES

ⓘ *Avenida de la
Constitución 21*

▶ *From Sevilla take the
NIV east for 32km (20
miles) to Carmona.*

❶ Carmona, Sevilla

The town of Carmona
stands on the highest point
of a flat plain. It has an old
Moorish fortress, which
holds a commanding posi-
tion over the town and
offers good views of the
countryside. Carmona is a
delightful little town and
has two old entrance gates,
known as the Córdoba
Gate and Sevilla Gate.

The Iglesia de Santa
María de la Asunción
(Church of St Mary of the
Assumption) is 15th-
century late Gothic, and
you can see the remaining patio
of the Great Mosque on whose
foundations the church was
erected.

The 16th-century Iglesia de
San Salvador is built in the
Churrigueresque style; the
baroque Iglesia de Clara has a
magnificently decorated interior, and the Santuario
(Sanctuary, 1525–51) is notable
for the retable adorning the
high altar. The Ayuntamiento
is attractively decorated with
Roman mosaics.

A Roman necropolis is
located west of the town. This
network of underground tombs
was hewn from the rock and
arranged in groups, with a
crematorium at the front. Look
out for the tomb known as El
Elefante for its unusual carving
of a young elephant.

The exquisitely coloured tiles
adorning the belfries of Écija

▶ *Continue northeast on the
NIV for 55km (35 miles)
to Écija.*

❷ Écija, Sevilla

The ancient town of Écija lies
at the end of a small basin on
the banks of the River Genil.
Thought to date back to Greek
times, it was known to the
Romans as *Astigi* and excavations of pottery, mosaics and
other items have given some
insight into its early history. Its
baroque belfries, decorated
with colourful tiles, can be seen
from quite a distance and are an
attractive feature of the town.
The Iglesia de Santiago (St
James) is entered through an
attractive 18th-century patio
and has interesting Mudejar
windows from a former structure. A fine Gothic retable
adorns the high altar. Several
handsome 18th-century palaces
in the town include the Palacio
Benamejí, which has a large
gateway in front; the Palacio
Peñaflor, which is beautifully
decorated with paintings on the
outside; and the Palacio
Valdehermoso, which has a fine
Renaissance exterior.

▶ *Continue on the NIV
northeast for 54km (34
miles) to Córdoba.*

❸ Córdoba,
Córdoba

Córdoba, a town of
narrow streets and alley-
ways, is situated on a
plain leading down to
the River Guadalquivir.
Overlooked by the
Sierra de Córdoba,
Córdoba suffers from
extremes of climate,
with very hot summers
and cold weather during
the winter.

Already quite promi-
nent when the Romans
arrived, the town contin-
ued to flourish and in
152BC became the capi-
tal of Hispana Ulterior.
It developed into a pros-
perous city under the Moors
and gained recognition as an
important cultural and artistic
centre of the western world.
The town fell to the Catholic
King Ferdinand in 1436, having
long been used by various
Christian leaders as a centre for
plotting the retaking of Granada
from the Moors. It was here that
Christopher Columbus was
granted the commission by
Queen Isabella for his first
exploratory expedition to the
New World.

The great Mezquita
(mosque) was constructed by
the Moors between the 8th and
10th centuries. It is one of the
largest mosques in the world
and is a remarkable achievement of Moorish architecture in
Spain. Its beauty lies in its interior. As you enter you are
confronted by hundreds of
columns made of onyx, marble
and other materials. They are
designed to catch the light,
forming myriad colours. The
columns are topped by capitals
and crowned with striking red-
and-white-striped arches, typical of Moorish art. An important
feature of a mosque is the
Mihrab, hollowed out from the
wall, where Muslims come to
pray. They are always built to

RECOMMENDED
WALKS

A detour north of Écija takes
you to the village of
Hornachuelos, which is on the
edge of a large game-hunting
area. This stretches away to the
north of the region and offers
some excellent walking.

Arts Museum) have interesting exhibits of sculptures and Roman antiquities in the first case, and a fine collection of paintings in the latter. Those with an interest in bullfighting will want to visit the Museo Taurino (Museum of Bullfighting). A statue of the celebrated Spanish bullfighter, Manolete, stands in the Plaza San Marina de las Aguas.

The Zoco (from the old Arab *souk*) has displays of traditional handicrafts and occasional flamenco performances.

A superb example of the Moorish style in Córdoba's ancient mosque

face Mecca in the east, although this one points more south than east, due to a miscalculation. From 1436 onwards, when Córdoba was taken by the Christians, the mosque was used as a cathedral. The Patio de los Naranjos (Court of Orange Trees) is particularly attractive in spring when it is filled with the fragrance of orange blossom. Through the Puerta del Perdón (Gate of Forgiveness) steps lead up to the baroque Campanario (bell tower) and a superb view of Córdoba and the river.

The Museo Arqueológico (Archaeological Museum) and the Museo de Bellas Artes (Fine

[i] *Torrijos 10*

▶ *Take the N432 southeast for 61km (38 miles) to Baena.*

4 Baena, Córdoba

The route continues through some of Andalucia's delightful *pueblos blancos*, or white towns. While sharing many common characteristics, each has its own character and style.

Baena is an oil-producing town and is typically Andalucian. A cluster of white-washed houses climbs up a slope, dominated by the remains of old Moorish battlements. The Gothic Iglesia de Santa María la Mayor dates back to the 16th century and is noted for its lateral aisle. The Convento de la Madre de Dios

(Convent of the Mother of God) was built in the Mudejar style and features an interesting carved retable.

▶ *Continue southeast on the N432. Close to the River Guadajoz turn south on the N321 to Priego de Córdoba.*

5 Priego de Córdoba, Córdoba

Priego de Córdoba is one of the region's little gems. Its dazzling white houses, flower-decked windows and tiny, winding streets give it a very Moorish look. Elegant 17th- and 18th-century mansions reflect former times when Priego was the centre of thriving silk and textile industries. Several churches are masterpieces of fine baroque architecture. Among them, the churches of La Asunción and La Aurora are noted for their wonderful baroque interiors. An abundance of springs here has resulted in the construction of the splendid Fuente del Rey (Fountain of the King).

Alcalá Zamora, first president of the Second Republic of Spain (1931–6), was born here in 1877. You can visit his former home, which has now been converted into a museum (Museo de Niceto Alcalá Zamora). A viewpoint from El Adrave, high up on the hill, shows the fertile lands that surround the town and the distant mountains.

▶ *Take the C336 west to Cabra, turning right on to the C327 for 2km (1 mile) for the town.*

6 Cabra, Córdoba

A pleasant park welcomes you as you enter Cabra. The Parque del Fuente del Río (Park of the Source of the River) refers to the River Cabra. The town is yet another Andalucian delight, with its white houses, red-tiled roofs and old narrow streets. Buildings of interest include the old Iglesia de San Juan Bautista, which dates back to the time of the Visigoths. The castle is now a college for a religious order.

▶ *Take the **C327** southwest for 11km (7 miles) to Lucena, which lies just off the road.*

Rising above the town of Estepa, the Torre de la Victoria is the last surviving feature of a convent

8 Estepa, Córdoba

Estepa is known throughout Spain for its excellent confectionery, especially its Christmas cakes, which are popularly known as *mantecados* and *polvorones*. The town lies among farmlands and has the typical Andalucian look. Monuments include the churches of Santa María la Mayor, La Asunción and Los Remedios. The 18th-century Palacio de los Marqueses de Cerverales (Palace of the Marquises of Cerverales) is worth a look, along with the Gothic interior of the old castle keep and the splendid Torre de la Victoria (Tower of Victory), which is all that remains of a former convent. There is a good view of the area from a nearby lookout-point called El Balcón de Andalucía.

▶ *Take the **N334** for 24km (15m) west to Osuna.*

9 Osuna, Córdoba

Osuna's history dates back to the time of the Iberians. Occupation by the Romans was followed by the Moors until 1239, when the town was captured by Ferdinand III. Of the many fine monuments to be seen here, special mention must be made of the Colegiata (Collegiate Church), an elegant Renaissance building from the 16th century, that houses valuable works of art.

La Universidad (University) is another noteworthy building which dates from the same period, with two circular towers built like minarets. The main churches are those of San Agustín, La Merced and La Victoria. The Casa de los Cepeda, the Palacio del Cabildo Colegial and the Palacio de la Antigua Audiencia are noted for their elegant façades. The Museo Arqueológico (Archaeological Museum) is housed in the old Torre de Agua (Water Tower).

▶ *Return to Sevilla on the **N334**.*

7 Lucena, Córdoba

Lying at the foot of the Sierra de Arcos is the attractive little town of Lucena, regional capital of this southern part of the province. The town is renowned for its bronze, furniture-making and copperware. Churches of major interest are the 15th-century Renaissance Iglesia de San Matéo, the Iglesia de Santiago and the Convento de San Francisco. Lucena was the scene of the capture of Boabdil, last of the Moorish rulers, by the Count of Cabra in 1483, during a revolt against the Christians.

▶ *About 2km (1 mile) west of the town take the **C338** for 45km (28m) to Estepa.*

on the road
SWITZERLAND

Switzerland is a nation divided by four main languages, but there is little division in the scenery, with most of the country given over to rolling Alpine meadows, impressive snow-capped mountain ranges, cool, blue, tranquil lakes and picturesque little villages.

Tour 43

A carpet of vines beneath the walls of Château d'Aigle

Genève (Geneva) is the geographic anomaly lying at the southern ripple of the Jura's flattening folds, a large city within a tiny canton (of the same name), almost entirely surrounded by French territory, which is strictly part of none of the three components

Page 269: top – typical painted Swiss wooden façade; bottom – view of Emmental farming village

of the country – the Swiss Alps, the Swiss Plateau (or Mittelland), and the Jura. Cynics might claim that it is not really part of Switzerland either, because this is one of those few cities which could arguably claim to belong to the world. Truly international in apparently every facet of its activities, more than one in

three of its residents is a foreign national and there are more international organisations based here than in any similarly sized community in the world.

The famous landmark of the cosmopolitan city of Genève (Geneva) is the towering Jet d'Eau, a plume of water forced up to a height of about 150m (490 feet) from an off-shore site close to the south bank of Lac Léman.

The city's other distinctive features are its elegant quays, promenades, parks and gardens. Prominent among the latter is the lakeside Jardin Anglais, with its celebrated flower clock, and the Jardin Botanique, which is host to a fine collection of exotic plants. The Promenade des Bastions is another fine open space, notable for its statues and monuments, and located on the fringe of the city's Old Town. Dominated by the 12- to 13th-century St Peter's Cathedral, this charming old quarter, with the quaint Place de Bourg-de-Four at its centre, is distinguished by art galleries, antique shops and antiquarian stores, as well as a comprehensive selection of bars and bistros.

The city' s other leading sights include the Tour de l'Ille, a 13th-century survivor of the original city fortifications, the 4th-century Eglise St Germain, the 16th-century Hotel de Ville, and the city's oldest house – the Maison Tavel. A generous choice of museums is devoted to natural history, old musical instruments, clock making and the Red Cross, and includes the famous Musée d'Art et d'Histoire.

Tour 44

The Jungfrau, the Mönch and the Eiger mountains are the highest peaks of the Bernese Oberland and their formidable presence states unequivocally why this region is acknowledged to be the jewel in the glittering crown of Switzerland's landscape. Their names translate, respectively, as the Virgin, the Monk and the Ogre, and the presence of the Mönch is supposed to guard the Jungfrau from the dishonourable intentions of the Eiger. The well-known resort of Interlaken is flanked by two Alpine lakes; the Thunersee in the west and the Brienzer See in the east. The high altitudes of the mountains provide year-round skiing in the region.

The elegant resort of Interlaken is celebrated for its wide tree-lined boulevards, stately Victorian hotels, tranquil waterscapes, flower gardens and – most memorably – dramatic mountain views of the Jungfrau massif. It was once famously dismissed by the 19th-century British travel writer John Murray as 'a sort of Swiss Margate', so popular had it become with English visitors.

Formerly known as Aaremühle because of its position on the banks of the River Aare, the town traces its origins to the founding of an Augustinian monastery in the early 12th century. All that remains of that structure, destroyed in Reformation, are the east walk of the 1445 cloister, the chapter house and the 13th-century Gothic chancel of the present St Mary's church. This cluster of historic buildings is located on the east side of one of the town's showpieces, the massive 'meadow' of neatly manicured lawns and colourful flower-beds known as the Höhematte. This is bordered to the north by the Höheweg, a wide and shady avenue lined by palatial hotels. In the built-up section between the Höheweg and the river is the famous pavilion-style Kursaal, a casino of 1859 with a splendid flower-clock in the midst of its landscaped gardens.

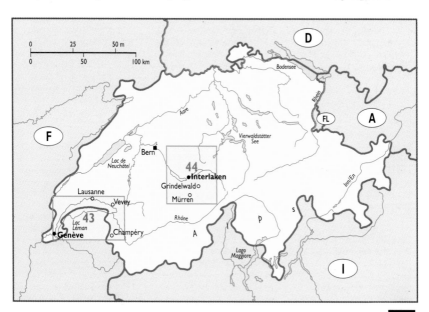

BANKS

Usual banking hours are 8.30am–4.30pm, Monday to Friday. In small towns and villages times vary, and banks may well close for lunch.

All banks are closed at weekends and on national holidays.

CREDIT CARDS

Most large stores, restaurants, hotels and petrol stations accept all major credit cards.

CURRENCY

The unit of currency is the Swiss franc. Notes are issued in denominations of 10, 20, 50, 100, 500 and 1,000; and coins are issued in denominations of 5, 10, and 20 centimes, and ½, 1, 2, and 5 Swiss francs.

CUSTOMS REGULATIONS

Switzerland is not a member of the EU and EU concessions for duty-free imports do not apply. Visitors from Europe are allowed to bring in 2 litres of wine, 1 litre of alcoholic beverages, 200 cigarettes or 50 cigars or 250g tobacco.

Visitors from outside Europe can bring in the same amounts of wine and alcoholic beverages, but 400 cigarettes or 100 cigars or 500g tobacco. These duty-free allowances apply only to persons over 17 years of age.

ELECTRICITY

The current is 220 volts, 50 cycles AC, on a continental two-pin plug. UK, Australian and New Zealand appliances need an adaptor; US appliances need an adaptor and transformer, if not fitted for dual voltage.

EMERGENCY TELEPHONE NUMBERS

Police: 117
Fire: 118
Ambulance: 117 (or 144 in some areas).

ENTRY REGULATIONS

Nationals of the EU, Norway, Australia, Canada, US and New Zealand need a valid passport. For stays over three months special regulations apply. Check with Swiss embassies or consulates.

HEALTH MATTERS

As a general rule vaccination and inoculation are not required by visitors entering Switzerland from western countries. As there is no state medical health service in the country, travellers are strongly advised to take out insurance cover against personal accident and illness.

MOTORING

Documents

A valid driving licence and the vehicle's registration details are needed by visiting motorists. Domestic motor insurance policies generally provide the minimum legal cover for driving in Switzerland, and production of a Green Card is not compulsory, but recommended.

Breakdowns

SOS telephones are located at regular intervals along all motorways and mountain-pass roads. The emergency breakdown number is 140. Breakdown and recovery insurance is strongly recommended because of the high cost of roadside assistance (especially high mountain passes). Most European breakdown organisations are affiliated to the Touring Club Suisse (TCS) which operates a nationwide 24-hour breakdown service. Carry warm clothes at all times if driving at altitude; breakdown vehicles can often take more than a couple of hours to reach a car on a mountain road.

Car rental

A circular giving details of rental charges is available from the SNTO. All the major rental firms are represented in Switzerland, and cars can be rented from all usual transit points. Booking in advance tends to be more cost effective than turning up at a car hire desk.

Motorway tax (vignette)

An annual road tax, known as the vignette, is levied on all cars and motorcycles using Swiss motorways. An additional fee applies to trailers and caravans. The green sticker is valid between 1 December of the year preceding and 31 January of the one following the year shown. It can be purchased at border crossings, post offices and service stations throughout the country and is valid for multiple re-entry into the country within the duration of the licence period. It is not advisable to drive on autoroutes in Switzerland without one; fines are heavy, and the relatively modest amount involved represents the cheapest form of toll-road driving in Europe.

Driving regulations

Vehicles must keep to the right-hand side of the road and overtake on the left. The wearing of seat belts is compulsory for drivers and all passengers (front and rear seats). Children under 7 must travel in rear seats. Motorcyclists must wear crash helmets. Foreign cars entering Switzerland are required to display their nationality plate at the rear of the car (and caravan). Driving with sidelights only in bad visibility is not permitted and dipped lights are compulsory in road tunnels. On mountain roads vehicles ascending always have priority, except for yellow post buses which have priority at all times. On bends their approach is signalled by a blast of their distinctive triple-note horns. Note that many mountain pass roads are closed from October to June. Conspicuous signs on all main

access roads indicate whether they are open (green) or closed (red).

The laws concerning speed limits, lighting and seat belts etc are strictly enforced and police are authorised to demand on-the-spot fines.

Speed limits
On motorways the speed limit is 120kph (74mph). Other roads, unless signposted otherwise, have a maximum speed of 80kph (50mph). In built-up areas and on secondary roads (even when not signposted) the limit is 50kph (31mph).

LANGUAGES
The national languages of Switzerland are German – 65 per cent (Central and Eastern Switzerland, locals speak a 'Swiss German' dialect); French – 18 per cent (Western Switzerland); Italian – 10 per cent (Southern Switzerland); Romansch – 1 per cent (Southeastern Switzerland). Many Swiss, especially those connected with travel and service industries, also speak English.

The serpent meanderings of a Swiss mountain road

NATIONAL HOLIDAYS
New Year's Day, Good Friday, Easter Monday, Ascension Day, Whit Monday, National Day (1 August), Christmas Day, 26 December. Different cantons observe different religious festivals, such as Corpus Christi.

POST OFFICES
Post offices in large towns are open from 7.30am–noon and from 2–5pm, closing on Saturday at 11am except in major cities. In small towns and villages times vary.

SWISS TRAVEL SYSTEM
Switzerland has arguably the most efficient and sophisticated public transport system in the world. Even if you are travelling by car you would be well advised to enquire into the various passes and cards which entitle the holder to unlimited travel, or reduced fares.

The Swiss Half-Fare Card, for example, enables the holder to purchase tickets at 50 per cent of the full fare for scheduled services of railways (including some mountain railways), post buses, lakeboats and some privately owned funiculars. Further details are available from the SNTO or any Swiss railway or bus station.

TELEPHONES
To operate a public telephone insert the relevant coin (or a phonecard called Taxcard which is available in post offices and newsagents). The dialling code for the UK is 0044; omit the initial digit 0 of the STD code. Otherwise dial 191 for details of dialling codes when calling abroad. Remember that there is always a surcharge when telephoning from hotels. There is a 24-hour English-speaking information line which will answer all queries about travelling and staying in Switzerland. Dial 157 50 14 from anywhere in Switzerland.

TIME
Switzerland and Liechtenstein observe Central European Time – one hour ahead of GMT in winter and two in summer, and six hours ahead of New York.

The Swiss
Riviera & Savoy
Alps

The crescent-shaped Lake Geneva (Lac Léman) shares its banks between France and Switzerland – with the latter having roughly two-thirds of the shoreline (and the fish). Some would also say that it has the best part of the deal. Most of the Swiss lakeside is on the sunny north bank in the canton of Vaud and the exclusive strip of land between Lausanne and Montreux has come to be known as the Swiss Riviera for reasons that will quickly become apparent.

4 DAYS • 757KM • 456 MILES

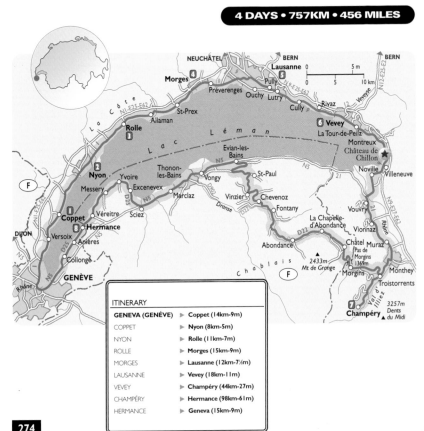

Lakefront sculpture at Ouchy

$\boxed{i}$ *Tour de l'Ile – also in station*

▶ *Follow blue road signs for Lausanne, taking road 1 – also signposted as Route du Lac – for about 14km (9 miles).*

❶ Coppet, Vaud

Earning modest notoriety as the anti-hero's Swiss HQ in the James Bond novel *Goldfinger*, this atmospheric little village is distinguished by its imposing 18th-century château. Set amidst a classically-styled park, its most celebrated owner was Louis XVI's Minister of Finance, who acquired it in 1784 and lived here until his death in 1804. The décor and furnishings of the public rooms date from this period. Otherwise the building is notable for its elegant courtyard, comprising stables and an orangery.

The village itself has a distinctive russet-coloured domed church which was built in the early 1500s, and a narrow main street of arcaded houses with brightly painted shutters. A regional museum is housed in a late Gothic building in the Grand-Rue.

▶ *Follow the lake road for 8km (5 miles) to Nyon.*

❷ Nyon, Vaud

A Celtic settlement, chosen by the Romans as the site for their first garrison town in this part of Helvetia, the former Noviodunum today owes much of its historical face to the influence of the Bernese. The 16th-century castle is their most obvious legacy, sitting squarely above the town with its five spired towers making a distinctive skyline. The view over the lake from the terrace is outstanding. One of the most important porcelain collections in Switzerland is housed within the castle walls – most of it manufactured by an 18th-century factory which still stands in the Rue de la Porcelaine. The town's Roman Museum features the remains of a 1st-century basilica, discovered in 1974, as well as an extensive collection of artefacts recovered from local excavations. The church of Notre-Dame, dating largely from the 15th century, has some interesting paintings on the north interior wall – pre-dating the main body of the building by an estimated 200 years. Elsewhere in the town, the Place du Marché is notable for its fine arcaded buildings, again in the Bernese style. Behind the Quai des Alpes stands the 11th-century Tour de César, a remnant of the town's original fortifications.

▶ *Continue on the lake road for a further 11km (7 miles) to Rolle.*

❸ Rolle, Vaud

This busy little lakeside town has a typically Savoyard-style 13th-century château, of trapezoid design with a rounded tower at each corner. The church of St Grat is of early 16th-century origin, subsequently altered in the 18th century. The majority of the buildings in the Grand-Rue date from the 16th century, with the rambling vintners' houses standing out as amongst the most handsome.

Lying a short distance offshore is the man-made Isle de Laharpe, constructed in 1844 and surmounted by a monument to local hero Frédéric de Laharpe – the military leader who delivered the fledgling canton of Vaud from the Bernese in 1798.

▶ *Follow the lakeside road for a further 15km (9 miles) to Morges.*

❹ Morges, Vaud

Once one of the biggest ports on the lake, Morges is still a

BACK TO NATURE

Nyon's Musée du Léman shows life in and around the lake over the centuries and features a remarkable aquarium which occupies the whole of one large wall. Fossils, fauna and fishing paraphernalia recovered from the lake, along with models of ancient fishing craft, comprise the core of a collection which offers an intriguing glimpse into this vital natural resource.

busy centre for the cantonal wine industry. Its commercial significance was somewhat reduced when freight began to be transported by rail rather than water, and now its 17th-century harbour is devoted predominantly to pleasure-boat traffic. The huge 13th-century

mansions on the Grand-Rue, is a comprehensive collection of antiquities including a unique set of engravings and etchings (20 of them by Rembrandt).

▶ Continue for about 12km (7.5 miles) on road 1 into Lausanne.

Lausanne's delightful old Quartier de la Citè

château stands close to the lake-front and shows obvious Savoyard influences with distinctive rounded towers at each corner of a robustly forti-fied square. Inside is a military museum with a collection of armaments and uniforms dating from the late 1700s. In the Musée Alexis Forel, housed in one of a number of handsome baroque and late Gothic

⑤ Lausanne, Vaud
Capital of the canton of Vaud, the former Roman camp of Lousonna offers impressive views across the lake to the mountainous Haute-Savoie from its commanding hillside position. By no means all of its contemporary architecture does justice to its enviable location, however, but this is a minor cavil set against the city's many seductive qualities – not least of them being its infectious energy and cosmopolitan atmosphere.

The acknowledged centre of commercial activity is the Place St-François which takes its name from the much-altered 13th-century church on its south side – the only surviving remnant of a Franciscan monastery which disappeared in the mid-16th century. North of the square, over a deep gorge, is the old Quartier de la Cité at the centre of which stands the city's most famous landmark – the cathedral of Notre-Dame which has fine views from its south terrace. The 12th-century structure, arguably the most impressive Gothic building in Switzerland, is unusually sombre inside. Distinctive features include the rose window (13th-century stained glass), the crumbling tombs of bishops from the same era and the 13th-century choir stalls in the south aisle. At the end of the latter is the first of 232 punishing steps leading to the top of the south tower. The view is almost worth the effort.

North of the cathedral square, via the charming medieval Rue Cité Derrière, is the Château St Maire, built in the late 1300s and extensively enlarged in the 16th century. A vast, squat structure of brick and sandstone, it is now the seat of the canton's government. West of the cathedral is the colourful market quarter of the Place de la Palud. Notable sights include the arcaded Hôtel de Ville, built in 1672, and the delicately sculpted Fontaine de la Justice. In the neighbouring Place de la Riponne is the handsome neo-classical Palais de Rumine, now the home of various museums (one of which contains the 12,000-year-old skeleton of a mammoth). Other interesting museums include the Musée Olympique, recording Lausanne's strong associations with the Olympic Games, housed in the new Cio building at Ouchy, and the extraordinary Musée de l'Art Brut in the Avenue Bergières which is a unique exhibition of unortho-